Culture in Dark Times

CULTURE IN DARK TIMES
Nazi Fascism, Inner Emigration, and Exile

Jost Hermand

Translated by
Victoria W. Hill

Berghahn Books
New York • Oxford

Published in 2013 by
Berghahn Books
www.berghahnbooks.com

Library of Congress Cataloging-in-Publication Data

Hermand, Jost.
    Kultur in finsteren Zeiten. English]
    Culture in dark times : Nazi fascism, inner emigration, and exile / Jost Hermand ;
translated by Victoria W. Hill.
        p. cm.
    German-language edition c2010 Böhlau Verlag … [as] „Kultur in finsteren Zeiten :
Nazifaschismus, Innere Emigration, Exil"—T.p. verso.
    Includes bibliographical references and index.
    ISBN 978-0-85745-590-1 (hbk. : acid-free paper)
    1. Germany—Intellectual life—20th century. 2. Fascism and culture—Germany—
History—20th century. 3. National socialism—Social aspects. 4. Ideology—
Germany—History—20th century. 5. Social distance—Germany—History—20th
century. 6. Exiles—Germany—History—20th century. 7. National socialism and art.
8. Arts, German—20th century. 9. Germany—Cultural policy—History—20th century
10. Germany—Social conditions—1933–1945. I. Title.
    DD256.6.H4713 2012
    943.086—dc23

                                                                2012012573

British Library Cataloguing in Publication Data

A catalogue record for this book is available from the British Library

Printed in the United States on acid-free paper.

ISBN 978-0-85745-590-1 (hardback)

Contents

Illustrations   vii

Preface   xi
    Three Claims to Cultural Representation

1. Nazi Fascism

Cultural-Political Preconditions   3

Enemy Stereotypes   6

Stated Objectives   15

The Ideal of an Eternally German Culture   28

Approaches to Practical Implementation   34

Consequences for the Arts   46
    Architecture   46
    Painting and Sculpture   55
    Music   72
    Literature   86
    Theater   103
    Radio, Film, and the Press   109

Class-Specific Successes of National Socialist Cultural Policies   122

2. Inner Emigration

Between Aversion and Accommodation   143

Forms of Artistic Expression   147
    Literature   147
    Painting and Sculpture   156
    Music   162

3. EXILE

Fragmentation of the German Exile Community   171

Places of Refuge   184

Possibilities for an Effective Antifascism   202

Consequences for the Arts   211
    Literature   211
    Theater   220
    Film   225
    Painting, Graphic Art, and Photomontage   231
    Music   238

Visions of a Liberated Culture in Postfascist Germany   246

Selected Bibliography   253
    NS Culture   254
    NS Architecture   255
    NS Painting and Sculpture   255
    NS Music   256
    NS Literature   257
    NS Theater   258
    NS Radio, Film, and Press   258
    Inner Emigration   259
    Exile   260
    Exile Literature and Press   260
    Exile Theater   261
    Exile Film   262
    Exile Painting   262
    Exile Music   262

Index   263

ILLUSTRATIONS

1. "Art is a sublime and compulsory fanatical mission." Plaque with a maxim propagated by Adolf Hitler at the NSDAP Cultural Congress on 1 September 1933.   xiii

2. "International Jewish Conspiracy." Caricature in the anti-Semitic smear-sheet *Der Stürmer* (1943).   11

3. Fritz Erler: *Portrait of the Führer*. Shown at the Great Exhibition of German Art (1939).   17

4. Germanic people of the early Bronze Age. From the book by Wolfgang Schultz: *Altgermanische Kultur in Wort und Bild* (Ancient Germanic Culture in Word and Image, 1934).   20

5. Oskar Martin-Amorbach: *Harvest Procession*. Shown at the Great Exhibition of German Art (1939) and purchased by Hitler.   22

6. Georg Sluyterman von Langeweyde: *Knight* (1943). "Victory or defeat rests in God's hands / We are the masters and kings of our own honor."   25

7. Hermann Giesler: Model for the *Hohe Schule* of the NSDAP on the Chiemsee (1939).   49

8. Albert Speer: Model for the *Great Hall* in Berlin (1938). © Bildagentur für Kunst, Kultur und Geschichte.   51

9. Cover image for the guide to the exhibition *Degenerate Art* in Munich (1937). The sculpture is *The New Man* (1912) by Otto Freundlich.   57

10. Karl Gries: *Summer* (1942). Tapestry.   62

11. Wolfgang Willrich: *U-Boat Commander Joachim Schepke* (1941). From the book by Wilhelm Westecker: *Krieg und Kunst der Gegenwart*, Breslau 1943.   64

12. Adolf Ziegler: *Goddess of Art* for Hitler's Chancellery (1941). From the book: *Was sie liebten. Salonmalerei im 19. Jahrhundert*, Cologne 1969.   66

13. Arno Breker: *The Fighters Depart* (1942).   69

14. Hans Liska: The state-supported studio built by Albert Speer for Josef Thorak in Baldham near Munich (c. 1938). From the book by KL Tank: *Deutsche Plastik unserer Zeit*, Munich 1942.   71

15. Cover image for the guide to the exhibition *Degenerate Music* in Düsseldorf (1938). © Bildagentur für Kunst, Kultur und Geschichte.   75

16. Hitler Youth trumpet parade. From the book by Otto Weber: *Tausend ganz normale Jahre. Ein Fotoalbum des gewöhnlichen Faschismus*, Nördlingen 1987.   78

17. Adolf Hitler with Winifred, Wieland, and Wolfgang Wagner in the garden of Villa Wahnfried in Bayreuth (1936). © Bayreuth, Nationalarchiv der Richard-Wagner-Stiftung.   80

18. Joseph Goebbels in conversation with Franz Lehar (c.) and Bernhard Herzmanowsky (l.) at the Ninth Congress of Composers and Authors in Berlin (1936). © Munich, Bilderdienst Süddeutsche Zeitung.   83

19. Hans von Norden: Postcard. "What the king conquered, the prince created, the field marshal defended, the soldier saved and united" (shortly after 1933).   91

20. Richard Schwarzkopf: *German Passion* (1936). From the catalogue of the Great Exhibition of German Art.   93

21. Arthur Kampf: *Hildebrand Overpowers Odoaker's Son*. From the book by Hans Friedrich Blunck: *Deutsche Heldensagen* (German Heroic Tales, 1938).   95

22. Werner Peiner: *German Soil* (1933).   98

23. Leni Riefenstahl: The Führer speaks. From the film *Triumph of the Will* (1936). From the book by Leni Riefenstahl: *Hinter den Kulissen des Reichsparteitag-Films*, Munich 1935.   108

24. Incarcerated radio directors and producers in Oranienburg concentration camp (August 1933). From right: Kurt Magnus, Hans Flesch, Hermann Giesecke, Alfred Braun, Friedrich Ebert Jr., and Ernst Heilmann. © Berlin, ADN Zentralbild.   110

25. Advertisement for the *Volksempfänger*. "All of Germany listens to the Führer with the radio receiver for the volk" (c. 1935).   112

26. Emil Lohkamp in the film *Hans Westmar* (1933) directed
    by Hans Wenzler. From the book by Eric Rentschler: *The
    Ministry of Illusion. Nazi Cinema and its Afterlife*, Cambridge,
    Mass. 1996.   116

27. Still photograph from the film *New Horizons* (1937)
    directed by Detlef Sierck with Willy Birgel and Zarah Leander.
    © Berlin, Bildagentur für Kunst, Kultur und Geschichte.   117

28. Scene from the film comedy *Roses in Tyrol* (1940) directed
    by Géza von Bolvary mit Hans Holt, Theo Lingen, and Hans
    Moser. © Bildagentur für Kunst, Kultur und Geschichte.   119

29. Heinz Rühmann collects for the winter relief organization
    in the Reich Chancellery on 1 May 1937. To the right of
    Hitler his adjutant Julius Schaub. © Munich, Bilderdienst
    Süddeutsche Zeitung.   128

30. Heinrich Hoffmann: *Vacationers on a KDF-ship* (1936).
    © Munich, Bildarchiv der Bayrischen Staatsbibliothek.   131

31. Ceremonial room in a community house designed by the
    Office for the Beauty of Work (1938). From the book by
    Anatol von Hübbeneit: *Das Taschenbuch Schönheit der
    Arbeit*, Berlin 1938.   133

32. Title page of the magazine *Kraft durch Freude* (Strength
    through Joy, 1938).   136

33. Mercedes-Benz advertisement (1940).   138

34. Rudolf Schlichter: *Ernst Jünger* (1937). From the book
    by Götz Adriani: *Ruldolf Schlichter. Gemälde, Aquarelle,
    Zeichnungen*, Munich 1997.   152

35. Otto Dix: *Landscape on the Upper Rhine* (1938). © VG-Bild-
    Kunst, Bonn 2010.   159

36. Ernst Barlach in his studio in Güstrow in front of the *Fries
    der Lauschenden* (Frieze of the Listeners, 1935). © Berlin,
    Bildagentur für Kunst, Kultur und Geschichte.   161

37. Thomas Mann and Albert Einstein in Princeton (1938).
    © Wikipedia Commons.   176

38. Johannes Wüsten: *Lenin* (1933).   186

39. Bodo Uhse, Lion Feuchtwanger, and Anna Seghers in the
    Bibliothek der verbrannten Bücher in Paris (Library of
    Burned Books, 1936).   188

40. Bertolt Brecht, Johannes R. Becher, Ilja Ehrenburg, and
    Gustav Regler at the International Writers' Congress "Zur

Verteidigung der Kultur" in Paris ("In Defense of Culture" in Paris, 1935). From the book by Werner Hecht: *Bertolt Brecht. Sein Leben in Texten und Bildern*, Frankfurt 1978.   191

41. List of new publications by Querido-Verlag in Amsterdam of works by leading German exile authors in fall 1933.   192

42. Title page of the 7 April 1943 issue of the journal *Orient* published in Tel Aviv.   195

43. Ruth Berlau: Bertolt Brecht and Lion Feuchtwanger in Pacific Palisades (1942). © Berlin, Hilde Hoffmann.   198

44. Arnold Zweig's membership card for the Schutzverband deutscher Schriftsteller in Paris (Association for the Protection of German Writers in Paris, 1936).   205

45. "Against the emigrants stirring up the muck." Poster of the Nationale Front in Zurich (1934). From the book by Werner Mittenzwei: *Exil in der Schweiz*, Leipzig 1978.   222

46. Ludwig Donath (r.) in the film *The Strange Death of Adolf Hitler* (1943) directed by James P. Hogan. © Los Angeles, Margaret Herrick Library Academy Film Archive.   230

47. Gerd Arntz: *Der Gegensatz Deutschland-Rußland* (The Contrast Germany-Russia, 1935).   232

48. Hanns Kralik: *Forced Labor in Börgermoor Concentration Camp* (1935). From the book by Wolfgang Langhoff: *Veensoldaten*, Amsterdam 1935.   233

49. John Heartfield: *Werkzeug in Gottes Hand? Spielzeug in Thyssens Hand.* Photomontage for the *Arbeiter-Illustrierte Zeitung aller Länder* (Tool in God's Hand? Plaything in Thyssen's Hand, 1933). © Berlin, Bildagentur für Kunst, Kultur und Geschichte.   234

50. Felix Nußbaum: *Selbstbildnis mit Judenstern und Identifikationskarte* (Self-Portrait with Star of David and Identification Card, 1943). © VG-Bild-Kunst, Bonn 2010.   237

51. Arnold Schoenberg in exile (c. 1935).   243

52. FBI file for Heinrich Mann (1949). © Washington, D.C., National Archives.   247

Images without copyright indications are from the author's own archive. In cases where the author could not locate the rightful owners of the other reprinted artworks and photographs, they should write to the author for claims of rights and/or compensation.

PREFACE
Three Claims to Cultural Representation

Let us begin with the central question of this book: why were the most artistically ambitious art forms still viewed as politically important by all cultured (or even semicultured) Germans in the period from 1933 to 1945, their ownership the object of a bitter struggle among key figures in the Nazi fascist regime, representatives of inner emigration, and Germans driven out of the Third Reich? This kind of esteem for the higher and highest manifestations of culture is barely comprehensible for people caught up in the hustle and bustle of today's mass media–related leisure and event industry. We have long since gotten used to the fact that the various forms of so-called high culture have become marginalized in that they continue to exist but no longer have any instrumental function in a nation's collective consciousness. The meaning of culture today, therefore, includes neither esteem for older masterpieces nor an attempt to come to terms with select remainders of what was once viewed as avant-garde, elite art. The concept of culture has expanded, and today almost everything that surrounds people in their daily lives is considered culture. When many neoliberal critics use this concept, they do not just mean so-called high or serious art; they also mean the cultural realms of entertainment, home décor, travel, and leisure and even food culture and bathroom culture. Culture has become a relatively noncommittal general concept in the course of the last sixty or seventy years; today's usage would have baffled the influential ideological opinion makers of the first half of the twentieth century.

Viewed from the perspective of social history, these evolutionary changes have both good aspects and bad. Among the good are the expansion of leisure time that followed the democratization of society as a whole and the concomitant high regard for aspects of everyday life. On the negative side, leisure time began to lose meaning as people increasingly viewed it from a consumer perspective; an inner void was created that was hard to fill with social values or values derived from high culture.

As a result, a need for distraction and amusement developed in large segments of the population and sought constant release in new technological innovations and pseudocultural commercial products. Even most representatives of the so-called cultured classes have lost all supraindividual objectives, whether related to the state, to religion, to partisan politics, or to artistic endeavors.

It is clear that everything was still functioning in a different way between 1933 and 1945 during what is often referred to as the Hitler era. During that period, talk of indispensable cultural standards was ubiquitous and unrelenting, especially in the upper levels of society, whether within or outside the Third Reich—as if these standards represented the absolute epitome of ideological values. What the leading opinion makers at the time considered culture was what found expression in the higher arts, or in art at its highest level; it was culture that imparted real value to both the state and the individual. To the ears of people concerned with social status, pronouncements to this effect sounded very convincing. However, had these political and aesthetic pretensions already been emptied of meaning following the penetration of the culture industry by commercially controlled mass media during the Weimar Republic? This is one of the unavoidable questions that will reappear often in the following pages. When people talked about culture at the time, did they really mean only high art? Might the National Socialist authorities have had something entirely different in mind when they made pronouncements about culture?

But let us postpone answering these questions for the time being. Between 1933 and 1945 most members of all three groups—the Nazi fascists, inner emigration, and exile—fought with equal fervor over who could definitively claim to represent the authentically great German culture. The ideologues of cultural theory among the Volkish-minded Nazis—members of the inner emigration with their recommendations for retreat to "the good, the true, and the beautiful" and the "better-quality Germans" from the sphere of high culture among the exiles from Hitler's Reich—all endeavored to appear as agents of the definitive German culture in an attempt to legitimate their claims to be Germany's representatives in the political as well as the cultural arenas. Because their statements often evidenced bizarre changes in direction or contradictions, it is not surprising that there are a number of hypotheses and theories about this set of problems, and it seems appropriate to discuss some of them briefly at this point.

In attempts to look back at the cultural claims of Nazi fascism, the following viewpoints usually predominated. People liked to point out that many Nazi leaders had been artists before they became involved with Nazism—this was true of the former painter Adolf Hitler and of a whole

Figure 1. "Art is a sublime and compulsory fanatical mission." Plaque with a maxim propagated by Adolf Hitler at the NSDAP Cultural Congress on 1 September 1933.

series of his most important followers and officers, such as the architect Alfred Rosenberg, the playwright and novelist Joseph Goebbels, and the poets Rudolf Hess and Baldur von Schirach. Therefore, the theory goes, these men always granted a particularly high status and even an evangelistic importance to ambitious forms of culture. In this context, it was often emphasized that most Nazi Party leaders found support in the theory posited by Houston Stewart Chamberlain and thoroughly exploited by Hitler that all great cultural achievements of the last four to five thousand years had been produced by race-conscious Aryans whose worthy descendants lived in Germany today. The Germans, these circles concluded, were entitled to claim worldwide cultural-political leadership to prevent the rest of humanity from sinking into a chaos without culture, ruled only by the baser instincts. Many of the ideological fanatics within the Nationalsozialistische Deutsche Arbeiterpartei (National Socialist German Workers' Party, NSDAP) really believed in these theories, whereas they were used by other more opportunistic groups simply to impart a higher sanctity to the Third Reich's political claim to world domination.

Some representatives of inner emigration made equally high-flown claims, but their claims, unlike those of the Nazis, did not imply a form of tyrannical imperialism. When the inner emigration artists referred to culture, they continued to mean very much the same thing as the upper middle class of the nineteenth century with its sense of entitlement to property and learning. They meant that idealized realm of civilized behavior outside the world of day-to-day politics, which Thomas Mann had tried to describe before World War I with the concept of "inwardness protected by power." Instead of venturing into what were considered the baser aspects of society as it really was, these groups performed an evasive maneuver into the realm of essentiality to remain as clean, pure, and apolitical as possible. This position was largely an ideology of nonideology—not inconvenient to the Nazi fascists because it made it easier for them to carry out their many crimes. Many representatives of inner emigration were aware of this, but it did not stop them from closing their eyes to reality and seeking refuge in what they considered eternal values, such as religion or art. It is therefore all the more important to recognize those among them who made an effort to insert some cryptically encoded elements of resistance in their ostensibly apolitical works because they did not want to be viewed as spineless fellow travelers or even sordid accomplices of the regime. When we talk about concepts of culture, it is important to distinguish among several groups here, as in the case of the Nazi fascists; it would be wrong to speak in general terms of a united front within inner emigration.

The same is true of representatives of the exile group. If we look more carefully, we see that the fragmentation into separate, ideologically very distinct schools of thought was perhaps even greater among them than among the artists and cultural theorists who stayed in the Third Reich. The contrast between those who had to flee abroad after 1933 because of their leftist viewpoints and those who had to flee because of their Jewish ancestry was just one thing among many that prevented any kind of consistent solidarity among the exiles scattered in many countries. There were also contrasts between rich and poor exiles, Christians and atheists, and bourgeois humanists and exponents of socialist viewpoints. Even so, most (with the exception of those in the film branch of the entertainment industry) clung stubbornly to the highest ideals of German culture to strengthen their own personal and ideological identities. In fact, clinging to German culture's greatest accomplishments gave some—even some of the Jewish-born, as they were called in Nazi parlance—the feeling that they were the better Germans. Inside the Third Reich after 1933, they asserted, a descent into the depths of philistinism, if not barbarism, had taken place. A substantial number of these Hitler refugees saw themselves as the definitive heirs of those essential German cultural accomplishments that had to be upheld even abroad. For this reason, they titled the first large antifascist conference during the exile years, which took place in Paris in 1935, "In Defense of Culture." Almost all the exiles were in agreement on this point, even if they often differed widely politically and ideologically. Especially the writers and composers among them felt the earlier works of German art, with their humanistic perspective, were still the most precious things left to them outside Germany.

Therefore, if we wish to undertake a sociopolitical analysis of the series of events set in motion by Nazi fascism between 1933 and 1945, it is certainly not illogical to focus on the phenomenon of culture. The object of this approach is not to divert attention from the concrete political, military, and racist crimes of the Nazis. On the contrary, perhaps if we analyze the highly complex interconnections among the cultural-political concepts of the various ideological groups between 1933 and 1945, we will better understand all the ideological positions that are usually circumscribed with terms such as opportunism, blindness, accommodation, taking refuge in higher things, public spiritedness, fanaticism, or the will to resist.

After all, not everything that was categorically labeled as culture deserved this distinction. There were many serious efforts within inner emigration and exile groups to maintain the dignity of German culture and deploy it as a weapon against the barbarism of Nazi fascism. But inside the Third Reich, despite all the lofty rhetoric, the concept was often debased, and the label of culture also applied to the most trivial products if it helped funnel false consciousness into the so-called broad masses. The Nazis' ideas of culture were ambiguous and, therefore, substantially more disparate than those of inner emigration or exile. Their tendency to split along class lines was one of the factors that helped them achieve a success that is still embarrassing to think about. The split reached from highest to lowest, offering the educated middle class, the workers, and the white-collar employees what was suitable for each of them. Inner emigration and exile groups had no access to the mass media with their wide impact, so they were forced to depend on the marginalized realm of high art. They therefore remained relatively ineffectual, and only in the process of coming to terms with the past after the Third Reich did they achieve some recognition and begin to have a political and an aesthetic effect.

1

NAZI FASCISM

CULTURAL-POLITICAL PRECONDITIONS

Culture probably appears more often in Nazi fascist propaganda than any other term, with the possible exception of *race* and *volk*. The movement's writings constantly mention German culture, Nordic culture, Aryan culture, volk-related culture, culture from blood and soil, and similarly constructed concepts. If you read carefully the many books, brochures, essays, and pamphlets devoted to the topic in which such terms were used—beginning in the terminal phase of the Weimar Republic and in absolutely inflationary numbers after 1933—expecting to find a coherent concept of culture behind this mumbo jumbo, you will inevitably be disappointed. Sometimes culture is used as an umbrella term defined primarily from a racist perspective, although it often remains unclear what actually makes up the cultural superiority of the Nordic race over all the world's other races—it is always simply characterized as a higher form of the spirit. Sometimes culture is understood primarily as an awareness of national tradition. Because the great achievements of older German art continued to be exemplary for the Nazi fascists, they now saw no need for pseudo-revolutionary upheavals. Sometimes, with exactly the same emphasis, they used culture to designate anything that tried to resist the demon of civilization located in the modern metropolis, with its liberalism, its materialism, and the examples of pluralistic degeneration they produced. In their writings about cultural politics, the Nazi fascists vehemently opposed as endangering culture everything they felt smacked of obscenity, prostitution, decadence, vice, greed, intellectualism, economic competition, anarchism, egocentrism, internationalism, technology, the subhuman, disintegration, class identity, Jews, or blacks. This catalog of the signs of civilizational degeneration that might lead to an ever-more threatening cultural decline could be extended for pages.

Admittedly, many of the targets of these strategic defensive maneuvers against so-called alien national characteristics could be subsumed under the rubric un-German. But that would just make the lack of conceptual clarity even greater. What does German mean? Is it just a theoretical construct that has been designated a priori as *of a higher nature* and that largely eludes any concrete sociological definition? Is something German if it is time-honored, unspoiled, based on traditional values, and untainted by the modern metropolis and its technological achievements? Was the effort instigated by the Nazi Party to clamber from the depths of the Weimar Republic's swamp culture to the peaks of a volkish civilization German? Or is German simply what the leaders of Nazi fascism, Hitler above all, thought it was? There are so many concepts—and just as many contradictions.

To beat a path through the confusing jungle of these theoretical constructions, we first need to look for enemy stereotypes put forward by exculpatory ideologies like these and then take a look at the objectives they pass off as positive. A critical analysis based on these two strategies can help us determine more exactly what made up the Nazi fascists' ideas of culture. Exploring this analysis is the only way to achieve a better understanding of their key political-aesthetic concepts. These concepts began with an emphasis on continuing venerable cultural traditions, but then either found a basis in fanatical belief systems or in clever efforts to attain power and hold on to it.

We will see—and this anticipates one of the main points of this book—that the contradictions in Nazi concepts of culture were based both on lack of ideological clarity and on the fact that the party functionaries responsible for cultural policy held conflicting views. Above all, the bitter struggle within the party between the Nordic-minded radical fascists and the pragmatists who were more ready to compromise played an important role. Among the former, a fanatical urge toward things of a higher Aryan nature dominated, while the latter tended to base their idea of a culture useful to the Third Reich on a realistic assessment of prevailing social conditions; they were even ready to accommodate the base entertainment needs of the so-called broad masses to avoid getting trapped in sectarianism from the start.

The first three sections of this book will include preliminary considerations of the enemy stereotypes developed by the Nazi fascists, the stated objectives of their theories of art, and the concept of an eternally German culture behind both. The following section will investigate the inevitable consequences of the opposition between the radical fascists and the more realistic pragmatists on how these cultural concepts were implemented in practice after 1933. The pragmatists proved to be stronger and thus more influential in these disputes, and so, despite constantly repeated slogans about the volk community (*Volksgemeinschaft*), the result was a highly visible split into high and low in the cultural sector of the Third Reich. These two concepts of culture diverged more and more drastically from the original idea of a high culture or a communal culture fed by fundamental Aryan-German impulses and led instead to a continuation of the situation that had prevailed in the Weimar Republic: the coexistence of a hypercultivated elite culture with an entertainment culture that was less discriminating and served primarily the lower classes' need for amusement. In subsequent sections, we will see what a powerful impact this class-specific differentiation had on the gradient within the various arts and what a resounding success the underlying cultural-political strategy achieved with this tactic.

ENEMY STEREOTYPES

At first glance, it seems that the communists and the Jews were the two main political and cultural adversaries of the Nazi Party. At any rate, it is their grotesque faces that are caricatured most often in satirical Nazi propaganda; they are ripped to shreds in both images and texts. Here, wide-open staring eyes, the facial features of a fanatic, fists clenched; there, hooked noses, bulging lips, and obese stomachs—they look like threatening politico-monsters or greedy parasites. A real German cannot trust them as far as he can throw them. In satires like the ones by Hans Schweitzer and Otto von Kursell that appeared in Nazi publications such as *Der Stürmer* (The Attacker) or *Der Angriff* (The Attack), nothing was sugarcoated. Unbridled hate set the tone and did not shrink from the most evil distortions.

Let us begin by considering the communists as enemy stereotype. The Deutsche Arbeiterpartei (German Workers' Party/ DAP) was founded in Munich on 5 January 1919, and from it the Nationalsozialistische Deutsche Arbeiterpartei (National Socialist German Workers' Party/ NSDAP) emerged in February1920. The party spoke out from the beginning against all the key concepts considered at the time to be Marxist. The attempt to found a *Rote Räterepublik* (red soviet republic) in Bavaria in April 1919 contributed to the intensification of their anti-communist position; the soviet republic collapsed only four weeks later due to resistance by the radical right-wing *Freikorpsgruppen* (volunteer groups) under the command of Baron Franz von Epp. To take the ideological wind out of the sails of other uprisings on the left, the followers of the German Workers' Party and later the Nazi Party pretended to be friends of labor; in other words, they played the role of nationalistic socialists, following the lead of Gottfried Feder and Dietrich Eckart in the defensive struggle against the threatening bolshevization of Germany. Adolf Hitler, named head of the Nazi Party on 29 July 1921, did the same; in his early years, he always sharply rejected communism, portraying himself as a supporter of people's socialism. He was supported in his efforts by the Estonian-German Alfred Rosenberg, among others. In 1922, Rosenberg published a book titled *Pest in Rußland. Der Bolschewismus, seine Handlanger und Opfer mit 75 Lichtbildern aus Sowjet-Rußland* (Plague in Russia: bolshevism, its leaders, its henchmen, and its victims with 75 photographs from Soviet Russia), which was grounded in the reactionary attitude of the *Freikorps* groups fighting the Red Army in the Baltic region.

Adolf Hitler took the same line in his book *Mein Kampf* (1925–27; *My Struggle*, 1933) where he portrayed the communists as the monstrous product of the Red International, determined to obliterate all the driving forces intrinsic to the different races and peoples and establish their own world empire, bastardized and without culture. "The most terrible example of this kind," he claimed, was Russia, where the communists "with truly fanatic ferocity, killed and starved to death almost thirty million people under conditions of inhuman suffering." The result was the unnatural "dictatorship of the proletariat," whose benefits had accrued not to the workers, but to "a gang of stock market bandits." In the years after the world economic crisis began in October 1929, Hitler's rhetorically exaggerated attacks on communism became sharper. To come to power legally, it was important to win over to his movement both the petty bourgeois frightened by communist ideology and industrialists who feared further growth of the Kommunistische Partei Deutschlands (German Communist Party/ KPD). So Hitler emphasized ever more strongly that the possible transformation of Germany into a bolshevist state was the main threat posed by the chaotic conditions the socioeconomic crisis had created within the Weimar Republic. Accordingly, the Nazi propaganda brochure *Ein Kampf um Deutschland* (A Struggle for Germany), which was published with a foreword by Hitler, stated that members of the German Communist Party intended to murder all the Nazi Party leaders—but that was not all. They also planned to blow up a series of public buildings, expropriate the wealthy members of the national community, do away with support for the unemployed, and establish a state ruled entirely by Communist Party big shots.

Due to propagandistically exaggerated statements like these, the Nazi Party, which had originally been oriented toward the proletariat and the petty bourgeoisie, became increasingly middle class. This shift led Hitler to give up his underclass perspective for strategic reasons in favor of the concept of a volk community (*Volksgemeinschaft*) that also embraced the upper classes. Those among Hitler's followers who were financially better off and part of the educated middle class welcomed this ideological policy change enthusiastically beginning in the economic crisis years after 1929 as the Communist Party gained adherents. These groups feared that if bolshevism advanced in Germany, it might bring with it a flare-up of the Novembrist tendencies they had bitterly rejected in the early 1920s. And that was not all. They were also afraid they would lose their political and economic hegemony if communism were to be victorious in Germany. So after 1930, although opposed to socialism, they defected in droves to the party claiming to be national socialists, now suddenly, in contrast to their previous party programs, portraying themselves as resolute defenders of existing property rights.

A similar development occurred in the Nazi Party's cultural ideas. So, for example, the Kampfbund für deutsche Kultur (Militant League for German Culture), founded in 1928 by Alfred Rosenberg, sharply rejected communist degradation of high art into something anti-bourgeois and therefore intellectually subaltern. Instead, it supported almost exclusively elite cultural concepts that tended toward idealism in the years that followed, hoping primarily to win over the conservative groups within the wealthy and educated middle class for their purposes. Because of its limited perspective, the league was denied any very broad appeal during its early years. We should not underestimate, however, how much it contributed between 1929 and 1933 to the Nazification of the upper social classes, who perceived everything leftist in the realm of the arts as endangering their property and lacking culture and therefore un-German in principle. Leftist and un-German art included, for example, Sergei Eisenstein's films, the red one-mark novels by Willi Bredel and Klaus Neukrantz, the photomontages of John Heartfield in the *Arbeiter-Illustrierte Zeitung aller Länder* (International Illustrated Newspaper for Workers, AIZ), plays by Bertolt Brecht and Friedrich Wolf, Hanns Eisler's red agitprop music, satirical drawings by George Grosz, and Communist Party organs such as *Die rote Fahne* (The Red Flag) and *Die Linkskurve* (Curve to the Left). These segments of the population did have to admit that some songs of the SA (Sturmabteilung/ Storm Troopers) were a bit primitive, too, but considered them politically quite appropriate under the circumstances. They welcomed right-wing student groups disrupting communist-inspired theater productions and the ensuing brawl, and they did not reject pre-fascist war novels, even though the books were not quite up to their aesthetic standards.

So when tens of thousands of Communist Party members and sympathizers were arrested by the police or by rampaging SA groups shortly after the transfer of power to Hitler on 30 January 1933 and carried off to prisons or concentration camps, most representatives of the upper classes did not view these actions as violent crimes. And they later supported persecuted leftists only in exceptional cases. After all, these groups—despite some liberal posturing—had in the majority been anti-democratic during the Weimar Republic; they welcomed Hitler's anticommunism as a turn toward the preservation of capital and a return to law and order in Germany after the turbulent years between 1929 and 1933. As a result, scarcely any in their ranks took a position after 1933 against the burning of left-oriented writings or the removal of paintings from German museums. The few protests against such actions, which were quickly repressed, came mostly from antibourgeois leftists. So when the propagandistic anticommunist exhibit *Das Sowjet-Paradies* (The Soviet Paradise) opened in Berlin in 1942, only a few members of the Kommunistischer Jugendverband Deutschlands (Communist German Youth League/KJVD) who belonged to the so-called Baum Group protested, and in some cases, they paid with their lives.

The arguments used by Nazi leaders when targeting the Jews were, if anything, even more caustic. An immense store of Jewish enemy stereotypes was already at the disposal of Hitler and his followers for their hate-filled tirades and campaigns. They did not use the tried and true Christian prejudices against the so-called despicable Jesus-murderers among the Jews. Instead, they emphasized almost exclusively the racial inferiority of these semitic subhumans in their anti-Semitic writings—following the lead of Adolf Bartels, Houston Stewart Chamberlain, Artur Dinter, Paul de Lagarde, Jörg Lanz von Liebenfels, Georg von Schönerer, and Richard Wagner, to mention just a few of their precursors. This racial inferiority supposedly manifested itself in the Jews' avaricious hustling, their hypocritical desire to assimilate, and their unrestrained sexuality—in other words, in their crass materialism, which was supposed to be the absolute antithesis of the attitude of the intellectually superior Aryan, who was always striving toward the ideal.

Because of this racially determined baseness, Hitler emphasized in *Mein Kampf* that "naked, unadulterated egotism" reigned among the Jews. If this "pack of rats" were to come to power, he declared full of hate, the whole world would "suffocate in dirt and filth." For him, it was a race interested only in "plundering their fellow men" instead of developing some concept of a state and a culture connected to it. Almost the same viewpoints can be found in books such as Wilhelm Stapel's *Antisemitismus und Antigermanismus* (1928; Anti-Semitism and Anti-Germanism), Alfred Rosenberg's *Der Mythus des 20. Jahrhunderts* (1930; The Myth of the Twentieth Century), Gottfried Feder's *Die Juden* (1933; The Jews), and Johannes von Leer's *Juden sehen Dich an* (1933; Jews Are Looking at You).

These books claimed that Jews had never been prominent as creators of culture; instead, they superficially imitate the culture of their host peoples or commercialize and degrade it. According to these writings, the Weimar Republic, oblivious to ethnic heritage, had granted Jews full civic equality with the long-established Aryan population. The Jews had shamelessly exploited this concession, flooding broad sectors of German culture with their pseudo-German garbage. Their crooked machinations had placed them in leadership positions in the new media—film, the press, the radio, popular theater, and the music industry—and in high art as well, where they had tried to force everything specifically German into the background in favor of a nonculture that leveled out all racial differences.

Beginning in the late 1920s, Nazi polemics pilloried scapegoats that represented attempts to infiltrate German culture with Jewish influences: the ostensibly corrosive literary criticism of Alfred Kerr and Kurt Tucholsky; Richard Oswald's film obscenities; houses such as Mosse and Ullstein in the publishing sector; in music, Kurt Weil's popular compositions and Leo Kestenberg's upper class affectations; and allededly trashy bestsellers by Lion Feuchtwanger and Stefan Zweig. Even in the realm of high art, which had always been the domain of pure Germanness, Jews such as the composers Arnold Schoenberg and Franz Schreker, the painter Max Liebermann, playwrights Walter Hasenclever, Ernst Toller, and Friedrich Wolf, and theater directors Leopold Jessner and Max Reinhardt had been up to mischief. In the country these Jews pretended was their homeland, these arts had struggled to reach the sublime; now their reputation had been stabbed in the back, and Germany could recover only through a rigorous elimination of this population.

So the Nazi fascists responsible for the cultural sector began as early as spring 1933 to confront the purported disastrous influence of Jews on German cultural life as forcefully as possible by removing all Jewish artists who had occupied influential state-funded positions from their posts. Even the 430 Jews who had joined one of the Reichskulturkammern (Reich Chambers of Culture) when they were founded in 1933 were expelled from them just one year later. At the same time, there was a series of infamous anti-Jewish boycotts, and in 1935, the "Law for the Protection of German Blood and German Honor" was passed, which branded both marriage and any extramarital sexual intercourse between Jews and non-Jews as illegal. In November 1937, the exhibition *Der ewige Jude* (The Eternal Jew) opened in the library building of the Deutsches Museum in Munich; its purpose was to demonstrate how Judaism corroded the culture of its German hosts. In fact, at this point, Rosenberg and associates were trying harder and harder, with the help of all available archival materials, to sniff out all the Jews in German history and intellectual life who had not yet been exposed. Even a declared anti-Semite like Goebbels, who viewed this kind of "Jew-sniffing" as ideological pedantry, wrote about such "excessive zeal" in his diary: "In the end, nothing will be left in our history but Widukind, Henry the Lion, and Rosenberg. That's not much."

But such temporizing viewpoints could not delay or weaken the anti-Semitic furor being constantly stirred up by Rosenberg as well as Heinrich

Figure 2. "International Jewish Conspiracy." Caricature in the anti-Semitic smear-sheet *Der Stürmer* (1943).

Himmler, Reinhard Heydrich, Julius Streicher, and other Nazi leaders with slogans like "Perish, Judah" or "The Jews are our misfortune." As we know, on 9 November 1938, this anti-Semitism led to the pogrom that has gone down in history as the *Reichskristallnacht* (Night of Broken Glass). Thereafter, the situation for Jews in Germany became increasingly intolerable from one year to the next. Anyone who did not voluntarily leave the Third Reich was transferred to one of the Jew houses, deported to Poland, required to take the given name Israel or Sarah, and required to wear the yellow Star of David after 1941. Following the infamous Wansee Conference on 20 January 1942, Jews were deported to the extermination camps in the East—Auschwitz, Chelmno, Majdanek, Sobibor, and Treblinka—where approximately 165,000 German Jews fell victim to the racial mania of the Nazis by 1945.

To make their anti-Semitic arguments as compelling as possible, some Nazi theoreticians went so far as to portray communism as a Jewish invention, pointing to Karl Marx, Rosa Luxemburg, and Leon Trotsky. Even before 1933, some Hitler followers characterized everything produced by non-Aryan political or cultural hustle—whether the source was communist or Jewish—as cultural bolshevism to discredit it as alien. Once again, it was Rosenberg who struck the most powerful blows. As he wrote in *Der Mythus des 20. Jahrhunderts*, bolshevism was simply the most acute form of "world revolution" to which the Jews aspired; they were an "oriental-Syrian race" who sought revenge on what to them was the "alien character" of the European mind. He accordingly characterized the USSR as a "Soviet Judea," where, thanks to the efforts of the "Jewish bolsheviks," the nefarious "idea of internationalism" appeared in its most sinister guise. If we fail to put a stop to these tendencies, he explained, we should not be surprised if Germany, too, falls victim to "Semitic world bolshevism." Rosenberg saw the most dangerous precondition for this eventuality in the ever-expanding swamp culture of the large industrial regions inhabited by proletarian subhumans. They were getting ready, under the leadership of Jewish communists, to destroy what little was left of a higher Aryan culture—or at least to drag it through the mire. In 1941, when Hitler both invaded the USSR and declared war on the United States, the world's leading industrialized nation, there were some overzealous anti-Semites in the NSDAP who described even dollar imperialism as the spawn of the worldwide Jewish conspiracy.

But these are by no means the only enemy stereotypes to be found in Nazi facists' writings on cultural theory. They wanted a national culture that was truly German, and from this perspective they condemned not only anything communist or Jewish, they condemned absolutely everything they perceived as alien and therefore incompatible with the essential nature of the Germans. Many of them followed in the footsteps of Carl Schmitt, who in his 1927 treatise *Der Begriff des Politischen* (The Concept of the Political, 1996) had spoken out against all pluralistic concepts of the state and of culture, characterizing all representatives of non-German thinking as "the others" or even "enemies" who had to be fought. Many Nazis also talked constantly about the need to confront tendencies toward egalitarian internationalism in the cultural sphere no matter what their ideological hue as forcefully as possible. So in addition to attacking communism and Judaism, they lashed out at all forms of pluralistically oriented liberalism, parliamentarianism, and democratic ideas that could threaten and finally destroy what was specific to the German nation and the race along with any state-based sense of order. Blood and soil advocates like Paul Schultze-Naumburg and some Rosenberg followers saw the primary site of this anti-spirit in the big cities of the time, where a process of de-Germanization was underway that was utterly indifferent to ethnic concerns. There, everything inherent to older ethnic-national ideas of culture was drowning in the egotistic and commercial hustle and bustle. There, a soulless functionalism ruled, they emphasized over and over, that did not hesitate to place even the highest cultural assets under the control of a civilization that was purely economically oriented, and, therefore, it degraded them to mere consumer products.

Those who held this view did not hold the Jews alone responsible; they also blamed Germans who were indifferent to their own ethnicity and had sympathized shamelessly during the Weimar Republic with an internationalism that took no account of German national traditions and cared only about world consumer markets. Nazi theorists of this ilk cited many manifestations of degeneracy within the un-culture industry of the Weimar Republic, chief among them the expansion of modernistically furnished department stores, the technically oriented functionalism of the Bauhaus in Dresden, abstract-modernistic painting, the Negroid element in commercial jazz, and, finally, everything in the realm of bestsellers and journalistic reportage they characterized as vapid asphalt literature.

Through this consistent devaluation of everything pertaining to modern civilization, even concepts such as secessionist modernity and critical reflection became negatively charged words in Nazi texts. The ideal of cultural creativity for these authors, as they repeated often, was neither the aesthete detached from society nor the socially critical so-called egghead; it was the Aryan complete human being whose actions and values depended on the inner voice of his own ethnic ancestry, not on temporary fads or the dictates of reason. As the third un-German enemy, along with communists and Jews, these theorists therefore denounced the rootless cosmopolitan intellectual. He was so far removed from his volkish origins that he could no longer muster any creative panache on his nation's behalf; he followed either his own subjective impulses or the faddish ideas dictated by those pulling the economic strings at the moment—usually in response to a non-Aryan greed for profits. In a Third Reich of a German type, these writings threatened, all of this would have to be eliminated.

Stated Objectives

This catalog of the Nazi cultural theorists' most important enemy stereotypes leads to a central question that needs to be addressed: what were the guiding ideological principles of true Germanness these writers posited as alternatives to the widely lamented foreign cultural infiltration, both before 1933 and then more forcefully after the transfer of power to Hitler? Most of them proceeded with enormous fervor and a lack of clarity of the same magnitude. But what else could you expect? After all, in the area of national psychology (*Völkerpsychologie*) at the time, interest centered primarily on the quintessential in-and-of-itself of certain nations. Thus, opinions, even when veiled in science, tended to be overgeneralizations and therefore questionable. So whenever the word *Germanness* appeared in texts of this kind, there were almost always very general nationalistic or chauvinistic ideas behind it. Much of this essentialist hairsplitting is reminiscent of equally problematic efforts by academic intellectual history and existential philosophy during the late 1920s and early 1930s to develop abstract concepts; they, too, were more interested in what was existentially being-appropriate *(seinsgemäß)* than in what history had actually produced.

It was especially popular in this milieu centered on cultural theory to use racial biology as a basis for portraying the truly German as an expression of an Aryan kinship community, following in the footsteps of Ludwig Ferdinand Clauß, Hans FK Günther, Alfred Rosenberg, Paul Schultze-Naumburg, Josef Strzygowski, and other Teuton enthusiasts. This group used as their starting point an intuition of essence (*Wesensschau*) that was German-conscious; they devalued all ways of thinking that were rationalistic—in other words, alien—as superficial and therefore unproductive.

What these theorists saw as specifically German was to be found not in historical developments through the centuries, but rather in whatever it was that had given inner greatness and cultural creativity and expressiveness to the Indo-Germanic race since time immemorial and whose worthiest representatives today were the Germans. In the end, this kind of genius cannot be rationally explained; it has to be recognized on the basis of a shared national spirit that is sensed instinctively.

If the goal was to return to the basic Aryan preconditions for what was truly German, according to many Nazi writers, cultural efforts in support of this goal had to be postulated on a rigorous enhancement of the race on an Aryan-Germanic basis, an enhancement that could not flinch from using sterilization and euthanasia. After the manifestations of cultural degeneracy in the recent past, according to these Nazi theorists, an Aryan culture of a higher type would be possible only when creative Germans could once again feel that the blood of their noble ancestors still pulsed through their veins. For this reason, their statements always invoked a radical rejection of any international mixing of the races within a modernistic urban civilization governed by the laws of functionalism, a civilization that had lost any relation to eternal being in the world. In declarations heavy with meaning, they explained that a serious pact of solidarity with forces from the wellspring of German being that had existed since the time of Germanic prehistory was now necessary. In its wake, an ethnically appropriate volk community would develop in Germany and with it a volk culture that would strive for the highest goals.

But for an upswing of this kind to occur, these authors repeatedly claimed, a rigorous exclusion of all alien influences and the establishment of a truly German-conscious Third Reich would be required; as the executor of these attitudes, they always envisaged a strong man from above. Even before 1933, both the older volkish groups and the young prefascists saw Hitler as that man. Only he, they emphasized incessantly, with his unique aura and irresistible charisma, could help Germany toward a cultural renaissance based on a radically executed program of racial improvement, thus preventing a descent into the modernism hazardous to the German ethnic type to which the communists and Jews aspired. Components of a personality cult were, thus, a major part of Nazi ideology in the cultural as well as the political sphere. In their writings they constantly invoked Adolf Hitler, who had been chosen by providence and in whom the truly German was magically experiencing a compelling resurrection. In the minds of these theorists, he had come from the depths of the people and knew better than anyone that elements of culture that were up to date, fashionable, economically determined, or smacked of revolutionary cultural bolshevism were deeply un-German. Therefore, they expected

Figure 3. Fritz Erler: *Portrait of the Führer.* Shown at the Great Exhibition of German Art (1939).

him to fall back on the traditional values in which the best aspects of German culture had found expression for centuries. Hitler, his countless supporters ceaselessly repeated, was a man who represented a race-conscious reawakening, not an upheaval that would be contrary to the ethnic nature of the people. Following him unconditionally was a necessity that could not be questioned; it was the only way to avoid continuing complicity in the downfall of the German spirit.

Because of this extreme dependency on the Führer, the NSDAP believed even before 1933, in contrast to other political parties, that they could dispense with a carefully formulated cultural policy. Instead of undertaking a concrete and rational analysis of the existing political and socioeconomic conditions in the cultural sphere, they consistently posited Hitler as their prototype, a Faustian-Nietzschian man of action and superman who embodied in his person everything the party considered exemplary. Thus, Hitler was not just their Führer, he was at the same time their program, their telos, their supposed utopia. His partisans viewed him as the man whose wholehearted devotion to the great cause provided a shining example to all Germans. While the chairmen of other parties fell back on dry, anachronistic programs, they wrote emphatically, Hitler was first and foremost a fighter, a savior, and a redeemer in whom one had to believe blindly, as Joseph Goebbels explained repeatedly, to grasp the true core of his message.

Because Hitler was devoting all of his strength to reawakening the German people to their ancestral greatness, his followers affirmed, it was not unreasonable for him to demand from those committed to him the same militant ethos in pursuit of his noble objectives. The speeches and writings of the leading officers of the party were therefore initially full of appeals to the willingness of the brown-shirted SA columns to struggle and sacrifice, while later they turned increasingly to the entire community of the volk. We read again and again of fealty, discipline, duty, manfulness, and, indeed, of willingness to sacrifice and courage in the face of death. All of this was to help the Germans (the worthiest representatives of the white race) in their struggle against subhumans with neither honor nor culture (represented primarily by the Jews, Slavs, Gypsies, and so-called negrified French) to find the *Lebensraum* they needed and with it the foundation for political domination in Europe if not the entire world.

In their speeches and writings, almost all Nazi fascists professed their devotion to the heroic ideal. At a cultural congress of the NSDAP on 1 September 1933, Hitler was already talking about the coming heroic age. In his opening address to the Reich Chamber of Culture on 15 November of the same year, Goebbels hoped that the works of art created in the immediate future would exhibit a "romanticism made of steel" that would of necessity be based in a "heroic attitude toward life." As we would expect, in his *Revolution in der bildenden Kunst?* (Revolution in the Visual Arts?) published in 1934, Rosenberg, too, advocated "heroism in the art to come," which should take the Aryan-Hellenic sculptures of the ancient Greeks as a model. Shortly thereafter, Paul Schultze-Naumburg simply equated Nordic-German man with heroic man in his book *Kunst aus Blut und Boden* (Art from Blood and Soil). In his volkish manifesto *Kultur ist Dienst am Leben* (Culture is Service to Life) from 1937, Georg Sluyterman von Langeweyde took an equally imperious stance, characterizing the Germans as "a people of comradeship" whose "spiritual foundation" was "a readiness to defend themselves." Even the German Christians repeatedly summoned their members to a "heroic Christianity" during these years. In accordance with these party proclamations, Nazi art historian Hubert Schrade titled one of his tradition-bound books published in 1937 *Die heldische Gestalt in der deutschen Kunst* (The Heroic Figure in German Art); it was celebrated by the Nazi authorities as a major work of the new art history.

Based on ideological concepts of this kind, many Nazis unleashed an absolutely merciless cultural war against everything communist, Jewish, Negro, urban-modernistic, and liberal-intellectual. The goal was to give what they considered their own inherently German counterproducts a semblance of the heroic idealism with which they tried to cloak their racist and imperialist objectives. Using pseudo-religious catchphrases like "the cleansing of the temple" or "preparing new tablets," they confronted their catalog of enemy stereotypes with a catalog of their own ideals that was equally long; their ideological justifications were both vaguely mythological and quintessentially racist. The approach of the overzealous among them was as demagogic as it could possibly be, in the cultural arena as in the political, if the two can be separated at all. Their vocabulary, which literally crawls with words like essence, type, soul, being, and meaningfulness, is enough to show that they were not concerned with rational methods of interpretation in this context. Instead of falling back on the kind of scholarly language generally rejected by the NSDAP, they used an "inherently Germanic intuition of essence" (*arteigene Wesensschau*), employing empty formulas loaded with pathos to create an impression of unfathomable depth. They sometimes even conjured up some Nordic "ur-womb" behind the often-apostrophized forces of blood and soil as the real wellspring of the Aryan race.

The ancient Germanic tribes, who are often evoked as role models or idealized images, seem especially indistinct to the reader. After all, we actually know precious little about the origins of these tribes. For this very reason, from an ideological perspective they could be misused with

Figure 4. Germanic people of the early Bronze Age. From the book by Wolfgang Schultz: *Altgermanische Kultur in Wort und Bild* (Ancient Germanic Culture in Word and Image, 1934).

great ease and effect as shining examples of heroism and cultural creativity, the two chief qualifications of the Aryan race. Many representatives of Nazi fascist Germanic studies sought an all-encompassing education of the entire German nation, trying to tear them away from lives of Christian quietism or petty bourgeois self-satisfaction and lead them back to a life based on an awareness of their Germanic origin. According to exponents of these views, every German needed to realize that Palestine was no longer the Holy Land, and the Teutons, not the Jews, were the most ancient of civilized peoples. Thousands of years ago on German soil they possessed a high culture of *Thing* sites, runic inscriptions, Germanic lur music, sagas, and Bronze Age jewelry equal to the later culture of the Greeks and Romans. In the early 1930s, for example, we read in the writings of Heinar Schilling, Josef Strzygowski, and Hermann Wirth that the time has come for Germany finally to show itself worthy of these noble ancestors and regain its original strength of will and its cultural superiority. These fanatics urged all Germans to stop allowing themselves to be dazzled by misleading effeminate concepts that were Judeo-Christian or humanistic-democratic. Instead, they were urged to return to the ur-Germanic values grounded in warlike heroism and cultural self-confidence, thus helping the elemental forces of the North to victory over Jahwe, the god of the Jews.

Still in the realm of concepts for racial enhancement, there were similar objectives behind the NSDAP's widespread cult of the peasant. Here the overzealous advocates of blood and soil could find support in an equally abundant supply of preexisting ideological approaches. Some among them were inspired in part by Otto Damaschke's efforts at land reform, Georg Hauerstein's ideas about tribal settlements, Willibald Hentschel's Mittgart mania, and the Eden Orchard Colony's Aryan worship. In addition, they could build on the activities of the Artamanen (the Artaman League) and the Jungdeutscher Orden (Young German Order), who had supported an effort at a permanent resettlement of the German people during the Second Empire and the Weimar Republic. In order finally to provide enough *Lebensraum* for a rising nation like Germany, most of these groups had already made two suggestions: first, an intensified domestic colonization and second, if this did not suffice, and aggressive colonization in the East, possibly reaching as far as the ancient lands of the Goths in the Crimea, a solution already put forward by the Alldeutschen (Pan-German league) under Georg von Schönerer at the turn of the century.

These concepts received a Nazi fascist interpretation primarily in Adolf Hitler's *Mein Kampf* and in many statements by Otto Bangert, Walter Darré, and Heinrich Himmler as well. Following in their footsteps, shortly before 1933, numerous Nazi authors advocated stopping German emigration overseas, which was ostensibly so damaging to the nation. Instead, they wanted to establish a large geographically unified and densely settled tribal empire so that not a single additional drop of Aryan blood would be lost. Much like Julius Langbehn had done in his manifesto-like book *Rembrandt als Erzieher* (1890; Rembrandt as Educator), which had fifty printings by 1926, these groups supported a thoroughgoing agrarianization of the entire German people, invoking an every more intensive symbiosis of blood and soil. Based on these views, they rejected, as many supporters of the Heimat-Kunst Bewegung (Homeland-Art Movement) around 1900 had done, the negative effects of modern industrialization and with them the anti-spirit of advancing urbanization, which they saw as diametrically opposed to the basic nature of the Aryan race with its peasant consciousness of being rooted in the soil.

For the Nazi fanatics who swore by the forces of blood and soil, all modernistic aspects of civilization showed a loss of homeland that was oblivious to what was inherently German and therefore reflected a process of de-Germanization. A death of the volk threatened; it had to be

Figure 5. Oskar Martin-Amorbach: *Harvest Procession.* Shown at the Great Exhibition of German Art (1939) and purchased by Hitler.

opposed, and those forces in Germany had to be strengthened that could build on primal ancestral tendencies to bring forth a Germanic agrarian culture. In the second half of the 1920s, those who followed this line found energetic support in two books by Walter Darré, who later became Reichsbauernführer (Reich Peasant Leader): *Das Bauerntum als Lebensquell der nordischen Rasse* (1928; Peasantry as Life-Source of the German Race) and *Neuadel aus Blut und Boden* (1929; New Nobility from Blood and Soil). They stressed values such as tribal consciousness, the ethos of the ancestral estate, and abundance of children as the most undistorted expression of the Germanic agrarian primal being. It was part of the program to dream that large parts of the German population would extend their roots into their native soil once again, and this process was often linked to gradually pushing back or even ruthlessly liquidating the Slavic subhumans of Eastern Europe to finally create the *Lebensraum* to which the German people were entitled. Often referring to the agrarian novels of Adolf Bartels, Gustav Frenssen, and Hermann Löns, Nazi writers emphasized two qualities they identified in the Aryan-German peasant: a hereditary love for their native soil and their warlike nature, so different from the decadent urbanites who had already been softened and were now luxuriating in the achievements of modern civilization.

Alongside the German peasant, an equally important role model for genuine Germanness was the German knight, usually either in the form of a Teutonic knight or of Albrecht Dürer's *Ritter zwischen Tod und Teufel* (Knight between Death and the Devil). The idea was to provide all the native-soil-loving agrarians with manful-minded Führer figures who could help the Eastern colonization succeed. Many Nazi fanatics cited the Teutonic knights of the late Middle Ages, linking them to ideas of new groups of heroic men who would come together as Nordic-minded liegemen in castles built for the orders yet to be founded and then ride into *Ostland* with concentrated force. Alfred Rosenberg was probably the main promoter of the concept of a state built on these orders, as was apparent in his speech at the Marienburg Castle in East Prussia in 1934, which attracted a lot of public attention. Rosenberg's NS Kulturgemeinde (National Socialist Culture Community) was an outgrowth of the earlier Kampfbund für deutsche Kultur (Militant League for German Culture); he characterized it as an order-council for the movement (*Ordensrat der Bewegung*) and believed that with himself as chancellor of the order the council could put Hitler's visions into social practice. Heinrich Himmler also paid tribute to similar ideas of an order during ritual gatherings with other SS leaders in the Wewelsburg near Paderborn. These views were kept strictly secret, however, to avoid contravening the populist concept of a national socialist community of the volk that was being widely touted. Even Hitler sometimes enthused about the idea of an order-state in private conversations, such as those with Hermann Rauschning, the NS leader in Danzig; his reference point was usually Wagner's *Parsifal*, whose Grail ideology he viewed as a specifically Nordic myth. To him, the blood in the Grail chalice was not Christ's blood, it was Aryan blood. Thus, he referred to the SS as "a brotherhood of Knights Templar around the Grail of pure blood," which would gleam once more only after German blood had been purified of all elements whose source was an alien race. Only when that effort was successful, he explained, would Germany be capable of assuming world domination.

Hitler, although he rarely admitted it, was firmly in the tradition of the Aryan zealots who tried to use the ancient myths of Atlantis and Thule as the basis for their idea that the Germans were a people chosen by destiny. This Grail-like elitism, this conviction that they belonged to a Nordic master race or even to a consecrated order of knights resulted in Hitler and members of his high command having an aristocratic sense of being among the chosen, a belief that veered more and more toward the lunatic as the years passed. The more ambitious the secret ideas of these circles became, the more they looked down on those peoples who were supposedly full of resentment—blacks, Jews, Mongolian-Asians, or bastardized Western Europeans—whose sole goal, they believed, was to eradicate the Aryan nobility step by step. Then they would be free to shamelessly indulge their purported base urges. From extravagant ideas of this kind some Nazi leaders extrapolated the entitlement of the Aryan-German race to rule over the entire world population, which would sink into a bleak racial and anti-cultural chaos for all eternity without the Aryans' guiding hand.

So in contrast to other autocrats of the era such as Francesco Franco, Benito Mussolini, Josef Klemens Pilsudski, or Joseph Stalin, Hitler's aspirations to power were based on imperialist as well as nationalist objectives. In most of his speeches, he referred only to the good of the German volk community, but from the very beginning, there were long-term objectives in the guise of lofty slogans that went far beyond a mere cult of Germanness. In his speeches, however, Hitler alluded to such visions of the future only when he talked about the thousand-year-Reich that he intended to found. Some social scientists see this as the actual utopia of Nazi fascism. After all, the vision of a Reich that lasts a thousand years is clearly reminiscent of many utopian fantasies since the sixteenth century. In contrast to the disastrously changeable fortunes of various systems of government, those writers had always proposed the concept of a society so well organized that it would prove to be immutable. In their political tracts, usually written in the form of utopian novels, these authors had

Figure 6. Georg Sluyterman von Langeweyde: *Knight* (1943). "Victory or defeat rests in God's hands / We are the masters and kings of our own honor."

included three requirements intended to put a stop from the outset to all internal conflicts that might lead to the overthrow of the existing social order: the rigorous avoidance of war, social equality of all citizens, and the abolition of existing property rights.

But none of this had any place in Hitler's Third Reich, which was supposed to last a thousand years. First, his idea of a Reich did not include the dream of eternal peace that had seemed indispensable to the utopian fantasies of Enlightenment writers. Second, there was no concrete foundation for the Nazi promise of a true volk community, which most earlier utopias had also propagated. Hitler's system of rule rested on a social Darwinist leadership principle based almost exclusively on the anti-utopian right of the stronger over the weak. Even on the question of property rights, the Nazis decided on an anti-utopian approach. They did not eliminate them, as utopian thinkers from Thomas More, Louis-Sebastien Mercier, and Morilly through Charles Fourier, Étienne Cabet, William Morris, Theodor Hertzka, and Edward Bellamy had recommended. Instead, as early as his first speech to the Reichstag, Hitler supported preserving the capitalist economic system and promised the better-off segments of society "the strongest possible support for private initiative and recognition of the right to private ownership."

This could not fail to disappoint all of his lower-class followers, who had welcomed the Nazi fascists' assumption of power with utopian expectations. These groups hoped until the spring of 1934 for a second revolution when Hitler would abolish capitalism to push through a social equalization of all German national comrades. But that proved to be an illusion, because Hitler was unwilling to risk frivolously the position of power he had achieved with the help of big business and the Reichswehr with plans for some kind of revolutionary transformation. A man like Otto Strasser, who before fleeing into exile had been a leader of the left wing of the NSDAP, later compared this change of course into anti-utopianism with the victory of the Girondists over the advancing Jacobins or the victory of the royalists over the Puritans under Cromwell. SA men, who had fantasized for years about the night of the long knives when they would eliminate all of the fat industrialists and transform their factories and office buildings into common property, were equally embittered about Hitler's procapitalist course and his aspirations to bourgeois respectability.

But just the opposite happened. Hitler had almost all the leaders of the NSDAP left wing murdered on 30 June 1934 and then spoke out against any form of un-German revolutionary activity at the subsequent Reich party congress in Nuremberg. Thereafter, within the hierarchy of the Nazi Party, an anti-utopian pragmatism triumphed over all the remaining utopian elements of what had been Nazi ideology up to that point. The true believers among the SA men were so disillusioned that in August and September 1934 alone one hundred thousand turned their backs on the brown columns of marchers that had previously strengthened their belief in a genuine volk community. Most of these men felt marginalized and withdrew increasingly into private life. Membership in the SA shrank accordingly, from 2.9 million in August 1934 to 1.5 million in October

1935. After that, the membership dwindled further, because no real political prospects remained for implementing genuine national socialist objectives.

The Third Reich was anything but the ideal state many of the older utopias had envisaged. On the contrary, except for the hypocritical slogans about equality in the early days of the Third Reich, it cannot be emphasized enough that its long-term objectives were more dystopian than utopian. Viewed critically, it is clear that a mythos of blood was almost always behind these objectives in keeping with the racial ideology on which they were based. In the final analysis, this myth implied warlike subjugation and the eradication of the alien and the weak; neither solidarity in the best socialist sense of the word nor individual self-realization were permitted, not even to volk comrades in the movement. It is not easy to explain why this Reich was nevertheless accepted by the majority of the German people and even welcomed enthusiastically by some. I hope the following chapters will help identify at least some reasons for this contradiction that is so disturbing to anyone attempting to interpret the phenomenon "Nazi fascism."

THE IDEAL OF AN ETERNALLY
GERMAN CULTURE

But let us return to the ideas about culture linked to the models we have considered: the cult of the Führer, the model of the heroic man, the mania for Aryans and Teutons, pride in the German peasant, the principle of the order-state with its knights, and fantasies about being the chosen people of the Grail. The people who supported these ideological concepts were united, albeit only in a vague and general way, by their will, often proclaimed energetically, to recreate German culture. After the modernist-internationalist foreign infiltration and degeneracy since the late nineteenth century, they wanted to create a culture that would reactivate those artistic forces in which the true nature of the Germans had realized its potential in its purest form since the beginning of the Germanic era and the Middle Ages. Instead of acting revolutionary, which most Nazi leaders rejected as too contemporary and therefore un-German, they were interested in what was tried and true in the cultural sphere. In their Reich, they wanted to strengthen what was tradition-bound, not what was subversive.

So they mobilized everything in the cultural-aesthetic realm that could be characterized as eternally German. In the political realm, they usually cited the Germanic warriors, the German emperors of the Middle Ages, or Prussian heroes like Frederick the Great, Otto von Bismarck, and Paul von Hindenburg—Adolf Hitler being the most worthy successor of all of them. In the cultural sphere, everything that ranked high in the classical period of the Hohenstaufen, the Reformation, the Beethoven era, the Goethe period, and German romanticism was painted with a fascist brush. Countless Nazi statements appeared that alluded incessantly to Young-Siegfried, the Bamberg Horseman with his heroic gaze, the Nordic chastity of Uta von Naumburg, the Aryan mysticism of Meister Eckehart, Dürer's *Knight between Death and the Devil,* the heroic German spirit of Beethoven's *Eroica,* Goethe's Faust as Nordic man of action, Schiller as Hitler's comrade in arms, the anti-French painter of the Wars of Liberation Caspar David Friedrich, or the creator of Germanic myths, Richard Wagner. All of these figures and their works had forfeited much of their earlier aura due to the modernistic emphasis in the cultural sector during the Weimar Republic. But the publications, press reports, concerts, and exhibits initiated by the Nazi leadership held them up as examples of eternal and, thus, timeless great works that were inherently German. They should be shown the reverence they deserved—as in the ostentatiously staged festival procession "Two Thousand Years of German Culture" that took place in Munich in 1939—and they should be lifted up to the inspirational level of artistic prototypes. By following these models, German artists were supposed to eliminate all elements that were contemporary, low, ugly, obscene, and subhuman, in short, Jewish-bolshevist, from the sublime realm of truly German art.

As ideal models for this kind of art, models that would serve a new resurrection of German culture, the Nazi authorities suggested in their bombastic style the immortal values of genuine classicism: human dignity, strength of will, noble-mindedness, strength of character, and physical comeliness. Following Hitler's lead, they pointed to the ancient Germanic tribes, but also to the Aryan Greeks; the similarity of their nature to that of the Germans had already been invoked by the poet Friedrich Hölderlin, as Rosenberg pointed out more than once. Nazi cultural theorists believed these general principles had been undervalued in the Weimar Republic. In their eyes, this had been a conscious attack on all that was higher by groups they denounced as oblivious to ethnicity, such as communists and Jews as well as all the mass media managers who before 1933, along with their greed for profit, had wanted nothing better than to obliterate the feelings of the people, who longed for spiritual exaltation. Instead of foregrounding the dignity and beauty of the Nordic race in art, these groups had supposedly been intent on increasing foreign infiltration and hence degradation of artistic strivings that were genuinely German. Their goal was to kill off any volkish consciousness left in the German people, thus instigating an internationally oriented mass production in the cultural sector and a corresponding process of alien trivialization.

What most of the leading cultural theorists of the Nazi movement hoped for even before 1933 was an art devoted to the highest ideals; in it, all members of the nation who were conscious of their ethnicity would see a reflection of the cultural superiority of their people over all other peoples and races. In view of the many commercial depredations of what had earlier been high culture during the phase of market-based prosperity in the Weimar Republic, the desire for a new resurrection of German culture cannot be condemned categorically. But the goal of liberating German culture from its degradation by mass media, consumerism, and marketability was coupled from the very beginning in Nazi cultural theories with a racist arrogance that could have dangerous consequences. But in the late 1920s and early 1930s, this tendency was still invisible to most members of the conservative educated middle class. They had withdrawn into the inner sanctum of traditional German high culture out of aversion to the depraved world of the mass media and the modernistic cultural sector with its deviations into the realms of expressionism, Dadaism, technology, musical theater, and leftist ideology. And so the high-sounding phrases of Nazi cultural theorists, which promised a turn toward noble sentiments and beauty, seemed quite appealing. Many felt this conversion in the artistic sphere would allow them to regain the entitlement to cultural leadership that was their due based on their level of education.

But how realistic was it for the educated middle class to believe that it could reestablish its earlier claim to be representative in cultural matters after power was transferred to the National Socialists? Was not the NSDAP—at least in their programmatic statements—a National Socialist German Workers' Party that had promised the lower classes more influence in the state during the Weimar Republic? Why did the party continue to emphasize the great achievements of earlier German art? It might have been more logical to aim instead at a volk culture that would conform to proletarian criteria and reflect a removal of the old class barriers in the artistic sphere as well. Or was the constant blather about the new resurrection of eternally German high culture on the part of Nazi cultural theorists simply a carefully calculated propaganda trick, an attempt to win over the largely apolitical educated middle class?

The main reason there is no obvious answer to questions like these goes back primarily to the relatively unclear objectives of early Nazi fascist ideological constructs, which tended to be anchored in the irrational rather than in clearly recognizable theoretical concepts. Despite some obvious constants, such as the rejection of everything that was communist or Jewish and the glorification of everything warlike, the leading Nazi cultural theorists did not agree on many basic issues up to the beginning of the Third Reich. This was partly because the more pragmatic among them limited themselves at first to interim goals that would not upset most Germans, keeping quiet for the time being about Nazi fascist long-term goals that were substantially more radical. To win over the educated middle class and white-collar workers as well as the broad masses, and despite all their slogans about community of the volk, they usually employed three strategies in the cultural sector that seemed to promise success: They promoted traditional high culture for the educated upper class. For the middle class, they propagated a so-called mainstream culture. And for the benefit of the lower classes, they tolerated the mass-media-based entertainment culture that had expanded during the Weimar Republic and which the pragmatic Nazis simply tried to purge of its more degenerate alien elements, i.e., everything Jewish or bolshevist.

And after 1933, this triple strategy proved extremely successful. Apart from those who were forced into exile for racial or political reasons, the majority of educated Germans welcomed the fact that the Nazi state was implementing a new resurrection of German culture in all areas and supporting it with high-sounding pronouncements. Almost all of the plays by well-established traditional authors were being performed regularly, museums were putting on important exhibitions of old masters, and the most important works of earlier German literature were constantly being reprinted. In addition, there were plenty of ambitious cultural periodicals, such as *Die Kunst im Dritten Reich* (Art in the Third Reich) and *Das Innere Reich* (The Inner Reich). During the early days of the Third Reich, you could often hear symphony and solo concerts of the masterpieces of classical or romantic music on the radio, which definitely appealed to those segments of society with more discriminating taste. None of these activities deviated from the traditional middle-class concern with nurturing tradition.

Another objective proved more problematic. The firm believers among the Nazi cultural theorists hoped to surmount the class ties reflected in earlier ideas about culture and use measures backed by the party to develop a widely authoritative German volk culture. This group issued a series of lofty pronouncements addressing the volk community they hoped to create, but they could never overcome existing educational barriers. Despite trends toward democratization that had begun during the Weimar Republic, the German population at the time was still split into too many different classes that had very different concepts of education and culture. After 1933, healthy popular sentiment was supposed to prevail in German culture, a culture that had existed since time immemorial and was now to be newly resurrected. As a social program, this sounded promising, but it could not easily be reconciled with either the artistic taste of the cultured upper classes nor with the entertainment needs of the white-collar workers and the proletarian masses.

Even after the transfer of power to the Nazis, the traditional split into an elite high culture and a relatively crude culture for the masses remained. The NSDAP cultural theorists may have enthused noisily about the objectives of the culture they were to initiate—an eternally German high culture for the volk in which a will to unity that emphasized Germanness would prevail by eliminating everything that was foreign, racially inferior, and politically subversive. But an ideal so infused with racism proved all too soon to be an illusion. In the cultural sector, the capitalistic principle of supply and demand was to a large extent preserved and provided many of the media corporations that continued to exist—despite the censorship laws—with a relative autonomy of which they made full use. Even after Hitler took power, the majority of Germans continued to follow their usual cultural practices. The upper class, thanks to its education, enjoyed works of traditional high culture as it had always done—i.e., experienced its aesthetic and spiritual pleasures in the theater, the opera house, and the concert hall, during a museum visit, or by reading challenging literary works. The lower classes, on the other hand, surrounded themselves with the blare of popular music, went to see B movies, paged through magazines, danced the shimmy or the Charleston, or read bestsellers and dime novels.

Imagine the ideological justifications the less pragmatically oriented Nazi cultural theorists had to come up with to advocate the ideal of an eternally German volk culture despite these obvious divisions and even subdivisions. Admittedly, some of these pragmatists really believed that the course of history could be reversed, in this sphere as in others. Thus, they usually advocated a retreat to the provinces, the small town, or the agrarian world. There the population was supposedly still homogenous, not yet tainted by the split into a bourgeois upper class, a middle class of white-collar workers, and a proletariat that was more or less depraved. There everyone got along in relative equality and therefore had the same cultural needs. There people were not yet living in a civilization that was inferior and alien to the volk, that was everywhere—in fashion, film, theater, and dance—guided by identical capitalist interests, so that the most vapid and destructive barbarism of all time was infecting the entirety of spiritual and intellectual life. This was the view reflected toward the end of the 1920s in the writings of many a volkish-minded Heimat artist, nationalistic and revolutionary peasant leader, or SA theorist, who, like Otto Bangert or Paul Schultze-Naumburg, opposed the reign of terror of the big cities, so lethal to the volk.

Language of this kind targeting the modernistic-commercial culture industry of the Weimar Republic was not ineffective, but it bypassed social reality. The moment they came to power, the more clever Nazi cultural theorists immediately recognized this as a problem if they were to avoid getting stuck from the get-go on the sidelines of society in the small-town provincial sphere. After this point in time, they had to make themselves understandable for all Germans—the upper class, the petty bourgeoisie, and the proletariat—whether they wanted to or not. They could not do this just by beating people over the head with agrarian or hyper-racist slogans; they had to adapt to the situation in the cultural sector as they found it. Most of the Nazi cultural concepts that tried to span all classes had to remain quite vague, even after 1933. This was true despite the rejoicing among the Nazi leadership, amplified in its propaganda, that they were at last living in a true volk community in which every German could feel part of the great whole—in contrast to the period after the November Revolution in which there was fragmentation into many parties and cultural needs. In reality, not even the activists among the Nazi fascists could immediately bring about a volkish-minded coalition of the classes, nor could they put together a new cultural team that would number in the thousands and agree with their ideas. Instead they had to adjust to the classes that continued to exist and make do with the artists who had not gone into exile and wanted to remain active in their profession under the new regime—some because they believed, some because they were opportunists, and some despite the antipathy they felt.

Along with a number of convinced Nazi fascists who tried to play a leading role in the emergence of the new volk community being trumpeted far and wide, the situation also created many halfhearted hangers-on and pragmatic hypocrites in the cultural sector during the years that followed. Chief among the latter were groups active in the cultural sector who continued to supply the broad masses with products of the established media industry—hit songs, operettas, film comedies, magazines, and dime novels. These groups gave very little thought to a volkish recovery or to racial enhancement of the German people in the context of a German culture grounded on the eternal values of the Nordic race. Even many of the discriminating creative artists active in the realm of high art did not view themselves after 1933 primarily as followers of the Nazi fanatics who swore by slogans about community; they saw themselves as artists who still followed the traditional bourgeois motto Lex mihi ars. The objectives of an eternally German culture on an Aryan foundation were proclaimed by the party and much discussed in theoretical pronouncements in Nazi writings. But they remained more or less marginal in broad categories of art in the 1930s because they contravened both the cultural needs that really existed in the different social classes in Germany and the view of art held by most discriminating writers, painters, and composers. Many Nazi cultural theorists tolerated this accommodation to existing conditions and to some extent even secretly welcomed it as a means of casting their spell over all social classes, be they educated, half-educated, or uneducated. As long as they took this approach, the cultural sector during the Nazi era ran relatively smoothly until the end of World War II and—once all of the undesirable elements had been ruthlessly eliminated—needed no further interference of a serious or violent nature.

Approaches to
Practical Implementation

The idea of an eternally German culture was already setting the tone in prefascist propaganda of the late 1920s; we have looked briefly at what we identified as the enemies of this culture and at its goals. But how were these goals implemented after the transfer of power to the Nazi fascists on 30 January 1933? After all, as we have just seen, widely differing cultural needs prevailed in the different classes within the German population, and it was difficult to find a common denominator. In summary, there had been three principle forms of culture during the Weimar Republic: (1) the culture of the educated middle class, which was largely traditionally oriented and based chiefly on the classical artists of the German cultural heritage whose works placed heavy demands on the general public; (2) the culture of the white-collar workers, which tended to adopt genres that corresponded to American middlebrow ideas; and (3) the culture of the underclass, which focused on the unsophisticated entertainment needs of the so-called uneducated classes and kept them supplied with mass media products grounded almost entirely in the profit motive. Admittedly, these approaches overlapped to some extent. During the 1920s, even some representatives of the educated middle class had allowed themselves excursions into the world of entertainment now and then, and not all white-collar employees and workers had been satisfied with the more or less crude products of the entertainment industry. But despite all the slogans that claimed to support democracy, the Weimar Republic as a whole was a class-based state where taste in matters of culture was largely specific to social class.

Although some minority groups tried to make their voices heard on the margins of these three dominant cultures during the same period, not much really changed. The two major groups on the left during the first turbulent phase of the Weimar Republic between 1918 and 1923 were the expressionists and the Dadaists, but their progressive and even openly revolutionary attempts remained by and large marginal and therefore ineffective due either to the bizarre formal aspects or the cynical edginess of their works. They were followed during the second turbulent phase of the Weimar Republic between 1929 and 1933 by groups of artists affiliated with the German Communist Party. But despite desperate efforts to check the NSDAP's race to victory, the meagerness of their financial resources alone sufficed to make them as ineffective as their expressionist and Dadaist predecessors.

During the less turbulent period of prosperity in the Weimar Republic between 1923 and 1929, there was a group of artists and cultural theorists who reached a somewhat broader public. They envisaged a liberal-democratic art and culture grounded on the median and therefore relatively well accepted by the more tolerant wing of the bourgeoisie. Their ideas about culture were based to a large extent on modernism, or New Objectivity, to use contemporary terminology, and were directed primarily at those segments of the bourgeoisie and the new class of white-collar employees who did not want to revert to Wilhelminian class-based ideas of rank. Therefore, they envisaged a culture that was neither bourgeois secessionist nor proletarian revolutionary; instead, it aimed for a broad effect that was reformist in nature, which in the context of this first German republic meant a democratizing effect. This school of thought did appeal to substantially broader sectors of society than the combative left-wing camp, especially toward the end of the prosperous period from 1926 to 1929. But it was marginalized by the world economic crisis that began in 1929 and by the political radicalization of the ensuing years, which encroached on the various cultural sectors as well.

Manifestations of German nationalist culture, or to be more precise, prefascist culture, did spread noticeably during the final years of the Weimar Republic. They turned with undisguised virulence against all cultural endeavors from the left and liberal bourgeois camps, denouncing them as cultural bolshevist or modernistic symptoms of decline. These viewpoints were supported by the Kampfbund für deutsche Kultur (Militant League for German Culture), which became active beginning in 1928 under Alfred Rosenberg's leadership. They were also promoted by a series of older Heimat artists and by young prefascists, most of whom belonged to the World War I generation whose national self-confidence had been shattered and who, inspired by the *Dolchstoßlegende* (the stab-in-the-back legend), were struggling to overcome the so-called shame of Versailles.

Thus, after the Nazi fascists finally came to power at the beginning of 1933, they found a very diffuse situation in the cultural sector that could not easily be synchronized (*gleichgeschaltet*). They could more or less rely on the majority of the educated middle class, to whom they promised energetic support for the traditional cultural heritage. But how should they handle the white-collar employees, who expected the cultural sector to supply cleverly packaged light entertainment? Or what was their attitude toward workers, most of whom had previously been on the left? In short, how could these three very different social classes be unified to the point that a homogenous volk community would emerge? And besides, did they have enough artists and creative people to develop a completely different volkish culture overnight and out of thin air that would not disappoint either the educated middle class or the white-collar employees and workers from the outset? What should they do to avoid facing the majority of the German people empty-handed, culturally speaking? Difficult decisions had to be made, and depending on the ideological orientation of the responsible party leaders making them, they tended to be either fairly pragmatic or veer into the realm of the fanatic and extreme.

The new masters within the top leadership of the NSDAP were relatively united at the beginning, at least on the question of what kinds of art should no longer be tolerated in the future. In accordance with their support of state capitalism, they first suppressed all the Marxist-oriented trends in the cultural life of the Weimar Republic. In their eyes, this category included in particular those authors and artists who were members of the Bund proletarisch-revolutionärer Schriftsteller (League of Proletarian-Revolutionary Writers, BPRS) and the Assoziation revolutionärer bildender Künstler Deutschlands (Association of Revolutionary Visual Artists of Germany, ASSO). But artists who had not belonged to those organizations but who, like Bertolt Brecht or Hanns Eisler, had sympathized with the German Communist Party, were also anathema. Even some writers with left-liberal or anarchist views, especially if they were Jewish-born, as the Nazis put it, were in danger as early as February/March 1933 of losing their passports, becoming stateless, or being imprisoned under inhuman conditions. At the same time, the first blacklists of undesirable or forbidden books appeared. Initially, there were few serious disagreements among the NSDAP leaders in this regard. After the Reichstag fire on 27 February and the first boycott of Jewish businesses on 1 April, there was no longer any place in the much-heralded Third Reich for authors who had declared themselves in support of cultural bolshevist or other volk-alien tendencies. This wave of defamation crested first on 10 May when members of the Nationalsozialistische Deutsche Studentenschaft (National Socialist Student Society) at many universities chanted *Feuersprüche* (fire slogans) as they tossed books by authors viewed as irksome into bonfires.

The new masters were no less rough with painters who—disregarding the German cultural heritage—affiliated themselves with the international trend toward modernistic, abstract, or even nonrepresentational art instead of continuing to use a form that was tradition-bound, meaning realistic, to express the soulful depths of the German volk spirit. By the spring of 1933, a series of bans on teaching and exhibiting had already been instituted, so that some painters were forced either to keep a low profile somewhere in the hinterlands or escape into exile. In 1933 and 1934, a series of exhibits of so-called November art was organized with the goal of finally opening the eyes of all Germans possessed of a healthy sensitivity characteristic of the volk to the debased nature of expressionist, Dadaist, or socially critical-veristic art. These were followed in 1937 by *Entartete Kunst* (Degenerate Art), a monster exhibit arranged in Munich by Adolf Ziegler, Hitler's favorite painter; it presented the most deterrent examples of aberrant works that were communist, Semitic, slutty, insane, or Negroid.

The Nazi fascists took equally severe measures against everything un-German in so-called serious music. Following many expulsions and performance bans, Hans Severus Ziegler staged an exhibition in Düsseldorf in 1938 with the title *Entartete Musik* (Degenerate Music), employing the same kind of vilification as the Munich exhibit *Entartete Kunst* of the previous year. It denounced all of the compositions from the Weimar Republic as un-German if they could be shown to have incorporated elements that were left-oriented or Jewish-synagogical or contained so-called Negroid jazz elements or technical abstractions; none of this had any place in a volk-based musical practice. And with this, the authorities felt they had made a clean sweep.

It was easy enough for the relevant authorities to set all of these actions in motion. But for the mighty among the Nazis, the task of determining what kind of culture they should oppose to such aberrations was substantially more difficult. These efforts, which were based on a specifically German-conscious point of view, adopted one of two main approaches during the early years of the Third Reich. One was nationalistic revolutionary, and acting in the spirit of an Aryan consciousness raised to the level of myth, it accepted only a high culture that was at the same time directly tied to the volk. The second was more pragmatic; it took as its starting point the existing and obvious split into high and trivial cultural needs and tried to overcome it using partial bans and careful tactics to influence the cultural life still to be created for the nascent Third Reich. Alfred Rosenberg was the authoritative cultural theorist behind the first approach; behind the second was Joseph Goebbels, appointed Minister für Volksaufklärung und Propaganda (Minister for Public Enlightenment and Propaganda) by Hitler in March 1933.

Rosenberg had paid the respect due to the traditional high arts in his Kampfbund für deutsche Kultur (Militant League for German Culture) founded in the late 1920s and in his manifesto *Der Mythus des 20. Jahrhunderts*, which had appeared in 1930. But in the end, he was not really concerned with a historically oriented nurture of the cultural heritage; he was interested in creating a culture for the future that was Germanic and sealed off from all international influences and that would provide every German with heightened self-awareness. In contrast to withdrawal into yesteryear, an approach espoused by older representatives of heimat culture such as Adolf Bartels and Paul Schultze-Naumburg, Rosenberg envisioned from the beginning an art and culture that would be a culture of the volk community and thoroughly forward-looking in its exaggeratedly utopian goals. It is true that he had to defend himself against some very vehement groups within the National Socialist German Students' League. Their nationalistic-revolutionary and therefore equally forward-looking ambitions led them to try to link to the wing of the expressionist movement they viewed as "Nordic-gothic" in art historian Wilhelm Worringer's definition of the term, and they invoked artists such as Emil Nolde and Ernst Barlach. But since Hitler, too, rejected such approaches, in 1934 Rosenberg was able to use the *Völkische Beobachter* (Volkish Observer) and his manifesto *Revolution in der bildenden Kunst?* (Revolution in the Visual Arts?) to vilify these groups as a cultural Black Front à la Otto Strasser and thus silence them.

At the outset, Rosenberg's Militant League for German Culture, which later became the NS-Kulturgemeinde (NS Culture Community), had the support of prominent people and organizations—authors such as Hanns Johst, Erwin Guido Kolbenheyer, and Emil Strauß; publishers such as Hugo Bruckmann and Eugen Diederichs; professors such as Andreas Heusler, Ottmar Spann, and Heinrich Wölfflin; the mistress of Bayreuth Winifred Wagner; and the Deutscher Pfadfinderbund (German Scout Association), the Werwolf, and the Deutscher Frauenkampfbund (Women's Combat League). But it proved less influential than Rosenberg had hoped in the first months of the Third Reich and was viewed by many pragmatists among the Nazi cultural theorists as unrealistic or even hysterical. Hermann Göring, for example, characterized the "philosophical belches" in Rosenberg's *Mythus des 20. Jahrhunderts* simply as "garbage," and Hitler himself sometimes privately called him a fussy old biddy. Heinrich Guthmann, who represented the NS Culture Community at the Berliner Volk-schaft publishing house and who was the author of a book titled *Zweierlei Kunst in Deutschland* (Two Kinds of Art in Germany), was a fanatic with a sectarian mind-set. He still quoted Rosenberg as an authority in 1936, citing his concept of an all-embracing mythical reawakening of German culture out of the primeval sources of German-Teutonic spiritual depth. Guthmann campaigned for volkish-minded oratorios and festivals, hoping to set himself apart from both the bizarre leftist aberrations of expression-ism and from the philistine middle-class contentment that characterized other forms of culture during the Weimar Republic. What he and his Bund der Verschworenen (League of Conspirators) demanded was a cul-ture as Rosenberg had imagined it in which a split into high and low was no longer possible and where all of the volk comrades would be moved by the same volkish exhilaration in the realm of culture.

But by 1936—after the murder of Ernst Röhm and Rosenberg's loss of prestige within the NSDAP—Guthmann was fighting a losing battle. Although Rosenberg, as the Führer's official appointee for supervising the entire ideological training and education of the NSDAP, tried repeat-edly to intervene in Nazi cultural politics with his German volkish views, even aspiring to become Reichsminister für Weltanschauung und Kultur (Reich Minister for Weltanschauung and Culture), he was nevertheless increasingly marginalized between 1934 and 1937. It was Joseph Goeb-bels who proved to be his main opponent. As Minister for Public En-lightenment and Propaganda, Goebbels was able to seize the reins of Nazi cultural politics as early as summer and fall 1933 and thus sideline Rosen-berg, that dense, obstinate dogmatist, as he called him. Even Rosenberg's NS-Culture Community remained a marginal phenomenon, and in 1937 Robert Ley, head of the Deutsche Arbeitsfront (German Labor Front) in-corporated it into his Kraft durch Freude (Strength Through Joy) organi-zation. And so within Nazi cultural life, less and less attention was paid to Rosenberg, the former chief ideologue of the Nazis, who was considered even by many old fighters among the Nazi fascists as too radical due to the one-sidedness of his anticlerical and Germanophile positions.

Joseph Goebbels was able to assert himself all the more strongly in the cultural sector both through his radio addresses and newspaper articles and through a series of very effective organizational measures. His most influential venture was the Reichskulturkammer (Reich Chamber of Cul-ture), which he established in summer 1933 and which he subdivided into seven chambers. In July of that year, he founded the Reichsfilmkam-mer (Reich Film Chamber) under Fritz Scheuermann as the first of the seven; Goebbels thought it would have the broadest effect and therefore be the most important for propagating Nazi ideology. The establishment of the other six followed in November 1933: the Reichstheaterkammer (Reich Theater Chamber) under Otto Laubinger, the Reichsschrifttumskammer (Reich Literature Chamber) under Hans Friedrich Blunck, the Reichskammer für Bildende Kunst (Reich Chamber for Visual Art) under Eugen Hönig, the Reichsrundfunkkammer (Reich Radio Chamber) under Horst Dreßler-Andreß, the Reichsmusikkammer (Reich Music Chamber) under Richard Strauss, and the Reichspressekammer (Reich Press Chamber) under Max Amann. So along with genres representing an elevated volkish art, the only important ones for Rosenberg, Goebbels established chambers not only for film, but for the press and radio as well—in other words, the media that could influence the uneducated masses. It is clear that Goebbels gauged the cultural situation much more realistically than did the NS-Culture Community. And that assessment had ramifications, first in terms of organization and second in terms of impact—of course, in many ways, they were linked closely to each other.

Let us begin with the organizational aspects. After the establishment of the Reich chambers of culture, everyone in the cultural sector—journalists, writers, painters, sculptors, architects, film producers, musicians, publishers, actors, booksellers, etc.—had to join one of the seven chambers; this requirement meant that Goebbels was able to bring the entire cultural life of Germany under his control all at once. In the press sector, this meant that approximately 3,500 daily newspapers, 15,000 magazines, and 470 company newspapers with a total circulation of over 100 million copies were put under the control of the pertinent chamber. In the case of radio, there were approximately seventy broadcasting stations with programs that could be received by over ten million radios that had to comply with the Reich Radio Chamber's guidelines. The approximately eleven hundred films that were made between 1933 and 1945 and shown in over 800 theaters and the approximately twenty thousand books published yearly by over three thousand publishing houses were the responsibility of the Reich Film Chamber and the Reich Literature Chamber.

This structure worked as a perfect surveillance system. And in general, that is what it was. Nevertheless, we should not picture official party control as overly strict. It is true that everyone active in the cultural sector had to apply for membership in one of the seven chambers, and that included about sixty thousand people. But neither party membership nor loyalty to Nazi fascist views was required to join; you simply needed proof of four Aryan grandparents. In fact, in his opening speech to the Reich Chamber of Culture on 15 November 1933, which attracted a great deal of attention, Goebbels emphasized that a certain amount of personal freedom was necessary in the cultural sector and not every creative artist had to follow party directives on every issue. "We do not want art," he explained, that "is nothing more than a dramatized party program. We have the courage to be generous and we hope our generosity will be rewarded by an equal generosity on the part of the artistic community."

In selecting presidents and managers of the various chambers, Goebbels also proceeded both strategically and pragmatically. Instead of calling on a party fanatic like Hans Hinkel in 1933, he invited the composer Richard Strauss to assume the presidency of the Reich Music Chamber, hoping to share in the composer's international fame. Strauss had been more or less apolitical up to that time and was generally considered to be a so-called Jew lover. Because of this situation, a bitter Rosenberg noted in his diary on 5 June 1934, "Everywhere I go everyone is complaining about the Reich Culture Chambers' lack of direction. Everyone in the country can see what a motley group has congregated there. Old Jewish comrades as president, lawyers for the Rotary Club in influential positions, incompetent 'National Socialists,' and here and there a few able people who feel worse than uncomfortable. Add to that speeches by Goebbels with no content, in a slick style, sidestepping all the problems. The situation is grim." And Rosenberg continued half hopeful, half resigned: "People put their hopes in me, but because a National Socialist is president of the Reich Chamber of Culture, it is hard to create another organization within the party structure."

He would prove to be right about that. As Rosenberg's influence waned in the period that followed, Goebbels' influence increased steadily. He avoided all the radicalisms with which the NSDAP might have unsettled both the culturally discriminating educated middle class and the less discriminating broad masses. With the Reich Chamber of Culture, he created an organization that cast its net widely enough to gather even those who had thus far shown no sympathy for the party into the various branches of Nazi culture. The motto seemed to be "If you bring a lot, you'll bring something for everyone"; it justified artistically valuable dramas, operas, and symphonies as well as less artistic hit songs and film comedies. A skilled political realist, Goebbels satisfied both the refined cultural needs of the educated classes and the substantially cruder entertainment needs of the lower classes.

But he went even further. There were seven thousand Jewish-born artists who were not able to join one of the Reich Chambers of Culture after 1934 because of their non-Aryan ancestry. But with the founding of the Kulturbund Deutscher Juden (Cultural Federation of German Jews), soon forced to change its name to Jüdischer Kulturbund (Jewish Cultural Federation), Goebbels created a sphere for cultural activity where approximately 110,000 Jews could participate in theater and opera performances as well as concerts, lectures, and exhibits through a system of subscriptions. At the beginning, members of the federation's support committee included the philosopher Martin Buber, the painter Max Liebermann, and authors Georg Hermann and Jakob Wassermann. Although all Jewish cultural federations were forced to shut down on 10 November 1938—one day after the so-called Night of Broken Glass—the Jewish Cultural Federation of Berlin was able to become active again on 20 November 1938 on Goebbels' order; it was not until 11 September 1941 that all its functions had to cease by order of the Gestapo. In the showpiece concentration camp Theresienstadt, too, the thirty-seven thousand Jews imprisoned there were permitted a rich cultural life with theater and opera performances and symphony concerts; they were even allowed to have a library of 180,000 volumes that was intended to give the Nazi authorities the appearance of being magnanimous.

In the beginning, Goebbels—in contrast to Hitler and Rosenberg—displayed a similar repressive tolerance even toward some of the expressionists; he credited them with healthy viewpoints and even included their works in his private collection. In general, Goebbels did not limit himself to advocating what was expressed in official party propaganda slogans, especially if they laid it on too thick. He was not primarily concerned with maintaining the purity of Hitler's teachings in *Mein Kampf*; he was looking above all for points of view that were strategically effective. With that goal in mind, he was ready to use a variety of means, even when it did not suit the ideologues concerned with the systematic enhanced Nordification of the German volk, who would have preferred to exclude anyone with dark hair from German life from 1933 on. In contrast, Goebbels issued requests at that same time for artists considering emigration to remain in Germany and supported with some success the return of prominent refugees. In contrast to an Aryan-race fanatic like Adolf Bartels, who refused membership in the Völkischer Kulturbund (Federation for Volkish Culture) he founded in 1933 to Jews and to "Freemasons, Rosicrusians, Illuminati, and Jesuits" as well, Goebbels was relatively broad-minded in his personal politics. When it suited his purposes, he sometimes even supported nonfascists, turned Jewish-born Germans into honorary Aryans, or tolerated composers and actors married to Jews such as Franz Lehar, Hans Moser, and Leo Slezak. He had substantially more success with this strategy than all the Nazi cultural functionaries who either did not have the same all-encompassing party organizations at their command as he did or were too narrow-minded in their Nazi fascist ideas to have a broad impact.

But despite the obvious differences in the cultural-political strategies employed by Rosenberg and Goebbels and their followers, both groups had the same goal—the creation of a true volk community, which, by returning to its ancestral Germanness, would dissociate itself from all influences emanating from alien races. The two sometimes diverged widely in their methods and therefore sometimes represented points of view that were polar opposites. This difference is explained by the fact that Rosenberg, a fanatic who thought in utopian terms, had his eye on the long-term objectives of Nazi fascist ideology, while Goebbels, a pragmatist who thought in realistic terms, was satisfied for the time being with achieving attainable short-term goals.

Hitler, therefore, who was also a clever strategist and a political realist despite his racist delusions, favored Goebbels for the most part. A premature implementation of Nazi fascist long-term goals, meaning enhanced Nordification of the German people through force, seemed unwise to Goebbels in view of the existing sociopolitical conditions. Hitler, too, realized that the ideological and cultural preferences of individual classes of the population could not be synchronized overnight. Therefore, in the early days of the Third Reich, he made a temporary pact with existing power blocs within large-scale industry, the Reichswehr (Reich Armed Forces), and the churches instead of trying to use rash measures to establish a state beyond existing power structures and class conflicts that would be based solely on the principle of an imagined community of the volk.

This perspective meant that Goebbels, who pursued the same strategy, could usually count on Hitler supporting his tactics, and unlike some of the old bushy-bearded Teuton enthusiasts and the Aryan fanatics befogged by "Thule fantasies," Goebbels was not relegated to the sociopolitical sidelines. On the contrary, he enjoyed the complete confidence of Hitler, who saw in Goebbels one of the most useful strategists for his plans in the realm of cultural politics. It is true that these plans were based on outlandish long-term goals, but both men wanted to provide them with a basis in real conditions by reaching certain strategic short-term goals in the meantime. Despite all the slogans about the volk community as the target of their aspirations, Goebbels tried to employ a series of very disparate but demagogically coordinated strategies to reach the different social classes. He hoped to gain the support of all Germans instead of concentrating on the approval of a single class, as the communists and social democrats had done.

It is therefore just as difficult to detect a coherent, logically structured cultural policy in the years after 1933 as it is to detect a coherent Nazi fascist ideology. There were blatant contradictions in both; they could not be reduced to a common denominator, but the end result was the same—to offer all segments of the German population what they desired if possible: blood and soil ideology for the farmers, retention of the capitalist economic system for the industrialists, assurance that religious practice would continue for the churches, an expansion of the German *Wehrmacht* for the army command, guaranteed full employment for the workers, and technical modernization for the financially better-off city dwellers. The objective was to achieve the mass acquiescence that the political realists among the Nazis considered the most important short-term goal.

As a consequence, Goebbels based his cultural policies to a great extent on the principle of limited pluralism. Accordingly, he tried everything he could—after eliminating all those who openly opposed the regime—to offer the various segments of the population what was suitable for them. Goebbels did not expect to eliminate with a single blow the split into high and low culture that existed in reality, and he did not aim at a revolutionary upheaval of existing conditions in the form of a volk culture based entirely on racist principles. Instead, he steered a course open to compromise in the interest of short-term objectives. While always keeping his propagandistic agenda in mind, Goebbels avoided everything that could be considered revolutionary; Hitler, too, after the murder of the followers of Röhm and Strasser, had rejected revolution as un-German in his notorious speech at the Reich party congress in Nuremberg in 1934. Instead, Goebbels kept his eye on current conditions as he considered the cultural situation. In short, he promised the educated middle classes increased support for the cultural heritage together with the option of inner emigration into nonfascism, and he promised the so-called broad masses a rather trivial entertainment culture in terms of films, radio, and light music to avoid confronting them with anything unfamiliar and to give them the feeling they were continuing to live under normal conditions.

And Goebbels did not have to wait long for this strategy to be successful. He was able to appeal to all segments of the population this way, while the race fanatics within the Nazi Party had tended to unsettle both the educated classes and the masses with their Germanophile ideas about culture. A lot was achieved with this strategy in terms of stabilizing the Third Reich's power in the cultural sector, but the long-term ideological goals of Nazi fascism, particularly that of a volk community that saw itself as socialist, were hardly mentioned. In the end, this strategy tended to maintain the split into an elite culture and a popular entertainment culture. In fact, as I said before, it offered an escape route to everyone: the store of traditional culture for segments of the upper class and the old familiar charms of the commonplace offered by an entertainment industry geared to mass consumption for the lower classes.

In fact, this was not the case just during the early years of the Third Reich when Goebbels was trying as a first step to offer all segments of the German population whatever appealed to them. The same approach continued even during the years between 1939 and 1945, when he called for a total war but simultaneously reinforced the entertainment aspects of Nazi culture, 70 percent of the total before 1939, to keep the so-called broad masses in a good mood. As a result, some of the Nazi fascists who were blind believers became insecure about their aggressively Nordic views as the years passed. Some even insisted on a decisive change in policy. But Goebbels was undeterred by these expressions of discontent. He continued to pursue his cultural politics of limited pluralism that could not be pinned down to a clear ideological position; it was based for strategic reasons, as it had always been, on class differentiation. So when Goebbels was asked at a press conference in Berlin in 1940 what the real essence of the National Socialist utopia was above and beyond the short-term goals already achieved, he answered cleverly that "it was essential to win first, and then we can take it from there." And this remained his attitude until the collapse of the Third Reich.

CONSEQUENCES FOR THE ARTS

Architecture

From the very beginning, Hitler saw the creation of a new architecture as one of the most important cultural tasks. In his opinion, the vulgar principle of arbitrariness had been the rule under the control of private capital during the Weimar Republic, with the exception of some publicly funded residential housing projects. In contrast, he was primarily interested in imposing public buildings that would reflect the new volkish sense of unity. So instead of continuing to give a free hand to large profit-hungry companies and the architects dependant on them, Hitler hoped to use a state management and investment policy for construction projects that seemed especially urgent to him; this, he thought, would give the new Reich a truly imposing or even an imperial external aspect. At the same time, as an adroit political realist faced with the continuing world economic crisis, he first needed to support construction projects that were as labor-intensive as possible. The effect would be to provide new scope for a construction industry that had been idle since 1930, thus reincorporating into the production process the millions of unemployed whom he had promised bread and work in his 1931–1932 election campaign. One good way to achieve this pledge was to carry out the plan developed in the late 1920s for a network of roads that would cover all of Germany; the plan was being promoted to the German people by Nazi propaganda organizations as the *Reichsautobahn* project, or the Führer's roads.

On 27 July 1933, Hitler issued the law authorizing construction of the *Reichsautobahn* and commissioned Fritz Todt, Generalinspektor für das deutsche Straßenwesen (Inspector General for German Roadways), to implement the plan. Hitler even participated in the start of construction of the first segment of this gigantic venture by picking up a spade on 23 September 1933 in Frankfurt am Main. After that, spurred on by Hitler personally, the project went forward at a frenzied pace. By October 1934, there were already fifteen hundred kilometers of autobahn under construction. Shortly thereafter, another twelve hundred were cleared for expansion. To keep the cultural aspect in mind, the responsible Nazi authorities, at Hitler's behest, often described the autobahns as a German *Gesamtkunstwerk*. Alwin Seifert, NS-Landschaftswart (Landscape Warden), was charged with making sure the new routes did not offend against the natural beauty of the surrounding landscape and that the embankments were planted with native flowers and shrubs. They also arranged for Paul Bonatz, a well-known architect, to take over bridge design. By 1936, there were already 125,000 people working on the completion of other autobahns, so that by 1939, approximately three thousand kilometers could be put into operation. All of this contributed in a major way to the image of Hitler as the genius who vanquished unemployment.

For the time being, the autobahn project satisfied the desire for new construction programs linked to realpolitik. But from the beginning, Hitler believed his much more important calling was to go down in German history, or world history, for that matter, as the master builder of great national public buildings. Here, too, the cultural aspect played a central role. As the first large-scale building of this type, Hitler commissioned the architect Paul Ludwig Troost in mid-1933 to construct a monumental *Haus der deutschen Kunst* (House of German Art) in Munich. With this project, he chose Munich, in his own words, not only as the "capital city of the movement," but also as the "capital city of art" in the Greater German Reich on which he had set his sights. Hitler participated in the laying of the foundation stone for this "consecrated hall" on 15 October 1933; here, he decreed, the annual Great German Art exhibits would take place. This edifice, 175 meters long with gigantic rows of pillars and columns, supported by donations of about eight million reichsmarks made by German banks and industrial concerns, was dedicated on 18 July 1937. Hitler emphasized that unlike most of the functionalist designs for large buildings during the 1920s, it did not call to mind "factories, district heating plants, train depots, or electrical sub-stations," as he disparagingly described them. He called it a temple of art in which the racial sense of beauty of the new Reich he had established could be expressed.

Also early on, Hitler envisioned—his third construction-related political scheme—the architectural configuration of large parade grounds, impressive *Thing* sites, temples of honor, and castles modeled on those of the Teutonic Order, all designed as an imposing backdrop for displaying the will to succeed of his NSDAP. The first of these to be put into use was the *Thing* site at Halle an der Saale in 1934, and that same year the architectural configuration of the parade grounds for the Reich party congress in Nuremberg was begun. Then on 9 November 1935, the dedication of the Temple of Honor on the Königsplatz in Munich designed by Paul Ludwig Troost and Leonhard Gall took place; its purpose was to honor the sixteen *putschists*-cum-martyrs who had lost their lives in the infamous March to the Feldherrnhalle led by Hitler in 1923. One year later the Dietrich-Eckart-Theater (now the Waldbühne) and the Olympic Stadium in Berlin, both designed by Werner March, were opened. At the same time, Clemens Klotz presented the Führer with the order castles Vogelsang in the Eifel region and Krössinsee in Pomerania built under his direction, and Order Castle Sonthofen in Upper Bavaria designed by Hermann Giesler soon followed.

What distinguished these buildings in Hitler's eyes was the fact that they clearly avoided the style employed by the leading architects of the Weimar Republic. That style, according to Hitler and other Nazi fascists, expressed an abject pursuit of modernistic internationalism and even cultural bolshevism, using constructivist architectural forms that had consciously dispensed with all traditions that reflected the greatness of the German spirit. Under the motto Down with Ornamentation, these architects had designed buildings that showed their opposition to all historical references and were characterized by their flat roofs, smooth, white walls, and glass-iron construction in the style of Adolf Loos, Walter Gropius, Mies van der Rohe, and also Le Corbusier, whom Alexander von Senger called the Lenin of architecture. The Nazi architects, in contrast, usually favored stone constructions with classicistic references; the purist-massive simplification they embodied was intended to convey monumentality and dominance.

With this style of construction, supposedly appropriate to the German inner nature, Nazi architecture tried to distance itself from all older concepts of style that focused on ornamental patterns and from the functionalism of the so-called New Objectivity as well. As Werner Rittich, a follower of Alfred Rosenberg and Paul Schultze-Naumburg, emphasized in 1938 in his book *Architektur und Bauplastik der Gegenwart* (Contemporary Architecture and Architectural Sculpture), architecture's "tectonic clarity, harmony of dimension, and balance in the relationship of load and support" should conform to the "feeling of the Nordic people," ever striving for purity. Instead of aiming for novelty at any price, as he and other like-minded Nazi cultural theorists explained, architecture should again be founded on a "sense of primal providence" that was striving for "organic unity" instead of lapsing into styles that were extravagant or arbitrary. And Rittich expressly cited Hitler, who had written in *Mein Kampf*

Figure 7. Hermann Giesler: Model for the *Hohe Schule* of the NSDAP on the Chiemsee (1939).

as early as 1925 that due to the obsession with novelty on the part of individual architects and the capitalist builders backing them, the archi- tectural design of contemporary large cities seemed unplanned and even chaotic. Soulless private homes and commercial buildings had been built everywhere, but—in contrast to the ancient world or to the Germanic Middle Ages—no magnificent public buildings had been constructed of which all Germany could be proud. Architecture, the highest and most important of the arts, as Hitler had said at the time, had not seemed to be emblematic of an idealistic community of the volk; instead it had degenerated to the point of being a sordid expression of the purely utilitarian. The "plutocratic functional buildings" of the 1920s, we read in *Mein Kampf*, reflected an unscrupulous desire for profit, profit that benefited not the broad masses, but a small group of wheeler-dealers, an uncultured clique made up of anti-German Jews and some modernists who had forgotten their fatherland and the fact that they were German.

In addition to individual buildings designed during the 1930s as a declaration of his will to political power, Hitler also began to think more and more about the reshaping of whole cities, the so-called Führer cities. Nuremberg, Munich, Berlin, and Hamburg were the first ones. Other cities to be reshaped were added later: Augsburg, Bayreuth, Breslau, Dresden, Düsseldorf, Graz, Hannover, Innsbruck, Cologne, Königsberg, Linz, Münster, Oldenburg, Saarbrücken, Salzburg, Stettin, Weimar, and Würzburg. Models of them were introduced to the public in 1938–1939 at the *Erste Deutsche Architekturausstellung* (First German Architecture Exhibit). One of the first cities to be rebuilt as part of this project was Nuremberg. Here, immediately after he took power in spring 1933, Hitler began to plan spacious parade grounds for the Reich party congresses. He first appointed Paul Ludwig Troost to carry out this task, but he was soon replaced by Albert Speer. Speer was the one who gave the project the streak of gigantism that Leni Riefenstahl attempted to highlight in her 1934 film *Triumph des Willens* (Triumph of the Will), which included massive parades, a sea of flags, and torchlight processions. Speer had the grounds enlarged to five times their original size so they encompassed a surface of thirty square kilometers. But after the parade areas were finished, much of the rest got stuck in the planning stage. The German Stadium designed by Speer, for example, was to be decorated with a martial Reich's eagle with wings eighty meters wide and would seat approximately four hundred thousand spectators when finished. The same mania for the gigantic was behind the plan to build stands next to the Märzfeld that would seat 195,000. And as a central structure that would extend into the surrounding landscape, Speer began construction of a Neue Kongreßhalle (New Congress Hall) that was 190 meters tall, had granite enclosure walls, and an amphitheater-like interior construction.

The designs for these structures and their ancillary grounds impressed Hitler so much that in early January 1937 he commissioned Speer to design the German pavilion for the Paris International Exposition, which was subsequently awarded the gold medal by the jury there. In addition, Hitler named Speer to the position of general building inspector with sole responsibility for the redesign of Berlin, the capital of the Reich, where over ten million people were supposed to live after its transformation into the largest city in Europe and its rechristening as Germania. By Speer's own report, he was asked to lay out two axis streets over thirty-eight kilometers long right through the existing city; in its center, the most imposing buildings of the New Reich were to stand to give Berlin the same imperial appearance as Rome or Paris. Speer—most certainly after a detailed discussion with Hitler—planned a Great Hall of the German People as the centerpiece of the entire design; its height was estimated at 220 meters, and there would be room for 160,000 to 180,000 standing volk comrades. Large-scale theater districts and artist colonies were also not forgotten in the plans for redesign. The plan to erect a six-meter-tall statue of Apollo, the supreme god of art, by Arnold Breker in the middle of the Runder Platz at the intersection of the two main axis streets was part of the same

Figure 8. Albert Speer: Model for the *Great Hall* in Berlin (1938). © Bildagentur für Kunst, Kultur und Geschichte.

deliberate exhibition of cultural consciousness. All of these projects were being planned and worked on up to the beginning of the war without a system of axis streets ever becoming visible. But in 1939 Speer completed—at Hitler's behest—the Neue Reichskanzlei (New Reichs Chancellory) in a record time of nine months; it was praised for displaying an austere order befitting a master builder while allowing plenty of scope for artistic elements. Numerous artworks testify to the accuracy of this description: the mosaic surfaces by Hermann Kaspar, the *Schicksalsschlachten der deutschen Geschichte* (Fateful Battles of German History) designed by Werner Peiner for the tapestries in the marble gallery, the statues by Arno Breker erected in the forecourt, and the central painting *Die Göttin der Kunst* (The Goddess of Art) by Adolf Ziegler, which Hitler himself had selected—all combined to highlight the new Führer's enthusiasm for art as well as his character as a powerful ruler.

The same mix of imperialism and aestheticism underlies the *Reichssportfeldgelände* (Reich athletic grounds) in Berlin and the stadium that was part of it, both designed by Werner March and both finished on time for the 1936 Summer Olympics; statues in the entrance areas by Josef Wackerle and Karl Albiker make an emphatically athletic impression. The Nazi authorities, and Leni Riefenstahl in her *Olympia* film as well, repeatedly emphasized the quintessential racial affinity between the art-loving ancient Greeks and contemporary Germans. To stress this affinity, March described the entire complex, which was intended to have a ceremonially solemn as well as an athletic character, with the following words saturated with cultural references: "Next to arena, the *stadion*, we find the Maifeld as a *forum* with the Langemarckhalle as *templon*, the Freilichtbühne as *theatron*, the Reichsakademie as *gymnasion*, the Haus des deutschen Sports as *prytaneion*, and the public recreational area as *palästra*. And even the sacred olive tree from the temple of Olympian Zeus, from whose branches a boy with a golden knife cut the victory wreaths, has experienced a recurrence in the German oak which greets visitors today at the Olympic gate."

Similar architectural transfigurations and new buildings were planned for Munich, Hitler's favorite city; they were to go far beyond the construction of the previously mentioned Temple of Honor on the Königsplatz in 1935. But most of these plans, like those for Berlin, got stuck in the beginning stages. It is true that on 21 December 1937 Hitler named Hermann Giesler, who was to build the advanced school for the Nazi Party leadership, to the position of Generalbaurat für die Hauptstadt der Bewegung (head of the Planning Office for the Capital City of the Movement), the architect's title in Nazi jargon; he was additionally commissioned with the architectural reconstruction of Augsburg, Linz, and Weimar. But projects of this kind never came to completion, because after the beginning of World War II on 1 September 1939, the realization of all the buildings that had been planned or begun was abandoned on Hitler's orders, and some had been, in any case, stuck in the planning phase.

The architectural projects Hitler targeted after that point tended to be pragmatic or influenced by considerations of realpolitik. For example, on 16 March 1940, he named Wilhelm Kreis, the tried-and-true builder of many clunky Bismarck towers, to the position of Generalbaurat für die Gestaltung der deutschen Kriegerfriedhöfe (head of the Planning Office for the Design of Cemeteries for German Warriors). In 1943, he had Joseph Goebbels transfer to Kreis the presidency of the Reich Culture Chamber for the Visual Arts so that he could design a plethora of memorials and halls of fame in which the World War II–enforced "unification of Europe under the leadership of the German people who are its heart" would assume a form that transcended time. Along with the dignified execution of these memorials, Hitler wanted to express his deep connectedness and concern for the families of soldiers fallen in the war. In 1940, with this in mind-set, he appointed Arbeitsdienstführer (head of the German Labor Front) Robert Ley to the position of Reichskommissar für den sozialen Wohnungsbau nach dem Krieg (Reichs Commissioner for Post-War Public Housing). But because the glimmer of hope for a final victory of the German *Wehrmacht* over the Soviet Union and the Western powers gradually faded after 1943, such plans were increasingly abandoned.

Especially painful for Hitler was the bitter insight that due to the rapidly worsening military situation he would not be able to undertake the rebuilding of Linz, his native city. Although Berlin was to be the political center for the reshaping of Europe, as late as 1943 Hitler still intended to use the construction of a gigantic museum facility to transform Linz into a European art center with which no other city in the world could compete. Here—after unscrupulous raids in all of the countries bordering Germany—Hitler wanted to "collect all the most famous works of the old and the new 'Germanic' classical periods for an exhibit that will overwhelm every visitor." To execute this plan, he had thousands of paintings, drawings, and prints put into storage in Kremsmünster Abbey and in the Altaussee salt mine toward the end of the war.

In summary, the imperial classicism of the large structures designed by Nazi architects, amplified by the use of torchlight parades and cathedrals of light, made the impression on the broad masses that Hitler and his chief architects had hoped for, but there were never enough of them to achieve the overall imperial effect that the Nazi leadership wanted. The time span between 1933 and 1939 had been much too short. Other art forms, be they paintings, books, films, or musical compositions, need a relatively brief period for development. In contrast, monumental public buildings and buildings designed to be showpieces, let alone redesigned city centers, require a substantially longer time for planning and construction. For this reason, it is difficult to speak at all of a significant National Socialist architecture. The intention is apparent, but there was simply not enough time to carry it out. A scant six years were not enough in the end to give the most important German cities a new architectural image.

Furthermore, many of these structures, like those in the Reich party congress compound in Nuremberg or the Great Hall in Berlin, which was planned to be seventeen times larger than Saint Peter's Basilica in Rome, were designed to be much too gigantic to take shape overnight. But we can see one thing clearly if we look at the fragments of Nazi architecture that were completed: the intent was to end once and for all the Weimar Republic's haphazard land speculation and addiction to architectural novelty. The Nazi leadership wanted to use architecture to replace both hunger for profit and undue emphasis on individuality and originality with an emphasis on community with an imperial aura. That is why they envisioned architecture that, as Hitler repeatedly emphasized, could hold its own in the eyes of eternity even when compared with Greek temples or the cathedrals of the Middle Ages. A worldview become stone would be expressed in these buildings; it would neither imitate older styles like a parvenu, nor would it serve soulless functionalism.

The buildings characteristic of Nazi architecture, many of which no longer exist, therefore did not imitate older stylistic models but instead attempted to express monumentality per se. With the exception of the eagle and the swastika—the two most important national emblems—the architects of these palaces, ministries, and museums dispensed with any further ornamentation and were content with the aesthetic effect of quarrystone, scratch coat left cement gray, shell limestone slabs, hewn wood, or roughly chiseled reliefs. In cases where these buildings avoided gigantism in the form of steeply jutting towers, immense cupolas, and schematic rows of pillars, there were individual exemplars that were certainly passable. Evidence suggests that the best of them were attempts to imitate existing buildings designed by members of the Deutscher Werkbund or their sympathizers such as Heinrich Tessenow and Peter Behrens.

More or less the same is true of the efforts at construction and ornamentation undertaken by the Amt Schönheit der Arbeit (Office for the Beauty of Work), founded in 1933 as a subsidiary organization of the NS-Kulturgemeinde (National Socialist Culture Community) or more specifically of the Deutsche Arbeitsfront (German Labor Front). Following the Werkbund approach, the office often saw to it that in the case of smaller construction projects, including city halls, courthouses, *Hitler Jugend* hostels, residential developments, and factory canteens, the designers avoided extremes (such as steeply soaring towers or palatial designs bristling with columns) and the prominent display of technological innovations; this restraint was welcomed by the majority of people living or working in these buildings. After all, the so-called International Style favored by the masters of the Bauhaus and by architects such as Ernst May, Erich Mendelssohn, and Bruno Taut seemed unusual or even alien to broad segments of the German population at the time. Thus, most of the buildings erected after 1933 caused little or no controversy in either the private or the public spheres. Most of the people interested in architecture either found these buildings beautiful in their dignified simplicity or at least inoffensive to their sense of taste. In any case, they saw a greater will to culture reflected in these buildings than in the functional buildings dating from the prosperous phase of the Weimar Republic, which they characterized as soulless.

Painting and Sculpture

We cannot really talk about specifically prefascist cultural politics with regard to painting until 1928. Admittedly, some volkish-minded cultural theorists and painters such as Ferdinand Avenarius, Julius Langbehn, Fritz Mackensen, Hans Thoma, Carl Vinnen, and others had been on a crusade against modernism in the visual arts since 1890. But it was the Nationalsozialistische Gesellschaft für deutsche Kultur (National Socialist Society for German Culture), founded by Alfred Rosenberg in 1927 and a short time later renamed the Kampfbund für deutsche Kultur (Militant League for German Culture), that gave such endeavors an obvious Nazi fascist slant. Paul Schultze-Naumburg's book *Kunst und Rasse* (1928; Art and Race) is a good example of this phenomenon. Schultze-Naumburg, after decades of relatively reasonable *Heimatsschutz* (homeland protection) publications, had begun to equate the images in expressionist paintings with the world of the mentally ill or the handicapped to be able to denounce them as racially inferior. And in other publications of this kind on cultural theory, the political and aesthetic vocabulary of the volkish old guard veered noticeably toward Nazi fascism. Previously, nationalistic circles had attacked nontraditional painting primarily as un-German, but now some representatives of this view increasingly used defamatory adjectives like degenerate, subhuman, Jewish subversive, Negroid, or cultural bolshevist when they took issue with the supposedly sorry efforts of modernist painting. So in Thüringen in 1930 when the National Socialist Party shared power for the first time in a coalition government of middle-class parties, Wilhelm Frick, who was NS-Innen und Volksbil-dungsminister (minister of the Interior and Public Education), used racist arguments and the support of Paul Schultze-Naumburg to have all the modern paintings removed immediately from the Weimar Schloßmuseum as marks of shame of an un-German Negro culture.

But it was after the transfer of power to the Nazis in spring 1933 that the dam actually broke. Expressionism, futurism, cubism, Dadaism, or sur-realism—all the art movements of the past twenty-five years that had been denounced as modernistic were suddenly viewed by many cultural theo-rists as alien to the volk or even hostile to the volk. Expressionism was still defended as artistically important and even revolutionary by some, including the journalist Paul Fechter, critic Fritz Hippler, museum ex-pert and head of the National Gallery in Berlin Alois Schardt, and many members of the radical left wing of the Nazi Party like Otto Andreas Schreiber in his journal *Kunst der Nation* (1933–1935; The Nation's Art). But it was nevertheless a special target for the blood and soil fanatics within the party, who attacked it more and more forcefully as instinctually uncertain, subhuman, alien to the species, racially divided, or papua-like. After 1933, for example, these groups characterized Emil Nolde's figures as Negroid, Ernst Barlach's as half idiots, and Karl Hofer's as decadent.

Faced with defamation campaigns of this kind, painters, graphic artists, and photomontage artists such as Max Beckmann, Heinrich Campen-donk, Lyonel Feininger, Raoul Hausmann, John Heartfield, Thomas The-odor Heine, Wassily Kandinsky, Paul Klee, Oskar Kokoshka, Johannes Molzahn, Felix Nußbaum, Kurt Schwitters, Johannes Wüsten, and others chose to leave the country either immediately or in the years that fol-lowed. George Grosz, a painter and graphic artist who had been a com-munist and then swung over to critical verism, had wisely already left Germany in January 1933. Those who did not leave voluntarily, like Willi Baumeister, Otto Dix, Max Pechstein, and Georg Tappert, were ruthlessly removed from their positions or honorary offices by the men with the proper authority in the new party. This happened even to a longtime Nazi Party member such as Ernst Nolde or to Ernst Ludwig Kirchner, who was living in Switzerland at the time, although they resisted these measures out of German-conscious motives. Even short-lived attempts to conform by Wassily Kandinsky and Otto Schlemmer were ignored by the Nazi au-thorities. "Newness for its own sake," as Hitler put it at the Reich party congress in 1933, would no longer be tolerated.

There were very few opportunities for either direct or indirect resistance to these views in the following years. After all, as early as 1925–1927 in *Mein Kampf,* Hitler had described the artistic efforts of Dadaism, futur-ism, and cubism as a "prostitution of art" in which a widespread "cultural degeneration" was made manifest. He instructed Joseph Goebbels and Alfred Rosenberg to put an end to this "nonsense that was harmful to the volk" without delay. The measures that were taken issued primarily from two organizations: the Reich Chamber for Visual Arts created by Goebbels in the fall of 1933 and its first chairman, architect Eugen Hönig, and from the NS-Culture Community headed by Rosenberg. Goebbels and those functionaries of the National Socialist German Students' League, the SS, and the Labor Front who had hoped for a second, much more profound national socialist revolution in the spirit of the Strasser brothers, had accepted the rebellious quality in the modernistic works of Emil Nolde, Karl Schmidt-Rotluff, and Ernst Barlach in the beginning. They had sometimes even portrayed this quality as exemplary and tried to make it accessible to German workers through secret exhibitions in factories into the early 1940s. Rosenberg and his supporters, in contrast, made no secret of their aversion to everything modern. And because Rosenberg and Hitler were of the same opinion on this point, Goebbels lost out in this internal party dispute. In fact, in his address at the Reich party congress in Nuremberg in 1934, which had a major impact on both the political and cultural sectors, Hitler distanced himself from all social-revolutionary ambitions within the NSDAP and committed himself very publicly to the forces of tradition. A short time before, Hitler had had Ernst Röhm and Gregor Strasser liquidated along with a hundred other representatives of his party's left wing and some opponents of the regime who seemed to him equally radical. He proceeded to suppress all efforts within the arts to portray Nazi fascism as revolutionary and to cite certain avant-garde artistic movements of the recent past in support of that view. In his speech, he accordingly denounced the "stammerings about art and culture" of the cubists, futurists, and Dadaists, whom he perceived as the most dangerous representatives of the "cultural bolshevist ism-art" he repudiated.

Subsequently, the condemnation of any kind of un-German painting

Figure 9. Cover image for the guide to the exhibition *Degenerate Art* in Munich (1937). The sculpture is *The New Man* (1912) by Otto Freundlich.

reached virtually apocalyptic intensity among Hitler's followers. Most of the pamphlets published by this group were either based on Hitler's own statements or they referred to Rosenberg's books *Der Mythus des 20. Jahrhunderts* (1930) and *Revolution in der bildenden Kunst* (1934). In these texts, that hyper-fanaticized Aryan enthusiast, following in the footsteps of Houston Stewart Chamberlain, ascribed the "intellectual syphilis" and "artistic infantilism" he saw manifested in expressionist "mestizo art" to the effects of the modern metropolis, including both "alienation from nature" and "racial bastardization." Pamphlets such as Paul Schultze-Naumburg's *Kunst aus Blut und Boden* (1934; Art from Blood and Soil) and Winfried Wendland's *Kunst und Nation. Ziel und Wege der Kunst im neuen Deutschland* (1934; Art and Nation. Destination and Pathways of Art in the New Germany) followed in Rosenberg's lead. But during the early years of the Third Reich, the most influential publication was probably Kurt Karl Eberlein's *Was ist deutsch in der deutschen Kunst?* (1934; What Is German in German Art?), which reads like a virtual catalogue of all the sins of pointedly modernistic painting. Closely aligned with Hitler and Rosenberg, Eberlein saw the absolute nadir of German art in the Weimar Republic. That era, he explained, was crawling with "art sybarites," "aesthetic lowlifes," and "art jobbers," who even in "the most sublime art" saw nothing more than "an end in itself, visual prostitution, and sensation." Much of this kind of painting was an "art for the upper classes" with a tendency to be bizarre and noncommittal—in other words, a folk alien "big-city art" or a commercialized fashionable art; its products had the same value for their profit-hungry owners as lucrative stocks. For Eberlein, the chief evildoers among the painters of the 1920s were not really leftist artists such as Käthe Kollwitz or the members of the Assoziation revolutionärer bildender Künstler (Association of Revolutionary Visual Artists, ASSO); the worst were the bohemian-elitist expressionsts whose hostility to the volk aimed for vile shock effects and whose tendency was to prostitute art in its entirety so that it awakened only revulsion. Many of them, he wrote, had painted primarily "wooden idols, criminals, dyspeptics, South Sea Islanders, Slavic-Russian peasants, village idiots, schizophrenics, nudists, mediums, whores, and pimps." Yes, some representatives of this movement had even begun to portray "godless criminal Jews as Christ and consumptive welfare sluts as the mother of God."

But it was possible to surpass even these tirades, as speeches and writings from subsequent years demonstrate. Some Nazi theorists liked to get especially upset about the cultural-bolshevist degeneracy and shameless obscenity of this kind of painting, which the expressionists had used to drag the pure German racial soul through the muck. Following a series of smaller so-called exhibits of shame bearing titles such as *Regierungskunst von 1918 bis 1933* (Government Art from 1918 to 1933), *Schreckenskammer der Kunst* (Art's Chambers of Horror), *Spiegelbilder des Verfalls in der Kunst* (Reflections of Decline in Art), or *Novembergeist: Kunst im Dienste der Zersetzung* (The Spirit of November: Art in the Service of Decomposition), this trend reached its climax in Munich in 1937 at the infamous monster show *Entartete Kunst* (Degenerate Art). The object of this exhibition was finally to open the German people's eyes to the general "decline of culture" during the years before 1933, as it was stated in the official guide to the exhibition. Bursting formal boundaries, defamation of religion, preference for ugliness, anti-bourgeois shock effects—absolutely all of expressionism's criteria for form and content that had been considered antibourgeois and therefore revolutionary between 1910 and 1922–1923 were denounced as "the spawn of madness, of insolence, of defenses undermined, of Jewish pathology, of incompetence, and of the bolshevist will to subversion," as Adolf Ziegler, the exhibition's organizer, put it. "These antediluvian prehistoric cultural cavemen and art-stammerers," Hitler jeered at the time, "can go back to the caves of their ancestors as far as we're concerned, and display their primitive scribblings there." Bruno E. Werner, a compliant and conformist journalist, wrote on 20 July 1937 in the *Deutsche Allgemeine Zeitung,* "With the exhibition *Entartete Kunst,* the Führer's will has put an end to an entire period."

Everything else followed with predictable logic. In 1937, for example, Wolfgang Willrich published "an artistic and political manifesto in support of the complete recovery of German art in the spirit of the Nordic type" titled *Die Säuberung des Kunsttempels* (The Cleansing of the Temple of Art). In this text, he attacked in the most offensive possible manner the expressionist writers of the journal *Aktion,* as well as the painters of the November Group, the cubists, and the Dadaists, with the goal of finishing off once and for all the anarchistic and red "artistic pestilence" of the 1920s. On the occasion of the opening of the *Zweite Große deutsche Kunstausstellung* (Second Great Exhibition of German Art) in Munich in 1938, Hitler used the same tone, sputtering once again about "the November chiefs of the Dada and Cubi tribes" as if he were talking about prehistoric subhumans. One year later, Bettina Feistel-Rohmeder and Adolf Dresler published their pamphlets *Im Terror des Kunstbolshevismus* (In Terror of Artistic Bolshevism) and *Deutsche Kunst und entartete Kunst* (German Art and Degenerate Art), in which they again claimed that painting during the Weimar Republic had consisted primarily of "blasphemies," "scribblings by cretins," and portrayals of "prostitutes, pimps, murderers, traitors, and maniacs."

In conformity with statements like this, a "law concerning the confiscation of products of degenerate art" was issued on 31 May of the same year, with the result that approximately sixteen thousand works of art were removed from public ownership. Many were ruthlessly destroyed or auctioned away to foreign buyers, as official parlance had it. On 20 March 1939 in Berlin alone, 1,004 paintings and 3,825 works of graphic art went up in flames in the courtyard of the main fire station. The Nazi Party leadership had other undesirable works publicly auctioned in Lucerne in June 1939—among them paintings and sculptures by Ernst Barlach, Max Beckmann, Marc Chagall, Lovis Corinth, Otto Dix, Paul Gauguin, Vincent van Gogh, George Grosz, Carl Hofer, Ernst Ludwig Kirchner, Paul Klee, Oskar Kokoschka, Max Liebermann, Franz Marc, Gerhard Marcks, Paula Modersohn-Becker, Otto Müller, Emil Nolde, Max Pechstein, and Pablo Picasso—and apparently "high spirits reigned like at a county fair."

In all of these actions that were well-organized according to the party's program, one ideology identified as among the most noxious—along with bolshevism and Jewish cultural subversion—was bourgeois liberalism, which supposedly resulted in an egotistical loss of all restraint. To prevent Germany from foundering in a metropolitan internationalist "civilization of filth and obscenity," Hitler and Rosenberg preached a radical religio in both the political and the cultural spheres, meaning a retrospective commitment to the "primal forces of the quintessentially German." Over and over, they asserted that the main achievements in the arts had always been based on national communal ideals; privatization that had an individualistic mind-set, on the other hand, tended to a "consumptive aestheticism" and hence of necessity led to ideological vagueness, intellectual smugness, or even degeneracy. Art should no longer be autonomous, they insisted, but must once again become conscious of responsibility and close to the volk. As you would expect, most Nazi cultural theorists wanted to assert principles such as comradeship, ethnic community, and public interest as the highest values in the visual arts. So instead of idolizing painters who separated themselves from the people in an elitist way to gain the favor of the "upper ten thousand," they supported those artists who attempted to appeal to the masses. "For that alone is true art," Hermann Göring explained with a pseudo-socialist turn of phrase, "which the common man recognizes and can understand."

NSDAP spokesmen liked to look back to painting in the decades before the beginning of the pernicious merry-go-round of isms around 1900; they portrayed periods like romanticism, Biedermeier, poetic realism, and the Gründerzeit (the Founder Epoch after 1871) as exemplary, because then art was still truly of the people. Not until around 1890, after these four periods, they claimed, did the progressive commercialization of the arts and a series of secessionist counter reactions to this trend lead to a pernicious polarization into educated and uneducated, esotericism and kitsch, and elite art and entertainment art. To counteract this development, Hitler and his followers incessantly promulgated the ideal of a new G-art, that is, a general art oriented to the tried and true primal force of the eternally German and contemptuously rejecting everything that was new, avant-garde, elitist, aestheticizing, or commercial. Hitler's opening address to the First Great German Art Exhibition of 1937 was therefore based almost exclusively on the opposing concepts modern and German. The first adjective represented decay, he emphasized, since the art corresponding to it had diverged increasingly from the primal forces of the German volk. The second adjective represented the rebirth of the ever same, specifically of that which is Nordic, Teutonic, and German. Hitler always portrayed everything specifically German as positive, ennobling, and uplifting. What he and his followers meant was a new-old German art that would be uplifting, not critical; down-to-earth, not intellectualistic; specific to German ethnic type, not international; and conscious of social responsibility, not free-spirited. The products of this art would be so significant, they explained, that they could only be valued, never evaluated, as Goebbels decreed with potential reviews of future exhibitions in mind.

Offhand, that all sounded very close to the volk, but in the final analysis it boiled down to very authoritarian ideas. Ultimately, this particular concept of being in the tradition of the volk (*Volkstümlichkeit*) was almost always based on an ostensibly indivisible symbiosis of volk and Führer. In the circles where these theories were developed, the proper usage was not "the volk wants" but rather "he wants," since it was generally asserted that the totality of the German people's will manifested itself in Hitler's aesthetic ideas in any case. There, explained the many Nazi fascists who had been transported into a state of enthusiasm during the first weeks and months of the Third Reich, German being had at last assumed its highest possible form. Even Martin Heidegger, rector of Freiburg University and a philosopher whose renown was based on his highly speculative book *Sein und Zeit* (1927; Being and Time, 1962), was in conformity with this view when he explained in 1933 to the students in the spirit of the new regime, "It is not theorems and 'ideas' that shall be the rules of your being; the Führer himself and he alone is German reality today and in the future, and its law."

Before 1933, Teuton fanatics of an older generation such as Paul de Lagarde, Julius Langbehn, and Ferdinand Avenarius had described an approach to art that was not quite so Führer-centered. In fact, some of the firmest believers in this group hoped that Nazi fascism would also produce a definite turn toward social concerns in art, and after the transfer of power to Hitler their writings began to express hope that a time had

Figure 10. Karl Gries: *Summer* (1942). Tapestry.

come when everyone, not just the upper levels of society, would develop a heightened interest in the highest achievements of German culture. In the beginning, some of these programmatic statements almost had a socialistic ring to them in the sense of an anticipated second revolution. In *Der Arbeiter und die bildende Kunst* (The Worker and the Visual Arts) for example, published in 1935 by the Strength Through Joy organization, it was stated that the Third Reich must also be concerned about "winning the workers for the visual arts." Here we read that instead of continuing to satisfy the needs of the broad masses for meaningful images with kitschy oleographs, socially conscious artists should be sent into the factories to show the workers that painting, too, was hard work and thus convince them of the value of real art. The same efforts were made with farmers. In 1936, the town of Mayen in the Eifel region, for example, invited a group of painters to live for a year in close comradely association with farmers and agricultural workers to learn from them. At the same time, the artists, through their paintings, were supposed to awaken a sense for the beauty of artistic creativity in the farmers, instead of being satisfied with continuing to create their works for the overeducated city slickers and aesthetes, who were only interested in satisfying their arrogant upper-class taste.

But positive attempts of this kind slipped further and further toward the margins after 1937 or were drowned in the gibberish of nonsensical racist ideological concepts. Wolfgang Willrich's book *Die Säuberung des Kunsttempels* (1937) illustrates this development; he points to the ideal of an art that is close to the people and nonindustrial, but otherwise babbles almost exclusively about the universally superior forces of the Nordic soul that should be expressed in art. Others did the same: Bruno Kroll in *Deutsche Maler der Gegenwart. Die Entwicklung der deutschen Malerei seit 1900* (1937; Contemporary German Painters: The Development of German Painting since 1900), Adolf Dresler in *Deutsche Kunst und entartete Kunst* (1938; German Art and Degenerate Art), Georg Sluytermann von Langeweyde in *Kultur ist Dienst am Leben* (1938; Culture is Service to Life), and Georg Schorer in *Deutsche Kunstbetrachtung* (1939; German Art Appreciation). All four enthused endlessly about the eternally German in art, and they spoke out as sharply as they could against the spirit of democratic agitation that had reigned in the hyper-modern pictures by "ethnically oblivious art-sters" during the Weimar Republic.

But this barrage of phrases, with their references to the Nordic nature of all true Germans, was not to last for long. After the beginning of World War II, as you would expect, the change in circumstances led such programmatic writings to emphasize the racial/unclear less and the heroic/concrete more. In 1942, for example, Hermann Stenzel posited the

Figure 11. Wolfgang Willrich: *U-Boat Commander Joachim Schepke* (1941). From the book by Wilhelm Westecker: *Krieg und Kunst der Gegenwart*, Breslau 1943.

mythos of heroism almost exclusively as the final objective of all German-conscious painting. In 1944, Wilhelm Westecker in his book *Krieg und Kunst* (War and Art) went so far as to challenge all volk-conscious painters to depict the tumult of battle as a grandiose spectacle.

In the preface to that volume, Bruno Brehm even had the nerve to write of the "magnificent horror of war." In Greater Germany's Struggle for Freedom, as World War II was officially called within the Third Reich, everything such dogmatists saw as essential to Nazi fascism came together: belief in destiny, the concept of a community of the volk, the cult of the Führer, heroism—heroism even to the heights of a Wagnerian *Götterdämmerung* or Nietzsche's concept of a tragic-dangerous life.

But what was the reality behind this grandiloquence? What did most Nazi fascist paintings actually look like? What did they portray? Who took notice of them? To whom were they sold? It is a good idea to avoid convenient generalizations and instead investigate the sequence of events between 1933 and 1945 somewhat more thoroughly. In the period immediately after the transfer of power, a certain lack of direction prevailed in the cultural sphere despite the enforced policy of synchronization. Along with graying volkish painters, such as Ludwig Fahrenkrog, Fidus, and Franz Stassen, or representatives of the right wing of the New Objectivity movement, such as Bernhard Dörries, Werner Peiner, and Georg Siebert, there were even some expressionists who pretended to be German-conscious in the beginning. The ecstatics tended to be supported by Goebbels, as I said before, and the volkish artists by Rosenberg. To defuse this conflict, Hitler criticized both the expressionist "daubers" and the volkish "backwardists" in his speech at the Nuremberg party conference in 1934 and pronounced a pseudo-Salomonic judgement: "To be German means to be clear!" Instead of taking sides in this argument, as self-appointed Führer in questions of painting, he simply elevated his own taste to the level of official guideline. And the artists who corresponded to his taste were primarily painters with clean and accurate styles such as Franz von Defregger and Eduard Grützner—in other words, the main representatives of realistic genre painting of the late nineteenth century as well as some historical painters and salon idealists from the Gründerzeit, such as Anselm Feuerbach, Franz von Lenbach, Hans Makart, Gabriel Max, and Karl Theodor von Piloty. In painting, too, Hitler did not support a revolutionary approach in any way; he preferred art that was consciously traditional.

This dictum led of necessity to a victory for the so-called field, forest, and meadow painters over any talented artists who were really committed and had viewed National Socialism as something more than merely a regime change. As a result, by 1934–1935, there had been a significant triumph of the opportunists, fellow travelers, the underprivledged, the provincials, and the small-town dwellers over the profound believers within Nazi fascist painting. The inevitable result of this trend was a noticeable comeback of tried-and-true genre painting; for the Nazi cultural theorists, this included landscapes, portraits, animals, still lifes, and genre scenes executed carefully with a paintbrush, a style that had become the dominant form of expression in European painting since the seventeenth century. Hitler knew that members of the middle class interested in the arts would surely have rejected volkish, Nordic, or anti-Semitic motifs as too ideological, meaning unattractive. On the other hand, they accepted conventional genre painting with the same delight as old-fashioned novels by authors such as Werner Beumelburg, Bruno Brehm, Ludwig Ganghofer, and Hermann Löns that had become bestsellers. This kind of painting therefore proved to be truly popular and sold like hotcakes. On this point, Hitler had firmly on his side both a majority of the opinion leaders among the educated middle class and members of the lower middle class who were interested in art.

Perhaps the most convincing documentation for this viewpoint was the First Great German Art Exhibition, which opened in Munich on 18 July 1937 parallel to the exhibition of Degenerate Art and was presented as a show that representated the artistic objectives of National Social-

Figure 12. Adolf Ziegler: *Goddess of Art* for Hitler's Chancellery (1941). From the book: *Was sie liebten. Salonmalerei im 19. Jahrhundert*, Cologne 1969.

ism. Landscape painting predominated in this exhibit as it had in the nineteenth century—landscape in its sentimental Biedermeier version, as a portrayal of an ideal world with no telegraph wires, no railroads, no factories, and no anything that might spoil the landscape. Approximately 40 percent of all the pictures in the exhibition belonged in this category. Next in terms of quantity were portraits and agricultural genre scenes with 35 percent and still lifes and pictures of animals with 10 percent. Only 5 percent of this overview remained for themes that were specifically Nazi fascist, including portraits of functionaries and members of the SA. The accent was clearly on depictions of the simple life—the uncomplicated, idyllic, and universally human genre scenes and landscapes that we still see today in the same or similar form offered as accessible to the general public in many frame shops and department stores or at flea markets. Not surprising, therefore, that works by painters such as Angelo Jank, Fritz Mackensen, Otto Modersohn, Leo Samberger, Rudolf Schramm-Zittau, Raffael Schuster-Woldan, and Heinrich von Zügel, which featured motifs that were typical of the turn of the century reflecting the world of peasant agriculture or salon idealism, were generally not viewed as old-fashioned at the Great German Art Exhibition in the late 1930s. Anyone not already familiar with them could easily have thought these were Nazi painters. This is particularly true for paintings with motifs from the world of agriculture, which made up about 20 percent of the entire show in 1937. What painters such as Carl Baum, Thomas Baumgartner, Georg Günther, Sepp Hilz, Oskar Martin-Amorbach, Hermann Tiebert, and Adolf Wissel exhibited here could just as easily have been painted twenty to thirty years previously (admittedly at a higher level of quality) by Fritz Boehle, Johann Vinzenz Cissarz, Albin Egger-Lienz, Karl Haider, and Hans Thoma. The world of the factory was represented in only 2 percent of the works in the exhibit; thus, the appearance that life was beautiful was not contravened, and the reversion to a tradition of painting that was ostensibly proto-German could be maintained.

But these picturesque depictions of the simple life, which were sometimes still meant quite seriously in the early years of the Third Reich, began to be in stark contrast to the lifestyle of the Nazi fascist elite as the years went on. The more secure the leaders and their functionaries felt in their domination of the people, the stronger the need for an outward representation that was ostentatious; this has often been characterized as the Makart spirit of these circles. This is most clearly expressed in their increasing preference for female nudes in paintings by Ernst Liebermann, Bernhard Müller, Paul Mathias Padua, Ivo Saliger, Johann Schult, Eberhard Viegener, and Adolf Ziegler, whose idealized portrayals are reminiscent of the Beaux Arts style of the late nineteenth century. In the course of the 1930s, a new class emerged relatively quickly from within the Nazi elite and found a parvenu's satisfaction in the public exhibition of their own wealth. At the beginning of the Third Reich artworks that were in particularly close conformity with the system were often described as property of the volk. But now illustrations of paintings by Nazi artists extolled as famous appeared in expensively produced art magazines with captions reading "Collection of the Führer" or "Collection of Reichsmarschall Hermann Göring." This parasitic cupidity became even more crass after the beginning of the Second World War, as many Nazi big shots attempted to enrich themselves with captured artworks; sometimes they even had some products of degenerate art carted off in secret to their private housing, thus degrading their constant appeal to the healthy sensibility of the volk and the ostensible refinement of artistic taste among the broad masses to the level of farce. Göring's art collection, for example, which included 1,375 paintings and numerous decorative art objects, was comprised in part of works from collections that had been Jewish or of works from among the 21,900 artworks that the Sonderstab Bildende Kunst (Special Staff for Visual Arts) had shipped out of the areas occupied by German troops to six protective storage facilities inside the Third Reich.

Was this also true for works of sculpture produced during these years? Because most sculptures are done in response to public commissions anyway, the influence of the Nazis in charge of cultural programming was even more noticeable in this sector than in painting. After all, this was an art form that was not intended primarily for private interiors and therefore limited to a small circle of observers; it was an art form that emphasized community because it was intended from the outset for installation in public squares and sports arenas as well as in front of ministries and other public buildings. There were no genre scenes to portray here, no scenes of peasant life, no intimate portrait-like subjects; here there was an urge to monumentalize and simplify. In sculpture, therefore, Nazi fascist elements could prevail in a more massive way—purely from the point of view of design—than in painting.

In the beginning, a state of uncertainty pertained even in this area. Most sculptors could certainly see that in the future their subject, too, would be an idealized portrayal of the people of a pure Nordic race who featured so prominently in statements by Hitler and his followers. But they were not yet sure what stylistic devices they should use to this purpose. They were well aware that lapses into styles that were expressionistic, critical veristic, or even abstract, in other words, into cultural bolshevist styles as they were now labeled, were not on the agenda. But such false steps had always been the exception in the realm of sculpture. The principle of

Figure 13. Arno Breker: *The Fighters Depart* (1942).

realism had dominated sculpture in the Weimar Republic, too, and this made these artists seem congenial to the new authorities from the outset. The only works of sculpture that did have to be eliminated after 1933 at the request of the Nazi authorities were some war memorials by Ernst Barlach that were considered unheroic; expressionistic sculptures by Max Beckmann, Otto Freundlich, and Ernst Ludwig Kirchner; the veristic figures of Joachim Kirsch; and the abstract shapes of Hans Arp and Rudolf Belling. Almost all other sculptors, among them Bernhard Bleeker, Fritz Klimsch, and Georg Kolbe, could continue their work relatively undisturbed. Admittedly, we can see a stronger tendency to idealize in the work of some sculptors after 1933, but we do not see blatantly obvious efforts to conform to Nazi fascist dictums about art. For a long time, for example, Georg Kolbe and his friend Richard Scheibe resisted the trend to monumentalism endorsed by the NSDAP. And Fritz Klimsch retained his graceful and moderate style in his female nudes; in other words, he avoided using broad pelvises to emphasize the fecundity of the Nordic woman. Much of what these sculptors were creating would have appealed even to nonfascist clients, because their works still exhibited a sense of the classicistic spirit that had conferred such esteem on Adolf von Hildebrand's statues around 1900.

But along with these sculptors, who tended to be older, some younger sculptors appeared on the scene around the middle of the 1930s who placed themselves entirely at the service of the NSDAP. Arno Breker and Josef Thorak, along with a series of lesser talents, particularly enjoyed the new masters' favor. Both were given oversized studios and innumerable assistants by the Nazi authorities. What they envisaged in responding to the wishes of their government clients were mostly figures of athletes magnified to a monumental level. They were intended to be manifestations of a fascist Olympus and remind the viewer of ancient Greek prototypes or works of the Hildebrand School, especially because these sculptors liked to present their male figures as Prometheus, Perseus, or Dionysus. But in the course of time, they began to look more and more aggressive and sometimes even barbarian. Breker and Thorak, who were invested with the title *Unersetzliche Künstler* (irreplaceable artists), received the most important commissions from Hitler and Speer. Breker's statues *Partei* and *Wehrmacht* were even positioned in the court of honor of the New Reich Chancellory in Berlin in 1939. Some of his works were intended to stand at the center of the north-south axis of the new German capital Germania. Breker remained faithful to a formal concept he had acquired during his early period in Paris that was distantly reminiscent of Aristide Maillol, but Thorak transitioned ever more strongly into a monumental style for his athletes and sword-bearers to express the triumph of the strong and healthy over the weak and sick. Some of the statues Albert Speer commissioned him to design for the Märzfeld in Nuremberg were intended to be seventeen meters high. They were an expression of the same mania of gigantism that Speer was aiming for in his Great Hall. In these works, as in the *Diskuswerfer* (Discus Thrower) by Karl Albiker and the *Rosseführer* (Horse Master) by Joseph Wackerle for the Reich Sports Complex as well as the *Fackelträger* (Torch-Bearer) by Willy Meller for the Ordensburg Vogelsang, the anti-spirit of Nazi fascism revealed itself in its crassest form as far as the visual arts were concerned—a form that was the expression of an omnipotent regime based purely on power, attempting through imperial gestures and pseudo-archaic scale to suffocate any dissent from the very outset.

During World War II, as most of the Nazi construction plans came to a standstill, what did continue to be produced and shown at the Great German Art Exhibitions in Munich were mostly small-scale sculptures and the always popular portrait heads, which seemed best in terms of quality. There were still a few statues from the same period by Breker and Thorak of grimly determined fighters or works by Adolf Wamper and Willy Meller bearing titles like *Wehrhaft* (On Guard) or *Kampfbereit* (Combat-Ready); these were intended as embodiments of heroic exertions of the will prefiguring the victory to come, but in contrast to the small-scale sculptures could only be characterized as emphatically violent.

What is true of Nazi fascist ideology in general is also true of works by the sculptors Hitler favored. The statues they created in response to a higher charge exhibit obvious contradictions. On the one hand, their striving for something higher was an effort to go beyond the realm of the private ego to that of a true community of the volk; on the other

Figure 14. Hans Liska: The state-supported studio built by Albert Speer for Josef Thorak in Baldham near Munich (c. 1938). From the book by KL Tank: *Deutsche Plastik unserer Zeit*, Munich 1942.

hand, they tended as time went on to a one-sided preference for what they viewed as warlike and racially viable; in the end, it came down to a fight against, indeed liquidation of, everything that was non-German or non-Aryan. Many statues that are products of specifically Nazi fascist ideas about art are therefore not just beautiful, not just perfect in form, as they were described at the time. They are at the same time conspicuously brutal, because they were based on a Weltanschauung that had to be willing to stop at nothing to assert itself.

Music

The Nazi cultural theorists believed it was much easier to define what was specifically German in music than in either painting or sculpture. Most of them simply invoked the undisputed international standing of German music, which had been consistently respected, even revered, in many countries throughout the world since the late eighteenth century. Many Nazi musicologists wrote with excruciating smugness about Germany's unsurpassable gallery of musical ancestors, beginning with Heinrich Schütz and Johann Sebastian Bach, continuing with Franz Joseph Haydn, Wolfgang Amadeus Mozart, Ludwig van Beethoven, Franz Schubert, Carl Maria von Weber, Robert Schumann, Richard Wagner, Johannes Brahms, and Anton Bruckner, and extending to Hans Pfitzner and Richard Strauss. These are the creators of tones, they claimed, who are unequalled in any other nation in the world. And once they had gone that far, it was a small additional step to insist in the same pretentious manner that music was the most German of all the arts, and in fact an ars sacra for any German with a volkish sensibility.

So much for modesty. The intent is clear, but what exactly, in the eyes of these music theorists, is really German in the works of these composers, all extremely important but at the same time very different? For the racist fanatics among the Nazi musicologists, there was only one explanation: their predisposition, in fact, the prerequisite for their very being, had to be Germanic. Anyone who viewed themselves as Nordic could not help but be musical, we read in many of the writings devoted to this topic by Walter Abendroth, Friedrich Blume, Richard Eichenauer, Walter Kühne, Hans Joachim Moser, Fritz Stege, and Guido Waldmann. The ancient Teutons had never been good at conceptual apprehension and intellectual processing of sensual impressions and instead had followed their inner instinct, which came from their soul and was therefore musical, these writers claimed. Thus, the Germans, descended from the Teutons, had always felt that music was their very own, and therefore their greatest artistic achievements were in this realm. In contrast to the music of other peoples, wrote Hans Joachim Moser with patriotic arrogance, in German music there is no "cunning dexterity by imposters who believe in nothing." In German music, there is always a soulful and turbulent struggle "to find the ultimate meaning" of life. That is why every true German, Moser asserted, scorns music that "has been licked till it is smooth, is outright emasculated, and is all too easy to understand." A true German seeks music that has the greatest depth, possesses the highest level of expression, and is the most suffused with meaning.

Some especially fanatic Nazi music theorists and their followers were concerned with helping the specifically German element in music—as a form of expression of the Germanic race that was bound to blood and soul—to return to its original greatness after the multiple depravations it had suffered during the Weimar Republic. With this in mind, from 1928 to 1933 and even more energetically after the official transfer of power to Adolf Hitler, they rejected absolutely everything in the music of the recent past they felt was un-German. And that was a lot. Included was music they rejected on the basis of their racist thinking as Semitic or Negroid, as well as everything that appeared to them to be leftist, atonal, or a reflection of New Objectivity, and therefore anti-Nordic. In the case of works with a text, these ethnically alien elements were relatively easy to determine. It was substantially more difficult for this group to zero in on what was specifically un-German in instrumental music, although much speculation was devoted to this question.

The Nazi fascist racial theorists were quite sure they could sort out what was Semitic. What they meant, without exception, was all works in the elite-music category by composers of Jewish descent—not just the volk-alien concoctions by contemporary composers such as Walter Braunfels, Hanns Eisler, Erich Wolfgang Korngold, Arnold Schoenberg, Franz Schreker, Ernst Toch, Kurt Weill, and Stefan Wolpe and the Jew operettas by Paul Abraham, Leo Fall, Emmerich Kálmán, and Oscar Strauss; they also rejected supposedly pseudo-romantic works by earlier Jewish composers such as Felix Mendelssohn-Bartholdy, Giacomo Meyerbeer, Max Bruch, and Gustav Mahler. They explained that Jews had never possessed music of their own, with the exception of their synagogic dissonances, and therefore had always depended on imitation. They had composed, in styles that were—subject to the fashion of the time—sometimes romantic, sometimes atonal, sometimes New Objectivist, sometimes agitprop, and sometimes purely for commercial purposes. Therefore the works of composers like these could no longer be played in the Third Reich. This was true even for Mendelssohn-Bartholdy's much-loved music for Shakespeare's *Midsummer Night's Dream*, which was replaced in 1939 by Carl Orff's Aryan incidental music for the same play. There were even attempts to replace Jewish opera libretti such as Lorenzo da Ponte's for Mozart's *Figaro, Don Giovanni*, and *Così fan tutte* with Aryan rewrites or underlay Händel's oratorio *Judas Maccabäus* with another text because of its glorification of a Semitic hero.

The Nazi cultural theorists proceeded just as severely against Negroid elements in the music of the Weimar Republic. They meant primarily jazz introduced from the United States, or nigger jazz, as they called it, which they characterized as manifestations of the lives of primitive Negro tribes, in other words as non-Aryan wails from the jungle. All the jazz elements that had proliferated in the wake of so-called topical operas (*Zeitoper*) such as Ernst Krenek's *Jonny spielt auf* (1927; Jonny Strikes Up) and Kurt Weill's *Dreigroschenoper* (1928; Threepenny Opera) were accordingly suppressed as quickly as possible after 1933. Dance music that had been influenced by jazz lasted a bit longer. Into the late 1930s, complaints can still be found in leading Nazi music magazines that German dance music was continuing to suffer from vulgar niggerizing. In dance halls and other entertainment venues, was the indignant complaint, you could still hear music that was advancing the cause of international decadence with its "nasalizing, yowling, blaring, and shrill tones" as well as its "muted horns, its hoarse or baying refrains, and the dislocation of the players' limbs"; all of this was diametrically opposed to the feelings of those Germans who were "concerned with the preservation of their health." Citing journals such as *Die Musik* or *Die Volksmusik:* all this music had to offer was titillation that could excite the nerves of those who were already "corrupt musically speaking"; for those who had a Germanic sensitivity, it was an abomination.

But that was not enough. After 1933, anything musical that contradicted "the occidental diatonic system with its clear progression in whole and half steps" and the "concern for harmony in its tonality and melody" was increasingly viewed as suspicious or rejected outright by the state. Of course, it was substantially more difficult to establish mandatory rules or criteria in the realm of instrumental music. Thus, some Nazi music critics teetered indecisively back and forth on the question of whether semimodern works by Boris Blacher, Werner Egk, Paul Höffer, Carl Orff, Hermann Reuter, Heinrich Sutermeister, Heinz Tiessen, Rudolf Wagner-Régeny, and Winfried Zillig should be characterized as condemnable because of certain lapses into atonalism—or should they be designated German-conscious? Most were helpless when Wilhelm Furtwängler, conductor of the Berlin Philharmonic, included relatively modern-sounding works by Béla Bartók, Arthur Honegger, Maurice Ravel, and Igor Stravinsky in his concert programs. The most difficult composer to judge proved to be Paul Hindemith, who after beginnings in expressionism and New Objectivity returned to a relatively tonal approach in the late 1920s. Hindemith accommodated the Nazi cultural theorists to some extent with his opera *Mathis der Maler* (1934; Matthias the Painter), with its evocation of one of the greatest German painters and its backdrop of themes related to the German Peasants' War; in addition, he enjoyed the support of Furtwängler, whom the Nazi fascists literally fawned over at the beginning because of his international prestige. But Hitler prohibited the performance of the opera as well as of other works by Hindemith, and in 1938, he was forced to follow his Jewish, avant-garde, and Marxist colleagues into exile.

For most Nazi fascist theorists and composers, the exhibit *Entartete Musik* (Degenerate Music) in Düsseldorf in 1938 was a watershed in distinguishing praiseworthy German music from non-German music that had to be rejected. The exhibition's chief organizer was Hans Severus Ziegler, who had appeared since the late 1920s in many German cities as an agitator for Rosenberg's Militant League for German Culture. As we would expect, the subject of this propaganda spectacle was primarily a critique of the ethnically alien Jewification and so-called niggeriza-

Figure 15. Cover image for the guide to the exhibition *Degenerate Music* in Düsseldorf (1938). © Bildagentur für Kunst, Kultur und Geschichte.

tion of German music during the Weimar Republic. This was made clear on the front cover of the pamphlet that accompanied the exhibit, where a black saxophone player wearing a Star of David was depicted so that the inferior racial fusion of these two musical forms could be pointed out in a bold and simplistic style. Posters mounted on columns offered equally harsh condemnation of Arnold Schoenberg's twelve-tone technique, the sinister influence of the Jewish musical dictator Leo Kestenberg, the cultural bolshevik Hermann Scherchen, the sexual pathology in Franz Schreker's works, the modernistic trends in periodicals such as *Melos* and *Anbruch* (Beginning), and futuristic or cubist stagings of Wagner operas. Even Igor Stravinsky's music, which had been tolerated up to that point, did not escape the exhibition unscathed. But some German non-Jews, such as the allegedly rootless charlatans Alban Berg and Paul Hindemith, were also treated harshly because of their new-music compositions.

This cabinet of horrors of musical bolshevism put an end for the time being to the protracted and complicated process of excluding un-German elements in favor of an Aryan-oriented music of the future. Many Nazi theorists believed they had finally achieved ideological clarification in this area. Succinctly formulated: from now on, anything that was Semitic, Negroid, left-oriented, or modernistic would no longer have any place in German musical life. What remained to be clarified with regard to both theory and composition was only the question of what had been specifically Aryan in German music until now and how it could provide a starting point for a new, genuinely Nazi fascist musical culture to develop that would be truly popular (*volkstümlich*) and at the same time spiritually elevated.

Some of the criteria that would later be decisive were already established in fall 1933 at the founding of the Reich Music Chamber. However this chamber, whose membership of 15,000 included 350 composers, never exercised the sweeping influence that many Nazi fascist theorists had hoped for. Just the fact that Joseph Goebbels named as its first president a bon vivant like Richard Strauss, who was musically highly gifted but ideologically noncommittal, instead of a volkish-minded fanatic like Hans Pfitzner, caused a noticeable weakening of overly severe anti-Semitic and anti-modernist policies. The Nazi fascists even permitted Strauss to premiere *Arabella*, the opera with a libretto by the Jew Hugo von Hofmannsthal that he had just completed, in 1933; he presented a fair copy to Hermann Göring a year later. Pfitzner, despite his firmly volkish-anti-Semitic attitude, received much less attention from the Nazi authorities. But Strauss was simply more famous on the international scene, and Goebbels was counting on a much greater gain in prestige because of Strauss's level of fame than if he had offered the position to Pfitzner. And Strauss, although he was not a convinced Nazi fascist, accommodated himself to the new political realities. Evidence is provided by one of his letters from this period, in which he explains in a very nonchalant and profit-oriented way: "For me, the people don't exist until they become an audience. It makes no difference to me whether the audience is made up of Chinese, Upper Bavarians, New Zealanders, or Berliners, as long as they have paid full price for their tickets." He showed himself equally opportunistic in a letter written 17 June 1935 to Stefan Zweig, the Jewish librettist of his opera *Die schweigsame Frau* (The Silent Woman), explaining that he was just "impersonating" the president of the Reich Music Chamber in order to "do good," but that he otherwise made sure not to "step forward politically." On the basis of this letter, which had been intercepted by the Gestapo and which Hitler found outrageous, Goebbels was finally forced a short time later to induce Strauss as gently as possible to give up the office of president and name the composer Peter Raabe, unimportant but ideologically much more stalwart, as his successor. Raabe issued occupational bans for three thousand musicians immediately after taking office, and in 1936, in his book *Kulturwille im deutschen Musikleben*

(Cultural Will in German Musical Life), he committed himself as clearly as possible to National Socialism.

Nevertheless, the political-aesthetic uncertainty in this area continued until 1938; as in almost all cultural sectors, it was based on the rivalry between Goebbels, who tended to think strategically, and the ideological overachiever Rosenberg. Goebbels tolerated even some works that sounded modernistic and tried to convince their composers, as long as they were Aryans, to stay in Germany and not go into exile. Rosenberg pitched a fit each time there was an offense against tonality within German-Aryan music. If he had been given a free hand, he would surely have thrown out even Boris Blacher and Carl Orff—and also forbidden the entire repertoire of operettas and hit songs, in which he saw only a depravation of the sublime Aryan spirit, rendering it vulgar and therefore un-German. But Goebbels—supported by Hitler, who appreciated *Die lustige Witwe* (The Merry Widow) as well as the *Meistersinger von Nürnberg*—proved more successful in these disagreements because he had a more pragmatic approach. And thus in music—in a countermove to the Nordic fanatics—a certain limited pluralism remained. Goebbels saw very clearly that if standards in this sector were set too high there was a danger of offending the taste of the lower segments of the population, which was very resistant to change. So along with the great works of the opera tradition, the symphonic and chamber music compositions of the classical tradition, and the agitprop music of the Nazi Party, Goebbels also tolerated the frothy music in the operettas of Eduard Künneke, Franz Lehar, Paul, Lincke, and Carl Zeller as well as mildly jazzy dance music and even pop songs that sounded sentimental or vulgar. The objective was to satisfy not just the party elite and the discriminating educated middle class, but in addition, as he often explained, to keep the so-called broad masses in a good mood with melodic music. For this reason, the Reich Radio Chamber, which was under his administration, was careful to broadcast pop songs and operettas on Hitler's birthday as well as symphonies and the "Horst-Wessel-Lied."

But it is important not to lose sight of the chronological order of the different cultural programs or of their artistic impacts during the period between 1933 and 1945, in music as in other areas. In the first two years of the Third Reich, the early party songs continued to play an important role within the Nazi music scene corresponding to the importance the SA still claimed for itself at the time. Among them were the numerous marches that still conveyed the national revolutionary spirit of optimism of the early NSDAP. Of central importance was the song written in 1929 by the SA leader Horst Wessel, who was murdered by Berlin communists in 1930: "Raise high the flag! Close ranks tightly! The SA marches with

Figure 16. Hitler Youth trumpet parade. From the book by Otto Weber: *Tausend ganz normale Jahre. Ein Fotoalbum des gewöhnlichen Faschismus*, Nördlingen 1987.

a tread that is calm and firm." On Hitler's orders, after July 1933, this song was always sung on solemn occasions following the *Deutschlandlied* (Song of Germany) as the second national anthem. The role the "Horst-Wessel-Lied" played for the SA was played for the Hitler Youth by a song with text by *Reichsjugendführer* (Reich Youth leader) Baldur von Schirach set to music by Hans Otto Borgmann: "Forward! Forward! Bright fanfares are sounding, / Forward! Forward! To youth, danger means nothing, / Germany, you will still stand luminous, / even if we perish." This song was used in the film *Hitlerjunge Quex* (1934; Hitler-Youth Quex) and resounded at a central point in *Triumph des Willens* (1935), a documentary film about the Reich party congress directed by Leni Riefenstahl. Many of these marching songs, based on a sharply accentuated rhythm, centered their texts on motifs that featured images and catchwords such as swastika, Hitler flags, drums, storm, blazing flames, flowing blood, or willingness to die to give them a combative character. After all, Rosenberg had often stated even before 1933 that the "German lifestyle" had to be the "style of marching columns." But this SA and Hitler Youth élan ebbed gradually as the years passed. After 1934–1935, celebratory and testimonial hymns sung with great pathos, older military songs rewritten for fascist purposes, and the traditional German folksongs that had already played a major role in the Wandervogel movement became predominant.

Hitler Youth parades with marching bands continued until the end of World War II, and they were really the only place where the marching column style continued to dominate—not surprising, because the music consisted primarily of blaring trumpets and large, crudely beaten drums. SA groups around 1933–1934 had loudly bellowed their marching songs, and Hitler Youth parades were often just as loud. In fact, the horrendous noise level in these parades and processions had something stimulating about it that was perceived by many youngsters as inspiring or even spellbinding. The attempts of some ideologically overheated Nazi fascists to reinstate the Bronze Age lur fared less well. This instrument was to be used for official party events or theatrical productions emphasizing the proto-Germanic, but the effect soon appeared contrived, and the playing of the lur was therefore discontinued at the instruction of the Ministry for Propaganda.

The party's cultural theorists accorded appropriate attention to Nazi songs and instrumental and march music during the late 1920s and at the beginning of the Third Reich when it was essential to help the NSDAP to victory and then to the implementation of their ideals. But the great music of the cultural heritage enjoyed undiminished esteem in all phases of the Nazi movement. The authorities used it to emphasize the international standing of German music as well as convince the educated middle class that the new masters were not just interested in the success of the "Horst-Wessel-Lied"; veneration for the musical masterworks of the past was equally important to them. There was no lack of exemplary performances of baroque, classical, and romantic music during the Third Reich, whether under the baton of Karl Böhm, Karl Elmendorff, Wilhelm Furtwängler, Herbert von Karajan, Hans Knappersbusch, or Clemens Krauss. There were also plenty of festivals in honor of venerable composers. In concert halls, in churches, on the radio, and on records: works by Bach, Händel, Haydn, Mozart, Beethoven, Schubert, Weber, Schumann, Brahms, Wagner, and Bruckner resounded everywhere in the Third Reich. In their writings, ideological zealots such as Friedrich Blume, Richard Eichenauer, and Fritz Stege liked to point out the Nordic disposition of these composers, which lent a greatness to their music with which no foreign composer could compete. But that was of only

Figure 17. Adolf Hitler with Winifred, Wieland, and Wolfgang Wagner in the garden of Villa Wahnfried in Bayreuth (1936). © Bayreuth, Nationalarchiv der Richard-Wagner-Stiftung.

tangential interest to most listeners in the educated middle class. They entered the concert halls with the same solemn reverence that had animated them even before 1933, without abandoning themselves to some sort of hyper-Aryan feelings of elation.

Both Nazi music critics and musicologists stressed that composers such as Bach, Beethoven, Weber, Wagner, and Bruckner were especially Nordic-spirited. They praised the vigorous proto-Germanic confidence of Bach's works, the heroic strain in Beethoven's *Eroica* and *Egmont-Overture*, the romantic-German quality of Weber's *Freischütz*, Wagner's preference for ancient Germanic myths, and the almost incomparable monumentality of Bruckner's nine sweeping symphonies. Since Hitler had admired Wagner more than any other composer since his "years of study and suffering in Vienna," as he stated in *Mein Kampf*, the music critics in thrall to him concentrated primarily on Wagner whenever they wanted to point out the proto-Aryan qualities in the main works of the German musical canon. Ignoring all of the revolutionary characteristics in Wagner's early work, they emphasized his preference for things Germanic, his anti-Semitism, his anti-liberalism, his hero worship, and his patriotic glorification of Nuremberg to celebrate him as one of the most important precursors of the Third Reich. Hitler himself, who had already established contact with the Wagner family in Bayreuth in the early 1920s, referred repeatedly to Wagner's *Meistersinger* with its "Wake up" chorus and Hans Sachs' final speech in which he opposes the greatness of German art to "foreign trumpery." Goebbels did the same, using a radio address during the intermission of a performance of *Die Meistersinger* in Bayreuth on 6 August 1933 to describe the thrilling character of the "Wake up" chorus as a "symbol of the reawakening of the German people from the political anesthesia of the years after November 1918."

Although Rosenberg, like Nietzsche before him, expressed some reservations about the Christian elements in Wagner's thought, everyone else in the Third Reich followed Hitler's lead and began to exploit Wagner's music without compunction at every possible official party occasion. "Der Walkürenritt" (The Ride of the Valkyries) from the second part of the tetralogy *Der Ring des Nibelungen* was commonly used as musical accompaniment for the stuka attacks shown in the weekly newsreels during the war. The funeral march toward the end of the *Götterdämmerung* (Twilight of the Gods) was often broadcast on the radio when some important Nazi had died. *Die Meistersinger* was the high point of the Day of Potsdam on 21 March 1933, an occasion staged by Goebbels with as much Nazi fascist pomp as possible to inaugurate the newly elected Reichstag. It was also the background music year after year for the German-volkish apotheosis of the Nuremberg Reich party congresses. *Rienzi*, Hitler explained, had made him aware that he, too, was destined to be a tribune of the people. Indeed, as Hitler emphasized in his conversations with Hermann Rauschning, he saw the grail of Wagner's *Parsifal* as a chalice containing not the blood of Christ, but Nordic blood. German economic leaders, hoping to emphasize their ties to Hitler, gave him the scores of the Wagner operas *Rienzi, Das Rheingold,* and *Die Walküre* for his fiftieth birthday on 20 April 1939.

In other words, hymns of praise to Wagner or other important German composers were common in Nazi writings. But when the time came to talk about contemporary music, these same music critics were more subdued. Despite strenuous efforts, they found little of which they could be proud. In the Soviet Union at the same time, highly important symphonies, concertos, and operas by composers such as Dmitri Shostakovich, Sergei Prokofiev, and Aram Khachaturian were being written and were recognized worldwide either immediately or a short time later. Almost none of the works composed in the Third Reich were noticed abroad. In terms of symphonic music, one could possibly mention the late works of Wilhelm Furtwängler such as his Second Symphony, written in 1944 and somewhat reminiscent of Brahms. In the realm of opera, almost nothing has remained in the repertory except a few works by Richard Strauss, among them his *Arabella* (1933) and *Capriccio* (1942). Admittedly, a few other operas, such as Rudolf Wagner-Régeny's *Der Günstling* (1935; The Protégé), Werner Egk's *Die Zaubergeige* (1935; The Magic Violin), Hermann Reutter's *Doktor Johannes Faust* (1936), Ottmar Gerster's *Enoch Arden* (1937), and Carl Orff's *Der Mond* (1939; The Moon) achieved short-lived *succès d'estime* in the Third Reich. But not more than that. Considering the 175 premieres of new German operas between 1933 and 1943 that was—despite much praise and great financial expenditures—a poor result.

These works were supposed to profess a romanticism of steel, but even the Nazi elite were disappointed by most of them. Many composers ultimately sought escape in fairy tales, fantasy, or religion—in other words, they preferred to compose operas that allowed them to remain ideologically noncommittal such as *Melusina, Das Herzwunder* (Miracle of the Heart), *Das Lambertusspiel* (The Lambertus Play), *Eulenspiegel,* or *Das Stuttgarter Hutzelmännchen* (The Stuttgart Fairy). Some even saw cultured middle-class isolation or haughty dissociation from all external hustle and bustle as an act of inner emigration. For this reason, some music critics are still arguing about whether we should view the few important works from this period, such as Carl Orff's oratorio *Carmina Burana* (1937) or Richard Strauss's opera *Friedenstag* (1938; Peace Day), as an integrated part of the system or not. The fact that these compositions were sometimes praised by Nazi music critics does not necessarily make them works that can be characterized as Nazi fascist. In the sphere of music, there was sometimes an especially broad repressive tolerance for something that was different.

A further indication of this relative broad-mindedness is the fact that Goebbels permitted German Jews, who could no longer become members of the Reich Music Chamber after 1934, to establish some symphony orchestras and chamber music ensembles and even stage some operas within the framework of the Jewish Cultural Association. And those within this group who were interested in music took advantage of this opportunity right away. This association organized 558 concerts

Figure 18. Joseph Goebbels in conversation with Franz Lehar (c.) and Bernhard Herzmanowsky (l.) at the Ninth Congress of Composers and Authors in Berlin (1936). © Munich, Bilderdienst Süddeutsche Zeitung.

and 57 opera evenings in approximately sixty German cities just in the six months between September 1934 and 30 May 1935. The Berlin Cultural Association was especially active, regularly arranging performances of operas or opera excerpts in the Theater in the Kommandantenstraße; they staged almost exclusively performances of German works until they were forbidden to do so and were forced to limit themselves to Italian, Russian, or French operas. The Nazi authorities also allowed the Jews who had been deported to the showpiece concentration camp Theresienstadt to establish an ambitious program of concerts. There were symphony concerts in the camp under the direction of Karel Ančerl and operas such as Mozart's *Entführung aus dem Serail* (Abduction from the Seraglio), Verdi's *Aida*, Puccini's *La Bohème*, and Bizet's *Carmen* that were performed by the prisoners. Even an important opera such as *Der Kaiser von Atlantis oder Der Tod dankt ab* (The Kaiser of Atlantis or Death Abdicates) by Viktor Ullmann, a student of Schoenberg, who had completed his opera *Der zerbrochene Krug* (The Broken Jug) a short time before, was rehearsed in the camp; in the end it was not performed, however, because the camp administration suspected it might contain a spirit of insubordination.

Now we come to the musical form that was most widespread in the Third Reich in percentage terms: popular music. At the beginning, it definitely gave headaches to some of the ideological purists within the Nazi elite. Because large segments of German music had supposedly been degraded to the level of substandard entertainment during the Weimar Republic, these circles had been asking since the late 1920s how popular music could be harmonized with the ideals they were touting of guiding the German people toward higher things. That kind of music seemed much too low from the start, much too frivolous, and much too cosmopolitan to serve the racial improvement of the German nation. Vacuousness appeared to be the dominant principle in music like this, or possibly even stupidity or at the very least giddiness—all qualities that were basically apolitical or even degenerate.

To confront criticism like this from the outset, Goebbels, who was a pragmatist interested in having a large impact, tried to place this art form in the service of the new Reich immediately after the transfer of power to the Nazi fascists. He was careful not to characterize the need of the broad masses for entertainment as something that could be ignored, because that might lead to a sectarian position outside the mainstream. He therefore supported serious music, but he supported so-called entertainment music just as emphatically—in other words, operettas, dance music, and hit songs. Based on this point of view, and anticipating potential criticism from the Nordic-minded fanatics within the NSDAP, he explained as early as 1933, "In order to counteract boredom and gloom, we want to avoid stifling the creation of minor amusements. No one should think about politics from dawn to dusk." Later, he expressed himself even more clearly, and admitted publicly that in general—if it was the wish of the majority of the people—"he had no objections even to kitsch."

Of course Goebbels had apolitical amusements in mind that had a thoroughly political purpose—that of keeping the so-called broad masses of the German population in a good mood, offering them the possibility of cultural free zones in which they did not always have to think about the hardships of the day or the demands of the party. Therefore, he even considered hit songs that were outrageous from an ideological viewpoint as politically meaningful entertainment that should be taken just as seriously as so-called serious music. He even participated personally in the composition of new hit songs by changing melodic lines or introducing new textual ideas, as Norbert Schultze, one of the most popular composers of hit songs during this time, later reported. In 1943, following the first defeats of the *Wehrmacht*, as half of Germany already lay in ruins, Goebbels had a competition announced for "hits to put us in an optimistic mood"; Franz Grothe won it with the title "We'll Rock the Baby Right."

Loosely speaking, although the music industry (in contrast to the film industry) was not nationalized in the Third Reich—in other words, it was owned by companies such as Deutsche Grammophon, Telefunken, and Electrola—the dissemination of hit songs took place largely under the control of the NSDAP. We should keep in mind that among the most popular hits of the period were all the talkie hits that played a central role in government-controlled entertainment films of the Third Reich and gave a level of fame that was hard to match to singers such as Hans Albers, Johannes Heesters, and Heinz Rühmann and female vocal artists such as the Hungarian Marika Rökk, the Chilean Rosita Serrano, and the Swede Zarah Leander. As was the case for popular radio programs on which the same hit songs were played, the party definitely had the right to a say and they made full use of it.

It is true that most of these hit songs did not have the impudent or risqué tone that songs and texts by Friedrich Holländer, Marcellus Schiffer, Mischa Spoliansky, or Kurt Tucholsky had in the mid-1920s; instead they tended to employ the same tried-and-true fire-desire or love-loss themes that evoked the stock illusions and moments of happiness provided by true love. This is evidenced by the titles of some of the hit songs, such as "I Know a Miracle Will Happen," "I'm Dancing into Heaven with You," "Every Day is Beautiful," "Let Me Have My Dreams," "You Are the World for Me," "Everything Passes, Everything Slips Away," "It Was Always so Wonderful with You," "I Would Give Everything for One Night of Bliss," "Sing Something for Me, Dance with Me," or "I Have You and You Have Me, What More Do We Need"; among the principle composers of these hits were Werner Bochmann, Franz Grothe, Michael Jary, Werner Kleine, Peter Kreuder, Eduard Künneke, Theo Mackeben, Willi Meisel, and Norbert Schultze.

The chief task of the inveterate dream manufacturers geared to the production of hit songs was to use these schmaltzy songs within the context of the soft wave of Nazi propaganda to give the German masses the feeling that they were living under normal social conditions; at the political level much might have changed, but on the private level everything was as it had always been. For this reason, the popular music industry even made some concessions to jazz, an approach that was taboo in serious music. Even critical remarks from Rosenberg's agency, which repeatedly complained that "lots of swing and jazz" was being played in some pubs and bars, had no effect. Goebbels was undeterred by such critical objections. In October 1941, he explained in a speech to the Hitler Youth that at "a time when heavy burdens and worries are being imposed on the entire nation," entertainment that is lively and therefore cheers people up has a particularly high value. A short time later he even confided to his diary, "A good mood is military equipment. In some circumstances it can be more than just strategically important, it can be decisive for the outcome of the war."

These brief comments about the politics of music in the Third Reich are proof enough that it is relatively difficult to speak of a coherent Nazi ideology in this sphere. Here requirements of an extremely racist nature and claims to represent interests of the educated middle class can be found together with pragmatic attempts to appeal to the taste of the broad masses. There seems to be no ideological consensus. Yet the most varied approaches, all designed to be strategically class-specific, boiled down to the same thing: a choice of products that was as varied as possible. True, there were no longer any leftist, Jewish, or extremely modernistic works, but there remained enough options so that each segment of the population, according to their varied tastes, could pick out what was suitable for them.

Literature

For the propaganda purposes of the Nazi fascists, the visual and acoustic art forms were much easier to use than the text-bound format of literature, as they themselves repeatedly emphasized. After all, poems, stories, and novels presuppose a reception at the level of the individual. Even plays are either read by individuals or observed by small groups in the theater. In contrast, representative buildings, sculptures, posters, mass-produced images, radio programs, films, hit songs, and marches always address much larger population groups, or even everyone within a particular country. This aspect is completely lacking in the literary sphere. Nevertheless, when they came to power in 1933, the Nazi cultural authorities subjected literature as well—or rather *Dichtung* (poetic writing) and *Schrifttum* (printed texts), as they referred to this material in the course of their linguistic Germanization—to a careful control by the state. It is true that they did not communalize the many privately owned book publishers, but they did interfere repeatedly in their ongoing production by applying censorship provisions; the main actor here was the central editorial office of Rosenberg's agency, whose head was Hellmuth Langenbucher. They also mandated that every publisher, bookseller, or author had to be a member of the Reich Literature Chamber.

Along with the novel, lyric poetry had played a substantial role in the literary life of the Weimar Republic; these two genres decreased somewhat in both quantity and importance in the years after 1933. For some of the ideologically overzealous Nazi cultural theorists, they were either not exciting enough or their appeal was not broad enough. They expected art to produce emotions that would stir the masses, not intellectual processes that would take place in the private sphere. And they believed such emotions could be induced much more easily through images and sounds than through protracted reading processes that took place at the individual level and had no community-building character. But despite these considerations, they perceived that even in the literary realm no effort should be spared to bring their ideological influence to bear on novel readers and friends of poetry as well as on theatergoers. They began, particularly in the sphere of higher culture, with the suppression, or rather the eradication, of all authors they viewed as cultural bolshevists, as modernistic, or as Jewish, so that they could institute a "purification in accordance with what was ethnically appropriate."

All of the writers who in their books, manifestos, or essays written since 1918 had espoused a change in political and social relations in a leftist direction with a flair that was Novembrist, expressionist, Dadaist, proletarian revolutionary, or even left liberal had to expect severe repressive measures by the regime as early as February/March 1933. Thus, many of them escaped immediately into exile to avoid being imprisoned in the course of the government-decreed protective measures. This included above all authors who had expressed themselves politically much more concretely in their writings than had painters in their pictures or composers in their musical works. The Nazi fascists confronted such writers at the very beginning of the Third Reich with a series of exclusionary measures and acts of violence that were in some cases more severe than the impediments or occupational bans to which other artists who did not conform to the system were subjected.

Arrests, expatriations, and the compilation of blacklists with the names of those authors who from now on would be considered undesirable or harmful to the volk began immediately after the transfer of power to Hitler. These actions peaked first on 10 May 1933, when public book burnings took place at many German universities, among them Berlin, Breslau, Göttingen, Cologne, Frankfurt, Hamburg, Munich, and Würzburg; most of them were organized by Nazi fascist student groups, and professors who had become especially fanaticized gave wildly inflammatory speeches. The books were burned to the sounds of the jeering crowd and SA bands. Books by Karl Marx, Karl Kautsky, Sigmund Freud, Magnus Hirschfeld, Emil Ludwig, Theodor Wolff, Alfred Kerr, and Carl von Ossietzky were burned; these works were about "provoking the class struggle," "soul-destroying overvaluation of the instincts," "volk-alien journalism of a democratic-Jewish character," "arrogant adulteration of the German language," and "distortion of our history and vilification of its great figures." Books by well-known writers of the Weimar Republic such as Lion Feuchtwanger, Ernst Glaeser, Erich Kästner, Heinrich Mann, Ernst Ottwalt, Theodor Plivier, Erich Maria Remarque, Kurt Tucholsky, and Arnold Zweig were also consigned to the flames. In Berlin, Joseph Goebbels, Alfred Bäumler, and Fritz Hippler, later director of the film *Der ewige Jude* (The Eternal Jew), participated in the book burnings and the speeches and *Feuersprüche* that accompanied them, denouncing the "shameful humiliation" of the German spirit in all these publications. The concerns that would set the agenda for German *Schrifttum* in the future would once again be "breeding and tradition," the "nobility of the human soul," the "schooling of the volk in the spirit of self-defense," and "striving for a community of the volk and an idealistic attitude toward life." In the center of other town squares, ideologically overzealous students put up what they called stakes of shame and nailed books by the same authors to them. Ten days later, the Berlin police reported proudly that they had confiscated approximately ten thousand centner of Marxist books and periodicals from bookstores, publishers, and book distributors.

Further measures of the same kind were not long in coming. With the assistance of Hanns Johst, Paul Kluckhohn, and Bruno E. Werner, the blacklists of all those books that could no longer be sold became longer and longer, finally totaling 6,843 titles, a quantity that was enthusiastically welcomed by the NS-Lehrerbund (National Socialist Teachers' Association) and the central leadership of the Hitler Youth. In addition, on 16 May 1933, all public libraries were requested to cleanse their collections of all books by authors whom the Nazi authorities found objectionable and therefore harmful to the volk. Included were well-known Soviet authors such as Maxim Gorki, leftist writers in the United States such as Jack London and Upton Sinclair, as well as the French anti-war novelist Henri Barbusse. In German literature, among others, they targeted authors such as Bertolt Brecht, Alfred Döblin, Klaus Mann, Ludwig Renn, Arthur Schnitzler, Anna Seghers, Ernst Toller, Jakob Wassermann, Franz Werfel, and Stefan Zweig—again primarily leftists and Jews. The Nazi authorities condemned these communist lovers, asphalt literati, Semitic sex maniacs for hire, and literary decadents, as well as all the authors who had, with the active involvement of Gottfried Benn, been removed from the literature section of the Prussian Academy in March 1933 because they had aledgedly supported cultural bolshevist subversion, pacifistic enfeeblement, and repulsive obscenity. These "fellows" have finally been forbidden to continue "poisoning our volk with their literary sewage," Will Vesper, the editor of the Nazi journal *Neue Literatur,* wrote triumphantly.

Following these radical purgative measures, the Reich Literature Chamber was founded in late fall 1933 with the volkish-minded novelist Hans

Friedrich Blunck appointed by Goebbels to be its first president. The chamber's guidelines applied to all public libraries, the Börsenverein des deutschen Buchhandels (German Publishers and Booksellers Association), and to all publishers, distributors, antiquarian book dealers, and lending libraries. Furthermore, from that point on only those three thousand authors (five thousand by 1941) who were registered members of the chamber were allowed to publish. Based on documentary evidence, there were five thousand publishers, seven thousand book dealers, ten thousand employees of publishing firms and bookstores, twenty-five hundred lending library employees, thirty-two hundred book salesmen, fifteen hundred public librarians, and four hundred editors—almost thirty-five thousand people in literature-related fields—who belonged to the organization. It was not necessary to join the party to become a member of the chamber, but after 1934 a state-attested Aryan certificate was required. Although Blunck spoke out against such discrimination in the beginning, soon anyone who was not a pure-race Aryan and was classified instead as a Semite could publish only with one of the publishing houses of the Cultural League of German Jews (later the Jewish Cultural League), which had over twenty-five at its disposal and issued approximately one thousand books up to 1938.

Exactly what the content of the new literature mindful of the nation should be, however, was not clearly defined in the Reich Literature Chamber's guidelines. Anything antifascist was, of course, ruled out from the word go. But Goebbels, in contrast to Rosenberg, took a relatively tolerant approach in this area, because he did not view literature as an instrument of propaganda equal in importance to radio and film; he took a much more active interest in purging those two mass media and in determining their ideological direction. Accordingly, there was talk in the communiqués of the Reich Literature Chamber about the volk community that might be brought about through literary means, but there was no attempt at a forced synchronization. Thus, Goebbels promoted even former expressionists such as Gottfried Benn, Arnolt Bronnen, and Hanns Johst, who had actually begun to move away from their earlier ideas by the later years of the Weimar Republic. Later he even named Hanns Johst as president in charge of the Reich Literature Chamber after the resignation of Hans Friedrich Blunck. But he went even further than that. There were also plenty of nonfascist and religious authors to whom he gave a free hand. In individual cases he even defended them against attacks in the SS newspaper *Das schwarze Korps* (The Black Brigade) or in Rosenberg's *Die Bücherkunde* (Book Lore); he wanted to avoid acting like an all-powerful dictator and thus running the risk of angering the traditional educated middle class. As a clever tactician, he was often more concerned with the literary prestige or the mass appeal of certain authors than with their political attitudes. He would have liked to see a writer widely admired by conservatives take over the chairmanship of the German Writers' Academy; he offered the position to Stefan George, who a short time before had sharply opposed the infamous years of the Weimar Republic in his volume of poetry, *Das neue Reich* (The New Reich), but George turned down the offer. It was also very painful to Goebbels that the militant nationalist Ernst Jünger largely withdrew from public view after 1933 into a sort of aristocratic inner emigration. Like Stefan George, he even refused an appointment to the German Writers' Academy; he did not want to be confused in the eyes of his readers with second-rate authors such as Werner Beumelburg, Hans Carossa, Hans Grimm, Erwin Guido Kolbenheyer, Agnes Miegel, Wilhelm Schäfer, Hermann Stehr, Emil Strauß, or Will Vesper, all of whom as members of the academy pledged themselves wholeheartedly to the new state.

What the new members of the academy and the leadership council of the Reich Literature Chamber posited as manifestations of new German writing were first of all declarations that Adolf Hitler was the highest incarnation of the German ethnic soul. He, so they constantly repeated, had shown exemplary determination in turning away from both the superficial materialism of the communists and the unholy intellectualism of the Jewish race to once again gaze into the depths of the abyss that was the Nordic soul. In the words of Otto Bangert, for example, Hitler the redeemer had "emerged out of the midst of the German people"; today, "everyone rallies around him," and "we therefore see him as the only one who can save us." Hanns Johst eagerly described the new Reich, in which Führer and volk, alienated for so long, were finally wed to each other again. "We stand united around Hitler," Ina Seidel avowed, in whom beats "the heart of the volk." Let "his work be ours" and "our work be his," wrote Hermann Claudius. According to Will Vesper, Hitler, "Germany's ablest son," had arisen "out of the midst of the volk" and "led the advancing army" like a king in the days of the ancient Germanic tribes. He had become the "champion" who bore the "fate" of all of us on his shoulders, we read in a text by Hans Carossa. Hermann Stehr asserted that a people "can fulfill and maintain itself only under the rule of a meaningful will, as followers of the Führer." Hermann Burte wrote with accents approaching religious ecstasy, "There is come a new man, out of the depths of the people, who hath prepared new tablets, and he hath created a new people, lifted from the same depths from whence the great poems rise: from the Mothers, from blood and soil."

Hitler, of course, was glad to go along with such adulation and expressions of devotion, and even encouraged them to surround himself ever

Figure 19. Hans von Norden: Postcard. "What the king conquered, the prince created, the field marshal defended, the soldier saved and united" (shortly after 1933).

more completely with an aura of infallibility. It may be true that Nazi fascism as an ideology had no real focal point; it consisted largely of clever tactical maneuvers employed to enforce the movement's ideological goals. But the new Reich could at least have an absolute fixed point in the towering greatness of Hitler's person. Accordingly, within the framework of this system, it inevitably fell to Hitler to give even the most blatant contradictions within Nazi ideology the appearance of having an internal logic through his personal bearing, his pompous rhetoric, his imperious gestures, and his simplistically Solomon-like gems of proverbial wisdom.

But it was impossible to create a new literature based solely on the principle, "A people becomes a people only when they obey," as Nietzsche had expressed it. The much-proclaimed belief in authority had to be joined by a whole series of other values to distinguish an author's works after 1933 as those of a national-minded poet. Nazi fascism saw itself primarily as a reawakening and not as a revolutionary upheaval. Its guiding principles came out of the ideological storeroom of the volkish opposition, which since the founding of the Second Reich had opposed the anti-spirit of civilization created by Germany's rapidly advancing industrialization and urbanization, and they did so in the name of tribal consciousness, racial purity, hatred of the big city, and awareness of their native soil. Whether Nazi literary works took the form of novels that were conceived as narrative chronicles, celebratory patriotic poetry, or solemn dramas, their literary embodiment of these values was also largely borrowed from the same storehouse and presented as the resurrection of a true German literature that had existed since time immemorial but had been temporarily submerged.

So in literature, as in painting and music, we cannot expect to see anything new or avant-garde in either form or content in the years between 1933 and 1945. Nazi fascist literature was not interested in overthrowing anything; its goal was to assist in establishing social relations that would not conflict with what had always been viewed as ethnically appropriate for German culture. Therefore it is only during the first months of the Third Reich that we can perceive a few halfway revolutionary sounds in authors from the far left wing of the NSDAP, and they were mostly suppressed after Hitler ordered the liquidation of the Röhm-Strasser group in the summer of 1934. Despite initial glorification of the Führer and militant optimism, a literature that was rather traditional spread during the 1930s; it displayed all of the elements of form and content that had played a central role in many works of bourgeois realism in the nineteenth century and in the nationalistic literature of the turn of the century. It was to be expected that Goebbels, as his master's faithful servant, did not oppose this development; instead he welcomed it as suited to his strategies that targeted short-term cultural objectives. He, like Hitler, wanted first of all to convince the German population that the NSDAP wanted to institute a purification process, but not a total revolution. And the middle-class majority interested in culture either thoroughly believed or at least benignly tolerated this approach. Such phrases led them to lose sight of the barbaric long-term objectives of the Nazi fascists and hope that the new government would consolidate their social and cultural positions—especially in view of the dangers of a communist threat.

During the Third Reich, actual party literature did not play anything like the role attributed to it later in the course of what is referred to as coming to terms with the past (*Vergangenheitsbewältigung*); at that point, a guilty conscience led to an overemphasis on either devoutly German or racist components within Nazi literature. These elements were most forcefully expressed in the hymns and marching songs originally written and set to music for the SA, the Hitler Youth, the Bund Deutscher Mädel (League of German Girls), and the Reichsarbeitsdienst (Reich Labor Service). The first texts of this kind were written by Dietrich Eckart, Hitler's early mentor and the founding editor of the *Völkischer Beobachter*. Most notably, his song "Deutschland erwache!" (Germany, Awake!) was immediately seized upon as a *Sturmlied* (attack song) by the SA, who added the cry, "Juda, verrecke!" (Die a miserable death, Jew!) to it. The "Horst-Wessel-Lied," written in 1929, proved equally effective ("Raise high the flag! Close ranks tightly! The SA marches with a tread that is calm and firm"); after July 1933 it rose to the status of second national anthem of the Third Reich. In contrast, the song "Es zittern die morschen Knochen" (The Brittle Bones Are Trembling) by Hans Baumann, which ends in the infamous refrain, "For today Germany is ours/ tomorrow the whole world," was sung primarily by the various age-specific groups within the Hitler Youth. Behind the evocation of marching columns in many of these songs, an image of Hitler escalated to a heroic level often appeared at a pivotal point. Typical are lines such as "Brothers, Hitler leads you / the Third Reich marches with us"; "Forward, fresh to battle / Adolf Hitler finds us ready for the struggle"; "Those who march today in clusters of bronze/ We ask no questions, we are the Führer's fist"; or "From a thousand eyes the final hope glimmered! / From a thousand hearts the dumb cry broke out: / The Führer! Enslave us! Master, make us free!" But these tones, in which the spirit of the early years of SA militancy still echoed, were already ebbing noticeably—like so many Nazi fascist fight slogans—during the stabilization phase of the Third Reich in the mid-1930s.

We can see this development even more clearly in the case of the *Thing-spiel* (*Thing* play). Some of the old volkish or Aryan-minded followers of Rosenberg within the Nazi Party after 1933 held great hopes for it, but Hitler and Goebbels soon began to view it as alien to the volk and force it into the background. The best known *Thingspiel* ampitheater at the time was the Dietrich Eckart-Bühne in Berlin designed by Werner March; there Richard Euringer's *Deutsche Passion* was performed in 1934 by hundreds of participants before twenty thousand spectators. But its form—that of a National Socialist worship service—with its half-revolutionary, half-pseudo-religious apotheosis of Hitler as the savior of the German nation from the depths of humiliation awakened misgivings in both church leaders and Hitler himself. Authors such as Rudolf Ahlers, Otto Erler, Kurt Heynicke, Eberhard Wolfgang Möller, and Heinrich Zerkaulen contributed a few more ritualistically oversimplified texts to the genre,

Figure 20. Richard Schwarzkopf: *German Passion* (1936). From the catalogue of the Great Exhibition of German Art.

but Goebbels viewed them to some extent as Nordic kitsch. Thus, this form of Nazi drama, based originally on expectations that a second revolution would occur, was officially discontinued in 1937.

In the end, middle-class tradition was victorious over volkish revolt in this sector too. Instead of promoting the Thing plays that could grip the broad masses, Nazi cultural authorities subordinate to Goebbels preferred to support existing state and local theaters, where primarily works by classic authors of world literature and the most familiar dramas and comedies from German literature were performed; the new masters used these works to try to convince the theatergoing bourgeoisie of the dignity of the new regime. And this effort led to the hoped-for results. This development suited the leaders of social opinion within the German population very well, because the *Thingspiele* reminded them of older forms of theater supported by the trade unions and the Social Democratic Party that they had despised. For this reason, the Nazi big shots were generally satisfied with brilliantly staged performances of tried-and-true plays in which popular actors and actresses such as Gustav Gründgens, Heinrich George, Emil Jannings, Käthe Dorsch, Käthe Haack, and Marianne Hoppe could appear in starring roles. New plays were hardly noticed by the majority of the educated middle class and therefore received very little support from the Reich Chamber of Culture. Only Hanns Johst's nationalistic action drama *Schlageter* was able to register a certain success in 1933. But this type of drama too soon faded into the background, despite the transitory efforts of Curt Langenbeck, Eberhard Wolfgang Möller, and Hans Rehberg.

The Nazi literary theorists took the novel quite a bit more seriously. After all, the novel—along with certain song lyrics—had been the most popular genre since the eighteenth century and reached substantially broader segments of the population than printed poetry, verse epics, or plays. It is important, however, to distinguish among a series of very different types of novel that should not be lumped together. Admittedly, this genre also included popular bestsellers, and it is difficult to determine from a sociological perspective who their reading public was. But in the case of most published novels, the authors and their publishers had a clearly identifiable readership in view from the beginning. Not all novels, even though they were portrayed as popular, were intended for a mass audience; many were directed at particular segments of the population. The Nazi authorities knew this very well, even if they hesitated to admit it for ideological reasons.

The responsible censorship board accordingly paid relatively close attention even to this genre, promoting mainly those works they expected would advance Nazi ideology either directly or indirectly. This included

Figure 21. Arthur Kampf: *Hildebrand Overpowers Odoaker's Son*. From the book by Hans Friedrich Blunck: *Deutsche Heldensagen* (German Heroic Tales, 1938).

all novels with Teutonic or agrarian-related subject matter that emphasized Germanic vigor, because these came closest to their blood and soil ideology. Equally popular with the authorities were war novels in which the heroic fighting man, Hitler's favorite idea of the true German, was at the center of the novel. In works of this kind, an ideology that emphasized ethnicity had to predominate at all times. But the same officials were much more lax in respect to other novelistic forms, where, as ever, the emphasis was on entertainment in the form of melodramatic amorous entanglements, humorous passages, or cleverly interwoven elements of suspense; here, they were much less strict and allowed many nonfascist texts to slip through their fingers.

Let us begin with the Teutonic novels. The only truly popular ones imitated Felix Dahn's *Ein Kampf um Rom* (1876; A Struggle for Rome), sticking relatively closely to the historical facts and recounting them in a suspenseful way. One of the best examples is Hans Friedrich Blunck's novel about the Vandals, *König Geiserich* (1936; King Geiserich), which was originally written as school reading material and to which primarily thirteen- to fourteen-year-old high school students were subjected. Other Teuton enthusiasts had a very limited impact. Among them were Johannes Arnoldt, Hermann Barthel, Rudolf Brunngraber, and Edmund Kiß. They tended to write novels set in prehistoric times that digressed wildly into utopian-obscurantist and pseudo-scientific modes, incorporating Herman Wirth's Thuate ideas, Hanns Hörbiger's glacial cosmogony, or the Atlantis myth with a racist tinge—all with the goal of emphasizing noble-born Aryans' claim to power over all other peoples of the world. Fantasizing about the ancestors in their blood corresponded perfectly with the party line supported by Rosenberg, but did not suffice to create a broad readership for these novels. They were simply too ideologically oriented and left the entertainment needs of broad segments of the population unsatisfied.

Somewhat larger reader groups were interested in the equally time-tested genre of the agrarian novel. Following in the footsteps of earlier bestselling authors, such novels had continued to appear in abundance after the end of the 1920s. Like earlier books by Adolf Bartels, Gustav Frenssen, and Hermann Löns, they described Nordic-minded people in Ditmarsch, Frisia, or Lower Saxony who had a deep respect for native German soil and could also boast of their heroic courage, proven in many wars. But whereas earlier examples of village literature had provincial and rustic features, these novels had been so strongly imbued with fascist qualities that many protagonists came across as peasants in Nibelungen boots in an effort to emphasize how gigantic and warlike they were. They described how the German people were slowly withering away or even dying off in the large cities, but many peasants had retained the Teutonic strength many theorists saw as the principle source of a long overdue volkish recovery. In these novels, both the long-established peasants on inherited farmsteads and the straw-blond settler couples distinguished themselves through their strong muscles and their overabundant production of children as the ones on which hope for a Nordic future state was pinned.

To put a stop finally to the overseas emigration of many Germans that was so damaging to the volk, authors of agrarian novels who adhered most closely to Nazi ideology supported an aggressive colonization in the east or an intensified internal settlement to be achieved by the reclamation of fallow moor and swamp regions. Their objective—like the earlier Pan-German movement under Georg von Schönerer—was not to dominate all of Europe or to conquer new colonies in Africa; it was a large, contiguous, and densely settled Germanic tribal Reich on an agrarian foundation. They therefore opposed the "juggernaut of the metropolis" and the "vampire of capitalism," which had led to a "devastating rural exodus" during the Second Reich and therefore to a Slavic infiltration of the German eastern territories. In the early years of the Third Reich, hoping to reverse this development, such writers proposed settling parts of the unemployed proletariat in the eastern territories, thus transforming them into worthy representatives of the Reichsnährstand (Organization for the Reich Food Supply). They also energetically supported the general rural labor service requirement introduced by the NSDAP that was intended to contribute to the gradual rustication of the German people and simultaneously create men with hard fists.

Hans Heyck, among others, addressed the topic of internal colonization in his novel *Robinson kehrt heim* (1934; Robinson Returns Home), while the political, social, and cultural concerns of the ethnic Germans in the Ukraine, Lithuania, Siebenbürgen, and Hungary were the subjects of Josef Ponten's trilogy *Volk auf dem Wege* (1933–1937; People on the Move), Heinz Gerhard's *Kameraden an der Memel* (1935; Comrades on the Memel), Erwin Wittstock's *Bruder nimm die Brüder auf* (1937; Brother, Take in Your Brothers), and Karl von Möller's *Grenzen wandern* (1937; Traveling Borders). In his novel *Gloria über der Welt* (1937; Glory above the World), Wilfried Bade went so far as to conjure up an agrarian kingdom of the future similar in concept to earlier utopias, where there would be neither selfishness nor technical tools and where the native soil would prove to be the sole basis of life. The more his new peasants understand this, the stronger the sense of a shared bond becomes. Instead of always thinking about themselves, in this future state everyone supports everyone else. And to top it all off, the peasants subordinate themselves to a Führer they all revere, who promises those gathered around him that he will transform everything from the ground up.

We can certainly get the message conveyed by novels like this, but what was specifically Nazi fascist about the concept behind them? Was it really the NSDAP's ultimate ideological objective to create a world without the achievements of civilization, a world with the most difficult rural living conditions, an existence characterized entirely by a mythologized

Figure 22. Werner Peiner: *German Soil* (1933).

native soil? Or was this idea, as reflected in many paintings from these years, nothing more than an ideological chimera? The old-time members of the volkish movement had long evoked it with all the fervor of their yearning for a real communality. Were activists like Bade, who had belonged to the revolutionary wing of the SA in the early 1930s, just trying to give it a new direction without thinking very deeply about the political and social feasibility of such projects? The more clever among the Nazi cultural theorists surely realized that although novels like this provided support for the blood and soil ideology loudly proclaimed by overzealous fanatics within the party, they did not provide a foundation for building a state. At the same time, the Nazi Party leadership began an immense wave of technological modernization to prepare Germany for a second world war, which led to an escalating rural exodus and therefore to an increase in the number of industrial workers—all in diametrical opposition to the volkish-minded cult of the peasant. Therefore, agrarian novels of this kind were promoted after 1933, but they were definitely not given priority, especially since they met with little response by the broader reading public, which was largely metropolitan and in favor of advanced civilization. If these groups read agrarian novels at all, then it was more likely to be works by Josef-Martin Bauer, Peter Dörfler, Friedrich Griese, Emil Strauß, or Karl-Heinz Waggerl, in which Nazi fascist elements were toned down in favor of idyllic, humorous, or local characteristics to make the novels more engrossing.

The many novels about World War I, with which a whole generation of male readers could identify based on their own experiences, were much

more popular. Between 1926 and 1929, during the final years of the stabilization phase of the Weimar Republic, works by Erich Maria Remarque
and Arnold Zweig with a critical perspective from the left were predominant within this genre. But after 1930, in keeping with the election victories of the NSDAP, it was primarily those novels in which a tendency to
glorify war dominated that were successful. Whether in *Aufbruch der Nation* (1930; The Emergence of a Nation) by Franz Schauwecker, *Gruppe
Bosemüller* (1939; The Bosemüller Group) by Werner Beumelburg, *Sieben
vor Verdun* (1930; Seven before Verdun) by Josef Magnus Wehner, *Der
Glaube an Deutschland* (1932; Belief in Germany) by Hans Zöberlein, or
similar works by Edwin Erich Dwinger, the subject of all of these chauvinistic novels about the battlefront was an unquestioned readiness for
action in support of the greatness of the German nation. Everything
in them existed in the context of authoritarian norms and blind self-
abandonment to fate. In these novels, the mass of ordinary soldiers always
willingly followed their leaders as part of an anticipated community of the
volk, and felt this validated their Germanness.

That these novels in particular proved extremely successful testifies
both to the continuing vitality of the battlefront spirit dating from World
War I and to the appeal exerted by the combative posture of the NSDAP
in the years between 1930 and 1933. Almost all the novels by these authors, which were widely promoted by party distribution channels after
1933 and set off a wave of new novels of a similar type, had print runs
in the hundreds of thousands. The idea of an agrarianization of Germany was not entirely abandoned in the course of the 1930s, although
it slipped into the background for reasons of realpolitik, but the NSDAP
propaganda machine continued to point consistently to the heroic self-
sacrifice that held sway in the war novels. The goal was to continuously
attune all the men between eighteen and forty-five who read novels to
the bellicose attitude conveyed by these works; the medium of literature
was intended to contribute to the ideological preparation for World War
II, which was being planned in secret since 1933. And the NSDAP was
proved right by the success of these efforts—German soldiers obeyed their
commanders after 1 September 1939 with the same subservience and belief in fate as they had in fall 1914 at the beginning of World War I. Of
course, the many fascist battlefront novels were not the only reason for
this, but they—along with numerous other factors—made a contribution
that should not be underestimated.

It would be misguided, however, to view works of this type as the only
popular novels of the Nazi period. All of the historical novels by Werner Beumelburg, Hans Friedrich Blunck, Bruno Brehm, Mirko Jelusich,
and Edwin Guido Kolbenheyer that used themes from the period of the

great migrations, the imperial magnificence of the High Middle Ages, or the history of Prussia with its consistent military victories, had a similar success. As was the case in novels about the battlefront in World War I, these novels usually emphasized elements that excited a nationalistic fervor, filling their readers with enhanced pride in the achievements of German willpower. Not limited to biographical facts or things that were historically verifiable, they were intended to demonstrate that great Germans were never solely concerned with material gains; they were also concerned with the implementation of higher goals that had lost nothing of their exemplary quality.

But this overview does not capture the entire range of novels written during the 1930s. It was primarily Goebbels and his followers who perceived that the broad masses needed to be entertained as well as educated and animated to keep them in a good mood even in the context of a social system heading toward another world war. Instead of just zeroing in on basic convictions, in other words, emphasizing too strongly the Nordic spirit of a heroic view of life, they also strongly endorsed ideologically unpretentious novels written to entertain. They did not mean "mind-numbing kitsch or mindless merchandise to provide entertainment"; they meant novels that were easily accessible and diverting and therefore put the reader in a cheerful mood— in other words, something that tempted readers to bury themselves in its pages and therefore was consciously designed to distract or kill time.

Heinrich Spoerl proved to be one of the most compliant authors of this type; his novels *Die Feuerzangenbowle* (1935; Wine Punch Flambéé), *Der Maulkorb* (1936; The Muzzle), *Wenn wir alle Engel wären* (1936; If We Were All Angels), and *Der Gasmann* (1940; The Gas Meter Reader) were welcomed by the NSDAP mainly because of their nonfascist amiability. Even Erich Kästner, up to that point known as a social critic, was still considered by many readers in the early years of the Third Reich primarily as a major humorist based on his novels *Das fliegende Klassenzimmer* (1933; The Flying Classroom, 1934), *Drei Männer im Schnee* (1934; Three Men in the Snow, 1935), and *Emil und die drei Zwillinge* (1935; Emil and the Three Twins, 1935). The larger reading public was equally interested in the wealth of suspenseful crime and detective stories that appeared during these years. And even novels by Karl May that had been popular for years such as *Winnetou, Old Shatterhand*, and *Der Schatz im Silbersee* (The Treasure in Silver Lake), all of which were among Hitler's favorite books, were once again published in large editions during the Third Reich. The same was true of the innumerable adventure and romance novels of the period. In contrast to similar works before 1933, they did not digress into sophisticated or erotic territory. But because of their escapades in the realm of illusion, they were viewed by the authorities in the same way as contemporary popular comedies for stage and screen—as a recommended balance to the daily grind, which often required hard work and self-denial.

Editors were not so concerned about whether works categorized as entertaining were by German or foreign authors. Along with novels by Rudolf G. Binding, Waldemar Bonsels, Ludwig Ganghofer, Rudolf Herzog, Reinhold Conrad Muschler, Felicitas Rose, Ina Seidel, and Richard Voß, there were also very popular novels by Archibald Joseph Cronin, Warwick Deeping, Sascha Guitry, Gunnar Gulbranssen, John Knittel, Selma Lagerlöf, Margaret Mitchell, Thyde Monnier, and Sigrid Undset; all conformed exactly to the ideological efforts at distraction that were welcomed by the Nazi authorities as helpful in conserving the system. They therefore did not object to the fact that almost three hundred thousand copies of Mitchell's *Gone with the Wind* sold within a very short time. On the contrary, that was exactly the kind of novel that carried readers off into an exotic clime beyond their tiring everyday lives where they could at least briefly abandon themselves to their longing for some kind of compensatory adventure or romance. As the need for recreational literature steadily increased after the beginning of World War II, the responsible authorities' aesthetic requirements for this type of literature were scaled back even further, especially when it came to supplying soldiers with reading material; instead, the trend toward entertainment increased rapidly. It was primarily Goebbels who supported this trend, writing in 1941 with a sideswipe at Rosenberg, "Above all, I make sure that the men in the U-boats get literature to read that is light and relaxing. There are still ideologues among us who believe that the U-boat man who comes out of the engine room filthy and covered with oil would like nothing better than to pick up a copy of the *Mythus des 20. Jahrhunderts*. That is utter nonsense."

Equally popular within this half-fascist, half-nonfascist, but never antifascist entertainment literature were works that were called futuristic novels (*Zukunftsromane*) in the Third Reich; this term was used to avoid the word utopia with its emphasis on progress as well as the Anglo-American concept science fiction. Along with relatively obscure authors such as Werner Chompton, Hans-Joachim Flechtner, Paul Alfred Müller, and Titus Taeschner, it was primarily Hans Dominik who was able to succeed as an opportunistic author of bestsellers of this type; the total number of his books published before and during the Third Reich reached 2.5 million. His novels, which seemed very suspenseful to readers of the time, were blatant expressions of what we would correctly characterize today, looking back at Nazi fascism, as reactionary modernism. For example, in his novel *Befehl aus dem Dunkel* (1933; Command from the Dark), the Japanese—at the time still regarded as the Yellow Peril—have invaded Australia; the "electronic strengthening of his brain," which now functions as a radio transmitter, enables a German engineer to use telepathy to keep them in check and finally to drive them off. To be armed against further incursions of "Asiatic hordes" in the future, "millions of white settlers" are subsequently channeled into Australia, as we are told at the end of the book. Although it was a single engineer's brilliant discovery that forced the "aliens of the yellow race" to retreat, the "strong peasant fists" of the German settlers will take over the task in the future—to satisfy the Nazi fascist native soil ideology.

It would have been hard to do a better job of exemplifying one of the main strategies of Nazi ideology—the embedding of the cult of peasants and settlers into the process of industrial modernization. It is impossible to determine today how many readers saw through this tactic at the time. The same is true of the novels of bestselling author Karl Aloys Schenzinger. Almost half a million copies were sold of his 1932 novel *Hitlerjunge Quex*. In 1937, he published the science-based novel *Anilin* (Aniline) about the scientist who discovered the chemical aniline; it was the most successful German language novel in the 1930s, selling 920,000 copies in the four years following its publication. This novel, which is about the promising manufacture of one of the most important source materials for the dye and pharmaceutical industries, perfectly captured the spirit of the time. Not only was it written in a suspenseful way, it radiated the kind of forced optimism which many of the Nazi elite believed would provide the most effective support for their ideology.

Most of these novels played exactly the role within the cultural sector of the Third Reich that the bigwigs had intended: they offered their readers distraction in the form of emotional escape into the realms of adventure and romantic bliss, agrarian elements appropriate to the theories of blood and soil, historical elements from the lives of the great men of Teutonic-German history, warnings against the pernicious consequences of life in the liberal and commercialized metropolis, stories consciously intended to be humorous, war experiences to created a mood of heroism, and finally novels about inventors and futuristic novels that portrayed the advances of German technology. None of this was particularly innovative. All of it had been present in the literature of the Weimar Republic, often in a form that was much more interesting. Missing were the novels from the period before 1933 with a critical perspective from the left that aimed at reform; almost all of those writers had taken to their heels after the transfer of power to Hitler. That was bad enough. But almost worse was the fact that the majority of readers hardly noticed that those writers were gone. The literature that remained still offered them—very deliberately—enough texts that were suspenseful, cheered them up, and took their minds off their problems, and the various sectors of the population were largely satisfied with that.

Theater

Following the transfer of power to the Hitler regime on 30 January 1933, it is not surprising that almost the same things happened in the realm of theater as in painting, music, and literature. Almost all theater managers, directors, and actors who had previously sympathized with "leftist" views or who were descendants of German Jews lost their positions a short time later. To avoid even harsher repression, those who were in the most exposed positions chose to escape into exile as soon as they could. Any Jewish members of this group who still remained in Germany either changed their profession or tried to continue being active in their métier through the Jewish Cultural League, in some cases until 1941. Some who had previously been on the left had a somewhat easier time in the theater if they could produce an Aryan certificate. If they kept quiet about their former views or even displayed remorse, their previous mistakes were sometimes magnanimously forgiven—out of pragmatic considerations.

Among the most well-known managers and directors who were forced to leave Germany at the time were Paul Barnay, Leopold Jessner, Leopold Lindtberg, Erwin Piscator, and Max Reinhardt. Many actors and actresses, including Albert Bassermann, Elisabeth Bergner, Ernst Deutsch, Tilla Durieux, Alexander Granach, Fritz Kortner, Wolfgang Langhoff, Peter Lorre, Grete Mosheim, Carola Neher, and Helene Thimig, shared the same fate. In this group were many of the most talented in the profession, who had given spectacular prestige to the theater of the Weimar Republic; for that very reason, Nazi fascist publications directed the vilest invective at them, hoping to erase them once and for all from the memories of the German-minded theater audience. Absolutely everything they had directed or performed was suddenly viewed as cultural bolshevism or alien to the German volk. They had been interested only in "rabble-rousing in the interest of class struggle," economic "greed for profit," or "a craving for sensation that stimulated the nerves," wrote many of the Nazi newspapers. In the theater, therefore, this "august cultural institution," it was high time, they claimed, to remember what might properly be designated as truly German.

It goes without saying that for the Nazi fanatics, groundbreaking theater in the future would be based on racial consciousness. "Our theater must become German-volkish or, even better, it must become Nordic-Germanic once again," was how Rosenberg's disciples put it; they viewed themselves as "the ones who had been roused to racial awareness," and they tried to take center stage forcibly following the chauvinistically orchestrated Day of Potsdam. They demanded a clear change from "an economic collective to a mythical one" in both politics and culture, and with it a sacrificial devotion to "the totality, the state, the race" as Gottfried Benn put it in his confessional statement *Der neue Staat und die Intellektuellen* (1933; The New State and the Intellectuals). The goal was no longer to disseminate enlightenment or education via the theater; these groups and the party supporters who sympathized with them longed for a retrospective link to what was prototypical or even to the cultic, all founded on an inner-directed vision and in the framework of a metaphysical community of faith. These theorists traced the racial decline of German theater largely to the pernicious trend toward anti-statism and thus toward the realm of private tragedy that had characterized both bourgeois-individualist and Jewish-oriented drama since the middle of the eighteenth century. What was needed to replace these tendencies from now on, according to the theorists whose thinking was primarily racially based, were broadly conceived national-level events that would promote a "heroic Weltanschauung" that all fellow Germans would view as "morally binding."

The Nazis fanatics, befogged by their political triumphs, saw the introduction of the *Thingspiel* with its Nordic inspiration as the most appropriate form of theater in 1933–1934; in it a day of judgment would finally be held over the enemies of the new Reich. Instead of putting a dozen "prominent individuals or universally known stars" on the stage, this group thought the entire volk should participate in such performances, experiencing their mythic awakening in the form of a festival. So those responsible made an effort to locate the first *Thingspiel* amphitheaters at ancient Germanic cultic sites such as the one on the Brandberge near Halle. By the end of 1934, five such *Thing* sites had been completed with fifteen more under construction. In 1936, nine more were added. But the construction of such facilities gradually came to a standstill, although especially devout Nazi fascists had originally envisaged four hundred of them. In 1936, performances took place only on the Dietrich Eckart-Bühne during the Berlin Olympics. After that, quiet reigned once again at the *Thing* sites.

Goebbels shared these views at the beginning—during the phase of national awakening that was still considered revolutionary—but as time went on he realized that in this sector of general cultural life, compromises had to be made to avoid putting the noses of the educated and therefore discriminating middle-class German theater audience painfully out of joint. In February/March 1933, he was still envisioning a Nazi fascist agitprop theater, and even hoped to win over an outspoken leftist like Erwin Piscator for the purpose. But by November 1933, he was already pursuing somewhat more moderate goals in the Reich Theater Chamber he had established. Otto Laubinger, whom he had named first president of the chamber, with Werner Krauss lending his support as representative of the actors, was much less radical than the theater critics from Rosenberg's Militant League for German Culture. On the one hand, he energetically opposed the mercantile interests and the liberal arbitrariness of the earlier Jewish theater managers and advocated the elimination of all un-German plays. On the other hand, he opposed a one-sided preference for party dramas in which ideology was laid on with a trowel and for Germanophile *Thingspiele*, both of which might bore or even repel the pampered taste of the theater audience.

Despite this development, Goebbels lowered himself to the level of founding a poets' circle to promote *Thingspiele* in the summer of 1934, but by a year later he mandated that mythic-sounding concepts like *Thing* or cult should be avoided in performances. The poetic form of the chant (*Sprechchor*), used in parades at the Reich party congresses in Nuremberg and characterized by Goebbels as "an advertising medium" that "was needed in a time of struggle to defeat the opponent," was already viewed by many Nazi theorists by the middle of the 1930s as behind the times and therefore superfluous. Nationalistic forms of theater such as the speaking chorus, the Reich autobahn theater, or the *Thingspiel* had been welcomed with high hopes by the popular socialist wing of the NSDAP at the beginning of the Third Reich; they were intended to finish off the elitist form of bourgeois theater and initiate a theater of ten thousand if not of the entire volk community in its place. But after this point in time, these nationalistic forms of theater ceased playing a central role. They were still popular with the Hitler Youth, the SA, the German Labor Front, and the Strength through Joy organization. But even there, they began to take the form of amateur theater performed as a leisure time activity instead pursuing the original goal of community building by molding the mass of the volk in the spirit of early Nazi fascist thinking.

From now on, Goebbel's Ministry of Propaganda paid less attention to the open-air theaters with their volkish ideology and instead gave ever-increasing financial support to all the state and local theaters already in existence that were subordinated to the ministry by the NS-Theater Law issued by Goebbels on 15 May 1934. Their subsidies increased accordingly from year to year, rising from nine million reichsmarks in 1934 to thirty-four million reichsmarks in 1942, while the subsidies for open air performances and similar events during the same period declined from 300,000 to 135,000 reichsmarks. After 1938, Goebbels supported the German-language theater in the so-called Reichs Protectorate of Bohemia and Moravia just as generously, providing it with 3.3 million reichsmarks in 1942. Expressed in percentages, Goebbels allotted the lion's share of all financial stipends in the cultural sector to the theaters—24.4 percent. The film industry was actually much more important to him, since it had a wider sphere of influence. But in contrast to the theaters, it supported itself to some extent and so received only 11.5 percent of the state subsidies. And this enormous outlay for the theater was not without effect. Later, the Nazi authorities could say with satisfaction that the number of theatergoers not only doubled but quadrupled or even quintupled during their tenure.

What Goebbels had achieved here was another victory for tradition over the efforts at revolutionary overthrow in the cultural sector intended by fanatics within the NSDAP. In 1933, Rosenberg was still imagining a "revolutionary drama of awakening" that would attune all Germans to the "Aryan myth of the twentieth century." But two years later, he was forced to look on bitterly while more pragmatic ventures increased in the theater sector as the Third Reich became more stable. In his speech at the national conference of the NS-Culture Community in Düsseldorf in 1935, he employed harsh words in opposition to this trend. He reproached Goebbels with providing existing theaters with financial support and permitting their administrators to engage in relatively liberal programming— in other words, programming oriented to the educated middle class—instead of attempting a drastic reorientation geared to volk-based socialist objectives. But by this point in time, it was already too late for proposals for change of this kind. In the meantime, Hitler had opted for the course pursued by Goebbels. And for the theater, that meant a rollback of all revolutionary trends in favor of a cultivation of the classical heritage.

Admittedly, some of the historical and partisan plays by Nazi dramatists such as Hanns Johst, Curt Langenbeck, and Eberhard Wolfgang Möller, most written before 1933, were still performed in the years that followed. But as time went on, they continued to lose ground to the theatrically effective dramas of the eighteenth and nineteenth centuries. The proportion of new works also remained substantially smaller than the number of foreign plays or of tried-and-true German tragedies, comedies, and light theater. Thus the deceptive glory days of the German theater dawned, celebrated exuberantly in the newspapers of the Third Reich. During these years, under the direction of Otto Falckenberg, Jürgen Fehling, Heinrich George, Gustav Gründgens, Heinz Hilpert, Eugen Klöpfer, and Lothar Müthel actors such as Horst Caspar, Friedrich Kayßler, Werner Krauss,

Bernhard Minetti, Will Quadflieg, and Paul Wegener and actresses such as Bertha Drews, Käthe Dorsch, Elisabeth Flickenschildt, Käthe Gold, Marianne Hoppe, Hermine Körner, Gisela Uhlen, and Elsa Wagener performed—many of them familiar to broad segments of the population through popular films. Managing directors such as Gründgens and George, who had been more or less on the left before 1933, sometimes mingled with the actors in the theaters they led, Gründgens as Mephisto and George as Götz von Berlichingen, the Great Elector, or Wallenstein.

The repertory included Molière's comedies and plays by Shakespeare—who was viewed by race fanatics like Adolf Bartels and Hans FK Günther as an exemplary man of the North and referred to since 1900 as Schüttelspeer by those who were particularly German-conscious. But it was works of the German classical period that were most important in the theater programming promoted by the Nazi authorities. In the 1936–1937 season alone, Goethe's *Faust* was performed a total of 220 times. Gründgens, who enjoyed the particular esteem of Goebbels as a privy counselor in the Prussian State Council, staged Büchner's *Dantons Tod* (Danton's Death) in 1939 and Schiller's *Die Räuber* (The Robbers) in 1944 as well as *Faust*. Jürgen Fehling also attracted attention with productions of Schiller's *Don Carlos* in 1935 and Hebbel's *Kriemhilds Rache* (The Revenge of Kriemhild) in 1936. Most managing directors refrained from any excesses in their productions that would seem too propagandistic. But once the final solution was already underway, Lothar Müthel in Vienna encouraged his star Werner Krauss to play the title role in Shakespeare's *Merchant of Venice* as a "pathological representation of the racial type of the Eastern European Jew."

In short, what was performed in the theaters of the Third Reich between 1935–1936 and 1943–1944—along with the unavoidable comedies with which the authorities hoped to put the audience in a system-integrated good mood—was above all the highlights of the dramatic tradition, performed for them by the best actors and actresses. The emphasis was on the big names and the prestige connected to them. And the audience, financially well-off and simultaneously aesthetically discriminating, and who still valued the theater much more highly than the movies, liked this very much. In these so-called holy halls, the pride they felt in their culture and education was confirmed, and they overlooked either intentionally or unconsciously the games that were being played with them.

Most people who attended the theater during this era hardly noticed that the real theater in the Third Reich was not taking place on the well-subsidized stages of national and local theaters. It was happening at the huge troop reviews, midsummer festivals, torchlight parades, and Reich party congresses that had been taking place primarily in Berlin and

Figure 23. Leni Riefenstahl: The Führer speaks. From the film *Triumph of the Will* (1936). From the book by Leni Riefenstahl: *Hinter den Kulissen des Reichsparteitag-Films*, Munich 1935.

Nuremburg since 1927. For these political stagings of themselves, the NS-DAP did not need any actors, just directors. Hitler, who liked to portray himself in effective appearances before the press as a friend of the theater, had recognized this early on. He did not want to watch a performance on such occasions, he wanted to be the principle actor. He was offered a good opportunity at the huge Reich party congresses, where he could give carefully prepared speeches to tens of thousands of eager listeners, including men from the Labor Service, soldiers, and Stormtroopers. These events—not productions of classic plays for the educated middle class—were the theater that really counted in Hitler's eyes, because there he was not a spectator, he was playing the leading role.

Radio, Film, and the Press

Radio, film, and the press had become the three most influential mass media in the course of the 1920s. Goebbels viewed them as so important that in 1933 he established three governing institutes for them that were equal in importance to the four culture chambers for the high arts: the Reichsrundfunkkammer (Reich Radio Chamber), the Reichsfilmkammer (Reich Film Chamber), and the Reichspressekammer (Reich Press Chamber). Every German citizen who wanted to be active in these areas had to first (it bears repeating) produce his or her Aryan certificate and then become a member of one of these chambers. Those employed in these rapidly growing media branches were not a series of individual artists; they were freelance workers in numbers so large they were difficult to assess. The number of members in these chambers climbed quickly into the tens of thousands, which inevitably led to delays in the approval of the membership agreements.

Here, as in the high arts, Goebbels put the main emphasis on acoustic and visual media (radio and film) and less emphasis on the print medium (the press). Of course, he did think reading books and newspapers was important, but not as influential with the masses as those forms of art and media that appeal directly to the human senses, above all the eye and the ear, and therefore do not require a particularly demanding reception process. Although he himself was active as a writer and newspaper editor for years, as Minister of Public Enlightenment and Propaganda his main interest was not the printed word; it was radio broadcasting, which was primarily acoustic, and sound films, conveyed both acoustically and visually, since these media had an effect that was both more sensually direct and more widely disseminated.

Radio proved easiest for Goebbels to get under his control. This medium—following its beginnings in the private sector—had been nationalized by the authorities of the Weimar Republic on 27 July 1932. Therefore it was primarily the functionalities of management and the programming that changed after 30 January 1933, not the ownership. In the personnel area, there was a series of major rearrangements and dismissals. There had

been few leftists or Jews at the management level in the various radio stations, so these affected primarily the reformist liberals, who were arrested
by SA troops immediately after Hitler took power. The new masters also
began to intervene massively in programming. Both the content of the
programs and the broadcast schedule and transmission ranges were determined in advance by Goebbels and his coworkers, among them Eugen
Hadamovsky and Horst Dreßler-Andreß in leadership positions; the goal
was to turn radio into an effective means for the propagation of national
socialist ideology.

The new government took several steps to make it easy for as many volk
comrades as possible to receive the restructured programs. They decided to
encourage production of relatively affordable volk receivers that cost first
76 and then just 59 reichsmarks instead of the 200 to 400 reichsmarks
radios had cost previously. They also encouraged workers and white-collar
employees to listen to important programs about national policy in large,
communal groups in pubs or staff canteens. They also had approximately
six thousand loudspeaker poles put up in suitable areas and generally tried
everything they could think of to encourage the majority of Labor Front
and Strength through Joy members to listen to the radio in their free time.
In the first year of the Third Reich, Hitler's speeches and those of his most

Figure 24. Incarcerated radio directors and producers in Oranienburg concentration
camp (August 1933). From right: Kurt Magnus, Hans Flesch, Hermann Giesecke,
Alfred Braun, Friedrich Ebert Jr., and Ernst Heilmann. © Berlin, ADN Zentralbild.

important followers were at the core of the broadcast programming. One speech by Hitler was broadcast each week. The beginning of autobahn construction, openings of politically important exhibits, and national socialist memorial days and holidays were acknowledged at length on the radio in the early days, which led to a noticeable cutback in the music and entertainment programs that had been popular up to that time.

A speech by Eugen Hadamovsky, the chairman of the national broadcasting company, may come closest to expressing the level of political enthusiasm in the programs broadcast by Nazi radio at the beginning of 1933 and the important role the authorities attributed to the medium. The speech was given in late fall 1933 on the occasion of the founding of the Reich Radio Chamber. Hadamovsky explained in a booming voice: "In Germany, radio was the hammer Adolf Hitler used after 30 January to forge a unified nation. It was the hammer he used to smash thirty political parties in Germany into a thousand bits and pieces. It was the hammer he used to crush the class struggle in Germany once and for all. It was the hammer used to vanquish Marxism and communism, not through a bloody class struggle but through compelling intellectual strength. And it was the hammer used to forge the German people, ruptured for two-thousand years, into a steel ingot that cannot be ruptured or divided, and that will rest in the heart of Europe today and for all eternity."

But by summer 1933 the so-called broad masses, who expected radio to provide an entertaining form of relaxation rather than a constant stream of ideology, had begun to respond to the partisan sledgehammer method with widespread expressions of discontent. Goebbels, as the strategist with responsibility for the cultural sector, took these utterances quite seriously. Toward the end of the same year, he explained in a talk before the new radio directors: "Whatever you do, don't be boring. No dreariness. Don't put your convictions on display. Don't think you can best serve the national government by playing blaring marches night after night. Convictions are important, but convictions don't have to equal boredom. Imagination must employ all possible means and methods to convey the new convictions to the ear of the masses in a way that is modern, up-to-date, and involved. Interesting and informative, but not didactic." So as early as late fall 1933 Goebbels decided to reduce the propaganda that had been piled on thickly in the chauvinistically overdone radio broadcasts in the first months of the Third Reich and include more challenging concerts and readings as well as more programs of light music and humorous skits. The upper classes would have the edification they wanted and the broad masses would have the relaxation they were demanding.

Due to these measures, radio achieved a level of popularity in the following years unimaginable up to that time. In 1932 there were barely four million radio participants. By 1939 their number had climbed to over 10.8 million and by 1942 to 16 million, making Germany's radio network the most highly developed in Europe after Denmark and Sweden. This can be traced primarily to the fact that Goebbels decided to appreciably reduce the number of what were referred to as audio reports (*Hörberichte*), including party leaders' speeches. After 1935, instead of supporting a continuous stream of ideology, he forcefully advocated offering radio listeners as great a diversity of programs as possible. An example was the program *Die Stunde der Nation* (The Nation's Hour), which was supposed to encourage intellectual and spiritual uniformity among listeners and was broadcast daily between seven and eight in the evening, the prime listening time. In early 1934, Goebbels had the program shortened and cut back to three times a week, and the following year he had it discontinued.

Figure 25. Advertisement for the *Volksempfänger*. "All of Germany listens to the Führer with the radio receiver for the volk" (c. 1935).

In the framework of the new cultural programming, symphony and opera broadcasts for the edification of listeners increasingly replaced stirring
ideological broadcasts. Instead of continuing to emphasize the revolutionary aspects of national socialism, the radio now offered, among other
things, all nine of Beethoven's symphonies as well as the entire *Ring des
Nibelungen* by Wagner. The quality of both the performances and the
sound reproduction was so high that such broadcasts were also picked up
by a series of foreign radio stations. But this overemphasis on high culture
seemed too challenging to many listeners from the lower classes. Before,
these groups had primarily spoken out against the dominance of partisan political broadcasts; now they rebelled against the music programs
that were too demanding for their taste. And Goebbels, always concerned
about having a large impact, lent a willing ear to these voices. In response,
he had the share of light music in the radio programming increased first
to 60 percent and then finally to 70 percent, allotting only 5 percent to
broadcasts of so-called serious music.

This did put some noses out of joint—those of middle-class listeners
who were fanatically concerned about education and those of volkish-
minded cultural traditionalists. But it gave the broad masses he was always invoking the desired feeling of living in a very normal society where
the stressful work day was always followed by some well-earned entertainment. Goebbels commented in 1936, "The radio program must be
configured so that it continues to interest the fastidious taste yet appears
pleasing and understandable to tastes that are more unassuming. It should
offer instruction, stimulation, relaxation, and entertainment in a mixture
that is clever and psychologically astute. Special consideration should be
given to relaxation and entertainment, because the vast majority of all
radio listeners are treated harshly and unsparingly by life, and they have
a right to find relaxation in the few hours of rest and leisure available to
them. In comparison, those few who want to be nourished solely by Kant
and Hegel carry almost no weight." A year later, Goebbels even supported
the trend toward rejecting all types of intellectual arrogance in programming even more strongly than before. "What does Furtwängler think he's
achieving with his 2,000 listeners in the concert hall?" he explained.
"What we need are the millions, and with the radio we have them."

Even after the beginning of World War II, this basic approach to radio
programming changed very little. True, the program now included Franz
Liszt's symphonic poem *Les Préludes* introducing proud reports of victory,
but the noncommittal tootling of light music did not decrease for all that.
On the contrary, as the state of the war worsened progressively after the
fall of Stalingrad in January 1943, music broadcasts intended to spread
a mood of optimism grew substantially on a percentage basis. The musi-

cal request programs, often lasting three hours, played an important role with their opera choruses, melodies from operettas, folk songs, carnival hits, waltzes, and military marches. They became more and more popular with soldiers at the front as well as with approximately 50 percent of the listeners on the home front as entertainment on evenings or Sundays. In addition, there were the many hits sung by popular favorites such as Zarah Leander, Hans Albers, and many others. They had catchy first lines such as "That isn't the end of the world," "I know a miracle will happen," "That can't bother a sailor," "We'll rock the baby right," or "At home, at home, we'll see each other again"—all intended to promote a stiff-upper-lip ethic that was finally revealed as meaningless at the end of April 1945 as one military defeat followed another.

Almost the same trends can be observed in the development of Nazi film production; only at the beginning were there some obvious differences. The radio was already in government hands before the transfer of power to Hitler, so the new government could put it in the service of their own ideology without too great an effort, but the entire film industry was still in the private sector in 1933. There were therefore substantial differences in the beginning in terms of how the employees of these two industries fared. In radio, leftists and Jews were a tiny minority of the employees. There were also very few leftists in the various film companies, but there were a great many Jews, who suddenly saw themselves marginalized. Well aware that they would not have any other professional opportunities under Hitler's thumb, there were approximately eight hundred directors, cameramen, and actors and actresses who left after the Third Reich was proclaimed on 30 January 1933, among them Fritz Kortner, Fritz Lang, Max Ophüls, Otto Preminger, Billy Wilder, and Fred Zinnemann. Most of them, after brief stays in France, England, and the Netherlands, went to the United States and in most cases to Hollywood, as Marlene Dietrich did. Later, in their periodical *Der deutsche Film*, the Nazis claimed that in the years preceding 1933, 70 percent of all screen writers, 50 percent of all directors, and 20 percent of all owners of film production companies had been Jews; these shocking percentages were cited with the intention of sharply underlining this supposedly deplorable state of affairs. These losses were a serious blow to the German film industry, which a short time before had been justified in claiming to be the second most important in the world after Hollywood. The half-Jew Fritz Lang, for example, was admired by the German-minded for his *Nibelungen* film (1924), and Goebbels would have liked very much to keep him in Germany to be utilized as a director of Nazi fascist propaganda films, but Lang refused.

Goebbels established a separate chamber for film in the process of creating the Reich chambers of culture in late fall of 1933. Film had long been considered a low genre, artistically speaking, and Goebbels liked to portray himself as a friend of the high arts, so this very fact shows how important he believed film to be. As minister for propaganda, he had to pay particular attention to the lower art forms that could more easily reach the so-called broad masses. While the educated middle class preferred to continue attending the theater and the opera, the lower classes were attracted by the movies; therefore Goebbels tried to win over these groups for the new regime right away through film as well as radio. He was well aware that the workers, who at the time made up almost 50 percent of the German population, had largely voted for the social democrats or the communists before 1933. So he tried everything he could to appear as a "friend of the worker" despite his own educational background, and to offer them the cultural products with which he could help them to a new consciousness with a maximum of speed and suggestivity. And for this purpose, the medium of film—along with radio—seemed most suitable to him.

The new government was thus faced with especially difficult tasks in this area. It was not enough just to establish the Reich Film Chamber. A number of questions arose to which there was no easy answer. Where could the NSDAP cultural authorities find new directors, actors, and actresses who could adapt to this genre? Where were there talented script writers who could give the new themes a powerful impact? And how would the lower-class audience react to these changes? Would they continue to demand sentimental melodramas or action films, musicals, costume dramas, and comedies? In short, how was it possible to convey the much-talked-about new national way of thinking to an audience affected by the world economic crisis and the unemployment linked to it? It hit the working-class segments of the population particularly strongly, and they expected the movies to provide entertaining suspense or escapism that verged on kitsch. These questions were not easy to answer.

Initially, the new regime adopted an emphatically revolutionary course, supporting the production of hard-core propaganda films. There were three of them in 1933: *SA-Mann Brandt. Ein Lebensbild aus unseren Tagen* (SA-man Brandt: The Image of a Contemporary Life), *Hans Westmar. Einer von vielen. Ein deutsches Schicksal aus dem Jahr 1929* (Hans Westmar: One of Many. A German Destiny in the Year 1929), and *Hitlerjunge Quex. Ein Film vom Opfergeist der deutschen Jugend* (Hitler Youth Quex: A Film about German Youth's Willingness to Sacrifice). All three were thematically based in conflicts between the SA or the Hitler Youth and the communist Red Front groups; in the end they all came down to either successful conversions or heroic martyrdom. But that did not make much of a splash with the lower class audience of the time, who were mostly

Figure 26. Emil Lohkamp in the film *Hans Westmar* (1933) directed by Hans Wenzler. From the book by Eric Rentschler: *The Ministry of Illusion. Nazi Cinema and its Afterlife*, Cambridge, Mass. 1996.

oriented toward the left. Only the film *Hitlerjunge Quex*, in which Heinrich George played a very impressive father role, achieved a certain level of success, whereas the other two met with either disregard or passive resistance.

Therefore Goebbels soon changed course in this area as in almost all artistic realms, and suggested to the filmmakers a much more deft mixture of propaganda and entertainment, and Hitler supported him in these efforts. He, like Goebbels, had highbrow cultural expectations but also like Goebbels felt the entertaining elements in Franz Lehar's operetta *Die lustige Witwe* (The Merry Widow) and Walt Disney's Mickey Mouse films were just as important as more serious elements. So instead of continuing to have heroic or tragically moving brown-shirt films made, Goebbels and his coworkers commissioned the leading film companies to produce entertaining films that were primarily humorous or melodramatic. These firms—Bavaria, Ufa, Tobis, and Terra—which came increasingly under state control in the course of the 1930s and finally became entirely state-owned, were all too happy to accept these commissions, from which they expected very high profits. They hired the best script writers, among them Axel Eggebrecht, Hans Fallada, Curt Goetz, Peter Huchel, Wolfgang Koeppen, Ernst von Salomon, Reinhold Schüntzel, and Günther Weisenborn, although these men were largely critical of or even hostile to national socialism.

As a result of this change of course, a vast number of well-made films appeared in the following years—comedies, love stories, Heimat films, musicals of various types, and film spectaculars—that were greeted with enthusiasm by the masses because they simulated a world beyond Nazi fascism in which a good life was obviously possible. The conversion agenda, which had predominated in the first three propaganda films, was now largely left to the newsreels and to some cultural and documentary films. These were sometimes based on scenes like those in Leni Riefenstahl's *Triumph des Willens*, made in 1934 at the Reich party congress; its cinematic quality garnered the German Film Prize and the Italian (1935) and French (1937) prizes as well. At Goebbel's directive, the propaganda elements receded in full-length feature films for the time being, increasing again in fall 1939 when it became essential to stress the German soldiers' courage and willingness to sacrifice at the beginning of World War II. Along with documentaries such as *Feldzug in Polen* (1939; Campaign in Poland), *Feuertaufe* (1940; Baptism by Fire), and *Sieg im Westen* (1941; Victory in the west), there were other full-length features such as *Kadetten* (1941; Cadets), *Kampfgeschwader Lützow* (1941; Bomber wing Lützow), *Blutsbrüderschaft* (1941; Blood brotherhood), *Stukas*

Figure 27. Still photograph from the film *New Horizons* (1937) directed by Detlef Sierck with Willy Birgel and Zarah Leander. © Berlin, Bildagentur für Kunst, Kultur und Geschichte.

(1941; Dive bombers), and *Himmelhunde* (1942; Dogs of heaven). Films intended to promote the so-called final solution or the NSDAP's euthanasia program were equally propagandistic, as were films that portrayed the Poles and the Russians as Slavic subhumans. The most well-known among these works were the three anti-Semitic films *Die Rothschilds* (1940), *Jud Süß* (1940; The Jew Süß), and *Der ewige Jude* (1940; The Eternal Jew); the assisted-dying film *Ich klage an* (1941; I Accuse); and the anti-Slavic films *Heimkehr* (1941; Homecoming) and *GPU* (1942; Soviet Secret Police).

In the anti-Semitic film *Der ewige Jude*, in which the Jews were compared to a plague of disease-infested rats, the propagandistic style was so crude that some especially bloodthirsty scenes featuring kosher butchers had to be cut out of consideration for female viewers. In the film *Ich klage an*, on the other hand, the mercy killing theme was suggested in such a veiled way that it did not arouse any disturbing unrest among the viewers, whether male or female. *Jud Süß* by Veit Harlan was probably the most popular of the propaganda films. This was based in part on the fact that important actors such as Heinrich George, Werner Krauss, and Ferdinand Marian as well as the Swedish actress Kristina Söderbaum played the main roles, but the screenplay was also of a higher literary quality than that of most other propaganda films. Among the propaganda films that were shot toward the end of the war, *Der große König* (1942; The Great King), a film about Frederick the Great of Prussia, bears mentioning. The most important, however, was *Kolberg*, a film about staying the course. Goebbels commissioned the film in 1943, and Harlan again filled the main roles with famous actors and actresses such as Horst Caspar, Heinrich George, Kristina Söderbaum, and Paul Wegener. After very elaborate filming operations, for which Harlan had a budget of eight million reichsmarks at his disposal, a sensational amount for the time, the film premiered on 30 January 1945 to mark the anniversary of the transfer of power to Hitler on the same day twelve years before.

There were many other films intended as propaganda, including historical films and films about major figures in science and culture such as Robert Koch (1939), Friedrich Schiller (1940), Ohm Krüger (1941), Andreas Schlüter (1942), Frederick "the Great" (1942), Bismarck (1942), and Paracelsus (1943). Much notice has been taken of these films, but in percentage terms they were only a small fraction of the 1,094 films made during the Third Reich. Approximately 80 percent of these were films located in some kind of realm far-removed from reality that gave viewers the possibility of abandoning themselves completely to their own dreams and wishful thinking. In some of these films, melodrama predominated, as for example in *Schwarze Rosen* (1935; Black Roses), *Zu neuen Ufern* (1937; To New Horizons), *La Habanera* (1937), *Das unsterbliche Herz* (1939; The Immortal Heart), *Die goldene Stadt* (1942; The Golden City), or *Romanze in Moll* (1943; Romance in a Minor Key). The whole point of others was fooling around and acting all lovey-dovey. Films of this ilk, such as *Wenn wir alle Engel wären* (1936; If We Were All Angels), *Hallo Janine* (1939), *Der Gasmann* (1940; The Gas Meter Reader), or *Frauen sind doch bessere Diplomaten* (1941; Women Are Better Diplomats After All) made with actors and actresses such as Hans Brausewetter, Evelyn Künneke, Theo Lingen, Hans Moser, Marika Rökk, Heinz Rühmann, Adele Sandrock, and Grethe Weiser, were liked as well or even better by most moviegoers, whose numbers climbed from 450 to 900 million in the years between 1938 and 1941.

Many of these films can hardly be distinguished from the musicals and comedies filmed in Hollywood at the same time, which could still be shown in Germany until 1940–1941. After the beginning of World War II, the Nazi leadership viewed comedies that were extremely innocuous as especially important for maintaining a generally optimistic mood within the German population. Particularly in the last phase of the war, in other words after the Stalingrad debacle, these films climbed from

Figure 28. Scene from the film comedy *Roses in Tyrol* (1940) directed by Géza von Bolvary mit Hans Holt, Theo Lingen, and Hans Moser. © Bildagentur für Kunst, Kultur und Geschichte.

47.8 percent of all film production to 55.4 percent, while the percent of films that were primarily propagandistic fell from 10 percent to 8 percent. Along with melodramatic films such as *Das Wunschkonzert* (1940; Music by Request) and *Die große Liebe* (1942; The Love of Your Life), it was the film *Münchhausen* (1943), with Hans Albers in the title role and a screenplay by Erich Kästner, that was particularly successful with the public. As Goebbels wanted, it offered everything that could distract from the bitter reality of the time: glorious adventures, sumptuously decorated palaces, Brigitte Horney as Czarina Catherine the Great, a ride on a cannonball (certainly something never seen before), an oriental harem with naked young women, a sprinter of unsurpassable speed, gondola rides through Venice, characters such as Cagliostro and Casanova, a balloon trip to the moon, and throughout, the incandescent charm of the eponymous hero, whom no woman could resist. A year later, millions of Germans were still laughing at Heinz Rühmann in the film *Die Feuerzangenbowle* (Wine Punch Flambéé) while all around them cities were being transformed into scenes of devastation.

The leadership of the NSDAP also paid considerable attention to the press. Goebbels established a Reich Press Chamber on 15 November 1933 as one of the Reich chambers of culture and named Max Amann, head of the official Nazi publishing house, as its president. But within the politically influential mass media, they did not attach the same importance to the press as they did to radio or film. They viewed newspapers, still primarily text-oriented at that time, as similar to books in requiring a more demanding and tedious reception process than the other two mass media, which functioned primarily visually and acoustically. The newspaper had a monopoly on opinion formation in the public sphere at the beginning of the Weimar Republic, but its importance had already gradually diminished in the course of the 1920s due to the impact of radio and film on ever larger segments of the population. Toward the end of the Republic, bankruptcy threatened even some of the newspapers that had previously flourished such as the *Berliner Tageblatt*, and that ended their political influence. Even Nazi newspapers such as the *Völkischer Beobachter*, the *Freiheitskampf*, *Der Stürmer*, and *Der Angriff* felt the impact of this problem, so that after 1933 the party leadership no longer attached the same importance to them as they had at the beginning.

Goebbels considered *Der Angriff*, which he had founded in 1927, as his personal newspaper, and he wrote innumerable lead articles for it. But after his appointment as Minister for Public Enlightenment and Propaganda, his interest in the newspaper, which continued to appear, diminished. By May 1933, he agreed to its transformation into the *Tageszeitung der Deutschen Arbeitsfront* and continued to write occasional articles only for the *Völkischer Beobachter* and the weekly *Das Reich*. This lack of interest was not only the result of the increasing dominance of the audio-visual mass media; it was also linked to the NSDAP's striving for respectability after its official assumption of power on 30 January 1933. In the late 1920s, when the Nazi fascists were still considered revolutionary, their newspapers had been unabashed propaganda organs, but now many of the leaders were struggling to give the new regime the appearance of having greater prestige. Nevertheless, they were not willing to give up any media with propaganda potential, so they tried to bring newspaper publishing under their control. They were somewhat more broad-minded here than in other areas. They even wanted to offer the status of honorary Aryan to the Jew Hans Lachmann Mosse, the owner of the internationally known *Berliner Tageblatt*, and to his Jewish chief editor Theodor Wolff as well if the two had been willing to continue managing the paper—of course omitting all comments critical of the regime. But both Lachmann Mosse and Wolff declined the offer, which had originated with Hermann Göring, and did not return to Berlin from exile. Because of the paper's international prestige, the Ministry for Propaganda simply allowed it to continue publishing, albeit under Aryan management, finally shutting it down on 31 January 1939.

Many other newspapers of the Weimar Republic were able to continue appearing after 1933, among them the *Frankfurter Zeitung* (characterized by Alfred Rosenberg as "boursianic"), the *Deutsche Allgemeine Zeitung*, the *Kölnische Zeitung*, the *Vossische Zeitung*, and the *BZ am Abend*. Only leftist papers such as *Vorwärts*, the *Rote Fahne*, and the *Arbeiter-Illustrierte Zeitung aller Länder* were forbidden. Of course all who worked for the newspapers that continued to appear, as well as their owners, had to become members of the Reich Press Chamber and produce an Aryan certificate. They also saw their editors forced to emphasize national ascendancy at all times. And in addition, the party authorities insisted that they give up two attitudes that had predominated until now in the bourgeois Jewish press: first, the sense of personal involvement that had its basis in the "rootlessness of subjective individual interests," and second, and in contradiction to the first, they were to ignore the commandment of "new objectivity," as the director of the Reich Broadcasting Company Eugen Hadamovsky explained in 1933. From now on, every journalist should feel they were first and foremost member of a national community and give expression to that feeling in their reports. But beyond that, not too many serious demands were made of this profession during the mid-1930s.

When it became important to spread a mood of optimism during World War II, newspaper editors too were given the task of writing articles that would cheer people up. In the wake of this reversal, the Propaganda Ministry stipulated that words such as *retreat* or *catastrophe* should be replaced by cleverly obfuscating euphemisms. But as I said before, a certain limited pluralism was preserved until the end of the Third Reich in the press as in the publishing industry and in magazines such as *Das Innere Reich*. Despite relentless attacks on the Semitic evil published in Julius Streicher's *Der Stürmer*, even the weekly newspaper of the Jews of Berlin was able to continue publishing until the middle of 1941. In its final issues you can still find ads by people seeking a marriage partner, which shows how resigned members of this group had become to the prevailing conditions and how they were trying to get along for better or for worse. But just a short time later, they were forced to recognize, appalled, that they no longer had any options for continuing to live in the Third Reich. Many of their Aryan fellow citizens, on the other hand, had been relieved of most of the routine dirty work by hundreds of thousands of foreign workers and prisoners of war. As their hope for a victorious end to the hostilities gradually disappeared after 1943, these people declared cynically, "Enjoy the war; the peace will be terrible."

CLASS-SPECIFIC SUCCESSES OF NATIONAL SOCIALIST CULTURAL POLICIES

Earlier historians of art and culture have long asked themselves: How was it possible that a highly cultured people like the Germans submissively allowed themselves to be synchronized absolutely overnight after 1933 by a half-educated terrorist clique like the Nazi fascists? Why were they ready to do anything to follow them, remaining loyal at great personal sacrifice until the catastrophe of 1945? First, the Nazi fascist leadership relied on a long tradition of nationalist-conservative or volklish-minded worldviews, whose ideological antecedents reached far back into the nineteenth century. Second, the German people had never really existed; there had always been a German population that was segmented into various classes and that did not readily coalesce into a homogenous community of the volk after 30 January 1933. And third, various segments of the population had very different expectations of art and culture based on their highly disparate educational backgrounds, and the Nazi authorities definitely took this into consideration by trying to offer something appropriate to each group.

In the years after 1933, there were many exceptions to the effort to synchronize everything related to cultural matters. Some historians and sociologists deny this, based on the assumption that the level of education of broad segments of the population today, often viewed as equalized by the mass media, was characteristic of the entire society of that time. This is not really true today and was even less true in the 1920s and 1930s, when only approximately 4 or 5 percent of the German population had any kind of secondary education, and the number of those who had completed university studies was even lower. In considering educational policy in the Weimar Republic and the Third Reich, therefore, we really have to speak of a social mélange in which any kind of democratizing trends were still quite weakly developed, particularly with regard to culture. To put it plainly, even the Weimar Republic was still a class-based state, despite the increase in white-collar professions that supposedly acted as intermediaries between the middle class and the proletariat. The individual segments of the population were more or less strangers to one another or even enemies in both election campaigns and in their cultural needs.

And the Nazi leaders were all too aware of this as they forced their way to power in the late 1920s. They were called the National Socialist German Workers Party, and they tried to win over the broad masses of the population, in other words, the proletariat. But they kept an eye on the upper classes and the petty bourgeoisie at the same time, hoping to gain an absolute majority in the Reichstag and thus come to power "legally," as Hitler explained under oath in 1930 during the Ulm Reichswehr trial. This attitude helps explain the many components of their ideology, some pro-capitalist and some anti-capitalist, to which analysts have often pointed. If we look more carefully, we see that there are no ideological inconsistencies behind these discrepancies. On the contrary; with their slogans that often contradicted one another, the Nazis were appealing first to one segment of the population and then to another, hoping to reconcile *all* Germans. And they were so skillful at this kind of demagoguery that ever broader segments of the population joined them—based on the world economic crisis that began in 1929–1930, the rapidly growing number of unemployed, and fear of a communist revolution on the part of those who were better off.

Their approaches to ideology were therefore not at all incoherent or bumbling; they were thoroughly suited to the given situation. These ideological systems rested on the motto "To each his own" on the one hand and on the motto "Public interest before self-interest" on the other. The goal was to attract both groups that were oriented to private capital and those whose opinions were socialist, and in this the opinion leaders within the NSDAP were astoundingly successful. What took place after 1933 in Germany was an incomparable success story that should be analyzed in the interest of understanding its complex nature. It is rare for the representatives of a mass strategy to succeed in coming to power, staying in power, and expanding their power within a very short time. In earlier times, a brutal military repression was often necessary to achieve this. The Nazi fascist coup, however, succeeded using democratic—in other words parliamentary-legalistic—means. This forces us to ask the question: How did they actually do it? Which tactics did they deploy to satisfy the justified demands of the lower classes for full employment and social protection and at the same time to win the hearts and minds of their followers through offers of leisure time activities that were as attractive as possible? In short, what role was played by art and culture, whose importance was constantly invoked by the Nazi elite?

The Nazi fascists wanted to avoid shocking the majority of the German population right away with their racist long-term objectives, which could be achieved only through an Aryan world domination requiring a second or even third world war. Therefore the more pragmatic Nazi fascists—after the elimination of the Communist Party and the first Jewish boycotts—limited themselves at first to achieving short-term objectives with which they expected broad agreement. So they did not emphasize the possibility of a new world war, the extermination of all alien races from the German population, or a return to blood and soil. Instead their programs talked about the hope for a new prosperity for everyone, the strengthening of traditional values, and state support for the arts, which had supposedly become depraved during the Weimar Republic. They were fully aware that the aggressive tendencies in their ideology would not suffice to consolidate their position of power, and in fact they might have dangerous repercussions. So beginning at the end of 1933 and more strongly in the following years, they muffled all of the pointedly combative or even revolutionary aspects of their ideology in favor of tradition-conscious views they expected would have a much broader appeal. This disappointed the nationalistic-revolutionary circles within their own party, whose leaders they ruthlessly had murdered by commandos of the Gestapo and SS between 20 June and 3 July 1934. But it won ever broader segments of the German population to their cause—groups who hoped the measures taken by the NSDAP would bring a return to calm and order after the turbulent years of the late Weimar Republic.

This resulted in some intraparty conflicts regarding the Nazi elite's concepts of culture; some of them were quite dramatic, but they were mostly concealed and therefore did not come to the public's attention. The fanatics within the NSDAP had expected a drastic overthrow of existing political, social, and cultural conditions and therefore had pressed for a second revolution from early 1933 to mid-1934, but they drew the short straw in the course of these confrontations. There were several of these groups: there were the old members of the volkish movement of the Wilhelminian period, there were the bushy-bearded Teuton enthusiasts for whom Hitler had a very low regard; there were the Strasser supporters with their national-bolshevist perspective; and there were the nationalistic revolutionaries within the SA. Then there was Alfred Rosenberg, who liked to play the role of chief ideologue. He had radical fascist objectives, hoping to overcome the split into elite versus entertainment cultures with his concept of an Aryan popular culture that would be exclusively in the service of a volk community yet to be created. These groups were all opposed to continuing an elite culture of erudition for the upper ten thousand and equally opposed to the largely commercialized culture of entertainment that had permeated the Weimar Republic. They primarily favored ideas of culture that emphasized community, in which the differences in taste among the educated middle class, the petty bourgeoisie, and the proletariat would fall away, and a universal culture would prevail in which every Aryan could recognize the ethnically specified determination of his basic nature. On the one hand, this could be viewed as democratic in a positive sense or even as an example of volk-based socialism, but it was also mainly based on a feeling of racist superiority with long-term objectives for dominance that would have very dangerous consequences.

In comparison, the ideas about culture held by Joseph Goebbels in his role as NS Minister of Propaganda and head of the Reich chambers of culture were much more pragmatic. He focused first on short-term goals that he could realistically advocate. Goebbels avoided putting the cart far before the horse; he often talked about a community of the volk that was worth striving for, but he realized that in the cultural sphere, ongoing class differences could not be ignored. Thus he promoted both a superior culture for the educated middle class as well as a culture based on entertainment for the so-called inferior taste. This has often been described as an indecisive vacillation between highbrow and lowbrow ideas of culture. Nothing could be further from the truth. On the contrary, this behavior reflected clever tactics. Under the motto "To each his own," Goebbels tried to please all segments of the population. And this approach proved to be much more successful in terms of the Nazis' short-term objectives than using concepts of synchronization or volk community that were essentially racist to try to force the highly differentiated segments of the population immediately into an Aryan brotherhood.

Based on these insights, Goebbels initially supported a limited pluralism in the cultural sphere. That term was not used, but it was what the social practice of the regime usually amounted to. After the undesirable elements had been eliminated—in other words the communists, the Jews, and the hypercivilized modernists—and the overenthusiastic Aryan fanatics no longer had the influence they had originally hoped for, Goebbels' various machinations enabled the same split into elite versus entertainment culture that had existed in the November republic so despised by the Nazis. Because educational levels hardly changed during the few years the Nazis were in power, the cultural needs of the various segments of the population also remained largely the same as before. What changed were the rules about language usage in this area. Before 1933, the term classes had been in common usage, but now the correct terms were workers of the fist and workers of the head, both of equal importance for the development of the Third Reich.

The chapters on painting, music, and literature in the Third Reich have already shown how effective this strategy was at the higher level. It was relatively easy for the Nazi cultural theorists, after they had eliminated leftist critics of the system and Jewish artists, to win over the majority of the educated middle class with their slogans reflecting a commitment to tradition. Many of these people had made no secret during the 1920s of their aversion to all modernistic deviations from the older forms of classical-romantic art, and now they thoroughly agreed with measures which amounted to a *Säuberung des Kunsttempels* (Cleansing of the Temple of Art), as a 1937 book on the topic by Wolfgang Willrich was titled. There were hardly any protests when expressionist paintings disappeared from museums and leftist and Jewish publications disappeared from libraries and bookstores. And almost no one in these groups mourned for Schoenberg's twelve-tone music, for the *Zeitoper,* a product of the New Objectivity movement, or the Negroid rhythms of jazz. On the contrary, they were happy that symphony orchestras were playing more Beethoven, Schumann, Brahms, and Bruckner again, the secondary schools were once again emphasizing German classical writers, and there was a notable renaissance of the painting of the Dürer period and of the principle works of nineteenth century romanticism and realism; in their eyes, these accomplishments represented the absolute zenith of German art's aesthetic will to create. Much of this enthusiasm for the great heritage was not at all hypocritical; it reflected the taste and the worldview of the nationalistic-conservative circles. They perceived many things about Nazi fascism as petty bourgeois or even half-educated, but they welcomed the Nazis' cultural politics, which praised everything that was German classical or German romantic as a long-overdue rectification of the depravation of the German spirit and intellect underway since the incursion of foreign isms into the world of German art.

These segments of the population therefore supported everything the Nazi government undertook for the promotion of high art. Like the Nazi fascist cultural theorists, they would tolerate no proletkult, no Nigger jazz, no obscenity-laden expressionist art, no Dadaist art mockery, no sexual enlightenment films like *Anders als die Anderen* (Different Than the Others), no bizarre freak shows such as *Das Kabinett des Dr. Caligari,* no smart-aleck New Objectivity, and no more frivolous hit songs. On the contrary, they hoped that what was great, important, and idealistic would finally take pride of place in art. They were enthusiastic when Hitler gave his speech at the Reich party congress in 1933 under the motto "German art is the proudest defense of the German people." Many of them, in a state of ideological blindness, saw Hitler and Goebbels primarily as artists—men of culture, in other words—who were mainly concerned with an aesthetic refinement of taste in the realm of art. They saw their feelings confirmed in the years that followed as state subsidies for theater, opera houses, and symphony orchestras grew steadily; Beethoven was usually performed on ceremonial occasions; the first major Nazi building constructed in Munich was the monumental Haus der Kunst; Wagner's Bayreuth achieved the status of a national pilgrimage site; and Hitler even prompted the establishment of *Musische Gymnasien* (high schools emphasizing literature and the arts) in Frankfurt and Leipzig. They enjoyed the feeling that they were the leaders of German public opinion in the cultural sphere as they had been in the Wilhelminian period; they believed they had reclaimed their earlier representative position in the realm of German art and culture.

But that was just one side of Nazi cultural politics, as I said before. To entertain the so-called broad masses after 1933, commercial entertainment art, which had become the dominant form of culture in the Weimar Republic, was not at all eclipsed; it received just as much state support as so-called high art. A propaganda artist like Goebbels, who had the most influence in this area, wanted to satisfy the relatively crude needs of the workers and white-collar employees as part of the volk community concept that was being trumpeted about. Admittedly, there were also a number of popular education movements within Nazi cultural politics. Some traditionalists tried with idealistic verve to familiarize these groups with the works of high art, employing government-sponsored visitors' organizations to tempt them into the theater, the opera houses, and the concert halls. Wilhelm Furtwängler even condescended to give challenging symphony concerts with the Berlin Philharmonic, now risen to the status of Reich orchestra, in factory buildings of the Siemens Corporation and other industrial concerns, during which the end of Beethoven's Ninth Symphony often resounded.

But entertainment was emphasized much more strongly in the various arts; it took the form of operettas, hit songs, lively dance melodies, best-seller novels, and film comedies—all to provide the hardworking men and women, as they were usually called, with the relaxation they needed and to avoid overtaxing them with cultural offerings that were excessively demanding. The authorities therefore avoided twisting people's arms in the cultural sphere. They neither wanted to constantly bombard the broad masses with Nazi propaganda slogans, nor did they want to impose on them a kind of art for which they did not have the necessary educational prerequisites. Instead, the Nazis considered it appropriate to use entertaining forms of culture that would appeal to these people. They were intended to view Nazi fascist society as normal, even something that was established with them in mind.

For all of these reasons, the landscape of entertainment culture in the Third Reich remained—except for the elimination of anything brash, obscene, or critically provocative—much the same as in the Weimar Republic. It, too, had been geared primarily to have a broad impact and to cheer people up. For that you needed a catchy hit tune blaring somewhere, dance music playing, or outrageous comedies at the movies to entertain the volk. Variety show theaters such as the Scala or the Wintergarten, where you could watch groups of half-dressed girls or acrobats amidst fairy-tale sets, had the same function. Given the general mood of nationalism that reigned during these years, there had to be a few emphatically German elements included in the mix. But this form of culture usually remained apolitical in the final analysis. Yet if we look more closely, the fact that it was apolitical was almost more political than propaganda slogans. The lower classes had largely been social democratic or communist before 1933. Now the Nazi institutions wanted to gear up the entertainment machine to put people in a good humor so they would not become insubordinate. And that was at least as political as the attempt to convince them to read Nazi training pamphlets or listen to propaganda broadcasts on the radio. This was what Goebbels meant in March 1933 when he said, "The most biased art is art whose creators claim it has no bias."

Large segments of Nazi entertainment culture therefore continued undaunted what had underlain the persuasive power of the Americanized mass media industry of the Weimar Republic. It is easy to see the reasons why. In the United States,

Figure 29. Heinz Rühmann collects for the winter relief organization in the Reich Chancellery on 1 May 1937. To the right of Hitler his adjutant Julius Schaub. © Munich, Bilderdienst Süddeutsche Zeitung.

where there were no feudalistic or even specifically bourgeois cultural traditions, such tactics had developed much earlier and more effectively. Thus, without hesitations or inhibitions, the market-based culture industry that Theodor W. Adorno would later call fascistoid had already developed there around the turn of the century. In the 1920s, the cultural critic HL Mencken had mocked it with the now-famous sentence, "Nobody ever went broke underestimating the taste of the American people." No wonder that as far as culture was concerned there were hardly any anti-American voices raised in the early years of the Third Reich. On the contrary, there were American newspapers and magazines on display everywhere in Germany during these years. In addition, the firm Blaupunkt produced an overseas receiver in 1937 with which you could receive a series of American short-wave transmitters even in the Third Reich. Until 1940, you could see a Hollywood film every week in all of the larger German cities; many German moviegoers were as familiar with stars such as Gary Cooper, Clark Gable, Buster Keaton, Charles Laughton, Joan Crawford, Greta Garbo, and Katherine Hepbur as with their favorites from German films. The same was true of Mickey Mouse, Goofy, and other Walt Disney characters, who amused even Hitler and who could be seen until 1940 in many film shorts that preceded the full-length Nazi films. Despite many objections by overzealous race fanatics, American swing was equally popular in the Third Reich. Even Negro spirituals such as "Old Man River" or jazz trumpeters such as Louis Armstrong appealed to many young people and were even broadcast on the radio. Coca-Cola, too, with its brightly colored advertising posters, was viewed as typically American and caught on in many German cities as a sort of people's drink.

So much for the Americanized components within Nazi mass culture; similar elements could be noted in other areas. The more pragmatic Nazi fascists, like many profit-based companies, did not hesitate in the slightest to promote cultural endeavors of the same kind that might cheer people up. They recognized early on that after the misery of the world economic crisis it would not be enough to try to satisfy the so-called broad masses with promises of full employment and with large-scale organizations such as the Winterhilfswerk (Winter Aid Organization), the Nationalsozialistische Volkswohlfahrt (National Socialist Public Welfare Organization), or the availability of state funds for low-income people with many children. Knowing very well that there were also psychological needs that remained unsatisfied, they deployed, along with imported products of the American mass media, their own entertainment industry, carefully supervised and also promoted by the appropriate Nazi authorities, which was intended to offer the majority of the population as much distraction and enjoyment as possible. This entertainment was intended to distract from the criminal long-term objectives of the NSDAP such as World War II, which had been envisaged early on, the expulsion or liquidation of all segments of the population that were racially alien, and the obliteration of the Soviet Union and its Slavic subhumans.

One of the prime movers in the strategy to cheer people up was NS-Gemeinschaft Kraft durch Freude (NS-Community Strength through Joy, KdF), founded on 27 November 1933. It was a subsidiary organization of the German Labor Front led by Robert Ley, which developed an extensive program of entertainment for workers and low-level white-collar employees. It included popular education options such as lectures, concerts, and free theater tickets. In addition, beginning in 1937, the program offered very inexpensive extended cruises to Madeira, the Italian Riviera, and the Norwegian fjords on specially equipped ships that were known as the White Fleet of Peace. And by 1936, six million workers and white-collar employees had been able to vacation cheaply in some of the most beautiful German tourist regions thanks to the Strength through Joy organization. Such opportunities were much appreciated by these groups; almost half of them had never left their hometowns before, and they had also been excluded from other similar pleasures such as riding lessons or support in remote areas by the KdF film busses. Ley declared with a self-satisfied undertone in his voice in a speech celebrating the fifth anniversary of the organization, "What we could only anticipate in 1933 is now reality; we have satisfied the wishes of the workers and responded to the longings of the broad masses, giving them what they had fought for decades long." And like so many Nazi theorists, he emphasized that he viewed this as a cultural obligation to satisfy the heart and the feelings of people who had been underprivileged up to now.

But the Strength through Joy activities alone did not suffice for stimulating feelings tinged with optimism and zest for life; the NS authorities had to resort to many additional measures. One of these was the Schönheit der Arbeit (Beauty of Labor) organization within the KdF. As with all of these cultural machinations, we should not lose track of the underlying ideological contradictions. On the one hand, these efforts, often portrayed as gifts of the Führer, brought about noticeable improvements in working conditions, since workplaces that were ugly with dust and dirt were cleaned up, junk and trash were removed, and washrooms were remodeled. On the other hand, they initiated an internal rationalization and therefore an increase in production in the service of the impending war. The Nazi authorities intended this program to marginalize the remaining elements among the workers still concerned with class struggle, and they used the aesthetic improvement of the working environment to give the so-called broad masses a sense of decisive participation in the production

Figure 30. Heinrich Hoffmann: *Vacationers on a KDF-ship* (1936). © Munich, Bildarchiv der Bayrischen Staatsbibliothek.

processes. This organization, like Strength through Joy, used slogans such as "Good light—good work" and "Hot meals at work," along with laying out gardens next to factories and installing artistically designed canteens and break rooms in an attempt to convey a new life-affirming cheerfulness to the workers. Following the brutal destruction of established workers' organizations, both KdF and Beauty of Labor contributed in an eminently political sense to the continuing efforts to end ideological involvement of large parts of the working class by providing them with a new ideology. Many workers were all too compliant in allowing themselves to be fooled, and up to the end of the war, no efforts were made within the factories to resist the Nazi leadership.

Thus, in this sector, too, the long-term objectives of the Nazi fascists disappeared behind a cultural façade resting—despite the obvious split into high and low artistic ambitions—on the deceptive semblance of a volk community that had already been achieved or at least was the goal. But that was not enough. In order to play it safe, as they put it, the NSDAP tried everything they could think of in other areas of social life to keep the volk comrades in a good mood. In addition to full employment, social welfare organizations, the programs of the KdF, and those of the entertainment industry with its hit songs, dance melodies, and film comedies, there were three additional state-supported efforts: (1) a strongly promoted cult of technology, (2) enthusiasm for sports, and (3) stimulation of the consumer goods industry. It is true that these efforts, under the label New Objectivity, had already played a central role in the Weimar Republic, particularly during the phase of the relative stabilization of capitalism between 1923 and 1929. Now they were intensified and supplied with nationalistic overtones. We must keep in mind, as always, the long-term objectives lurking behind the Nazi fascists' short-term goals to avoid the mistaken conclusion that all this was primarily a general effort to make the volk happy. But this was not recognized by most Germans at the time, and they allowed themselves to be led blindly and without many scruples into World War II and the resulting catastrophe.

If we go beyond the technology cult that characterized New Objectivity to that of the Nazi fascists, we find—along with the introduction of modern communication devices and household appliances, which had already begun to some extent in the Weimar Republic—that the express train, the car, and the airplane were of central importance. Other technological achievements were usually embedded in the sphere of ordinary consumption and elicited a benign contentment, but no deeper level of enthusiasm. But these three so-called wonder-mobiles, which outdid each other in terms of speed, could be used to constantly set new records that would thrill the broad masses and contribute to a new and effective pride in German achievements. In addition to architects, engineers, and technicians such as Albert Speer and Fritz Todt, locomotive operators, race car drivers, and airplane pilots were celebrated as stars or pioneers of the future by the Nazi leadership and a public that was all too eager to follow them.

Figure 31. Ceremonial room in a community house designed by the Office for the Beauty of Work (1938). From the book by Anatol von Hübbeneit: *Das Taschenbuch Schönheit der Arbeit*, Berlin 1938.

The first sensation in this category was an express train named the *Flying Dutchman* that reached a top speed of 160 kilometers per hour on the railway line between Berlin and Cologne in 1933 and was proclaimed the best express train in the world. In the race car category, the *Silver Arrows* made by Autounion and Mercedes-Benz broke one record after another in the 1930s. In January 1938, when a universally admired race car driver named Bernd Rosemeyer was killed in an accident as he attempted to drive faster than 330 kilometers per hour on one of the autobahns recently opened to traffic, the Nazi press treated it almost as a national tragedy. But it was flying, in which Hitler himself liked to indulge, that garnered the most attention. Many Germans in the Third Reich saw flying as one of the most important cultural achievements of the day. Along with the speed of individual airplane types, with which firms such as Heinkel and Messerschmitt set several world records in 1939, it was the aura of adventure and daring that made flying so fascinating for the majority of the population at the time. It quickly became a central topos in Nazi popular culture, illustrated among other things by film comedies such as *Quax der Bruchpilot* (1941; Quax the Crash Pilot) with Heinz Rühmann and war films such as *Stukas* (1941) or *Junge Adler* (1944; Young Eagles).

The Nazi leadership hoped that their further encouragement of the pre-existing enthusiasm for sports would have a similar influence on the nationalization of the broad masses. The Summer Olympics, which took place in Berlin in 1936, offered one of the most effective preconditions for this effort; almost all countries of the world that participated in sports took part, with the exception of the Soviet Union. In this setting, feelings of national superiority could be strongly stimulated. At this Olympics, there were 1,929 competitions in nineteen types of sports on a particularly artistically landscaped terrain. The German team had 248 athletes participating, and they won a total of thirty-three gold medals, twenty-six silver medals, and thirty bronze medals, occupying first place by a large margin ahead of the United States in the national rankings. Television, which had been developed by German technologists in 1935, was deployed for the first time on the occasion of these games. Television rooms were especially set up for viewing this festival of beauty, as the party called it; along with those listening on the radio and attending in person, as many volk comrades as possible could be convinced of the new Reich's potential for achievement. Leni Riefenstahl's four-hour film *Olympia*, which celebrated these events, had the same purpose; the film was premiered on Hitler's birthday on 20 April 1938. The triumphs of individual German sports aces were exploited in an equally chauvinistic way by the Nazi mass media; one example was the victory of the German world champion boxer in all divisions Max Schmeling over the black United States boxer

Joe Louis in 1936. The NSDAP liked to portray these kinds of events in the popular media as cultural achievements because their emphasis on the vigorous body enabled a certain proximity to a Hellenic spirit. The same purpose was served by Nazi organizations such as Glaube und Schönheit (Belief and Beauty), whose performances allowed people to admire the well-formed bodies of young girls and women; in fact, all sports related to gymnastics or eurhythmics, whether ice dancing or artistic gymnastics, had the same effect.

In the beginning, very few people perceived that the party, after dissolving the bourgeois and communist sports clubs, had as their long-term objective the regeneration of military strength—as had Turnvater Jahn, the father of gymnastics, in the preparatory phase of the Wars of Liberation against Napoleon. Most Germans admired the setting of new records in sports as in other areas. Many did not limit themselves to a passive response, turning on their radios for such events or reading the sports pages in their local papers the following day. They participated actively in the athletic fun activities for leisure time organized by the NS-Strength through Joy organization, which for the first time offered workers the opportunity to participate in what had previously been considered elitist categories of sports, such as tennis, skiing, riding, and golf. For this purpose, hundreds of new playing fields, gymnasiums, swimming pools, and shooting stands were built, consciously giving millions of volk comrades the opportunity of dulling their minds by devoting their leisure time to the physical exercise being universally praised, all the while believing naively that the state meant them well.

But all of this—the products of the entertainment industry, the enthusiasm for technology, and the fascination with sports—would not have sufficed to keep the majority of the population in a good mood for years if there had not been a noticeable expansion of the production of consumer goods at the same time. Both Hitler and Goebbels recognized very early that the satisfaction of civilizational needs, as they called it, was just as important as direct political control. And meeting these expectations played an eminently important role in the Nazi press and in Nazi advertising. The expansion of consumption promoted by the NSDAP was portrayed not only as a triumph over the old class barriers; it was also viewed as a cultural achievement by the new Reich. Government agencies and private firms continually emphasized how many people the increased industrial production in the Third Reich had enabled to acquire a car, a radio, a refrigerator, a telephone, a camera, a washing machine, an electric hair dryer, and similar cultural assets. Commercials appearing in 1939 announced with patriotic satisfaction that there were more telephones and radios in operation in Germany than in any other European country

Kraft durch Freude

Rechtsrheinische Ausgabe

Monatsheft der Deutschen Arbeitsfront · NSG. „Kraft durch Freude"   Gau Düsseldorf

Folge 4
April 1938
5. Jahrgang

Preis 10 Pf.

Figure 32. Title page of the magazine *Kraft durch Freude* (Strength through Joy, 1938).

and that there were already 3.63 million volk comrades who owned a car, among them an Opel P4, an Opel Kadett, or a Ford Eiffel. In the years to come, so the relevant communiqués explained, this number would surely climb rapidly, since new volkswagens would be available for a weekly payment of five reichsmarks. With equal pride, the directors of propaganda pointed to the continuous expansion of the autobahns, on which more and more people were able to enjoy the lure of faraway places. Even the increase in household appliances and furniture brands occupied a large space in these boastful advertising campaigns. The Siemens vacuum cleaners, the AEG refrigerators, the washing machines, the radios, and the wicker furniture—there were very few products that did not reap praise in these advertisements as evidence of a new German lifestyle.

Although much of this was targeted propaganda that did not correspond to the real distribution of these products in any way, it gave the broad masses hope that they would soon be able to acquire most of these things. The Nazi machinations in the spheres of consumption and leisure were in many ways a continuation of the New Objectivity movement during the Weimar Republic. In any case, it was not blood and soil slogans, anti-Semitism, and breeding programs to improve the race that were dominant in the mid-1930s. Instead, expressions of reactionary modernism were dominant—a term coined in part due to the constant emphasis on achievements in the realm of technology during the Third Reich. This undoubtedly contributed to Nazi fascism's history of success in satisfying both material and emotional/spiritual needs. During this period, at least until the beginning of World War II, a large majority of the German people felt at home in a society that was not constantly requiring one privation or another. Instead, the entertainment industry and availability of consumer products allowed them to have a life they viewed as apolitical, because it was a life that permitted a gradual increase in standard of living and the enjoyment of consumer goods that were life-enhancing or at least made life easier. At the same time, they could enjoy the delights of the ordinary offered to them by the leisure industry, which was operating in high gear.

In reality, property and income conditions changed very little and the system dominated by private capital persisted. But during this period, most people were very cleverly led to believe that despite all class differences, they were living in a community of the volk in which earlier relations among social classes would increasingly disappear. Thus by 1936–1937, the Nazi leadership had more or less achieved their short-term objectives in the sphere of cultural ideology. They had won over the three segments of the German population—the middle class, the white-collar

Figure 33. Mercedes-Benz advertisement (1940).

employees, and the workers—by engaging in a clever and strategic real-politik that emphasized their various cultural achievements and offered the people socialism on a foundation of private capital. It is true that during the same years the NSDAP did not shrink from violent measures such as the construction of concentration camps and the use of euthanasia and sterilization, but these they kept mostly secret in order not to violate the glossy veneer of their cultural and leisure programs. And with this approach, they speeded up the movement toward a mass-media-dominated consumer society rather than encouraging the establishment of a true community of the volk. They repeatedly postponed programs with long-term goals requiring much more brutal measures and instead limited themselves to the expansion of the position of power they had achieved. This strategy disappointed the racist fanatics among them, but it satisfied both the upper social class by extolling the values of high culture and the lower classes by offering mass-media-based leisure activities and a series of relatively affordable consumer goods. Accordingly, many if not most of the people in this state did not feel they were living in a violent regime of ideological extremes; they felt they were living in a society that offered culture and consumer goods appropriate to their needs. And therefore, even during the early days of World War II, they put up with the hardships and sacrifices they viewed as temporary without much resistance.

Not until 1943–1944, as it became increasingly clear that Germany would lose the war, did some oppositional groups form. But they were unable to achieve anything against the firmly established power structure of the Nazi regime and the security forces stationed everywhere in the Third Reich, and they were quickly liquidated. The vast majority of the German population therefore hardly noticed such protests and fought or worked with unrelenting doggedness until the last days of the war. We can only understand this attitude if we consider how quickly the Nazis were able in the early days of their rule to attune both the upper and middle classes as well as the broad masses to a cleverly shammed sense of community; this feeling made the German population relatively immune to any socially concrete assessment of their own situation. Despite obvious class divisions, it is absolutely beyond doubt that the glossy veneer of Nazi culture, along with the expansion of consumption and the attendant increase in prosperity, played an important role in building this sense of community. This kind of strong connection to the state does not just hark back to older ideas about authority shaped by Prussia or by Protestantism, as is often claimed. Otherwise, German soldiers, who had grown up as Wilhelminian subjects in similar authoritarian conditions, would not have begun a revolution against the ruling Hohenzollern regime in November

1918. That there was no such revolution before 8 May 1945 and that it required the military superiority of the Western powers and the Soviet Union to force the *Wehrmacht* under Hitler to capitulate is still a source of humiliation. Viewed from this perspective, the Nazi facists, although they may have lost World War II, were successful to the end with their political tactics and their powers of ideological persuasion.

2

INNER EMIGRATION

BETWEEN AVERSION
AND ACCOMMODATION

For decades, people have argued about which areas of German culture inside the Third Reich have earned the designation inner emigration. Certainly not everything that can be characterized as nonfascist in a superficial sense should be so designated; if we used that criterion, almost two-thirds of the art works created between 1933 and 1945 could be subsumed under this relatively positive-sounding concept. Therefore, we should exclude two phenomena a priori if we are discussing inner emigration during these years in a more precise sense: first, the cult status of German classical artists in the eyes of the cultured upper classes; and second, the often banal entertainment culture with which the Nazi authorities tried to distract the lower classes from thinking about where their real interests lay.

The enormous esteem in which the Nazi elite held the masterpieces of what they referred to as the cultural heritage was aligned directly with the cultural consciousness of the educated middle class, which was dominant in this sphere; they had long felt that this art was the most venerable link in the ancestral chain of the German spirit. These groups had by and large rejected everything modernistic before 1933 and had not needed Nazi fascism to force them to reject all art works that were expressionist, futurist, cubist, Dadaist, realistic/socially critical, or communist as degenerate. They had already done so, and therefore most of them welcomed the Nazis' staunch opposition to this kind of art. Their cultural consciousness was based almost exclusively on Gothic art and works of the Dürer era, on the music of Beethoven's time, on the literature of Weimar classicism, and on the paintings, compositions, dramas, and novels of the romantic and realistic movements in nineteenth-century German art. Accordingly, they did not see the NSDAP's ambitious cultural programs as tyrannical measures; they viewed them as a long-overdue purification process through which the truly important works of the German cultural tradition would regain their rightful place of honor. It would be wrong to characterize this viewpoint as either Nazi fascist or as an expression of inner emigration. Underlying it was a nationalistic-conservative attitude based on these bourgeois and anti-democratic circles' belief that they were entitled to be dominant in matters of culture—a claim that the members of this class had been trying to assert in their own self-interest since the late eighteenth century.

The entertainment culture that the Nazis strongly supported for the less discriminating lower classes was not an expression of inner emigration either. The Nazi cultural authorities allowed these segments of the population to escape into the delights of the ordinary and did not attempt to synchronize them ideologically right away. Above all, they wanted to keep the so-called broad masses, as Goebbels always said, in a good mood. From a historical perspective, this aim was nothing new; the same ultimate goal of providing diversions had also set the tone in the mass media during the Weimar Republic. The strategic maneuvers of the new masters were simply more purposeful, as they tried in every way they could think of to distract the population from the brutal long-term goals of the NSDAP. Thus, the culture of entertainment, which permitted many people inside the Third Reich a welcome escapism, should not be characterized as an expression of inner emigration. It was—particularly in the form of hit tunes, film comedies, and bestselling novels—much too noncommittal. There was a pretense of being nonfascist, but there was also a withdrawal into the realm of entertainment and very seldom did the products of this entertainment culture give any recognizable signal of agreement or disagreement with the Nazi system. This largely excludes entertainment culture from consideration as part of inner emigration. In terms of the lower 80 percent of the population, this was—as under many regimes geared to the masses—the art and culture of the conformists, the fellow travelers, or of those who paid almost no attention to politics and who after a hard day's work just wanted something to provide a little laughter or suspense during their leisure time.

If we speak at all of an art specific to inner emigration in which critical or even oppositional attitudes are perceptible—and this within the culture of the Third Reich, where enforced accommodation was the rule— then we can do so only to a very limited extent. In percentage terms, such works lagged far behind what we could characterize in a narrower sense as specifically Nazi fascist art. And there was not even an exorbitant amount of that. During this period, the majority of both the upper classes and the so-called broad masses largely rejected art that was expressly politicized. Either they wanted to feel that their cultural self-image was being confirmed, or they wanted to be entertained, distracted, or diverted.

The art of inner emigration developed, in contrast, in that ideological gray area between aversion and accommodation, a gray area based on a nonconformist attitude that cannot be classified as either unambiguously private or unambiguously openly antifascist. Had it simply been restricted to the private sphere, it would not deserve the name inner emigration. If it had been openly antifascist, it would have to be labeled resistance art. But under the circumstances, there were very few artists who mustered that kind of courage, and they usually had to pay for it with occupational bans or prison sentences. So only two possibilities remained for the artists of inner emigration: either encode anything that was critical of the regime so carefully that it would be overlooked by the ever-watchful eyes of the Nazi censors or relinquish from the outset any attempt to reach the public, waiting instead with works that had been written, composed, or painted in secret for the time that would follow the collapse of the Third Reich.

Most of the works we know about that were written from this perspective were not by blue- or white-collar workers; they were created by artists who still saw themselves at the time as members of the traditional educated middle class. For this reason, the culture of inner emigration developed, if the word *develop* is even appropriate in this case, largely in the realm of high art. In the entertainment industry between 1933 and 1945, a producers' perspective geared to a market economy was dominant. The industry made a conscious attempt to create distractions, but more important, its attitude reflected those of the managerial sector, interested as always in success and profit and eager to adapt to any regime. The artists of the so-called inner emigration, in contrast, still viewed themselves as discriminating creative writers, composers, and painters. They were not concerned with financial advantages or social prestige; they were concerned with achieving a subtle effect; they wanted to warn their fellow citizens not to allow the new regime's gleaming façade to blind them to its repressive short-term measures or its brutal long-term goals. They were well aware that they could do this only by using a style that was symbolic or encrypted. Still, the best among them tried to use these techniques to influence people who were educated enough to read between the lines in literary works, to understand the meaning in indirect messages conveyed by images in paintings, and discern in disharmonious sound patterns a dissatisfaction with the forced efforts at harmony that characterized Nazi music.

All of this presupposed an understanding of art that was present only in an extremely small segment of the educated middle class. From the outset, this fact alone sufficed to deny inner emigration a larger sphere of influence; it was a marginal phenomenon that did not play a central role in cultural politics. Nevertheless, it would be wrong to ignore it entirely. Among its representatives were a number of admirable artists who—for various reasons—abandoned all the trappings of success and opportunities to advance in the Third Reich and chose instead, in some cases risking their lives, to create art that would not make them complicit in the crimes of the regime. This did require certain strategies of accommodation or even partial compliance. But this way these artists hoped to keep their consciences clear and avoid sinking to the level of ideological stooges of a regime they viewed as tyrannical or even devilish, satanic, or demonic.

The opportunities for the works they produced to have an impact varied, and it is important to point out the differences between writing, painting, and music in this regard. The writers of inner emigration had the most difficult time, because their works were almost always subjected to a careful preliminary censorship by the Nazi authorities. Any openly antifascist statements in written texts were therefore excluded a priori, unless these works were going to remain in a drawer or in some other hiding place. Everything intended for publication had to be so carefully encoded that often the secret messages were scarcely perceptible even to contemporaries interested in political issues. When they were recognized and communicated to others, it sometimes led to disastrous consequences for the authors. Inner emigration composers had it a bit easier, especially if they limited their compositions to instrumental music and hinted at their opposition to the regime in power through a more or less concealed use of labor songs, twelve-tone series in the style of Schoenberg, or melismas that were specifically Jewish. So in the sphere of music, there were at least a few options for the sounds of opposition. But who detected them—except for a few specialists? The situation in painting was completely different. Even oppositional artists who decided in favor of a retreat into inner emigration could continue to work undisturbed; they had to forgo public exhibitions, but could sell their works to private collectors as they had always done. Many of these works did not reach the public until after 1945; they contributed to an honorable posthumous reputation for the artists but were almost entirely unnoticed during the Third Reich. We need to keep these differences in mind when we make generalizations about the art of inner emigration. The impact (insofar as there was any) of its artistic works was limited to those circles of the educated middle class who tried to maintain a certain distance to the Third Reich and also were cultured enough to recognize the hidden meaning of the messages in these works.

Forms of Artistic Expression

Literature

Literature occupies the most space in the inner emigration art we know about, but it played a relatively marginal role in the culture of the Third Reich as a whole. It is easy to see why. First, it was denied access to most of the mass media outlets from the outset. Second, even in its more harmless manifestations, literature often ran into the barriers of censorship the Nazi authorities had erected. Third, critical statements had to be so encoded that very few readers could decipher them. And fourth, many of the most important works remained in the drawer until the end of World War II, and therefore did not reach interested reader groups until after the collapse of the Third Reich.

All of this is true of resistance literature as well. It is often mentioned in this context and sometimes equated with the literature of inner emigration, although there is so little of it. All authors who attempted to revolt against fascism using the medium of print had to rely on activities that could only take place in the underground and only in certain districts of some large cities. And even that was very dangerous. Most who decided to try it had belonged to the KPD, which was now banned. For example, some members of the earlier Bund proletarisch-revolutionärer Schriftsteller (League of Proletarian-Revolutionary Writers/BPRS)—among them Elfriede Brüning, Werner Ilberg, Louis Kaufmann, and Karl Maron—published an illegal mini-newspaper under the title *Hieb und Stich* (Slash and Thrust) in Berlin from August 1933 to early 1935; it reached only approximately 350 to 500 readers. Jan Petersen's antifascist novel written during this period, *Unsere Straße. Geschrieben im Herzen des faschistischen Deutschlands* (Our Street: Written in the Heart of Fascist Germany) belongs in this context, although it had to be printed abroad. Other texts, such as the antifascist poems written in prisons and concentration camps, were lost, were read only inside the camp, or reached only a handful of readers; the *Moorsoldaten-Lied* (Song of the Moor Soldiers) by Johann Esser and Wolfgang Langhoff and the *Moabiter Sonette* (Sonnets from Moabit), written in 1944–1945 by Albrecht Haushofer, are examples. It is therefore very difficult to talk about an effective resistance literature at all. We have to respect individual efforts, but under the conditions that reigned within the Third Reich, they remained largely politically ineffective.

The literature of inner emigration was somewhat more extensive but not much more politically effective. Because these writers were forced to forgo all openly antifascist statements and remained in a twilight zone between aversion and accommodation, they were usually tolerated by the Nazi fascist guardians of German ethnicity. The Nazis' generous gesture was intended to convince inner emigration authors of the ideological broad-mindedness of the new regime or to lure them gradually into the Nazis' own belief system. Ultimately, after the forcible expulsion of many important authors in early 1933, the Nazi authorities had no desire to create even more martyrs in the years that followed. They preferred to style themselves as a party dedicated to tradition in the literary sphere, who showed even the apolitical works that were middle-class favorites a respect that was sometimes real, sometimes feigned. Sheltered under the umbrella of this respect, an ambitious literature developed after 1933–1934 by writers who exploited the anti-revolutionary spirit of the NSDAP and held fast to their prior cultural and religious convictions. No one was forced to become a party member just because they were a member of the Reich Literature Chamber. An approach indebted to tradition and founded on an appreciation for the German cultural heritage sufficed to satisfy many of the Nazi literary bigwigs. If we exclude the modernists who had been given star billing in the liberal or left-liberal literary sector of the Weimar Republic, then this was the position that many of these solidly middle-class authors had always taken, and they therefore did not see the regime change in 1933 as radical. They tended to see it as a confirmation or even as a reinforcement of their own ideological convictions with regard to literature.

Their views were similar in many ways to those of the nationalist-conservative authors invited by Hans Grimm to his Lippoldsberg writers' congresses or by Börries von Münchhausen to his Knights of the Rose festivals in the Wartburg. The principal works by most of these writers, among them Rudolf G. Binding, Hans von Gabelentz, Joachim von der

Goltz, Heinrich Lilienfein, Ernst von Salomon, Wilhelm Schäfer, Hermann Stehr, and Leo Weismantel, had appeared before the transfer of power to Hitler, but some of them also had large print runs in the Third Reich. Although they usually did not have an openly fascist bias and took a nonfascist or even a universal humanist position that reflected their bourgeois detachment, their works should not be counted as part of inner emigration. Otherwise, we would have to categorize a large part of the literature published during the Third Reich as belonging to the movement. If we look carefully, we see that the majority of authors who were publishing in Germany between 1933 and 1945 either remained true to their traditional nationalist-conservative convictions or they chose apolitical themes as they had always done, and they were not above incorporating elements that were humorous or at least entertaining to reach as large a group of readers as possible. After all, writers such as Georg Britting, Hans Carossa, Manfred Hausmann, Ina Seidel, Frank Thiess, and many others did not want to relinquish the literary successes they had achieved during the Weimar Republic even in the Third Reich. To this end, they were sometimes willing to make a few minor concessions to the new regime.

But now we move into that gray zone between aversion and accommodation we mentioned earlier—the zone in which authors had to operate if their nonfascist position incorporated views that rejected or opposed the ideology and violent acts of the new regime. The nature poetry of Wilhelm Lehmann and the Protestant poems of Rudolf Alexander Schröder have usually been included here, as has the nonfascist literature of the young generation—authors such as Stefan Andres, Johannes Bobrowski, Günther Eich, Max Frisch, Rudolf Hagelstange, Felix Hartlaub, Gustav René Hocke, Peter Huchel, Marie Luise Kaschnitz, Rudolf Krämer-Badoni, Wolfgang Koeppen, Ernst Kreuder, Karl Krolow, Horst Lange, Wolf von Niebelschütz, Wolf Dietrich Schnurre, Eugen Gottlob Winkler, and others. These writers published many novels, short stories, radio plays, and poems with content that was not Nazi fascist for the most part, and sometimes these works even included formal elements that Nazi authorities viewed as un-German or even degenerate. But on the other hand, not many elements in their works are specifically oppositional either. Therefore, to view these works as expressing strong aversion to the regime in power would be an exaggeration.

Many of these authors did not begin writing until after 1933, so the democratic-liberal and leftist tendencies in the literature of the Weimar Republic were for the most part foreign to them. For them, who were neither leftists nor Jews, fleeing into exile or joining the political resistance was more or less out of the question. At first they simply accepted the conditions after 1933, which were not threatening to them personally. They tried to find a niche inside the Third Reich where they could pursue their individualistic literary inclinations as undisturbed as possible. And there were plenty of publishing houses and periodicals glad to publish that kind of literature: houses such as Goverts, Rauch, Rowohlt, and Suhrkamp, and journals such as *Neue Rundschau* (New Review), *Europäische Revue* (European Review), *Deutsche Rundschau* (German Review), *Das Innere Reich* (The Inner Reich), *Hochland* (High Country), and *Eckart*. Even the feuilleton editors for the *Frankfurter Zeitung*, the *Kölnische Zeitung*, the *Magdeburgsche Zeitung*, and the *Rheinisch-Westphälische Zeitung* were favorably disposed toward this group of writers. They withdrew into subject matter that was purely intellectual and individualistic, and they avoided all topics related to politics of the day, an approach that gave the journal *Das Innere Reich*, for example, its high literary reputation. The Nazi censors obviously considered works by these authors harmless. Therefore, members of this group seldom came into conflict with the Nazi authorities, were left largely unscathed, and were sometimes even promoted by the state.

However the state immediately homed in on anyone who ventured out of the realm of pure intellect and onto the slippery slope of social criticism. Because it did, this is the point at which we can begin to talk about the literature of inner emigration in the strict sense of the term. It is still important to differentiate among several disparate manifestations of this literature. Except for a few leftist proletarian authors who had remained in the Third Reich and who tried to create political solidarity in the underground, the inner emigration group consisted almost entirely of bourgeois outsiders who felt a literary responsibility only to their own consciences. Unaccustomed to subordinating themselves to party programs of any ideological hue, each one expressed his or her own personal aversion to the regime change that had taken place on 30 January 1933. Although these authors had minimal contact with each other and tried to go their own way in the end, it is possible to distinguish six different directions taken.

First, there were those writers who had already made names for themselves before 1933; they had been in the spotlight in the literary public sphere and now, despite a few or even many reservations, were trying to become more comfortable with the new regime, as they said at the time. Leading the way was Gerhard Hauptmann; we have documentation of both profascist and antifascist statements by him after 1933. His friendship with Jews such as the publisher Samuel Fischer and the painter Max Liebermann, which he maintained after 1933, was viewed as a serious flaw by Nazi fascists such as Alfred Rosenberg; Goebbels, on the other hand—because of Hauptmann's international prestige as a Nobel Prize winner—

was much more broad-minded. A more precise look at Hauptmann's late works, in which he turned to mythological and dreamlike themes, reveals few elements that seem to express resistance. The playwright Georg Kaiser, in contrast, who had been much celebrated during the Weimar Republic, was much more openly oppositional after 1933 in his antifascist poems, which were reproduced only as hectographed copies. He put himself in danger of being arrested and had to escape to Switzerland in 1936. Hans Fallada, who had become a bestselling author with his novel *Kleiner Mann—was nun?* (1932; Little Man, What Now? 1933), took the risk of including some socially critical passages in his novels *Wer einmal aus dem Blechnapf frißt* (1934; Who Once Eats Out of the Tin Bowl, 1934) and *Wolf unter Wölfen* (1937; Wolf among Wolves, 1938). Goebbels did not find the passages disturbing at all, but they were only reluctantly tolerated by Alfred Rosenberg, Will Vesper, and Hellmuth Langenbucher.

Most Nazi authorities were equally tolerant of authors who clothed their criticism of particular measures taken by the Third Reich in the form of aesthetic dissociation. The best-known example is Ernst Jünger, who was much courted by some Nazi fascists. His writings from the 1920s that glorified war—such as *In Stahlgewittern* (1920; Storm of Steel, 1929), *Der Kampf als inneres Erlebnis* (1922; Struggle as Inward Experience), *Das Wäldchen* (1925; Copse 125, 1930), and *Feuer und Blut* (1925; Fire and Blood)—were frequently reprinted well into the 1940s. Even when Jünger, who characterized himself as a "lone wolf who wandered the forest," withdrew into an "aristocratic form of inner emigration," as he later explained, the regime did not really hold it against him. His novel *Auf den Marmorklippen* (On the Marble Cliffs), which he published in 1939, was reprinted often until 1942, although many of his well-educated readers perceived the arrogant dissociation from the real existing conditions in the Third Reich that underlay the book as critical of the system. The same claim is still being made today. But judgments of this kind, with which some of Jünger's adherents hoped to grant him a denazification certificate (*Persilschein*), should be examined very carefully. Arrogance in and of itself does not constitute resistance. We need to keep this in mind when we evaluate similar exercises in ornamental calligraphy—some of the classicistic poems by Joseph Weinheber, for example, who wrote a series of highly elaborate sonnet cycles after 1933 and who was a thorough Hitlerite ideologically. Gottfried Benn, whom Heinrich Himmler himself defended against attacks by the Rosenberg clique in the fall of 1937, is a similar case. In October 1944, after the Nazi fascists had expelled him from their ranks, he wrote the aesthetically perfect poem "Chopin," a psalm of praise to the artistic perfection attainable only in solitude. But this does not excuse his testimonials to Nazi fascism, his mockery of those

who chose emigration, and his positive view of the breeding and euthanasia measures of the Third Reich.

Admittedly, most inner emigration writers were not as linguistically
gifted as Jünger and Benn. But that is no reason to disdain or dismiss

Figure 34. Rudolf Schlichter: *Ernst Jünger* (1937). From the book by Götz Adriani:
Ruldolf Schlichter. Gemälde, Aquarelle, Zeichnungen, Munich 1997.

them. When our main concern is a writer's attitude toward Nazi fascism, our judgments should be based on political belief as much as on formal skill. Benn liked to use the dismissive bon mot, "Well-meant, but worthless from a literary viewpoint," but it has no validity in this context. What counts is the antifascist attitude behind these works. Between 1933 and 1945, that attitude is found in the works of authors who laboriously concealed their dislike of Nazi fascism behind their convictions—be they religious, humanistic and nationalist-conservative, antimilitaristic, or left-critical, instead of choosing to escape into aestheticism.

Most authors belonging to these four groups employed religious motifs in their work. They rejected an organized and violent struggle against the Nazi fascists. But like Werner Bergengruen, Albrecht Goes, Jochen Klepper, Elisabeth Langgässer, Gertrud von Le Fort, Luise Rinser, Reinhold Schneider, and Ernst Wiechert, whether they were Catholic or Protestant, they wanted to keep their consciences pure. Before 1933, they had not acted as social critics and had usually avoided making political statements; therefore, the Nazi fascists did not see them as oppositional in the beginning. But in the course of the 1930s, as some of them assumed a position that was critical of the regime—by rejecting the persecution of the Jews, the crushing of religious associations, the imprisonment of recalcitrant clergy such as Martin Niemöller, the euthanasia measures, and the obvious preparations for war—the Nazi authorities became increasingly suspicious of them.

The author in this group who attracted the most attention was probably Ernst Wiechert, who had published a series of nationalistic works during the 1920s along with several novels with religious overtones. The Nazi authorities saw him as a welcome ally in the beginning if for no other reason because of his enormous popularity. He was even more appealing to them because, in comparison with others, Christianity was just a pale glimmer in the background in his works. This very quality, along with his simple, unadorned language, had made Wiechert so popular he began to think he could permit himself a few liberties after 1933. A speech to students in Munich on 6 May 1935 was especially charged. Because some measures being taken by the new system of government in Germany were moving into lawless realms, he called on his listeners not to submit to them too willingly. Because of this speech, Wiechert was subsequently kept under increasingly strict surveillance. Until 1938, they hesitated to arrest him. But when he spoke publicly against the arrest of Martin Niemöller, he was put in Buchenwald concentration camp for six weeks. After his release and a coerced reconciliation with the regime, he published one more work in 1939 that attracted attention, the novel *Das einfache Leben* (The Simple Life). In it he described a modest, reclusive life on an island as a counter image to life under the influence of fascism.

The book could be interpreted from a religious or from a general ethical perspective and expressed sympathetic consolation; it therefore achieved wide distribution among the quiet in the land who, although they did not agree with national socialism, had already capitulated to its ideological superiority.

Literary success of the same magnitude was not granted to other authors in this group. This is true even of Werner Bergengruen, whose works were published in relatively large printings. His opposition to the Third Reich is less marked than that of Wiechert, and it is also overlaid by a stronger devotion to the will of God. Thus, his novels *Der Großtyrann und das Gericht* (1935; A Matter of Conscience, 1952) and *Am Himmel wie auf Erden* (1940; In Heaven as on Earth) were approved for publication without difficulty. This occurred even though Bergengruen was married to a woman who was three-quarters Jewish and was therefore temporarily excluded from the Reich Literature Chamber as a person married to someone of non-Aryan ethnicity. Jochen Klepper did not emerge quite so unscathed. In his novel *Der Vater* (1937; The Father), he opposed the Nazi fascist view of King Friedrich Wilhelm I of Prussia as a Führer type to the image of an ethical educator of the volk who, acting purely out of Christian motives, wants to prevent all future wars among the peoples of Europe with his plan for an eternal peace in Christendom. Friedrich Wilhelm I had traditionally been referred to as the soldier king, and his image was overlaid with militaristic clichés. Klepper's view of him did not fit at all into this tradition, and he was expelled from the Reich Literature Chamber soon after the novel appeared, finally committing suicide in 1942 together with his Jewish wife, who had been threatened with deportation.

Because of his Catholic beliefs, Reinhold Schneider opposed the racist antispirit of fascism even more clearly in his novel *Las Casas vor Karl V. Szenen aus der Konquistadorenzeit* (Las Casas before Charles V: Scenes from the Time of the Conquistadors), which was published in 1938. In the novel, he clearly implied that the extermination of the South American Indians by the Spanish bore a close resemblance to the Nazis' hatred of the Jews. In 1941, his works were subjected to a print ban by the Nazi authorities. This ban did not stop him from distributing other oppositional texts in hectographed copies, participating in the founding of the nationalist-conservative Kreisauer Kreis (Kreisau Circle), and offering antifascist pastoral counseling. In 1944, he was put on trial for high treason for undermining military morale, but in the chaos of the final months of the war, the trial could not be completed.

While the literature of inner emigration based in Christianity found its most forceful expression in the works of Wiechert, Bergengruen, Klepper, and Schneider, it is not entirely clear whether Elisabeth Langgässer's works should be included in this group. Langgässer was a half Jew who had been baptized as a Catholic and was also the mother of a daughter who was three-quarters Jewish; thus, she was under threat immediately after 1933. Nevertheless, she tried to get by in Berlin as a freelance writer of short stories and radio commissions, but after her novel *Gang durch das Ried* (Path through the Marsh) appeared in 1936, she was forbidden to continue publishing. Today she is considered part of inner emigration chiefly due to her novel *Das unauslöschliche Siegel* (The Indelible Seal), which she wrote between 1936 and 1945 and which appeared in print in 1946. One focal point in the novel is a Jew named Lazarus Belfontaine who has been baptized as a Catholic. Like a modern Job, he is subjected to the trials of Satan, but despite the indelible seal of his baptism remains an Israelite in the end. Another central figure is Father Lucien Benoit, who represents the fixed pole of the Catholic faith. The novel, despite its inner contradictions, can be read as offering hope for a religious transformation and thus as a work of resistance against satanic Nazi fascism. That covers, at least to some extent, the religious voices who were part of the literature of inner emigration.

As the most admirable writer of the humanistic nationalistic-conservative wing of the movement, Ricarda Huch deserves mention. She voluntarily resigned from the Prussian Academy of Arts in April 1933, openly rejecting the boastful self-importance and the brutal methods of the new regime as un-German. In the years that followed, she remained true to this view, publishing little except memoirs of her youth and several works on early German history with Atlantis Verlag in Zurich. Despite her unyielding direct opposition to the Nazi fascist racial doctrines, nothing happened to her during the Third Reich; the Nazi authorities responsible for her case continued to see her as a patriotic, if nonconformist, author based on her earlier publications on German romanticism.

Anyone who expressed convictions that were antimilitarist or critical from a left perspective, in contrast, did not get off so lightly. This was true of Adam Kuckhoff, for example, who had already become known as a socially committed writer during the 1920s. The Nazis just barely tolerated his novel *Der Deutsche von Bayencourt* (1937; The German from Bayencourt), in which he supported an agreement between the French and the Germans to avoid further wars. But he was arrested in 1942 after he joined the antifascist resistance group around Arvid Harnack and Harro Schulze-Boysen, usually called the Rote Kapelle (Red Orchestra), and was executed at Berlin-Plötzensee Prison shortly thereafter. Günther Weisenborn almost met the same fate. His novel *Barbaren* (Barbarians) had ended up in the bonfire in 1933, and he decided to escape temporarily as a writer into subject matter that was noncommittal. Like Kuckhoff, he later made contact with the Harnack-Schulze-Boysen group on the basis of his earlier leftist convictions. When the group was exposed in 1942 by the Gestapo, he *only* received a three-year prison sentence. The experience of Werner Krauss was similar. He joined the same group and also ended up in prison. There, in 1943–1944, living under inhuman conditions, he managed to write his novel *PLN. Die Passionen der halkyonischen Seele* (PLN: The Passions of a Halcyon Soul) without getting caught. Using a style that was both satirical and encoded, he portrayed the activities of a catacomb society within a totalitarian regime, a scenario that corresponded in many ways to the activities of the Red Orchestra against the fascists.

In summary, due respect must be paid to all of these attempts to oppose the Nazi fascists based on religious, national-conservative, anti-militaristic, or left-critical beliefs. But unfortunately, due to the overwhelming success of the Nazi propaganda machine, these attempts were not sufficient to establish an effective culture of inner emigration, let alone a culture of resistance. In the end, the level of approval the Third Reich enjoyed among the majority of the German population can hardly be overestimated, and faced with this approval level, these attempts at opposition remained isolated phenomena that occurred only sporadically. They intensified toward the end of the war, but even then they failed to trigger any broad-based opposition.

Painting and Sculpture

Following the transfer of power to the Nazi fascists on 30 January 1933, they immediately homed in on the visual arts along with literature and music. After all, both Hitler and Rosenberg saw themselves as visual artists, one as a painter, the other as an architect, so they attributed to themselves the ability to pass professional as well as ideological judgment. Anything that clashed with their ideas of what truly German painting and sculpture should be, whether it was leftist, Jewish, expressionistic, or abstract, was in danger of being suppressed, eliminated, or eradicated after March/April 1933. Pursuant to these views, even painters who were famous at the time, such as Max Beckmann, Otto Dix, Karl Hofer, Emil Nolde, Max Pechstein, Karl Schmidt-Rottluff, and many others, were immediately and publicly labeled degenerate artists. First, permission to teach was withdrawn from some of them. In addition, they were excluded from the academies, banned from exhibiting, and were forced to look on as the Nazis removed their works from galleries and museums and denounced them as "un-German, Semitic, Negroid, or tinged with cultural bolshevism" at the infamous Munich exhibition of Degenerate Art. In fact the Nazis did not hesitate to burn thousands of these artists' works in Berlin or auction them away in Switzerland.

What were the consequences for individual artists? Did they go into exile, resist openly, or disappear into inner emigration with its characteristic combination of accommodation and aversion? In contrast to writers and composers, there were very few Communist Party sympathizers or Jews among German painters before 1933, so most of them remained in their ancestral fatherland. After initial hesitation, some did leave the Third Reich: a few nonconformist verists and leftists and the Swiss Paul Klee, the American Lyonel Feininger, and the Russian Wassily Kandinsky, who were the principle representatives of abstract or nonrepresentational painting. An equally small number of critical leftists continued secretly to include oppositional motifs in their works. Along with Hans Grundig and Oskar Nerlinger, Otto Nagel is the main artist who should be mentioned in this context. In close conjunction with the Assoziation revolutionärer bildender Künstler Deutschlands (Association of Revolutionary Visual Artists of Germany, ASSO), he had painted almost exclusively scenes from working-class life in Berlin-Wedding; after spring 1933, he was immediately subjected to a series of house searches, interrogations, and imprisonments, especially since he had dared to exhibit some of his paintings in Amsterdam in 1934 together with works by Käthe Kollwitz and Heinrich Zille.

Nagel was one of the few who took actions that put their lives in danger. Most of the other visual artists rejected by the Nazi fascists tried to disappear as inconspicuously as possible into anonymity after 1933. The relatively unknown among them, unable to promote themselves through exhibits in galleries, either led a fairly wretched life or accepted whatever offers came their way from the advertising industry. Practitioners of the kind of abstract painting that had developed primarily in Bauhaus circles had a particularly hard time. Their works were largely met with incomprehension after the realistic New Objectivity style caught on in Germany and many other European countries in the late 1920s. Painters such as Max Ackermann, Willi Baumeister, Georg Meistermann, Oskar Schlemmer, Theodor Werner, and Fritz Winter could hardly find patrons or wealthy art collectors after 1933 who would buy their nonrepresentational works. Since the frequently cited "death of Expressionism" in 1922–1923, well-heeled art lovers had preferred realistic paintings, whether they sympathized with the Nazi ideology or felt a certain antipathy to the excesses of the Nazi regime. Therefore, many painters belonging to the New Objectivity movement were very successful in these circles. Even artists who had been ostracized or marginalized by the Nazi authorities, if they had made a name for themselves before 1933, could continue to do a good business.

Most of these painters had a middle-class orientation and therefore had mustered very little interest in democratizing trends during the Weimar Republic. They rejected even more strongly ideas about being nonprofit or even collective put forward by leading cultural theorists in the Third Reich. Despite conscious or unconscious ties to contemporary styles such as New Objectivity, most still paid tribute to the ideal of the totally independent freelance artist. One example among many is Karl Hofer, who ranted repeatedly against the "hollow-chested and feeble-minded pseudo-republic" of the 1920s. He was equally sharp-tongued in early 1933 in his article "Kampf um die Kunst" (Struggle for Art) in the *Deutsche Allgemeine Zeitung* when he opposed the emphasis on "traditional and folksy" elements shown by especially fanatic Nazi fascists: "We must destroy cruelly and completely the illusion that art must first and foremost be popular. The greater and more important art is, the less it can be an art for the masses; it never was and never can be."

The inevitable followed quickly: Hofer lost his teaching position in 1934, was forbidden to exhibit, and was forced to leave the Prussian Academy of Art, and his works were removed from all German museums. But as a freelance artist—in contrast to the writers and composers who were subject to the board of censors—this did not harm him in the slightest. Unlike them, he was not dependent on government-supervised book or music publishers and was therefore not forced to chose between refusal and conformity. As long as he was left in peace, he could pursue his own artistic inclinations alone in his studio. Because of this isolation, he had never painted so much and "never sold so much as at that time," as Hofer wrote later in his memoirs. It would be difficult to find a better description of the situation of painters who were already well-known and who were forced to live a life of inner emigration under the Nazi regime. Although they were ostracized by the state, they lived relatively "free in the interior rooms of their art," where they were not subject to public approval and could devote themselves completely to their own predilections and to those of their middle-class patrons and collectors.

Otto Dix, an equally famous artist, was a similar case. Because of his antiwar paintings and his obscene portrayals of high society during the Weimar Republic, his permit to teach at the Dresden Academy was withdrawn in 1933, and in 1934 he was forbidden to exhibit. Some of his paintings were denounced as un-German in the 1934 Stuttgart exhibition entitled *Novembergeist. Kunst im Dienste der Zersetzung* (The Spirit of November: Art in the Service of Decay) and in *Entartete Kunst*, the

Figure 35. Otto Dix: *Landscape on the Upper Rhine* (1938). © VG-Bild-Kunst, Bonn 2010.

monster exhibit in Munich. At first he reacted to these measures as he did in his paintings *Die Sieben Todsünden* (1933; The Seven Deadly Sins) and *Triumph des Todes* (1935; The Triumph of Death), for example: his depictions were allegorical and could definitely be interpreted as bitter satires of Nazi fascism, but they could not be shown anywhere and brought him no income. In response, Dix turned to painting portraits and landscapes in the style of the old masters; these conformed exactly to the tradition-bound taste of middle-class collectors and, because of their lovely painting style, were easy to sell. Even NS-Foreign Minister Joachim von Ribbentrop acquired a liking for this type of painting in the mid-1930s and did not hesitate to have Dix secretly paint portraits of his children.

Other inner emigration painters found themselves with similar problems. As I said before, those among them who had the fewest difficulties were the New Objectivity realists. They did not earn as much through private sales as Hofer and Dix, but they could not really complain about the demand for their paintings, especially for portraits and landscapes. As long as they did not belong to the verist or leftist wing of the movement, they remained more or less unscathed and were not urged in any way by the NSDAP to give the motifs in their paintings a Nazi fascist bias. Therefore they saw no reason to oppose any measures of the new regime that did not affect them personally. Here, as in other artistic categories, there were exceptions. One of the most laudable was the painter Franz Lenk, who came out of the Dresden realist tradition and after 1933 was active in the presidential council of the Reich Chamber of Culture. In 1935, however, he and Otto Dix mounted a minimally disguised protest exhibition in the Nierendorf Gallery in Berlin. In 1937 he refused to take part in the *Große Deutsche Kunstausstellung* in the Munich Haus der Kunst, and one year later he relinquished his teaching position and withdrew to the countryside, where he made his living selling meticulously painted landscapes. In contrast, the socially critical verists in the New Objectivity group—painters such as Karl Hubbuch, Franz Radziwill, and Christian Schad—did not have an easy time continuing to live in the Third Reich. They had to conform, find bread-and-butter jobs, or avoid the problem by producing art that was pleasing but noncommittal. The abstract painters had an even more difficult time. After the major shift from expressionism to a more realistic art, they were already having difficulty finding buyers for their work in the second half of the 1920s, and later most of them were forced to hire themselves out in other professions.

When we talk about inner emigration painting, we need to keep its stylistic diversity and the contingent variation in financial circumstances of individual painters in mind. What connected these artists with other representatives of inner emigration was their more or less overt aversion to Nazi fascism based on a fundamental dislike of every kind of collective solidarity and a corresponding insistence on the principle of artistic exceptionalism. Almost all of these painters had been individuals before and wanted to remain individuals after 1933. This kind of attitude served a protective function during the Third Reich, because the executive organs of the Nazi administration usually suppressed any sort of group formation immediately. But it was also connected to the specifically bourgeois view of art that was based on an exaggerated appreciation for the personal uniqueness of the individual artist. Thus, as was the case with literature, no broadly effective counterculture or oppositional front developed here; they were simply coexisting but helplessly isolated artists caught between aversion and accommodation. Nevertheless—considering the repressive measures taken by the state—we should not deny them the relatively modest label of inner emigration.

The situation was similar for the much smaller number of sculptors who maintained some distance to the cultural politics of the Third Reich; they included artists as diverse as Ernst Barlach, Hermann Blumenthal, Joachim Karsch, and Christoph Voll. Voll and Karsch tried to cling to the "realism" of New Objectivity even in the Third Reich instead of striv-

ing for the kind of Greco-Roman ideality of the human body à la Arno
Breker that the Nazi fascists favored. Voll became more and more demor-
alized by constant hostility from the NSDAP. Karsch had to be satisfied
with a life on the margins and even saw his *Lesendes Paar* (1933; Couple
Reading) removed from the Folkwang-Museum in Essen in 1937 as degenerate because of its supposedly unattractive shape. Blumenthal, whose
style tended to be more classical, had a somewhat easier time of it and
even found some wealthy buyers for his sculptures because of their impressive beauty. Nevertheless, his sculpture *Stehender Jüngling* (Standing
Boy) was also removed from the Folkwang-Museum in 1937 because of
its supposedly bizarrely exaggerated posture and also because of Blumenthal's contact with proscribed artists such as Käthe Kollwitz and Gerhard
Marcks. Kollwitz, who turned to sculpture more and more during these
years, never had a chance to exhibit any of her works publicly; they usually portrayed figures who were lamenting or grieving.

Ernst Barlach, the greatest of the inner emigration sculptors, towered
above the others. For this very reason—primarily due to his unheroic war
memorials and the Slavic-Mongolian facial features of his figures—he felt
the lash of the Nazi fascists who were committed to Alfred Rosenberg

Figure 36. Ernst Barlach in his studio in Güstrow in front of the *Fries der Lauschen-
den* (Frieze of the Listeners, 1935). © Berlin, Bildagentur für Kunst, Kultur und
Geschichte.

with particular force. They confiscated his book *Zeichnungen* (Drawings), published in 1934 by Piper-Verlag, forced him out of the Prussian Academy of Arts, and imposed a general ban on exhibiting his sculptures and drawings. Nevertheless, Barlach decided not to leave Germany. In 1937, he wrote a letter from Güstrow, a safe haven he had chosen a long time before; the letter was written shortly after his house had been searched for evidence that he was hostile to the regime. He wrote, "In my own fatherland, I have been forced into a kind of emigrant existence. The only options remaining for me are to really go into exile or decide to assert my right to exercise my profession freely, whatever it may cost. I have never even considered the former and thus the latter has become an absolute necessity for me. There is no salvation for me elsewhere, even if I were to be successful. You may be forced to flee, but then you have to consider, shuddering, that in a strange country you will be estranged from yourself—wasting away in a state of homelessness."

But the decision to remain in Germany under dishonorable conditions wore Barlach down in the end. He found a wealthy patron in the industrialist Hermann Fürchtegott Reemtsma, but even so, he was not able to pull himself together to the point of open resistance to the regime that oppressed him. He had to look on as the religious and nationalist circles that had admired him in his early years gradually turned away from him; they even allowed the Nazi district administration to remove his famous angel of peace with the facial features of Käthe Kollwitz from the east choir of the main church in Güstrow and melt it down for military purposes during World War II. Thus, not even Barlach was able to have a major impact; he remained an isolated representative of an inner emigration whose noble sentiments were unquestionable, but who due to their marginal position, whether self-chosen or imposed, had no chance to oppose the Nazi fascists in an effective way.

Music

It is not easy to find musical works composed during the Third Reich that can be characterized as examples of inner emigration in the same way as works of literature or paintings. Plenty of music critics characterize this art form—because it lacks words and images—as a retreat to the realm of vagueness and emotionality, even inexplicability; you cannot come to grips with it, they believe, through rational or social scientific interpretation strategies. It behooves cultural historians who think in more concrete terms to contradict this way of listening to music as firmly as possible; its romantic-reactionary origins are all too obvious. In instrumental works, music may appear to be removed from the world. But it is always part of either the dominant or the oppositional culture, whether it exists within a totalitarian state or in a class-based social system. This is also true of the music composed in Germany between 1933 and 1945.

The dominant forms of music performed during the Third Reich can be classified in four somewhat crude categories: (1) German compositions since the late seventeenth century, usually characterized as baroque, classical, or romantic, and all the subsequent trends up to Hans Pfitzner and Richard Strauss; (2) Protestant church music by composers such as Hugo Distler and Ernst Pepping, tolerated and even supported by the Nazi fascists; (3) hit songs, dance music, and film music, all widespread since the Weimar Republic; and (4) songs and marching music purporting to be national socialist. Since the NS authorities had eradicated all left-critical, Jewish, and modernistic elements from German musical life, we have to ask how a compositional style could develop in the interstices between the four officially recognized musical forms and successfully create a spirit of insubordination toward Nazi fascism in the broad masses. Could a musical composition protest the split into elite music and entertainment music that the Nazi authorities were promoting, perhaps by turning conspicuously against derivative classicism and late romanticism? Because the state monitored performance conditions so carefully, such efforts were inevitably condemned to failure. The only options left to serious composers in this situation were either to try to adapt to prevailing conditions by semiaccommodation or forgo performing in Germany between 1933 and 1945 and simply stash compositions away in a drawer for the time being. Among composers at the time, it was primarily Paul Hindemith who took the first approach and Karl Amadeus Hartmann who took the second.

While the Hartmann case continues to be relatively obscure, there are already extensive libraries of material about the Hindemith case. Hindemith composed a large quantity of works during the 1920s that provoked highly diverse reactions from music critics. He first appeared on the scene as an expressionist enfant terrible with his short operas *Mörder, Hoffnung der Frauen* (1919; Murderer, Hope of Women) based on a play by Oskar Kokoschka and *Sancta Susanna* (1921) based on a play by Gustav Stramm. Then in quick succession he paid tribute to New Objectivity's ideal of functional music, set texts by authors as different as Gottfried Benn and Bertolt Brecht to music, performed a *Zeitoper* entitled *Neues vom Tage* (1929; News of the Day), which was considered obscene because of a bathroom scene in the second act, temporarily joined the musicians' guild inspired by Fritz Jöde, and finally, after 1930, began to develop a musical style that can be characterized in general terms as tonal half modern.

So when the Nazi fascists came to power in 1933, he had both supporters and bitter enemies among them. One group hoped that because
he had turned away from the various forms of modernistic music after
1929–1930, he might develop into a major composer of national socialist music; the other group, with Alfred Rosenberg once again leading
the pack, could not forgive his previous musical excesses and urged a
total Hindemith boycott. Because in this case Hitler shared Rosenberg's
negative viewpoint, fierce disputes between the two camps were unavoidable. They were sparked primarily by Hindemith's opera *Mathis der
Maler* (Matthias the Painter), which he had composed between 1932
and 1934. The conductor Wilhelm Furtwängler, who was politically a
nationalist conservative, liked the work so much that he wanted to give
the first performance in Berlin in spring 1935. In an attempt to propitiate
Hindemith's critics, he included the three relatively accessible preludes
to the work in one of his concert programs as the *Mathis-Symphonie*. This
caused a massive backlash among the composer's opponents and brought
about a performance ban of the opera that even Goebbels was forced to
support. In protest against the ban, Furtwängler refused to continue acting as vice president of the Reich Music Chamber, and he resigned from
his offices as director of the Berlin State Opera and as head of the Berlin
Philharmonic as well. A coerced reconciliation between him and Goebbels was reached a short time later because for tactical reasons Goebbels
still saw Furtwängler as a useful "walking advertisement for our artistic
beliefs," as he put it. But Hindemith's position in the musical life in the
Third Reich did not change; on the contrary, it continued to be highly
insecure.

Actually, his *Mathis der Maler*—with just a few deletions and changes—
could have become a major work of Nazi fascist music. It is based on a
stringently tonal method of composition, uses early German folk songs
and chorales in its arioso sections, has as its subject matter the peasant
uprisings of the early sixteenth century that were always glorified by Nazi
historians, and centers almost exclusively around Mathis Neithardt, called
Grünewald, who belongs to the universally admired great masters of early
German painting. In principle, these qualities should have appealed to
the music critics of the Third Reich. So why was the work banned? Surely
one reason was Hindemith's past involvement with expressionism and
risqué elements of New Objectivity. Another was the libretto, written by
Hindemith himself, which begins by displaying a clear sympathy for the
rebellious peasants but turns away from social reality toward the end and
retreats into a half religious, half aesthetic-melancholy solitude that pre-
cludes any hope for a political modification of the conditions portrayed
in the opera.

After this scandal, some of Hindemith's compositions continued to appear in print into the early 1940s, but there were fewer and fewer performances of his works. Therefore, the composer, who was constantly shuttling back and forth between Germany and Turkey between 1935 and 1937, increasingly adopted the attitude characteristic of inner emigration. Instead of currying favor with the Nazis, he composed only noncommittal-sounding instrumental works such as small suites for orchestra, quartets, and sonatas. In 1937, he defended his style of composition in the relatively formal *Unterweisung im Tonsatz* (The Craft of Musical Composition) and finally retreated to Switzerland in 1938 and then to the United States in 1940, where he remained as apolitical as in previous years—in other words, he did not compose any antifascist works. You would have to be broad-minded to label Hindemith's conduct as belonging to the inner emigration that developed in the gray area between accommodation and aversion. In the final analysis, the question is still open as to whether Hindemith may have secretly hoped—until 1938 when he was denounced as a "rootless charlatan" at the exhibition *Entartete Musik* in Düsseldorf—to be recognized by the Nazi authorities as one of their own and qualified to assume a leading position in German musical life. He certainly never took any action that would contradict such a supposition.

Karl Amadeus Hartmann's conduct toward the Nazi fascists was much more unambiguous. He rejected every accolade proffered by the new rulers from the beginning, and between 1933 and 1945 composed only works that clearly expressed opposition to the Third Reich. His situation in 1933, it is true, was completely different than Hindemith's. Hartmann was substantially younger and at that time was still completely unknown outside Munich. Shortly before, because of his left-critical viewpoint, he had moved to a style of composition that was related to Hanns Eisler's music and Bertolt Brecht's theories of epic theater. The fact that his views had gradually become more and more radical was expressed both in his vocal works such as the *Profane Messe* (Profane Mass) and a cantata based on texts by Karl Marx and Johannes R. Becher as well as in some instrumental works reminiscent of Eisler. In fact, immediately after the transfer of power to the Nazi fascists, affronted by the racist politics of the new regime, he specifically focused on Jewish music and incorporated a series of traditional Jewish folk melodies in his First String Quartet written during the months that followed.

Nevertheless, Hartmann decided to remain in Germany instead of going into exile like others who shared his views, who were either members of the Communist Party or Jews. "I will not go abroad," he wrote shortly after 1933. "In my fatherland I'm forced to feel like an emigrant, and actually worse than a real one because all the wolves are howling at me."

And the howling had serious consequences for him. As a former cultural bolshevist, he was viewed as a suspicious character by the Nazis from the beginning and so could not expect that any of his works would be performed in Germany. The NSDAP expected young composers like him to display staunch fidelity to their views; he was simply not well enough known for the party to grant him limited freedom for reasons of prestige. After all, even in the infamous Hindemith case the Nazi authorities had been very severe. Thus, Hartmann could only hope that his works would be performed abroad, which also had its risks, or he could hold them until the fascist dictatorship had ended.

A close look shows that Hartmann was not entirely unsuccessful with this strategy. His symphony *Miserae*, which he dedicated to his friends in Dachau Concentration Camp, premiered in Prague in 1935 under the direction of Hermann Scherchen. His First String Quartet premiered in 1936 at a chamber music festival in Geneva. In 1937, his cantata *Friede anno '48* (Peace Anno '48) was honored by the Emil Hertzka Foundation in Vienna. Ernst Klug first performed his *Musik der Trauer für Violine und Streichorchester* (Music of Mourning for Violin and String Orchestra) in St. Gallen; later it was also titled *Concerto funèbre*. Subsequently, between 1941 and 1943, Hartmann composed his sweeping triptych for orchestra, *Sinfoniae Dramaticae*, with its three parts entitled *China kämpft* (China Struggles), *Symphonische Hymnen*, and finally *Vita Nova*, which included a final section in which he quoted the International as a sign of his resistance to the Nazi regime.

Hartmann made temporary contact with Anton Webern, a pupil of Schoenberg's who had remained in Austria, but he was disconcerted both by Webern's serial composition technique and by the subservience he displayed to the Austrian authorities. In contrast, he viewed Hermann Scherchen, a left-leaning conductor in exile, as his musical mentor. It was from him that Hartmann got the idea, during a conversation in Switzerland in September 1934, of composing an opera based on *Simplicissimus*, a novel by Hans Jakob Christoffel von Grimmelshausen, which seems in many ways to be in diametrical opposition to Hindemith's *Mathis der Maler*. The opera is about young Simplicius, who grows up in the chaos and turmoil of the Thirty Years War. But unlike Hindemith's Mathis, he does not withdraw from the world of political conflict into hermit-like solitude. Instead, in a strongly anachronistic turn of events, he joins forces with a troop of insurgent peasants in the end; they simply massacre their former exploiters and demand a socially just society in the spirit of Thomas Münzer.

In order to emphasize the work's political radicalism in musical terms, Hartmann sacrificed everything middle-class opera subscribers had always expected. This work is neither a feast for the eyes nor a treat for the ears. It presents the "torments of a hopeless time" in images and sounds that display no formal consistency and no inner coherence. Sometimes the listener hears street songs, sometimes chorales, sometimes spoken texts delivered in a clipped style, sometimes quotes from Bach, Borodin, Bartók, and Prokofiev, sometimes references to Stravinsky's *Histoire du soldat*, and much more besides. Hartmann wanted to express a condition "of restlessness, of anxieties, and of grief." He wanted to remind the audience of the oppressive situation after 1933, when everyone who was politically suspect was led off to prison or to a concentration camp, when members of the SA roamed the streets smashing the windows of Jewish stores, when Nazi students burned books the regime did not like, when women who had sexual relations with men the Nazis considered racially inferior were pilloried, and when, in the midst of all this tumult, the danger of a second world war began to be apparent, a war that would destroy culture and civilized behavior entirely.

Still, his *Simplicius Simplicissimus* is anything but a vision of horror. "If you hold up a mirror to the world so that it perceives its own hideous face," Hartmann wrote later about this work, "maybe at some point in time it will think of a better way." And as a utopian who was prepared to fight, he added the following sentence to his declaration: "Despite all the political storm clouds, I believed in a better future; that is what the apotheosis at the end of my *Simplicius* is intended to express." Faced with all the terrors that filled the year 1933 which in his view pointed ahead to the most terrible of "crimes," a new world war, Hartmann explained with grim determination, "I recognized that it was necessary to make a declaration—not out of desperation and fear of that regime, but as a counter-reaction."

Hindemith's *Mathis der Maler* and Hartmann's *Simplicius Simplicissimus* are the two most striking examples of the range of styles and themes within what is generally labeled music of inner emigration. One, hoping to be performed, glorifies withdrawal into an apolitical attitude; the other, with no hope of being performed, uses a historical setting to call for a revolt against the tyrannical power assumed by the ruling class. So much for obvious contrasts. But what the two works have in common is their form, which belongs to the sphere of high culture; both are musically challenging operas that in the final analysis cannot achieve a broad political impact. Both works, as different as they are, assume that you can intervene in current events using a genre like opera that is already a half-ossified museum piece. The idea of culture underlying them is still based on the claim of the middle class to be representative and to be trend-setting in all-important matters of culture. Both Hindemith and Hartmann still felt they were artists outside the rapidly expanding media culture that eluded all the requirements of high art, and therefore could set their own standards. Neither of them scorned traditional and folk-like elements in their music or their themes, but both tried to present them in a highly artistic form. This may have been admirable in terms of their own ideas about culture, but the two operas would inevitably have missed their target audience even if they had been performed in the Third Reich. Who were the people being addressed by these operas: the upper or the lower class? In the context of the cultural sector of the time, split as it was into elite art and entertainment art, this was an unavoidable dilemma connected to the socially precarious marginality of opera per se; neither Hindemith nor Hartmann can be held responsible.

3

EXILE

FRAGMENTATION OF THE
GERMAN EXILE COMMUNITY

There was a wave of emigration in 1933 without parallel even in German history, which had seen many similar expulsions. During the French Revolution, the restoration at the time of Metternich, the period after the Revolution of 1848, and the years of the anti-socialist laws under Bismarck—all were times when individuals or small groups tried to avoid imminent arrest by fleeing abroad. But after the Nazi takeover in Germany, thousands, tens of thousands, or even hundreds of thousands of people were in danger of being subjected to constant repressive measures or incarcerated in the prisons and concentration camps of the new regime because of their politics or their race. Communists and Jews had the most to fear. But there were also many social democrats, Christians critical of the system, left-liberal intellectuals, so-called asphalt literati, and painters and composers with modernistic views who suddenly felt threatened and looked around for potential places of refuge. But not even fleeing abroad seemed to offer a 100 percent guarantee that their lives would be saved. Some leading Nazi fascists who had condemned the exiles as un-German referred to them as cadavers on leave whom they would pursue to the ends of the earth.

Because the transfer of power that took place on 30 January 1933 was so drastic and largely unforeseen, the refugee groups, who were generally distraught, terrorized, and split into many ideological camps, were unable to consolidate immediately into a humanistic or antifascist front. A state of isolation, fragmentation, and general chaos reigned during the first weeks of exile, since neither the committed leftists, the exiles who were apolitical, nor even the Jewish-born had predicted such a series of events.

In February/March 1933, particularly after the Reichstag fire and the atmosphere of persecution and pogrom it triggered, sheer survival was the first thing on the agenda, not a common initiative of any kind. Looking back at this period, Wolf Franck wrote bitterly in 1935 in his *Führer durch die deutsche Emigration* (Guided Tour through German Emigration), "Emigrant and emigrant, from the very beginning they were not the same. Businessmen wanted nothing to do with politicians, social democrats wanted nothing to do with communists, those with connections wanted nothing to do with helpless aliens, and the rich definitely wanted nothing to do with their poor companions in misfortune." In a nutshell, as Lion Feuchtwanger put it in his 1940 novel *Exil*: "The German emigrant community was more fractured than any other." The later autobiographies of these Hitler refugees, as they were called at the time, provide revealing evidence of this disunity; their tone ranges from strident to lackadaisical, from elegiac to sentimental, and from religious to pessimistic. Their differences are illustrated by the titles they chose, among them *Streitbares Leben* (Combative Life), *Vom tätigen Leben* (An Active Life), *Ein Mensch fällt aus Deutschland* (A Person Falls out of Germany), *Sehnsucht nach dem Kurfürstendamm* (Longing for the Kurfürstendamm), *Gestohlenes Leben* (Stolen Life), *Dunkle Jahre* (Dark Years), *Schicksalsreise* (Fateful Journey), *Flugsand* (Drifting Sand), *Odyssee* (Odyssey), *Aus gutem Hause* (From a Good Family), *Du Land der Liebe* (Oh Land of Love), *Alte, unnennbare Jahre*, (Earlier Ineffable Years), *Meines Vaters Haus* (My Father's House), *Der verlorene Sohn* (The Prodigal Son), or *Heimkehr zu Gott* (Returning Home to God).

Immediately after 30 January 1933, the refugees were concerned first with their own safety and that of their families; only then could they look at the situation from a broader perspective. A minority, in blind, calculated optimism, hoped the Nazi regime would last six months at the most and that they would then be able to return to their homes; surely a highly cultivated people like the Germans would soon be laughing at a political puppet and Hofbräuhaus rowdy like Hitler. But a majority of the exiles saw a bleak future ahead. And their general state of mind became more depressed when they read in newspapers from Prague, Paris, or Switzerland or learned from the reports of other refugees how quickly the transition to a one-party dictatorship had been accomplished and how great was the rejoicing of large segments of the German population over the reduction of unemployment and the process of volkish recovery.

Many of the more serious artists had already felt isolated and marginalized during the Weimar Republic as people turned increasingly to commercialized mass media, and now in the exile years that followed their feelings of alienation intensified. Many exiles found themselves in countries that seemed exotic, where languages they did not understand were spoken, and where there were sometimes completely different ideas of culture than those they had been used to during the Wilhelminian era or the Weimar Republic—in short, where they encountered nothing that was familiar or appealing. In addition, what country wanted to admit them in the midst of a continuing world economic crisis? Because their economic structure was based on private enterprise, the other European countries barely had the necessary public funds to take care of their own unemployed; the Soviet Union with its socialist government was the exception. And most refugees from Germany were either leftists or Jews, or sometimes even Jewish leftists. They were not welcome even in the Western democracies, where anticommunism was fomented by the dominant opinion makers and there was much latent anti-Semitism. As a result, almost all refugees from the Third Reich had to struggle constantly with visa, affidavit, or work permit problems. Even when they were granted a residence permit, it was usually subject to a time limit, and reapplication was necessary to renew it to avoid the danger of being deported to another country or even back to Germany.

Particularly among the poorer artists in exile, a feeling of existential hopelessness increased in the following years, and nothing seemed to replace what they had lost. This feeling led some of the refugee writers to assert, as Alfred Polgar did, that their homeland was increasingly becoming a foreign country, while at the same time no foreign country could offer them a new homeland. They had grown up in a national culture that was rich with tradition, a high culture that certainly showed no signs of the globalization that would begin fifty to sixty years later. Even their ability to express themselves verbally better than other exiles provided them no support, since this talent was not in much demand in foreign countries. Painters and composers, whose works did not encounter linguistic barriers because they used pictorial and tonal means of expression, had a somewhat easier time of it in exile than their wordsmith colleagues and could in some cases continue to work as teachers or conductors even abroad. And an impressive number of filmmakers made their fortune in Hollywood. But German-language authors, most already advanced to an age when learning a foreign language is extremely difficult? Were they condemned to despair from the outset? Yes and no. Some despaired, but some were hopeful; some were plagued by thoughts of suicide, but some were born fighters; some hated everything German, and some glorified everything that was good in Germany's past; there were Zionists who viewed Germany simply as Hitler's country, and there were also Jewish refugees who viewed themselves as the so-called other, better Germans and tried to cling to the ideals of German culture and civilization.

These deep splits explain why many of the artists who fled Germany were not able to agree on a term that expressed their status within the political and cultural activities in exile. They employed a number of very different terms depending on their own ideological orientation, taking into consideration the obvious fragmentation of those who had fled Germany or had been expelled. Those who were more or less apolitical usually used the term emigrants. The activists, on the other hand, preferred terms such as exiles, displaced persons, or outcasts. In their ears, the word emigrant sounded too much like a "voluntary expatriate," as Bertolt Brecht explained in his poem, written in the mid-1930s, "Über die Bezeichnung Emigranten" (On the Term Emigrants). Therefore, it is ideologically problematic to speak in a general way about the testimonials left by the Hitler refugees as exile art or exile culture. Thomas Mann and Bertolt Brecht, Else Lasker-Schüler and Lion Feuchtwanger, Arnold Schoenberg and Hanns Eisler, Robert Musil and Anna Seghers, Max Hermann-Neiße and Johannes R. Becher, Paul Klee and Felix Nußbaum—an examination of the nature of their political commitment shows that they had hardly anything in common. The fact that they were all antifascists did not suffice as a basis for solidarity. Even in exile, there were dubious figures such as Bernard von Brentano and Ernst Glaeser whose behavior was not unequivocal, even on this one point. Alfred Döblin, Thomas Mann, and Franz Werfel made statements in fall 1933 that sounded equally ambivalent because they wanted to cleanse themselves of the suspicion of engaging in antifascist activity to avoid causing trouble for their Jewish publishing house S. Fischer in Berlin.

How can we categorize exile art in particular schools of thought, when active commitment appears next to timid despair, noble heroism next to personal inadequacy? Were there actually clearly recognizable groups, or was it all a chaos of individual voices? The exiled artists themselves did make categorizations when they talked about militant art versus resigned art. Alfred Döblin made one of the first attempts at this kind of breakdown when he tried to identify the exile artists as either conservative, humanistic bourgeois, or intellectually revolutionary. These categories are not entirely incorrect, but they leave no room for Marxist-oriented writers such as Johannes R. Becher, Bertolt Brecht, Willi Bredel, Anna Seghers, Erich Weinert, and Friedrich Wolf; for leftist composers such as Hanns Eisler; or for leftist graphic artists such as Gerd Arntz, John Heartfield, Max Lingner, and Johannes Wüsten. In our discussion here, it seems preferable to categorize the exile artists based on the factor that led to their expatriation—the level of their political opposition to the Third Reich—into three groups: resigned escapist, culturally aware humanistic, and actively antifascist.

The first group appears especially heterogeneous. They took an escapist position in exile—in other words, they withdrew into private life, for a variety of reasons: (1) because they had always been largely apolitical, (2) because they gave up in the face of the political and military superiority of the Nazi regime and the wait-and-see appeasement policies of most Western democracies vis à vis Hitler, or (3) because they suddenly found a new "Heimat" in Zionism or in the bosom of the Catholic Church.

Chief among the apolitical artists and creative people in a broader sense who had been expelled from the Third Reich were many fugitive filmmakers who after 1933 simply looked for more or less lucrative positions in the dreamland of Hollywood. They tried, as they had previously done in the German film industry, to rent their talents to the local corporate chiefs, an approach that Bertolt Brecht disparagingly characterized as the Tui behavior of intellectuals who "rented their brain" to the ruling class. Some writers, such as Albrecht Schaeffer and Richard Beer-Hofmann, simply continued their work—albeit without any intention of making a profit—at the point where they had been torn out of their poetic interior spaces by the transfer of power to Hitler. Others, such as Else Lasker-Schüler, Karl Wolfskehl, and Max Hermann-Neiße, got bogged down in gloomy lamentations about the obscurity of the exile fate had imposed on them or they confined themselves, like Robert Musil, to keeping egocentric diaries where they bemoaned their literary insignificance. Kurt Tucholsky was one of those who saw the Third Reich as the perfect realization of the hoary longings of German Philistines and therefore simply laid down their literary swords. As early as 4 March 1933, Tucholsky wrote to his friend Walter Hasenclever, "You can fight on behalf of a majority that is being oppressed by a tyrannical minority. But you cannot preach something to a people that is the exact opposite of what the majority of them want (the Jews too)." The attitude of graphic artist and painter George Grosz in exile was even more disillusioned, even cynical. He, like Tucholsky, had been among the sharpest critics of the chauvinistic Free Corps movement and looming Nazi fascism before 1933. Now he not only made fun of the marching troops of brown-shirted Philistines, he also mocked the goody-goodies among the exiles who had still not realized, as he wrote in a letter to his friend Ulrich Becher, that babble about a "humanistic" oppositional stance or "blah blah about human improvement" was nothing more than "a kind of mush with rationality gravy." Therefore, all antifascist "cultural efforts" and "appeals for solidarity" made him "want to vomit." But few exiles expressed themselves in such nihilistic terms. Others, who were equally disgusted by the Philistine faintheartedness of the Germans yet had to face their own ideological disorientation at the same time, found a new support in their Catholic or Jewish beliefs; they wanted to distance themselves from any kind of faith in Germanness or hope for progress in this world. This group was primarily made up of older expressionists such as Alfred Döblin, Franz Werfel, and Arnold Schoenberg, who had displayed a certain tendency to irrationalism even before their flight into exile.

The humanistic defenders of culture, as they were called, formed another group of Hitler refugees who were equally apolitical, at least in the beginning. The group consisted primarily of solidly middle-class or upper-middle-class artists who emigrated into a state of genteel reserve insofar as they could afford it. Many among them continued to believe in the myth of Germany as the land of poets and thinkers and therefore supported the theory that good art is always the best politics. Some of them liked to cite Thomas Mann, the self-selected representative of bourgeois high culture, in this context. In his essay *Richard Wagner und der "Ring des Nibelungen"* written in 1937, Mann rehashed his earlier thesis from the *Betrachtungen eines Unpolitischen* (Reflections of a Nonpolitical Man) of 1918 that the "German mind is essentially uninterested in social and political questions." According to Mann, "the work of art" emerges from "the innermost depths." Therefore art alone, and not politics, should be

Figure 37. Thomas Mann and Albert Einstein in Princeton (1938). © Wikipedia Commons.

recognized as "authoritative." You can find similar statements by others of these cultural aristocrats in exile who, as Heinrich Mann wrote, had been largely taken by surprise in their "civilized state" of cultural bias and concomitant ideological defenselessness in 1933 by the Nazi fascists. Ludwig Marcuse, for example, later admitted openly that he "didn't know the first thing about political ranting and raving" at the time. Max Brod confessed with the same honesty that he had viewed himself shortly before 1933 as an optimistic representative of "a coming epoch of cosmopolitanism." Klaus Mann explained in deep disappointment after the Nazi dictatorship was over, "The majority of 'our emigration' consisted of dutiful citizens who saw themselves first and foremost as 'good Germans,' then secondarily as Jews, and last of all, or not at all, as antifascists."

Just how fundamentally apolitical these previously well-situated members of the educated middle class were is clearly demonstrated by their attitude toward the brutal and even homicidal aspects of Nazi fascism. The most sensitive among them reacted, as did many representatives of inner emigration, in a purely emotional way. Without any deeper insight into the historical, social, and economic dimensions of the phenomenon, they saw Hitler primarily as a demon who had emerged out of nothingness and plunged Germany into darkest barbarism inexplicably and overnight. This was how the philosopher Ernst Cassirer, who had fled into exile in the United States, described it to Henry Pachter in all seriousness, as if there had never been any prefascist trends in Germany: "This Hitler is an error in history; he does not belong in German history at all." When these circles said anything about the Nazi fascists, they did so in terms of a mind-set based in the history of ideas or in demonology; they were limited to an apolitical-metaphorical approach, in other words, a view of the phenomenon of fascism as pathological, demented, or devilish. Walter A. Berendsohn, for example, spoke of the Third Reich as "the crudest of sub-humanity"; Ludwig Marcuse used the term "plague-infested region"; Oskar Maria Graf wrote of "bestial Hitler-barbarianism"; and even Klaus Mann used terms such as "Hell," "repulsive fraud," and "horrible homecoming to night and death."

These group members saw themselves, in contrast, as the worthiest, although final, representatives of the legacy of the humanistic tradition; its best-known manifestations had been Goethe's cosmopolitanism, Beethoven's Ninth Symphony, and Kant's idealism; in their own formulation, they were the other, better Germans. Of course this sometimes led to rather arrogant attitudes with an obvious touch of the upper class about them. "German culture is wherever I am," Thomas Mann is reputed to have said at the time without the slightest touch of irony. One of the documents most representative of this mind-set is his novel *Lotte in Weimar*

(1939), which specifically emphasizes Goethe's conservative and culturally aristocratic qualities. No mention is made of the progressive elements in Goethe's works; instead he is singled out as a great individual—one who viewed the Wars of Liberation as a national hoax and advocated a traditional class-based order with a cosmopolitan superstructure. In this novel, the essence of the other Germany is still the inwardly directed personality in which we can see a cultural but not a political counter image to fascist Germany.

In the first years of exile, the only really political statements came from the activist camp, which insisted on unmistakable commitment, even in art. As early as 1933, Bertolt Brecht wrote, for example, "Literature has almost never experienced such consideration from the state: the fascists show their deference with kicks. I hope that German literature will prove itself worthy of these exceptional courtesies." Accordingly, the left-oriented *Neue deutsche Blätter* published the following statements a short time later on the theme "Anyone who writes also acts": "Today, writing of distinction has to be antifascist," and "Anyone who remains silent condemns themselves to social and artistic sterility." Exile periodicals such as the *Neue Weltbühne* (The New International Stage) and *Internationale Literatur* supported the same commitment with contributions by Ernst Toller, Anna Seghers, and Heinrich Mann. Even the formerly conservative author Joseph Roth wrote in 1934, "Today, a writer who does not struggle against Hitler and the Third Reich is without doubt a small, weak person and probably also a worthless writer." And Ferdinand Bruckner, who wanted to set himself apart from apolitical authors such as Franz Werfel and Carl Zuckmayer, stated with appropriate emphasis at the New York PEN meeting in 1939, "Only when literature becomes a weapon will a better life become possible."

So instead of writing novels set in the past about "Pippin the Middle or Melanie the Odd," as Kurt Hiller put it with a dig at Hermann Kesten and Stefan Zweig, instead of painting vacuous landscapes or composing symphonies with neutral contents, the activists on the left among the artists in exile strongly supported a militant art based on the principle of antifascist solidarity. They had two objectives: to create works for the inner German resistance and smuggle them into Germany or to enlighten the countries in which they resided at the moment about the atrocities of the fascist reign of terror. Although there were limited opportunities for a militant or resistance art of this kind, at least they tried. The exile anthology *Deutsch für Deutsche* (German for Germans 1935), which includes texts by Johannes R. Becher, Willi Bredel, and Anna Seghers, provides evidence of these efforts. Other examples are Bertolt Brecht's "Fünf Schwierigkeiten beim Schreiben der Wahrheit" ("Writing the

Truth: Five Difficulties") and the *Gedichte* (Poems 1938) by Rudolf Leonhard, camouflaged as a volume in the Universal Library series published by Reclam. Leonhard's *Gedichte* was smuggled into the Third Reich, but remained largely unnoticed, as did John Heartfield's Hitler satires. Other texts, primarily poems and short reports that appealed for resistance to Nazi fascism, were broadcast in Germany over the German Freedom Station 29.8, which had been founded by communists in exile. Similar forms of agitprop art developed during the Battle for the Saar (1935), the Spanish Civil War (1936–1939), and above all on the Eastern Front (1941–1945), where Johannes R. Becher, Willi Bredel, Adam Scharrer, Erich Weinert, Friedrich Wolf, and others participated in the production of pamphlets, radio broadcasts, and come-on-over-to-our-side poems (*Kommrüber-Verse*).

These activists—in contrast to the apolitical humanists—based their struggle on hard-hitting analyses of the socioeconomic foundations of Nazi fascism, not on a defensive emotional reaction. This is apparent on the first page of the *Neue deutsche Blätter* (New German Pages), where we read, "Many see fascism as an anachronism, an intermezzo, a reversion to Medieval barbarism; others talk about a mental illness of the Germans or of an anomaly. We on the other hand do not see fascism as a random formation; we see it as the organic product of a terminally ill capitalism." Their efforts to educate people in the Western democracies therefore boiled down to denouncing Hitler as a henchman of anticommunist, profit-hungry, large-scale industry who used the hypocritical catchphrase of a new volk community only to take the wind out of the sails of the left, as Ernst Bloch put it in his 1935 book *Erbschaft dieser Zeit* (Heritage of Our Times). These groups saw very clearly that German fascism was not a form of socialism; it was a state capitalist dictatorship attempting, with the help of nationalist and racist ideas, to implement its objectives throughout Europe. Many of them believed they would not be the only ones to see through this political strategy; surely the majority of the German people would too. Particularly in the beginning, the leftist camp cherished great hopes that this would happen and insisted repeatedly that Nazi fascism emanated from a small clique of gangsters and was trying to rule over a people who was in the majority opposed to the new regime. Even Heinrich Mann, who usually thought quite clearly in other contexts, reflected this illusion when he wrote in 1933: "The national socialists would get only 20 percent of the vote in free elections, and the communists certainly more than 60 percent."

In accordance with this perspective, many activists on the left among the artists in exile put their trust almost exclusively in the German working class. As conveyed by the title of a brochure published in Paris in

1938 by Lion Feuchtwanger, Rudolf Leonhard, Heinrich Mann, and Gustav Regler, *Deutsche Arbeiter! Ihr seid die Hoffnung!* (German Workers, You Are Our Hope!), the left expected a strong resistance to the capitalistically oriented Nazi regime. They almost completely omitted the bourgeoisie, from which the other two exile groups primarily emanated, from their deliberations and from their works. In retrospect, this omission seems amazingly shortsighted or at least one-dimensional. But what other support could these activists hope for in their struggle against the brown tide? The support of German industrialists and large landowners, who because they feared communism had chosen Hitler as the militant guarantor of their property rights? The support of the German educated middle class, most of whom were dazzled by the Nazi fascists' tradition-bound concepts of high culture? The support of the German petty bourgeoisie, who were not politically organized before 1933 and therefore were all too ready to follow any loudmouthed demagogue who lured them into his clutches with better employment prospects, slogans touting prosperity, and entertaining options for their leisure time? The support of the Western democracies, who made one concession after another to Hitler as part of their policies of appeasement? What other options did these activists have than to place their hopes in the power of resistance of those workers who had voted for the German Communist Party before 1933 and to whom the Soviet Union, extolled as a state without unemployed, had been advertised as a model for the future?

The most active phase of these antifascist efforts occurred between 1935 and 1938 as a popular front movement began to assert itself temporarily in France and the eyes of many of the apolitical artists in exile were opened to the true nature of German fascism and to the related anticommunist attitude in the Western democracies. After all, almost all of those who had been forced out of Germany or had fled between 1933 and 1935 had bitter and even humiliating experiences in the countries of refuge that pretended to be liberal. Almost none of these countries welcomed them with open arms. Most of them had to live with temporary residence permits that could be revoked at any moment. They had seen Hitler's prestige grow in response to the Nazi-friendly politics of Hermann Rauschning, president of the senate of the free city of Danzig, the concordat with the pope signed in July 1933, the Haavara Agreement with the World Zionist Organization in August of the same year, the overwhelming electoral victory of the NSDAP in the Saar region in 1935, and the Olympic games in Berlin in 1936. Eye-opening political events followed shortly afterward, such as the fascist victory in the Spanish Civil War, the so-called Anschluß of Austria, the disgraceful Munich Agreement, and the military occupation of Czechoslovakia.

Many exiles concluded that the West not only grudgingly tolerated the advance of Nazi fascism, they were already trying to use Hitler as an ally in their struggle against communism. Foreseeing this development, Kurt Tucholsky had written in 1933 to Arnold Zweig about the Third Reich that had just been founded, "This regime is being supported by the whole world because it's acting against the workers." After the events of the years 1936 through 1938, even some bourgeois authors such as Thomas Mann experienced their political Damascus. His essay *Dieser Friede* (1938; This Peace), which was highly important from the point of view of contemporary politics, was written after the Munich Agreement between Adolf Hitler, Benito Mussolini, Édouard Daladier, and Neville Chamberlain. In it, he wrote that up to that point he had "not been enough of a politician" to figure out that the "non-intervention comedy to aid and abet Franco" and the "betrayal of the Czechoslovakian republic" were examples of English "knavery." "Fear of socialism and of Russia," he explained, had brought about the "self-abandonment of democracy as an intellectual-political position" in the course of the year. It suddenly dawned on him that "this Europe doesn't really want the downfall of the national socialist dictatorship." After this, he posited "social democracy," not liberal democracy, as the real antithesis to fascism.

Some of the staunchest opponents of Hitler among the exiles and their new allies derived their concepts of culture from this position. Admittedly, even among the supporters of a popular front who wanted to bring all Hitler refugees under one ideological umbrella, there was no clearly recognizable political line. Although the activists on the left and the individual bourgeois artists who sympathized with them were generally united in their antifascism, they propagated cultural and aesthetic ideas that were quite different, even during these years. Those who came from the more or less apolitical camp continued to believe that a cosmopolitan attitude was the best position from which to oppose Nazi fascism; therefore, they emphasized everything in Germany's cultural heritage that could be characterized as humanistic or as concerned with social issues in a liberal-democratic sense. Of course, they always stayed within the framework of high culture, paying no attention to low agitprop forms of art. Those seemed to them too vulgar or possibly even fascist or fascistoid. They believed that only the highest cultural achievements were good enough to set against the cultural void that was Nazi fascism, against what they believed was a barbarism that scorned all forms of serious art. They pitted cultural greats such as Albrecht Dürer, Johann Wolfgang Goethe, and Ludwig van Beethoven against Hitler, not Bertolt Brecht, Charlie Chaplin, and Hanns Eisler, and certainly not Karl Marx, Friedrich Engels, and Rosa Luxemburg.

Even most of the antifascist activists who were leftists had nothing against the highly esteemed giants of traditional German culture. Since Franz Mehring, an undisguised cult of the classical writers reigned even in their ranks, but it was based not only on a feeling of uncritical veneration, but on the principle of dialectic sublation in Hegel's sense as well. And this double perspective led to many political-aesthetic differences among the exiled artists on the left. The Moscow Group around Georg Lukács continued to venerate the culture of Goethe's time and largely rejected modernistic art, leading Thomas Mann to characterize Lukács later as "the most important literary scholar of the twentieth century." Activists such as Bertolt Brecht, on the other hand, insisted on pointing out the middle-class attitudes reflected in this position. Instead of "simultaneously rescuing and distorting" the humanistic ideals of Goethe's time into socialism, as Brecht put it, we should be targeting an art and a culture that correspond to socioeconomic relations that have been fundamentally transformed by the development of industrial modes of production and the emergence of the proletariat. A socialist viewpoint is essential, according to Brecht, but he also advised leftist artists to adopt the avant-garde stylistic devices used by the very contemporary art Lukács condemned.

It was primarily in 1937 on the occasion of the so-called expressionism debate that controversy arose between these two positions. Georg Lukács and Alfred Kurella supported the thesis that an unrevolutionary irrationalism, which had later proved advantageous to Nazi fascism, was fundamental to almost all avant-garde types of art—and they listed primarily expressionist authors such as Gottfried Benn, Arnolt Bronnen, and Hanns Johst as examples. But that was not all. In the end, Lukács and Kurella condemned any kind of modern art—art that was elitist, unrealistic, or led to a disintegration of form—as alien to the volk and therefore symptomatic of the decadence of a dying bourgeoisie. This viewpoint was contradicted by exile artists and theorists such as Bertolt Brecht, Ernst Bloch, and Hanns Eisler, who continued to value stylistic elements of the avant-garde left. This led unavoidably to a split into groups that attacked each other more or less openly, calling each other orthodox or formalist, respectively.

However, the political events that followed on the heels of this debate—the Moscow show trials, the so-called Anschluß of Austria onto the Greater German Reich, the Munich Agreement, *Kristallnacht*, the occupation of Czechoslovakia by German troops, the German-Soviet Nonaggression Pact, and the beginning of World War II—prevented these two groups from reaching an agreement or even some kind of coerced reconciliation. After the invasion of Poland by the *Wehrmacht* on 1 September 1939, hardly any further cultural debates occurred in the exile community. As in early 1933, all those who had been driven out of Germany and Austria and in many cases had been staying in the countries around the perimeter of the Third Reich now had to save their own lives first of all. Most of them had to flee overseas—to Shanghai, Mauritius, Cuba, Mexico, or to the United States.

This displacement led unavoidably to a completely different attitude toward Nazi Germany. Due to the distance from Europe, almost unimaginable at the time, as well as to the beginning of total war and reports about extermination camps such as Auschwitz, the exiles' relationship to politics—even among those who had thus far been activists—became more strongly imbued with emotion. The feeling that they were Germans too at a time when the whole world suddenly hated and condemned Hitler Germany unnerved almost all the artists in exile—both conservative Hitler refugees such as Franz Werfel and Emil Ludwig, who now supported the thesis of collective guilt at meetings and in radio speeches, as well as a number of leftists who had hitherto been actively militant. There was a danger that the exiles, even the actively antifascist groups, might abandon the catchphrase of the "other, better Germany." In the context of the changing political conditions, it had become all too clear that the fact of being German in and of itself did not bind together. Now, even Hitler opponents in the left-liberal to left camp began to speculate about what was German in and of itself. This led some to a fundamental renunciation of their "fatherland which had gone to the devil years ago" and thus to an abandonment of the cultural concepts they had held thus far. For some of the former activists, the feeling that they were living in exile suddenly diminished. After 1945, despite the possibility of returning home, many therefore remained in their respective host countries. In the final analysis, only the ideologically unshakeable core of this group decided to return to Germany. Most of them returned to the Soviet Zone of Occupation and not to the western part of Germany, where an anticommunist ideology vigorously supported by the United States spread after 1946–1947 and opposed all concepts of culture based on democratic socialism.

PLACES OF REFUGE

For the writers, journalists, filmmakers, painters, composers, conductors, and musicians driven out of Germany after 1933, the decision about which place of refuge to choose was dependent on two factors. Either they went to countries in which they had friends or relatives who offered them the necessary initial financial assistance or they chose countries where they hoped to find a meaningful sphere in which they could have an impact in accord with their professional training or their political orientation. Both decisions were relatively difficult, because at that time most Germans, even the artists among them, had few connections abroad. This was particularly true for those writers, journalists, and actors who up to that point—still with no inkling of the globalization that was looming—had remained mostly in German-speaking areas. But even many painters and composers had exhibited or performed their works almost exclusively in Germany before 1933 and therefore had only come into contact with other cultures in exceptional cases.

"Now Where?" was the anxious question which Heinrich Heine had used almost one hundred years before as the title for one of his poems following the failed Revolution of 1848. This question was also a difficult one for most of the artists who were expelled from the Third Reich. After the events in January/February 1933, many of them initially hoped or believed that the Hitler scare would not last long. Therefore, they remained for the time being in countries that bordered directly on Germany where they could follow the events in their former Heimat as closely as possible. These countries—primarily the Soviet Union, Czechoslovakia, Switzerland, France, Belgium, Holland, England, Denmark, and Sweden—received them more or less reluctantly. Some of them went to Austria because of the language if for no other reason, but they did not last long there due to the quickly increasing level of fascism in that country. Although they had large German-speaking populations, both Hungary and Poland were excluded from the outset as an option for the activists among the exiles because of the reactionary regimes in power in those countries.

The hard core of artists who sympathized with the KPD or were even party members went first to the USSR after 1933. Among them were Johannes R. Becher, Klara Blum, Willi Bredel, Ernst Fischer, Alexander Granach, Julius Hay, Alfred Kurella, Theodor Plivier, Gustav von Wangenheim, Erich Weinert, Friedrich Wolf, and temporarily also Ernst Busch, Hanns Eisler, and Erwin Piscator. A short notation by the Marxist literary critic Ernst Fischer perhaps expresses best the feelings of many of these leftist artists and cultural theorists who had viewed themselves as partisans of the Soviet Union at their arrival in the country: "What a happy feeling—a country exists whose national anthem is the International, a country in which all the things have triumphed for which you are shot, tortured, or imprisoned in capitalist countries. We are not arriving as guests, we are arriving as people who are in need of their homeland."

But these exuberant feelings were not to last long. This was already apparent in 1934 at the All-Union Congress, where Maxim Gorki spoke in support of the doctrine of socialist realism, and where the German left was represented by the Moscow Group and also by Oskar Maria Graf, Gustav Regler, and Ernst Toller. The communists who had been driven out of the Third Reich and who had lost the final battle with the Nazi fascists one year before were paid little attention, in contrast to the leftists from France. Hanns Eisler and Erwin Piscator, both part of the artistic avant-garde, could see that the effects of this congress would limit any possibilities for them to have an impact in the future, and they soon left the Soviet Union. Red architects, too, such as Ernst May and Bruno Taut, were not able to tolerate living in the USSR for long. Later, there was a series of German language theater productions in Moscow and in Engels, the capital of the German Volga Republic. And there were journals such as *Internationale Literatur* and *Das Wort* (The Word), which published important exile novels by Willi Bredel, Lion Feuchtwanger, Theodor Plivier, and Anna Seghers and in which influential statements concerning cultural policy appeared. But the initial wave of enthusiasm for the Soviet Union gradually died down in the course of the 1930s even among those German artists in exile who were the most convinced communists. The primary reasons were the Moscow show trials, the shooting, imprisonment, or deportation of so-called Trotskyites and other opponents of Stalin, and the German-Soviet Nonaggression Pact of 1939, all of which prompted the exiles to have serious doubts about the views they had held up to that time. Therefore there were few German refugees who went to the Soviet Union after 1938–1939, and the cultural activities of the exiles who had remained in Moscow ground largely to a halt. This group had still been convinced in the mid-1930s that the popular front policies they were actively supporting would make an important contribution to a spirit of militant antifascism. But now a sense of ideological paralysis set in, which was replaced by a new spirit of activism only after 1943 as the *Wehrmacht* was forced, following the debacle of Stalingrad, to yield step by step the territory they had conquered. This development gave the German artists in Moscow the hope that after the collapse of the Third Reich they might be able to construct a socialist culture in their former homeland that would remain free both of degeneration into Nazi fascist racism and of any capitalist-inspired commercial perversions as well. The cult of the German classics, which was in favor in the USSR, provided them with prototypes, and in the new works they planned to create, they intended to apply the doctrines of socialist realism, which had been the foundation of Soviet cultural policy since 1934.

Because Czechoslovakia was overrun by Nazi troops in March 1939, the German exiles had little time to develop anything on a grand scale there. Nevertheless, the extent of the antifascist cultural activities they initiated in the short period of time between 1933 and 1938 is beyond astonishing. In Prague, they published left-oriented newspapers and journals such as *Der Gegenangriff* (The Counterattack), *Die neue Weltbühne* (The New International Stage), the *Neue deutsche Blätter* (The New German Pages), and the *Arbeiter-Illustrierte Zeitung aller Länder* (The Workers' Illustrated International Newspaper) with editors such as Hermann Budzislawski, Oskar Maria Graf, Wieland Herzfelde, Willi Münzenberg, Willi Schlamm, and Anna Seghers. They also performed compositions by Hanns Eisler and Karl Amadeus Hartmann and exhibited a series of extremely

Figure 38. Johannes Wüsten: *Lenin* (1933).

aggressive Hitler satires by John Heartfield in the Galerie Mánes despite objections by the Nazi embassy. They tried to continue the work of the League of Proletarian and Revolutionary Writers with the collaboration of Willi Bredel, Louis Fürnberg, Oskar Maria Graf, Stefan Heym, Ernst Ottwalt, Adam Scharrer, Alex Wedding, Franz Carl Weiskopf, Johannes Wüsten, and Hedda Zinner. They founded a Hans Otto Club and a Bertolt Brecht Club and staged plays and scenes by dramatists who had been expelled from Germany in the Urania Society in Prague. The former Dadaist and communist Wieland Herzfelde was even able to re-establish his Berlin Malik-Verlag in Prague, where he published the first two volumes of Bertolt Brecht's early plays in 1938.

All of this was possible in part because after the dissolution of the Habsburg empire in 1918 approximately 25 percent of the population living in the Czechoslovakian republic still spoke German. In addition, the liberal Prague government under Tomaš Masaryk and Eduard Beneš did not curry favor with the Nazi regime by pursuing a policy of appeasement; on the contrary, they granted Czech citizenship to individual exiles such as Heinrich and Thomas Mann to guarantee their personal safety and also open unlimited travel possibilities to them. In individual cases, they even showed support for the antifascist bias of the German-language newspapers being published in Prague. They did not intervene, for example, when the editors of the leftist *Neue deutsche Blätter* published the first issue in 1933 in the spirit of the motto "Anyone who writes, acts" with the following statement: "In Germany, the National Socialists are on a rampage. We are in a state of war. There is no neutrality. Least of all for writers. Even those who are silent are participating in the struggle. Anyone who, shocked and stunned by events, flees into an existence that is solely private, anyone who uses the weapon of words as a toy or as ornamentation, anyone who subsides into detached resignation—those persons condemn themselves to social and artistic sterility and yield to our opponent. Therefore: literature of distinction today must be antifascist." The ideas about culture developed by the activist exile artists who had fled to Prague largely conformed to the statements made by the Moscow Group up to the signing of the German-Soviet Nonaggression Pact in fall 1939. Of course, the Prague exiles had to retreat to other countries, primarily France, in spring 1939 when German troops marched into Czechoslovakia.

In Paris, a large colony of refugees had established itself in 1933; they did not enjoy the same goodwill on the part of the government as the Prague group did, but they still organized impressive activities that were in most cases left-oriented. Citing earlier German exiles such as Georg Forster, Ludwig Börne, Heinrich Heine, and Karl Marx, who had also lived in exile in Paris, many of these Hitler refugees continued to view France as a country with a highly significant cultural tradition and also as the country in which (before the Russian October Revolution of 1917) most progressive revolutions had taken place. Here they hoped to find energetic support from both local artists and broad sectors of the French population for their struggle against Nazi fascism. Although they experienced numerous disappointments in this regard, they continued to appeal to the French left again and again for support. And they succeeded to some extent, because there was a relatively strong Communist Party in France that even supported the incumbent government during the so-called popular front period in the mid-1930s; nothing comparable occurred in other Western countries.

Thus it was in Paris that the *Braunbuch über den Reichstagsbrand und Hitlerterror* (Brown Book on the Reichstag Fire and Hitler Terror), which challenged the reader to a sharp confrontation with the Nazi regime, was published by Editions du Carrefour headed by Willi Münzenberg as early as 1933. It was the most successful book of the entire body of exile literature; it was translated into fifteen languages, and by 1935, six hundred thousand copies had been printed. At the same time, an Association for the Protection of German Writers under the chairmanship

Figure 39. Bodo Uhse, Lion Feuchtwanger, and Anna Seghers in the Bibliothek der verbrannten Bücher in Paris (Library of Burned Books, 1936).

of Rudolf Leonhard was founded, also in Paris. It represented the publishing rights of various exile authors and also organized several political lecture series with the slogan "German writers of all countries, unite"; Johannes R. Becher, Ernst Bloch, Walter Benjamin, Alfred Döblin, Lion Feuchtwanger, Heinrich Mann, and Friedrich Wolf, among others, participated as speakers. In addition, a library of burned books was opened in Paris in 1934 with the support of André Gide, Romain Rolland, Bertrand Russell, and HG Wells; it was later called the Deutsche Freiheitsbibliothek (German Freedom Library) and had an inventory of twenty thousand books. Several German-language periodicals were published in Paris in subsequent years, including the *Neues Tage-Buch* (New Daily Diary) edited by Leopold Schwarzschild, Hermann Budzislawski's *Neue Weltbühne*, which had transferred from Prague to Paris, and the *Pariser Tageblatt* and *Pariser Zeitung*, in which cultural politics, of special interest to many of the exiles, played a significant role. There were even scattered productions of German exile plays; Bertolt Brecht's *Die sieben Todsünden* (The Seven Deadly Sins), *Die Gewehre der Frau Carrar* (Senora Carrar's Rifles), and some scenes from *Furcht und Elend des Dritten Reiches* (Fear and Misery of the Third Reich) in particular did not go unnoticed.

But the real high point of German exile activity in Paris was the popular front conference In Defense of Culture held on 21–25 June 1935; approximately one hundred writers from no fewer than twenty-eight countries took part. Although the stimulus for the conference came from the French side, fifteen Soviet and twenty German authors, among others, participated. A particular sensation was created by the communist underground author Jan Petersen, who had traveled to the conference from Berlin. He covered his face with a mask, and his text was read by André Gide in French translation. In accordance with the title of the conference, all the lectures were concerned with the question of how culture could be used most effectively to oppose National Socialist barbarism. With the exception of Robert Musil, who advocated a strict separation of politics and culture, almost all the other speakers declared their support for literary activism that invoked the inviolable fundamental values of tried-and-true humanism—love of freedom, dignity, and justice. Most of the German-speaking participants were members of the educated middle class, and they still believed high art possessed a force that could transform the world. But it was, they claimed, in danger of being brutally obliterated under the Nazi fascist regime. Bertolt Brecht, who felt that the one-sided appeal to humanism was Tui-like, was one of the few to broach the materialist topic of property rights with the intent of being provocative. His leftist comrades tried immediately to point out to him, however, that since they were trying to develop a popular front strategy, it was no longer appropriate to express support for a proletarian united front. In the struggle against Nazi fascism, it was necessary to ensure the support of "bourgeois-progressive artists" as well, as Alexander Abusch formulated it in his *Die Verteidigung der deutschen Kultur und die Volksfront* (The Defense of German Culture and the Popular Front). The concept of culture that emerged from this conference did not go so far as to separate politics and art, but it did continue to endorse an artistic endeavor that proceeded from lofty literary imperatives even in its struggle against the low-minded anti-spirit of the Nazi fascists. No serious attention was paid to the kind of agitprop art in the spirit of Bertolt Brecht or Hanns Eisler that would also involve the broad masses.

But at least the beginnings of solidarity among the widely scattered exiles had been established at the Paris conference. In other democracies of Western and Northern Europe, similar activities were paid little attention or were prevented from the outset by local authorities, who usually viewed them as an attempt at communist infiltration and who also hoped to avoid any political confrontation with the German fascists and their diplomatic missions. This was particularly true in Switzerland. There, traditional German culture continued to be widely esteemed. But among the educated middle class—based partly on an inveterate awareness of tradition and probably also based on their fear of the overwhelmingly powerful so-called German brother country in the north—a rather inhospitable feeling toward the German exiles spread. The Frontists, who were fascist sympathizers, held public protest demonstrations in which they opposed the alleged agitation of the emigrants. They campaigned against the Jewish emigrant cabaret Die Pfeffermühle (The Peppermill), founded by Erika Mann in November 1933, and against productions in Zurich of Friedrich Wolf's *Professor Mamlock* and Ferdinand Bruckner's *Die Rassen* (The Races), demanding a radical "purging of the entire foreign emigrant vermin from Switzerland." The local authorities shared these prejudices, and urged that the infamous red J should be stamped in the passports of all Jewish exiles.

Even non-Jewish emigrants, such as the antifascist playwright Georg Kaiser, were not received very favorably in Switzerland. Their options for publishing literary works were restricted, for example; the goal was to prevent the distribution of political writings—in other words, writings opposed to the Third Reich. Not until the second half of the 1930s did these neutralizing appeasement policies yield to somewhat greater tolerance. But even then there were clearly defined limits. Thomas Mann and Konrad Falke were able to publish *Maß und Wert* (Norm and Value), the "bimonthly journal for free German culture," in the Oprecht publishing house in Zurich beginning in 1937. But they adopted an apolitical stance,

Figure 40. Bertolt Brecht, Johannes R. Becher, Ilja Ehrenburg, and Gustav Regler at the International Writers' Congress "Zur Verteidigung der Kultur" in Paris ("In Defense of Culture" in Paris, 1935). From the book by Werner Hecht: *Bertolt Brecht. Sein Leben in Texten und Bildern*, Frankfurt 1978.

avoiding any statements that might sound activist. In this journal, art and culture were understood as the highest expressions of the bourgeois ethos that could be fielded against what was described in generalized terms as the opinionated trash that was increasingly polluting contemporary cultural life. In 1940, however, as fear of unspecified greater German cravings on the part of the Nazi government increased following Germany's victory over France, even *Maß und Wert* had to be discontinued. In 1942 the Swiss immigration authorities, having already substantially reduced the right to asylum in 1937, decided not to allow any further refugees into the country. As fear of the big brother to the north gradually diminished in the following two years due to the first defeats of Hitler's armies in the Soviet Union, the Swiss authorities decided to grant the German exiles who were already resident some possibilities of having an impact. This was particularly true for the Zürcher Schauspielhaus (the Zurich theater), where several Brecht plays were performed for the first time toward the end of World War II with the participation of Therese Giehse, Wolfgang Langhoff, and Leonard Steckel.

Some other West European and North European countries took similar stances as the first Hitler refugees began to arrive. The Belgian government also adopted a temporizing position of appeasing the Third Reich. In 1938, Belgium, like Switzerland, issued a ban on any kind of political activity by the German exiles and even threatened to expel them or de-port them to Germany if they violated this order. Holland was somewhat more tolerant toward the refugees, especially because there was a Jewish minority there with distinctly liberal views. The energetic support provided to fugitive writers by the Amsterdam publishing houses Querido and Allert de Lange is evidence of this tolerance. With the help of Fritz Landshoff and Walter Landauer, they published a considerable number of works by authors who had published with Kiepenheuer, Ullstein, Insel, and Rowohlt in Germany; they also published the antifascist monthly *Die Sammlung* (The Collection), established in fall 1933 by Klaus Mann with the patronage of Heinrich Mann, André Gide, and Aldous Huxley. As a result, a remarkable series of the books now considered to be the most important works of German antifascist exile literature appeared in these two publishing houses—works by authors from Günther Anders through Bertolt Brecht, Alfred Döblin, Lion Feuchtwanger, Leonhard Frank, Hermann Kesten, Irmgard Keun, Egon Erwin Kisch, Heinrich Mann, Gustav Regler, Joseph Roth, Anna Seghers, and Ernst Toller all the way to Arnold Zweig.

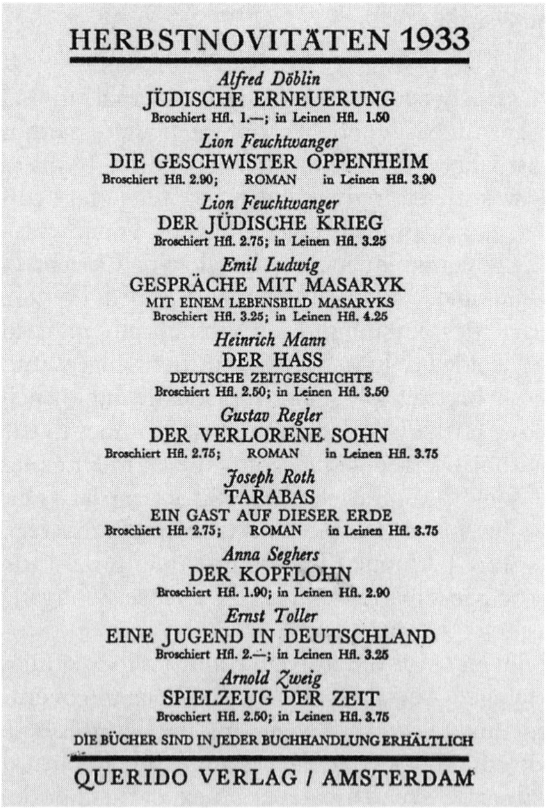

HERBSTNOVITÄTEN 1933

Alfred Döblin
JÜDISCHE ERNEUERUNG
Broschiert Hfl. 1.—; in Leinen Hfl. 1.50

Lion Feuchtwanger
DIE GESCHWISTER OPPENHEIM
Broschiert Hfl. 2.90; ROMAN in Leinen Hfl. 3.90

Lion Feuchtwanger
DER JÜDISCHE KRIEG
Broschiert Hfl. 2.75; in Leinen Hfl. 3.25

Emil Ludwig
GESPRÄCHE MIT MASARYK
MIT EINEM LEBENSBILD MASARYKS
Broschiert Hfl. 3.25; in Leinen Hfl. 4.25

Heinrich Mann
DER HASS
DEUTSCHE ZEITGESCHICHTE
Broschiert Hfl. 2.50; in Leinen Hfl. 3.50

Gustav Regler
DER VERLORENE SOHN
Broschiert Hfl. 2.75; ROMAN in Leinen Hfl. 3.75

Joseph Roth
TARABAS
EIN GAST AUF DIESER ERDE
Broschiert Hfl. 2.75; ROMAN in Leinen Hfl. 3.75

Anna Seghers
DER KOPFLOHN
Broschiert Hfl. 1.90; in Leinen Hfl. 2.90

Ernst Toller
EINE JUGEND IN DEUTSCHLAND
Broschiert Hfl. 2.—; in Leinen Hfl. 3.25

Arnold Zweig
SPIELZEUG DER ZEIT
Broschiert Hfl. 2.50; in Leinen Hfl. 3.75

DIE BÜCHER SIND IN JEDER BUCHHANDLUNG ERHÄLTLICH

QUERIDO VERLAG / AMSTERDAM

Figure 41. List of new publications by Querido-Verlag in Amsterdam of works by leading German exile authors in fall 1933.

Not even England, one of the other liberal democracies during these years, can boast of having contributed as much to the publication and distribution of German exile literature as these two Amsterdam houses. As we know, a policy of appeasement toward the Nazi Reich was maintained relatively strictly in England during the mid-1930s until the Munich Agreement in 1938. For this reason, many German exiles had substantial visa problems on arrival there. Like France, it had suffered for a long time from the effects of the world economic crisis, and most refugees could only flee to England if they had already submitted a work permit from a British government agency or from a private firm. Still, many of the exiles who held liberal or middle-class views preferred to try to get a residence permit in England, whatever the cost, rather than going to the far-off United States, to restive France, suffering from a so-called plague of leftists, or to the Soviet Union. It is not surprising, therefore, that most of the exiled German artists in England tried to hold on to their earlier cultural concepts. With this in mind, they founded a series of cultural organizations in London in which they could keep mostly to themselves. Probably the most important was the Freie Deutsche Kulturbund (Free German Cultural League), founded in 1938 with the significant participation of Oskar Kokoschka, Berthold Viertel, and Stefan Zweig. But by 1940, its activities dropped off significantly as approximately seventeen thousand Germans who had fled to England were interned on the orders of Winston Churchill, with his imperious directive, "Collar the lot!" The Neue Deutsche PEN-Sektion (New German PEN Section) under its president Alfred Kerr as well as a group of independent authors around Kurt Hiller also tried to make themselves heard. But they did not attract much attention. And the British took hardly any notice of performances by small theaters and cabarets founded by writers in exile.

Considering all the difficulties German expellees faced in the Soviet Union and in some of the Western democracies, we have to ask why so few German artists went to Palestine after 1933. After all, an overwhelming majority of them were Jewish born, as it was termed at the time. We might think that would have moved them to seek a new home in the land of their origins. But for the following reasons, very few even considered this option. First, in 1933, Palestine—in contrast to Prague, Paris, or London—seemed simply much too far away to most of them. Second, most of them were assimilated Western Jews, and they feared that in Palestine they would end up in the same orthodox ghetto that their ancestors had finally eluded by relocating from Eastern Europe to the Habsburg empire or to Germany. And third—and this was usually the decisive reason—they as former members of the German educated middle class did not want to move to a tropically hot country settled mostly by

Muslims, a land purportedly without culture, where there were neither theaters, opera houses, symphony orchestras, museums, nor libraries and where there was no German language press. In addition, almost none of them understood a word of modern Hebrew, a language that because of its ostensibly peculiar letters seemed much stranger to them than French or English. Even those German-Jewish artists who had developed Zionistic leanings during the Weimar Republic or in the crucial year of 1933 decided almost without exception against emigrating to Palestine. In Paris, Alfred Döblin joined the Yiddish-speaking Freyland-Bewegung (Movement for a Free Territory), which had no intention of returning to Palestine; instead, because they were representing the so-called territorialists, they were seeking overseas settlement colonies for the Jews in Angola, Argentina, or Madagascar. Even a rabid Zionist like Arnold Schoenberg realized after some hesitation that there would be no scope for him as a modernist composer in a presumably culturally backward country like Palestine, and he therefore decided to emigrate first to Paris and then to the United States.

Among those who did go to Palestine were Max Brod, Louis Fürnberg, Else Lasker-Schüler, and Arnold Zweig. In 1925, Zweig had written in his book *Das neue Kanaan* (The New Canaan) a description of a utopian Jewish state on Palestinian soil in which Jews, Christians, and Muslims would someday live together in peace as in a "small leftist Switzerland." But even he could see shortly after his arrival in Haifa that he was in a foreign place. After all, in this area, German was viewed as the language of Hitler and not as the language of Goethe; thus, many right-wing Zionists, consistent with their efforts on behalf of an integrated nation, confronted the German emigrants in a militant tone with the slogan, "Speak Hebrew—or die!" Despite everything, Zweig, together with Wolfgang Yourgrau, founded the *Unabhängige Wochenschrift für Zeitfragen, Kultur, Wirtschaft* (Independent Weekly for Current Issues, Culture, and the Economy) in 1942—which by order of the British Mandate had to be titled *Orient*, although its layout was intended to remind readers of the earlier *Weltbühne*. His intention was to confront the widespread Germanophobia, but the right-wing Zionists, in their hatred of everything German, simply blew up the journal's printing plant. Full of bitterness, he let himself get carried away to the point of characterizing them in his letters to Lion Feuchtwanger as Jewish Nazis. After the end of World War II, Zweig left Palestine and, being a resolute antifascist, moved to East Berlin. He had written in *Orient* that Germany should be given the opportunity to do a "political turnaround" after the war and perhaps even to change over to "communism," instead of being condemned wholesale.

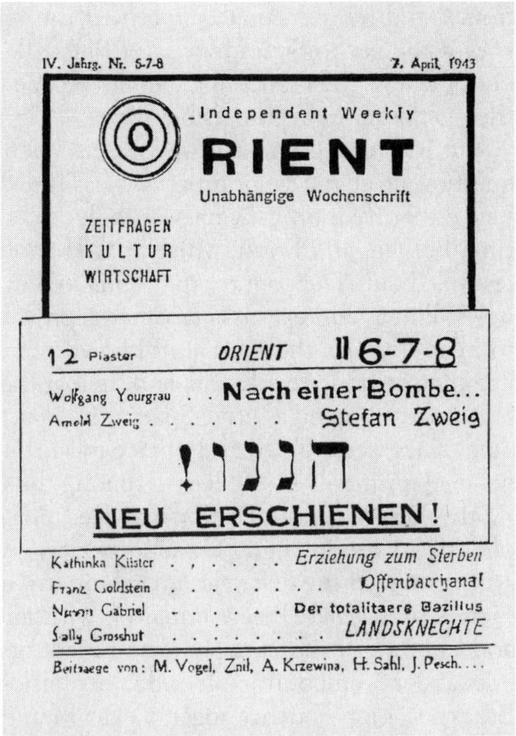

IV. Jahrg. Nr. 5-7-8 — 7. April 1943

Independent Weekly

ORIENT

Unabhängige Wochenschrift

ZEITFRAGEN
KULTUR
WIRTSCHAFT

12 Piaster — ORIENT — II 6-7-8

Wolfgang Yourgrau . . Nach einer Bombe...
Arnold Zweig . . . . Stefan Zweig

הננו!

NEU ERSCHIENEN!

Kathinka Küster . . . . Erziehung zum Sterben
Franz Goldstein . . . . Offenbacchanal
[illegible] Gabriel . . . . Der totalitaere Bazillus
Sally Grosshut . . . . LANDSKNECHTE

Beitraege von: M. Vogel, Znil, A. Krzewina, H. Sahl, J. Pesch. . . .

Figure 42. Title page of the 7 April 1943 issue of the journal *Orient* published in Tel Aviv.

Between 1933 and 1938, it was usually individuals or small groups who left Germany to go into exile, but after 1938, the number grew larger from one month to the next. This mass exodus was the result of several events: first, it was the Austrian Anschluß, then the so-called Kristallnacht, the occupation of Czechoslovakia, and finally the invasion of Holland, Belgium, and France by the *Wehrmacht*. But wherever the exiles turned, they were almost always met with an outcry of protest: "The boat is already full." After 1937, even refuge in Palestine was closed to them; British authorities rejected further Jewish immigration because they did not want the area to become a flash point for political, religious, and ethnic tensions. Approximately twenty thousand Jews who had been turned away everywhere decided in their desperation to go to distant Shanghai, where there were few visa problems. For others, the path disappeared into darkness. We have the best information about the fates of those artists who were in Paris in 1940 when the German troops began their blitzkrieg against France. Most of them retreated to southern France. But this withdrawal did not help them much because the government that the Nazi fascists had installed there under Marshall Philippe Pétain was both anti-left and anti-Semitic. His slogan was "Better Hitler than the popular front," and he immediately interned the refugees in camps from which they could get to Spain by way of Marseille or the Pyrenees and then—out of fear of the Franco regime—to escape to a Portuguese port city and then get as far away as possible.

But where to go next? They were suddenly confronted with the same question as at the beginning of the Third Reich. Almost everyone believed that their only escape was to flee overseas. South America, Argentina, Bolivia, and Brazil, which balked at admitting them, were more or less ruled out. The country that remained was Mexico, which at the time was still in a half revolutionary mood; previously it had even given refuge to Leon Trotsky, the most well-known representative of the ideology of communist world revolution, and then at the end of the Spanish civil war to twenty thousand fugitive Spaniards. Approximately two thousand German exiles were able to find a place in Mexico. After 1942, this group was made up primarily of the leftists among the German artists who, inspired by the heroic resistance that the Red Army in the Soviet Union was offering to the invading German troops, continued to have communist sympathies. In the first year after their arrival, they founded the monthly *Freies Deutschland* (Free Germany), with an emphasis on cultural policy and militant antifascism. Under the editorship of Bruno Frei and later Alexander Abusch, it published contributions by Ernst Bloch, Ferdinand Bruckner, Lion Feuchtwanger, Oskar Maria Graf, Leo Katz, Egon Erwin Kisch, Theodor Plivier, Anna Seghers, Bodo Uhse, and Paul Westheim. To compensate for the lack of European culture, which they experienced as a bitter loss, many members of this group banded together in a Heinrich Heine Club. Under the leadership of Egon Erwin Kisch and Bodo Uhse, the club organized readings, concerts, and theater performances in Mexico City for over four years. But in their eyes the founding of the El Libro Libre publishing house, which soon became the primary German-language exile publisher in all of Central and South America, was their most significant activity. After 1942, it published the most important exile novels by Lion Feuchtwanger, Leo Katz, Heinrich Mann, Ludwig Renn, Anna Seghers, Bodo Uhse, and Franz Carl Weiskopf in rapid succession. These were the same authors who collaborated on the journal *Freies Deutschland*, which was soon to be renamed *Neues Deutschland*.

But the majority of the artists who had fled from Germany, Austria, and Czechoslovakia went to the United States after 1939–1940. Here, too, they had to surmount difficult obstacles in the beginning: there were relatively strict quotas and isolationist—in other words, xenophobic—press campaigns. But in this country, there were also counter-reactions. Several Jewish aid organizations were the most energetic in countering such difficulties, and they even financed the cost of passage for a series of prominent refugees. In addition, there was an American Guild for German Cultural Freedom active in the United States which for a time espoused the establishment of a German Academy of Art with Thomas Mann as its president. Efforts of this kind, including the easing of immigration regulations through the relentless activity of a newly constituted Emergency Rescue Committee, had a definite impact. As a result, after Arnold Schoenberg and Thomas Mann had relocated to the United States in 1934 and 1938, respectively, a vast number of other German and Austrian artists arrived in New York, Los Angeles, or other American port cities, among them Hermann Broch, Bertolt Brecht, Alfred Döblin, Hanns Eisler, Lion Feuchtwanger, Bruno Frank, Leonhard Frank, Oskar Maria Graf, Paul Hindemith, Ernst Krenek, Heinrich Mann, Erich Maria Remarque, Franz Werfel, and Carl Zuckmayer.

Glad to have escaped persecution by the Nazis and European wartime atrocities, these exiles first took a breath of relief, little knowing what awaited them. This was the land of legendary unlimited opportunities, was it not? It had welcomed innumerable persecuted and miserable people as immigrants. But in propounding such sentiments, the large American corporations had always been concerned primarily with recruiting a cheap workforce, not with increasing the number of creative artists. Since the mid-1920s, what had developed in the way of high art in the United States had been forced to accommodate itself with very few exceptions to the desire for profit of the so-called leisure industry or culture industry; in other words, under the pretext of serving democracy, they had to serve the entertainment needs of the broad masses, which promised to be profitable. In most European countries, many artists were still embedded in a cultured middle class or, in some cases, a socialist tradition where they believed themselves to be respected or even leading representatives of their class or of their nation. In the United States, on the other hand, they had arrived in a country where even artists—embedded in a fordist system of mass production—were judged based on their ability to entertain and their income level. This was the attitude that led some Americans to ask the newly arrived exiles naively, "And how much does Hitler earn a month?"

Almost all of the exiles suffered initially from culture shock after their arrival in the United States. While they had at least felt tolerably at home in a cultural sense in most European countries of refuge despite their existential endangerment, they had now ended up suddenly in a country that had neither feudal-aristocratic nor middle-class cultural traditions and therefore placed little value on serious artworks—be they operas, symphonies, plays, lyrical poems, or oil paintings—all of which were considered too arty in the United States. What counted here were musicals, film comedies, bestselling novels, swing, burlesque shows, and comic strips; with them, so it was said, you could make a fast buck. Only an author of popular biographies that would sell well such as Emil Ludwig or a highly paid Nobel Prize winner such as Thomas Mann were met with a certain amount of respect. But what about the other artists among the German and Austrian exiles? Even those who had been fairly well-known in Europe had little or no name recognition in the United States and suddenly sank to the status of nobodies. Bertolt Brecht, for example, was asked again and again, "Mr. Breckt, how do you spell your name?" Arnold Schoenberg provides another example. The composer, who was very famous in Europe, was seated at a banquet in Hollywood to which he had coincidentally been invited. From the mouths of some unimportant but highly paid film composers who sat down next to him came the greeting, "Hi Arnie, who are you? Never heard of you. But your stuff must be good, because otherwise you wouldn't be sitting here."

For most of the artists who had fled to the United States, this meant a decline from an artistic point of view as well as from a social point of view. In this country, where separation between the entertainment industry and politics reigned, who was interested in their works? As a result of latent anti-Semitism and a long-lasting policy of appeasement, Jewish and antifascist themes in the arts were not especially popular in the United States during the 1930s. Benjamin Huebsch, owner of Viking Press, for example, had earned a tidy sum of money on translations of Arnold Zweig's novels about World War I. But knowing that there were approximately one hundred anti-Semitic organizations in the United States, he turned down Zweig's *Bilanz der deutschen Judenheit* (Insulted and Exiled: The Truth about the German Jews) in 1935 as being unacceptable in the United States because of its philo-Semitic bias. Other

Figure 43. Ruth Berlau: Bertolt Brecht and Lion Feuchtwanger in Pacific Palisades (1942). © Berlin, Hilde Hoffmann.

publishing houses as well as the Broadway theaters and the film companies were equally intractable with regard to any works that attacked the Third Reich until the end of 1941, when the United States finally gave up their policy of appeasement. Even then it remained difficult for exiles˙ who had a left-critical viewpoint to present their work in public. Bertolt Brecht, for example, could not find a New York theater in which to produce his plays *Der aufhaltsame Aufstieg des Arturo Ui* (1941; The Resistible Rise of Arturo Ui) and *Schweyk im Zweiten Weltkrieg* (1943; Schweyk in the Second World War). And there was no money to be made in the United States with avant-garde compositions either. The works of Arnold Schoenberg, as well as those by Ernst Krenek and Stefan Wolpe, were almost never performed.

Inevitably, some exiled artists reacted to being underappreciated by developing a cultural arrogance that they displayed openly and that got on the nerves of many Americans. Ernst Bloch, for instance, stated in a speech to the Association for the Protection of German Writers in New York in 1939, for example: "We are full of Europe, there we know what we're doing, we are Athens." But other less pretentious exiles, too, emphasized often that culturally speaking, everything was much more intellectual and sophisticated "at home in Berlin" ("*bei uns in Berlin*") or "at home in Vienna" ("*bei uns in Wien*"), which led many Americans to refer to them as the beiunskis. This was most true of the German or Austrian artists who had gone to Los Angeles because they hoped to make a subsistence income there at least temporarily in the city's enormously bloated film industry. But even that proved to be a false hope in most cases, since almost all of the film scripts they produced so laboriously were rejected by the film companies as not entertaining enough. Even authors such as Heinrich Mann and Alfred Döblin, who were extremely famous in Germany, led an obscure and marginal existence in Los Angeles. In a city where even Hanns Eisler had to hustle with his compositions, a leftist like Bertolt Brecht felt like "Lenin in the Prater." For this reason, while he was in Los Angeles, Brecht gave up his plan to write a Tui novel about all of the European intellectuals and artists who had unabashedly hired out their talents to the ruling class. Everybody here was a Tui, proud to hire out his or her talents as lucratively as possible to the corporate bosses. How could art develop under these circumstances? In these climes, he asked bitterly, had not good art been devalued to art goods long ago? Only once had he seen an "object that resembled art" in this city, he wrote in a cynical-arrogant tone in his *Briefe an einen erwachsenen Amerikaner* (Letters to an Adult American). It was a "candy-colored" banner fluttering behind a motorboat off the Santa Monica beach. But unfortunately, it was actually an ad for a company that made skin lotion. The composer

Paul Hindemith, who was much less politically engaged, expressed himself in an equally ironic style about commercial art in the United States, writing to his wife that there was only one true artist in this country, and he was still underestimated, namely the animator Walt Disney.

Theodor W. Adorno, an elitist admirer of the highest forms of culture, let himself be tempted into making more cutting remarks. In his essay *Kulturindustrie. Aufklärung als Massenbetrug* (The Culture Industry: Enlightenment as Mass Deception), he denounced the shoddy products of the music and film corporations in the United States as the expression of "a society alienated from itself" that applied social engineering strategies that were almost comparable to the propaganda products geared to ideological manipulation in the Third Reich. All of the so-called cultural sector in the United States, he wrote, was dependent on the big corporations' emphasis on conformity with the goal of maximizing profits; they were concerned only with mass production that was as widely marketable as possible. Accordingly, a nonculture dominated in this country, while in Germany—despite the capitalist economic structure that was dominant there as well—the "universities, the artistically influential theaters, the great orchestras, and the museums" had been exempt from the system, at least until the beginning of the Nazi fascist dictatorship. In contrast, a "cult of cheapness" oriented exclusively toward advertising ruled in the United States. He declared apodictically in his essay that the technical and economic "conflation of advertising and the culture industry" in the United States had led to a "demoralization" of the masses and thereby created a commercialized unculture of the worst kind.

Admittedly, not all exiles expressed themselves so sharply about the products of the American leisure industry and the tendency to ideological conformity that governed it. But most German and Austrian exiles were in agreement that there was just no culture in this country. Nevertheless, in contrast to Bertolt Brecht and Theodor W. Adorno, there were some leftists and left liberals who at least found the helpfulness in the private sphere as well as a number of basic democratic assumptions of political and social life to be quite positive. Some even indulged in certain illusions, little suspecting how carefully they were being observed by the agents of the Federal Bureau of Investigation. But it was not until after the end of World War II that the consequences of this surveillance would become ticklish for them. Until that time, even many of the artists who were leftist activists continued to live lives in which their labors attracted hardly any attention, writing works intended for postwar Europe, not for the United States. There were in fact few or no theaters in which their plays could have been performed, no symphony orchestras that could have played their compositions, and no publishing houses that could have published their works in German. So many of them bided their time, without acculturating, as it was characterized even then, and after 1945, as soon as conditions permitted, they tried to return to Europe to help in their own way with the construction of a nonfascist high culture in their former homeland.

Possibilities for an
Effective Antifascism

Neither Joseph Goebbels nor Alfred Rosenberg thought that the leftist and Jewish artists who had been driven out of Germany would react as they did. Faced with the rapidly solidifying power of Nazi fascism and the cautious appeasement policies of many European states, and despite all the difficulties they faced in their countries of refuge, some exiles began immediately in 1933 to expose the brutal and inhuman nature of the Third Reich using both propagandistic and artistic means. Granted, there were also artists among them who simply tried quietly to keep a low profile in their new country; they changed their names, denied their national origin, and adapted to the lifestyle in their new surroundings as best they could. But there were the others, too, who remained Germans even in exile, who thought German, wrote German, and tried to counteract the events inside the Third Reich both politically and artistically. Their thinking usually centered around the following three questions: (1) What had happened to cause a breakdown of the German-Jewish symbiosis in Germany? (2) How had the Nazi fascists achieved such a high level of popularity? (3) How was it possible that a "half-educated, noisy, troublemaker" like Adolf Hitler was welcomed and even worshiped by both the broad masses and many of their highly educated compatriots, who saw him as a charismatic redeemer figure?

Their answers were as diverse as their analyses of fascism. In their interpretive models of German fascism, the exiled artists who thought in Marxist terms usually emphasized the disastrous effects of unemployment since 1929, the political fickleness of the petty bourgeoisie, and the financial support of Rhine-Ruhr industrialists such as Fritz Thyssen for the

Nazis in election campaigns. The bourgeois liberals, on the other hand, rarely considered the socioeconomic reasons for the undeniable successes of NS policies. Their assessments remained largely limited to theories about the superstructure. Most of them tended to interpret this phenomenon, as they referred to it, from the perspective of the history of ideas. In other words, they attributed it to trends toward intellectual leveling or even nihilism; their answer was to confront these trends with a heightened cultural consciousness to avoid contributing to the "decline of the West" that Oswald Spengler had evoked at the beginning of the 1920s. For them, with their restrictive viewpoint based on their class, the chief bastion against the anti-spirit of the brown masters was usually to lay great stress on a high culture of the old stripe, which they saw as the essential foundation of an effective strategy against Nazi fascist barbarism.

Because their views of the Hitler regime varied, these two groups sometimes supported very different strategies for resisting the threat of the brown flood. But they agreed on one point: in any attempt at resistance, the cultural aspect should not be forgotten. Both the bourgeois liberals and the committed leftists among the exiled artists saw themselves as the so-called other, better Germans—as representatives of a culture that was truly concerned with social issues or at least had a serious intellectual content. They wanted to distinguish themselves as clearly as possible from the depraved anticommunist or racist unculture of the tyrannical regime that had set the tone in Germany since 1933. Whether as individuals or in small groups, they wanted to provide for themselves and their co-exiles the feeling of a Heimat of the spirit in which they could better survive the dark night of fascism than if they stood idly by and watched the tyrannical operations of Hitler and his minions. Many assumed that it was their task to defend the honor of German culture even in countries where they had not been welcomed with open arms, and from this they derived a justification of their continuing existence. Many hoped that this position and the works they created in support of it would win allies with similar political views in their respective host countries. They also hoped to create the prerequisites for a future German culture that would emerge after the collapse of Nazi fascism, building on the bourgeois-humanist, liberal-democratic, or socialist traditions of culture during the Weimar Republic.

Let us look first at individual actions against Nazi fascism by the left, which began as early as 1933. Among the most difficult were attempts to smuggle antifascist publications that had been printed abroad into Germany or maintain contact with members of the League of Proletarian-Revolutionary Writers who had gone underground after 1933. Attempts to call attention to Nazi barbarism at international writers congresses abroad were also seldom successful. In late May 1933, for example, the playwright Ernst Toller, who had fled from the Third Reich, spoke out at a conference of the International PEN Club in Ragusa against the book burnings that had taken place a short time before and against the imprisonment of antifascist authors such as Erich Mühsam and Carl von Ossietzky. But the Austrian and Swiss delegates left the room during his speech, and during the subsequent vote on his proposal that crimes of this kind should be publicly condemned, the conservative majority of PEN Club members abstained from voting.

Other exiled writers made similar individual efforts in the name of intellectual freedom for art, but they usually learned that even in the Western democracies, very few were interested in being enlightened and some welcomed rather than condemned the Nazi fascists' anticommunist repressive measures in the cultural sphere. So when Klaus Mann tried to intervene once more on behalf of writers imprisoned in the Third Reich at a PEN Club congress in Barcelona in 1935, the British author HG Wells opposed him, warning the assembled delegates emphatically that that they should not turn the International PEN Club into a club of leftists because the greater danger for literary freedom emanated from the communists and not from the fascists. Similar scenes took place at subsequent congresses of the International PEN Club. A notable example was their congress in Paris in 1936, where the majority of the assembled members attempted to keep everything political out of the debates as far as possible. Only Lion Feuchtwanger got permission to speak in support of Carl von Ossietzky once again; the other German authors in exile who were present—Egon Erwin Kisch, Ludwig Renn, and Anna Seghers—were not allowed to address the congress.

Those exile artists who were politically involved, finding little sympathy in most of the Western host countries, were therefore forced from the outset to found their own associations or clubs and hope they would prove more effective. The founding of the Association for the Protection of German Writers in Paris in October 1933 marked the beginning of this approach, with the word *protection* having a much more literal meaning than it had in the identically named association in the 1920s. The association saw itself as a comprehensive organization for all German writers who had not been brought into line by the Nazis, and approximately 150 authors joined. At the beginning, the leftists, presided over by Johannes R. Becher, Alfred Kantorowicz, Egon Erwin Kisch, and Anna Seghers made up the largest contingent. Shortly after the Communist-inspired popular front policy began in 1934, they began to pay attention to humanist and left-bourgeois exile authors. At that point, Heinrich Mann, who was revered by all ideological contingents, took over the chairmanship of the association.

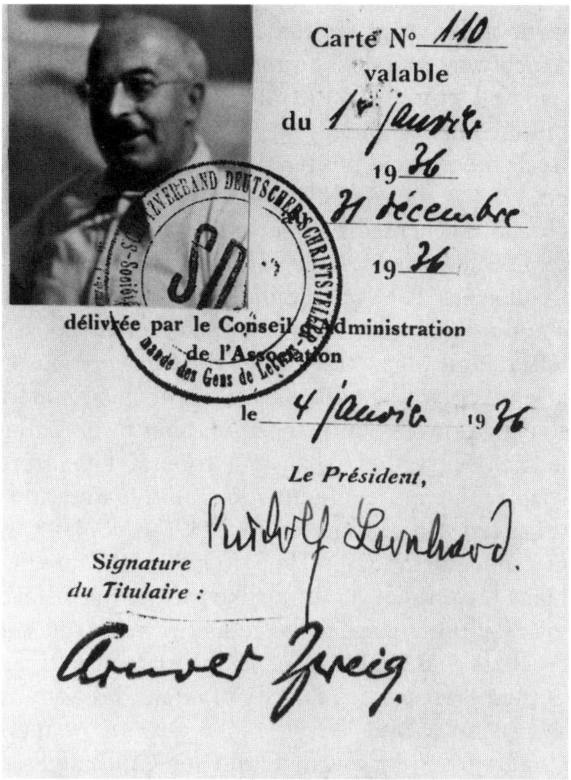

Figure 44. Arnold
Zweig's membership
card for the Schutz-
verband deutscher
Schriftsteller in Paris
(Association for the
Protection of German
Writers in Paris, 1936).

But that remained an isolated case. In other exile organizations of this
type, frictions arose repeatedly between the leftist and bourgeois artists
despite the popular front policy. Even at the popular front congress In Defense of Culture in Paris in 1935, where the mood was rather conciliatory,
these frictions could not be entirely suppressed. In fact, there was not
even unity on the left on some issues at events of this kind. The Union of
the Twelve, for example, which Wieland Herzfelde initiated in Prague—
which was to include himself along with Johannes R. Becher, Bertolt Brecht, Hanns Eisler, Oskar Maria Graf, George Grosz, John Heartfield, Egon
Erwin Kisch, Erwin Piscator, Franz Carl Weiskopf, Arnold Zweig, and a
sculptor yet to be named—was doomed to remain a utopian project. The
same was true of the antifascist Diderot Society that Bertolt Brecht was
contemplating in March 1937; potential members were artists as varied
as WH Auden, Slatan Dudow, Sergei Eisenstein, Hanns Eisler, George
Grosz, Fritz Kortner, Nikolay Okhlopkov, Erwin Piscator, Jean Renoir,
and Sergej Tretjakov. It, too, never made it out of the planning stage.
Even Arnold Zweig, who was located in Palestine, advocated associations
like these, but was able to reach only a relatively small circle in the frame-

work of the Lepac Cultural Federation and through the Liga V (Victory), which were founded during the war.

The Heinrich Heine Club in Mexico City, which approximately two hundred exiles joined, was somewhat more successful. Although most of its members were politically on the left, in response to the popular front policies of the Association for the Protection of German Writers the club also accepted bourgeois liberals as long as they pledged themselves to a resolute antifascism. The Free German Cultural League, founded in London in 1938, was similar. Its most active members were communists, among them John Heartfield, Werner Ilberg, Jürgen Kuczynski, Jan Petersen, and Max Zimmering. For this very reason, the league was generally boycotted by exiled social democrats. Alfred Kerr, its first president, stepped down from his position after a short time out of aversion to the leftists. Nevertheless, over a thousand registered members joined the league. The anticommunist counterorganization of independent authors that Kurt Hiller founded in 1939, in contrast, managed to attract only fifteen members. Club 1943, founded by Grete Fischer, Monty Jacobs, and Hans J. Rehfisch out of dislike for the leftist leadership in the Free German Cultural League, also remained relatively small.

There was similar dissention between leftist and liberal exiles in the United States. The majority of artists did not arrive in this country until 1939 after World War II broke out. Two American organizations—the conservative American Guild for Cultural Freedom and the socialist-oriented League of American Writers—gave them a hand; both supported humanitarian aid programs, but differed clearly from one another in their programmatic statements. While Thomas Mann was close to the American Guild for Cultural Freedom, the leftists joined the German-American Writers' Association. The ideological discrepancies between these groups did not come to the fore as sharply between 1939 and 1942 as they did toward the end of the war. At that time, the leftists seized the leadership in both the Deutsch-Amerikanischer Kulturverband (German-American Cultural Association) and the German-American Writers' Association, and this change caused most of the social democratic and bourgeois artists to withdraw, leading to a distinct weakening of both associations. The German-American Emergency Conference, which was initiated in response by Lion Feuchtwanger, Oskar Maria Graf, Alfred Kantorowicz, and others, remained marginal. The same is true of the Nationalkomitee Freies Deutschland (National Committee for a Free Germany), which became active in 1943. After a brief period of solidarity, it broke apart again; Thomas Mann, the most politically influential of the German writers in exile in the United States, withdrew his signature from the founding proclamation one day after he signed to avoid suspicion of being a pinko or commie.

In summary, we can say that the leftists, the group most aggressively pursued by the Nazi fascists, were dominant in the most important organizations of German exile artists, whether it was the Association for the Protection of German Writers, the Bert Brecht Club, the Heinrich Heine Club, the Free German Cultural League in London, or the German-American Cultural Association. Nevertheless, they tried to win over bourgeois-humanistic artists whose sympathies were clearly antifascist to their objectives in the interest of an antifascist front that was as strong and broad-based as possible. It was inevitable that many crises and disputes resulted, some referring back to ideological antagonisms of the Weimar Republic and some anticipating confrontations in the period after World War II. In the end, there was a series of political and cultural associations, but never the united front incorporating all the artists who had fled or been expelled from the Third Reich of which some had dreamed in the beginning. The ideological differences between the individual groups were simply too great, despite the popular front concept that had been advocated at many levels. It remains remarkable that any coalitions at all could be formed in the midst of the universal misery of exile and that based on their left-democratic or bourgeois liberal beliefs artists were still prepared to join resistance groups that might be politically dangerous for them in order to engage in the struggle against the homicidal right-wing radicalism of the Third Reich.

On the conservative side, which usually upheld the freedom of the individual and nothing else, there were hardly any efforts to organize artists in exile. The adherents of the elitist George Circle, who actually despised the masses, were the one exception; even after 1933, they maintained a certain group solidarity outside the borders of Germany. Under the circumstances, associations of this kind seemed almost like indirect testimonials to the reactionary collective spirit of Nazi fascism in the eyes of other bourgeois artists. So the nonleftist exiles preferred to remain loners and trust in the general principle of unfettered subjectivity that had always been invoked by middle- or upper-middle-class artists in similar situations. Although it had not worked for them during the Weimar Republic, it seemed to them to be the only nonideological position and one that would allow them to preserve their artistic integrity.

Most of the cultural activities of these leagues and associations were hardly noticed outside the narrow circle of their members, but this was not just the result of ideological disputes. The lack of support from their respective host countries also played a role, as did the limited possibilities for communication; the exceptions were the situations in Prague and Paris in the mid-1930s. Even in the early years in Moscow and during World War II in Mexico City, where they were not confronted with a carefully strategic policy of appeasement, these associations remained largely is-lands in an alien environment because they were German-speaking, if for no other reason. Now that they were living abroad, many of their mem-bers clung even more tightly than before to the familiar traditional ideas of German culture so that they would feel more at home, at least within their confined circles. Thus, it was inevitable that most of the activities of these exiles were inwardly directed and reached only the circle of those who were seeking political and cultural support in these organizations.

The fact that many writers were able to publish at least some of their literary works with foreign publishers changed this situation very little. Whether they were published in Switzerland, Sweden, Holland, or Mos-cow, most of these books appeared in German and so were more likely to be read by co-exiles than by the foreign population groups the politically involved exile authors hoped to enlighten with their works. Admittedly, there were a number of translations, but they were a miniscule fraction of the whole, and seldom specifically antifascist. Instead, theses transla-tions were usually well-written biographies or historical novels—the most popular genres in book production at the time—which were most likely to produce a lucrative profit for the foreign publishers. But after the be-ginning of World War II, the translation and publication in Europe of original works in German essentially stopped. Only in the United States did a few more translations of works by German exile authors appear. Along with Viking Press, the publisher Alfred A. Knopf played an im-portant role. But the situation in the US publishing sector was unfavor-able due to the continuing world economic crisis and the war effort that began shortly afterward. And in any case, there was very little interest in publications with a European background in this country. The result was that politically engaged exiles had only a very slight chance of be-ing published. Aside from the works of Thomas Mann, only works that would move quickly off the bookstore shelves—in other words, were cus-tomer friendly—were published, and no pivotal exile works were among them. For this reason, a group of authors around Wieland Herzfelde who were politically on the left decided to initiate their own German-language publishing house in New York, the Aurora Verlag; the principle authors involved were Ernst Bloch, Bertolt Brecht, Ferdinand Bruckner, Alfred Döblin, Lion Feuchtwanger, Oskar Maria Graf, Heinrich Mann, Ernst Waldinger, Berthold Viertel, and Franz Carl Weiskopf. When Aurora Verlag was founded, these writers were already thinking about the time after World War II in which they hoped to build German culture anew in their earlier homeland.

If we want to talk about the Hitler refugees having a political impact beyond the ideological and cultural disputes among themselves, then we have to talk about the exile press, not about exile literature, although some works by Thomas Mann, Lion Feuchtwanger, and Anna Seghers are possible exceptions. Journals such as *Die Sammlung*, the *Neue Deutsche Blätter*, the *Neue Weltbühne*, *Das neue Tage-Buch*, *Das Wort*, or *Internationale Literatur* were paid more attention in the host countries than most German exile novels, let alone the few paintings or compositions with a political message that were created in exile. But because the authors who expressed themselves in these publications differed widely, the journals, too–because of the very antifascist liberality they supported—were often little more than reflections of the ideological disputes within the exile community. Even during the phase of so-called popular front policy during the mid-1930s, contributors to these publications only seldom coalesced into politically effective groups. The journals and newspapers supported by the social democrats who had fled into exile continued to distance themselves from each other, representing the views of the executive committees of the Sozialdemokratische Partei (Social Democratic Party), the group Neu Beginnen (Begin Anew), the Sozialistische Arbeiterpartei (Socialist Workers' Party), the Volkssozialisten, or the Internationales Sozialistisches Kampfbund (International Socialist Combat League). In the same time frame, there were substantial splits among the communists into Stalinists and anti-Stalinists that were very difficult to hush up. Above all, the Moscow show trials caused a profound ideological crisis for many German communists; in the case of some writers—Arthur Koestler, Manès Sperber, and Gustav Regler for example—the result was a radical rejection of communism. Willli Münzenberg, for example, had been the main organizer of the communist exile press in Prague and Paris. In 1937, he published *Propaganda als Waffe* (Propaganda as Weapon), in which he called upon all leftist exiles who sympathized with the popular front to oppose Nazi propaganda with an equally effective "counter-propaganda." But a short time later, faced with the ominous course of political events that ultimately led to the German-Soviet Nonaggression Pact and the invasion of France by the German *Wehrmacht*, he gave up his political activities and committed suicide in 1940.

But where exactly could the journalists among the German exiles have published newspapers, journals, or political pamphlets after the start of World War II? Because most of them had fled to the United States, they suddenly faced a publishing world whose conditions were unfamiliar. It was difficult to place articles in German except in *Aufbau*, a newspaper that was published first by the German-Jewish Club and then after 1940 by the New World Club. In general, there was much greater pressure to integrate in the United States than in the European countries in which most exile writers and journalists had been living before. Commercialism, not political activism, was dominant in US journalism, as it was in the world of publishing. And there was little interest in what the exiles viewed as culture. As a result, Klaus Mann's cultural journal *Decision*, which he founded in the United States at the beginning of 1941, went under after only twelve months.

Despite the substantial number of German exile artists who fled to the United States after the beginning of World War II, often with great difficulty, their influence on this country remained relatively slight. The parents and grandparents of many German-Americans who had emigrated to the United States in the late nineteenth century had been demonized as barbaric Huns during World War I. They had finally regained a certain sense of self-esteem through the rise of Adolf Hitler, the economic upswing he stimulated, and the resulting full employment, which even many Americans admired. Most of them were averse from the outset to all supporters of leftist ideologies. They also did not share the exiles' ideas about culture, which seemed too challenging and even arrogant to them. If they read German-language books at all, they read novels such as *Horst Wessel* by Hanns Heinz Ewers, *Der Arzt Gion* (Doctor Gion) by Hans Carossa, and *Volk ohne Raum* (A Nation Without Room) by Hans Grimm, as well as nonfiction books by Alfred Rosenberg and Oswald Spengler, advertised proudly by the German bookstore B. Westermann in New York in the mid-1930s. These segments of the population were therefore aghast as the United States was drawn into World War II at the end of 1941; now everything connected to Germany was again viewed as barbaric and its nationals were portrayed simply as aggressive, leading to the widespread theory of collective guilt à la Henry Morgenthau and Robert Vansittart. Most German-Americans, as I said, no longer had any sense of German-European culture they could hold on to during this period of crisis as the artists and intellectuals among the Hitler refugees were able to do. So most of them simply turned their backs on their Germanness and became 100 percent *Amurricans*, as everyone said at the time. Many of the politically engaged artists among the exiles, in contrast, tried as so-called beiunskis to hang on to their ideas about culture. But they received no political backing either from the Americans, whom they viewed as Philistines, nor from the German-American groups. So they turned their attention increasingly to Germany after 1943–1944, where it would be important to establish a high culture based on social humanism after the crimes of Nazi fascism.

CONSEQUENCES FOR THE ARTS

Literature

The writers were the largest, the best-known, and also the most important group of artists among the Hitler refugees. Without them, it would be almost impossible to speak of a culture of the other, better Germany in exile. They wrote a number of works that should not be overlooked, which were published in German or in translations in many European countries after 1933 and even overseas after the beginning of World War II. But that was not all. They were the only ones who joined together in antifascist groups in Moscow, Prague, Paris, London, and Mexico City; they wanted to retain a feeling of ideological solidarity among themselves and also to demonstrate to people in their so-called host countries who sympathized with them politically that not all Germans had become slaves to Nazi fascism. We know that their success was limited in most Western democracies because of policies of appeasement toward the Third Reich. And still, nevertheless, despite everything, they did contribute to a culture of resistance, which is remarkable and deserves lasting appreciation.

It goes without saying that this kind of appraisal cannot be based on aesthetic criteria alone. These writers were not working in a realm of inwardness protected by power, at desks surrounded by high bookshelves; most of them were working in insecure circumstances, "changing countries more often than their shoes," according to Bertolt Brecht's formulation in his poem "An die Nachgeborenen" ("To Those Born After Us"). Their passports expired, their visas or residence permits were not extended, their options for earning a living were endangered, their family ties loosened, and the groups they formed collapsed again and again. In the USSR, they were subject after 1936 to Stalin's repressive measures, while in 1940 in England and France many of them were temporarily interned. Even the United States showed itself to be a country that accepted them, it's true—after many difficulties surmounted—but where the dollar reigned and where their high cultural standards left them feeling quite lost in the beginning. Yet the best and most engaged among them did not give up, despite all the toils and tribulations, and tried to continue their defense of culture as well as they could to oppose Nazi barbarism by offering the counter image of an essentially better Germany.

It is true that there were victims in the years between 1933 and 1945. Authors, publishers, and cultural theorists such as Walter Benjamin, Carl Einstein, Walter Hasenclever, Willi Münzenberg, Ernst Toller, Kurt Tucholsky, Ernst Weiss, and Stefan Zweig committed suicide. Others fell silent because resistance to the powerful ascent of Nazi fascism seemed pointless. Others did not want to be reminded of their German origins in exile and changed their names to names that sounded French or English. There were even exiles who had been liberals but now tried to find a new Heimat in orthodox Judaism or in the arms of the Catholic Church. But along with them, there were other authors who spoke up over and over again, who viewed the exile they found so oppressive simply as a way station on the path to another better Germany where they hoped to collaborate after the collapse of the Third Reich on the reconstruction of a German culture founded on the best humanistic, left-liberal, or even socialist traditions.

This will to return was strongest among the left-oriented exile writers. The fact that they, too, failed to form a united front is not just the result of personal animosities, confused feelings, or wrong decisions. Objective factors such as the widely dispersed places of refuge and the resulting lack of possibilities for communication also played a role. This is why both the social democrats and the writers who had been further to the left split into several groups. They continued to hold fast to the idea of a different postwar Germany uncorrupted by Nazi fascism, but they developed concepts that were quite different. Most of these writers had sympathized with the KPD or even belonged to the party; since the late 1920s, they had viewed Hitler as the most implacable communist hater and the Soviet Union as the only state strong enough to achieve a military victory in the war to come and prevent all of Europe from becoming fascist. With this in mind, they were even willing to accept a leader like Stalin. But they were sorely tested. First it was the Moscow show trials, then the German-Soviet Nonaggression Pact in 1939 that led many of them to withdraw from the political sphere or engage in strident anti-Stalinist diatribes. But there were a number of leftist authors who held onto their convictions during this period. They joined the Thälmann-Brigade in the Spanish Civil War, as did Erich Arendt, Willi Bredel, Alfred Kantorowicz, Egon Erwin Kisch, Ludwig Renn, Bodo Uhse, and Erich Weinert. In Mexican exile or in Moscow, they professed their communist convictions openly and consistent with those convictions went to the Soviet Zone of Occupation at the end of World War II, as did Johannes R. Becher, Willi Bredel, Hans Marchwitza, Ludwig Renn, Anna Seghers, Erich Weinert, and Friedrich Wolf.

Among the authors in exile who clung to their bourgeois humanist ideas of culture, there were very few coalitions based on political aesthetics. They sometimes presented themselves, as Thomas Mann did, as representatives of the other, better Germany, but usually did so as individuals, without entering into any group commitments. Many authors in this category, Robert Musil for example, withdrew entirely to their solitary ego and firmly rejected any link between literature and politics. They did view themselves as exiles, but they did not write militant exile literature; they rejected even the thought of a broad-based popular front policy because they saw it as a turn toward collectivism and therefore a leftist orientation.

What literary forms did these authors adopt in exile to express their cultural and political opinions? The situation was definitely most difficult for the poets and the playwrights. Poems in particular, which according to long-standing tradition had been the expressions of subjective feelings, were rejected by many of the more politically engaged exile writers as not interventionist enough. You could have a political impact with poems, they claimed, only if you reduced them to epic or epigrammatic elements or had them put to music in a memorable way so that they were quotable or singable. In contrast to many poets—including Rose Ausländer, Hilde Domin, Max Hermann-Neiße, Karl Wolfskehl, and even Else Lasker-Schüler and Nelly Sachs—Bertolt Brecht was one of the few who actually succeeded in doing this. As early as 1934, he published a volume of memorable songs, poems, and choruses (*Lieder Gedichte Chöre*) that included accompanying music by Eisler in the hope of reaching a larger audience. And Brecht was also the one who considered his own ideological situation in exile in some of his later poems such as "Schlechte Zeit für Lyrik" ("A Bad Time for Lyric Poetry") or "An die Nachgeborenen." He emphasized in his lyric poetry that he, too, given better circumstances, would have preferred to write poems about the beauty of nature. But because of the unfavorable situation, he was forced to take up primarily political themes to use the poetic genre in the front lines of the antifascist struggle.

It was equally difficult for playwrights who had been highly appreciated in the Weimar Republic to find ways to have an impact in the various countries of exile. Georg Kaiser and Carl Zuckmayer, who had been among the most frequently performed German playwrights before 1933, were largely thrown back on their own resources after their expulsion. Ferdinand Bruckner, Ernst Toller, and Friedrich Wolf succeeded in having at least some of their antifascist plays, such as *Die Rassen* (The Races), *Pastor Hall*, and *Professor Mamlock*, performed. But none of them could regain the name recognition they had before 1933. Bertolt Brecht had the same experience. The world-famous author of the *Dreigroschenoper* (The Threepenny Opera) was lucky that at least his *Rundköpfe und Spitzköpfe* (Round Heads and Pointed Heads), his *Mutter* and *Die Gewehre der Frau Carrar* were staged in exile, though in productions that were scattered and received little notice. Some of his great classical dramas, such as *Der gute Mensch von Sezuan* (The Good Person of Szechwan), *Mutter Courage und ihre Kinder* (Mother Courage and Her Children), and *Herr Puntila und sein Knecht Matti* (Mr. Puntila and His Man Matti), which he had written in the 1930s in Scandinavian exile, were performed only toward the end of the war in Zurich in productions on which he had no influence and without the general public taking much notice. In contrast, his later exile plays such as *Der aufhaltsame Aufstieg des Arturo Ui*, *Die Gesichte der Simone Machard*, (The Visions of Simone Machard), *Schweyk im Zweiten Weltkrieg* (Schweyk in the Second World War), and *Der kaukasische Kreidekreis* (The Caucasian Chalk Circle) remained unperformed during Brecht's exile years in California because none of the producers there supported them; "Stage hyenas like them," in the words of the exiles, found these plays uninteresting for an American theater audience because of their European background. Moreover, plays in comic or burlesque styles were much more in demand in private theaters in America in the 1930s, on New York's Broadway, for example, than they were in most European theaters. For this reason, even Brecht's plays had very little chance to be performed in the United States, although they were, despite their seriousness, full of comic scenes. His was a humor that alienated the viewers into a socially critical perspective and was therefore not at all innocuous; it would probably have upset rather than amused an American audience. As a result, the most successful playwrights and directors in exile were the ones who limited themselves from the outset to satirical revues or slapstick comedies in clubs they had rented or on cabaret stages without making any claim to being high culture.

What did succeed in exile was the novel, which had gained acceptance as the prevailing literary form on the book market since the eighteenth century and—if its authors took up themes that were trendy at the time— promised substantial sales. Therefore, the most successful exile authors were novelists such as Vicki Baum, Lion Feuchtwanger, Hermann Kesten,

Heinrich Mann, Thomas Mann, Franz Werfel, and Arnold Zweig, whose works appeared both in German-language editions in exile publishing houses such as Oprecht, Bermann Fischer, Querido, and Allert de Lange as well as in translations published by Alfred A. Knopf and Viking Press. So-called historical novels sold the best by far, among them Heinrich Mann's *Die Jugend und die Vollendung des Königs Henri Quatre* (1935–1938; Henry Quatre, King of France, 1938), Lion Feuchtwanger's *Der falsche Nero* (1936; The Pretender, 1937), Arnold Zweig's *Erziehung vor Verdun* (1935; Education before Verdun, 1936), Hermann Kesten's *Ferdinand und Isabella* (1936) and *König Philipp II* (1938; I, the King, 1939), Thomas Mann's *Joseph in Ägypten* (1936; Joseph in Egypt, 1938) and *Lotte in Weimar* (1939; The Beloved Returns, 1940), and Franz Werfel's *Die vierzig Tage des Musa Dagh* (1933; The Forty Days of Musa Dagh, 1934). Well-crafted biographies of famous historical figures also proved in some cases to be highly marketable; examples are Stefan Zweig's *Maria Stuart* (1935), *Triumph und Tragik des Erasmus von Rotterdam* (1934; Erasmus of Rotterdam, 1934), and *Magellan* (1938) and Emil Ludwig's *Hindenburg* (1935), *Cleopatra* (1937), *Roosevelt* (1938), and *Simon Bolivar* (1939). Some exile writers, such as Kurt Hiller, who preferred to treat subjects that were political and topical and who were mostly unsuccessful, characterized this kind of publication as a shameful "flight from the challenges of the day" and pleaded for novels with a clear contemporary relevance. This led to an internal debate among the exiles in the mid-1930s about the ideological relevance of the historical novel. At the time it was primarily Georg Lukács who defended the importance of the historical novel and used works by Heinrich Mann and Lion Feuchtwanger to demonstrate that such works did not need to be apolitical at all and that any observant reader with political interests could certainly find parallels to contemporary events in them.

Along with historically themed novels, some exile novels appeared during the same period that dealt very directly with the authors' present circumstances. Primary among them were works that confronted the situation within the Third Reich from a critical perspective. An opening salvo that attracted a lot of attention was the novel *Die Geschwister Oppenheim* (The Oppermanns) by Lion Feuchtwanger, which appeared in late fall 1933 and had already sold 20,000 German copies and 270,000 copies in several foreign-language versions by summer 1934. It centers on the helplessness of an old, established Jewish family in the face of Nazi fascism as it advances from one victory to the next. The family, which has accumulated substantial wealth and is German nationalist in its political views, had long regarded fascism as a laughable petty bourgeois phenomenon whose agents would never succeed in seizing power in Germany.

Only the widely extended family ties provide the Oppenheims a certain support after the disastrous events of January 1933. Apart from that, they are forced to recognize that the rug is being pulled from under their feet, in an economic sense too. The same realistic style is used to portray the non-Jewish cultured middle class and its equally defenseless position as the brown flood rises. Feuchtwanger singles out a high school teacher as an example. This character tries to cling to his humanistic educational ideals, and in his credulous naivety thinks it is impossible for a half-educated man like Hitler, whose book *Mein Kampf* is written in miserable German, to govern a highly educated people like the Germans. All of this is described with great insight, but not in a way that would provide guidance for potential antifascist actions inside Germany or in exile.

In contrast to Lion Feuchtwanger, communist authors such as Willi Bredel, Heinz Liepmann, and Walter Schönstedt were not concerned with the fate of individual Jewish or non-Jewish citizens during the first months of the Third Reich. In their novels based on current events (*Zeitromane*) that were published a short time later, their subjects were either individual workers or groups of workers who decided to engage in an illegal struggle against the brown dictatorship despite the Nazi fascists' superior power. They described how small resistance groups distributed pamphlets, wrote provocative slogans on the walls of houses, and raised red flags on tall buildings at night. But at the same time they were realistic enough to portray the fact that these measures had not brought about any thoroughgoing shift to the left in opposition to the victorious Nazis; on the contrary, they showed how quickly the brown hordes had succeeded both in gaining power and stabilizing it with ever-new terrorist measures. These works proved to be noble documents of political resistance, but they, too, failed to offer their readers any kind of effective guidelines for action. In addition, were there any readers for works of this kind in other countries? After all, few workers had been driven out of Germany; it was mostly well-known intellectuals and artists along with the majority of middle-class Jews who had been forced into exile. So these books were published in small editions, while a novel like *Die Geschwister Oppenheim*, which centered on the fates of bourgeois refugees, addressed a much broader audience which included both German exiles as well as intellectuals in the nonfascist countries who sympathized with them.

But the series of exile novels that addressed political and socioeconomic events within the Third Reich continued. In his novel *Mephisto* (1935), Klaus Mann confronted the shameful issue of intellectual fellow travelers who fell into line with the Nazi regime. The subject is the career of an unprincipled actor who adapts to every regime. It is reminiscent of the life of Gustav Gründgens, who became a National Socialist member of the Prussian State Council, but it also reminds the reader of the ideological opportunism of other artists who remained in the Third Reich, such as Gottfried Benn. Several writers satirized the same urge to conform among the German petty bourgeoisie, among them Irmgard Keun in her novel *Nach Mitternacht* (After Midnight) and Oskar Maria Graf in his *Anton Sittinger,* both of which appeared in 1937. With nightmarish intensity, they portrayed the resentful nature of this class, whose members thought they could participate in power through the petty bourgeois leader Adolf Hitler and not need to continue bowing down to the masters from the upper classes. But the only way out of this claustrophobic atmosphere offered by Keun is flight into exile.

On what else besides exile could anyone set their hopes at this point, be they bourgeois, petty bourgeois, or proletarian? Only later were there scattered efforts at resistance—by the Red Orchestra, the Kreisau Circle, the White Rose Group around Sophie and Hans Scholl, and the 20 July Plot—as the conviction spread toward the end of World War II that the Third Reich was rushing toward its demise. But in the years between 1933 and 1941 at the high point of Nazi dominance, flight into exile was the only way to escape the terror of the NS regime. This situation was probably expressed most intensely in the series of scenes *Furcht und Elend des Dritten Reichs* (1935–1938; Fear and Misery in the Third Reich) by Bertolt Brecht, which describes the oppressive and conformist conditions under Nazi fascism, which finally lead a Jewish woman to decide to leave Germany never to return. And in *Das siebte Kreuz* (The Seventh Cross) by Anna Seghers, which was begun in 1938, a man who escapes from a concentration camp has no choice in the end but to evade the clutches of the Nazi henchmen by fleeing abroad, despite some evidence of solidarity on the part of people with leftist views.

Probably the most ambitious attempt to portray the political, socioeconomic, and cultural conditions inside the Third Reich was made by Arnold Zweig in the novel *Das Beil von Wandsbek* (The Axe of Wandsbek), which he wrote, or rather dictated, in the early 1940s in Palestinian exile. It includes representative figures from all walks of life inside Germany: intellectuals, civil servants, nouveau riche Nazi fascists, pastors, bankers, SA functionaries, white-collar workers, petty bourgeois, officers, and workers. The plot centers around a conformist petty bourgeois, the butcher Albert Teetjen, who is threatened with economic ruin due to the increasing monopolization of the food industry. So for a meager amount of money, he agrees to act as the executioner of four communists who have been condemned to death. The reader also learns much about the attitude of the so-called good Hanseatic citizens, who, like the prison warden Koldewey and the doctor Käte Neumeier, try to cope with the

Nazi regime in their own way. After conforming initially, their insight into the atrocities of the masters in brown uniforms and their pronounced cultural awareness give them courage to act in a way that goes beyond typical inner emigration behavior. They find help by thinking back to the Hamburg of the eighteenth century, when Gotthold Ephraim Lessing tried to found a German national theater in the city, Friedrich Gottlieb Klopstock was inspired by the ideas of the French Revolution, and Matthias Claudius published his half-enlightened, half–emotionally inspired *Wandsbeker Boten* (Wandsbek Messenger)—in other words, a time when confidence in the "oneness of the human race, in humanity, enlightenment, philanthropy or human kindness, and the power of reason" still reigned. In comparison, Hitlerism seems to them more and more like a "hysterical system of delusions," of the kind Sigmund Freud had exposed in his studies of the Schreber case. In the beginning, Koldewey invokes his favorite author Friedrich Nietzsche, who had often emphasized that it was only "the riffraff who liked" to "question the inevitable." So as a cultivated person, Koldewey shuts his eyes to the terrorist acts of the Nazi regime for a long time. But toward the end of the novel, he decides to leave the ivory tower of inner emigration and adopts an attitude characteristic of the men involved in the July 20 Plot. Using art and culture that float above reality to oppose fascism has now come to seem like a hopeless illusion to him. But just as in earlier works of this kind, and despite the novel's critical left perspective, there is no hint of what actions might result from this insight.

The same is true of the novel *Doktor Faustus*, which Thomas Mann began toward the end of the war. Although the author had actively confronted conditions inside the Third Reich in his radio addresses *Für deutsche Hörer* (For German Listeners), which had been broadcast to Germany since 1942 by the BBC transmitter, there is little evidence in this novel of any kind of critical perspective on fascism. Nazis appear only on the margins and then only in the character of intellectuals. Even less attention is paid to the political or socioeconomic foundations of Nazi fascism. The narrator, Serenus Zeitblom, is a representative of inner emigration and is also a relatively close friend of the protagonist, the composer Adrian Leverkühn, whose compositions resemble the cold aestheticism of many Nazi artists. Zeitblom maintains a compassionate sympathy with Leverkühn until the composer's death and therefore there is neither a careful analysis of fascism nor a description of any situations in exile. Instead, although the author keeps one eye on the events of the 1930s and World War II, the novel ends with a typical Protestant plea that the mercy of forgiveness be granted both to the deceased Leverkühn and to his German fatherland. All of this is embedded in a grandiose plot that has the crisis of German cultural consciousness as its central theme, but that completely ignores the primary aspects of Nazi fascism.

What escape routes did other authors among the Hitler refugees see as they attempted to portray the ideological consequences of their own exile situation in their novels? Did they take more concrete positions vis-á-vis Nazi fascism? Or was that impossible a priori due to their oppressive living conditions—the fact that they really lived nowhere? What do works of this kind tell us? The novel *Exil* (1940) by Lion Feuchtwanger is particularly instructive for answering questions like this. Despite being multilayered, this book, which takes place in exile circles in Paris, is basically an artist's novel. The novel forcefully expresses the misery of exile, which for many refugees led to social isolation, loss of socioeconomic status, and political apathy. These people had been forced to exchange their cultivated bourgeois comfort for an insecure existence in small emigrant hotels in Paris, and now they dreamed of returning to their earlier circumstances. But with equal force, the novel points to those exiles who viewed their situation as refugees as the opportunity for a new beginning and not only as an oppressive stroke of fate. In Feuchtwanger's novel, the central figure in this group is the composer Sepp Trautwein. As an educated middle-class liberal, he believes in a kind of humanism—a humanism that relies on reason to successfully assert principles based on justice against relationships based on force characteristic of dictatorial forms of government. In conversations with his leftist son Hanns, Trautwein gradually realizes that in his Wartesaal-Sinfonie (Waiting Room Symphony) he had withdrawn into a kind of "nihilistic aristocratism," which is ineffective in the end. It becomes clear to him that intellect and power are not irreconcilable opposites and that instead of perpetually waiting, you can also use music in the struggle against fascism. In other words, a self-critical examination of the fundamental positions of bourgeois art becomes the main theme of the novel. Instead of creating pure art as an antithesis to the barbarism of the Nazi fascists, Trautwein comes to see that art and culture should no longer be privileges of the ruling class; they should adjust to the social behavior of the broad masses of the people. But he also recognizes that this is not yet possible under the conditions of exile and can be realized only in a socialist state of the future.

The perspective on the role of art in exile that underlies the novel *Transit* (1943) by Anna Seghers is similar and yet different. *Transit*, too, centers around the miserable conditions of exile in France. In this case, however, the protagonist is a German worker, who is telling an anonymous listener about his flight out of Germany, his internment by the Vichy authorities, and his continued flight to the south of France, still not occupied by the *Wehrmacht* at the time. At first glance, this seems to be a true-to-life escape story much like the one in Seghers' *Das siebte Kreuz*. But the set of issues surrounding art plays an important role at many levels here as it does in Feuchtwanger's *Exil*. Because this particular worker is carrying with him the manuscript of a novel by a bourgeois exile writer who committed suicide when the German troops invaded Paris, he becomes a "worker who reads," although he had not previously been a "literature lover." In reading the novel, he realizes it is not just the bourgeois literary heritage that Georg Lukács and Alfred Kurella were praising at the time that is important. The worker in *Transit* confronts these two theorists both directly and indirectly when he comes to the conclusion that a contemporary novel can be just as important as the constant invocation of Goethe and Schiller, the two grand masters of bourgeois classicism. It is fitting, then, that at the end of the novel Seghers' worker does not flee abroad to more secure climes because he is afraid of the Nazi fascists; he decides to remain in France and establish contact with resistance groups.

Many critics will object that this does not amount to much. But you could not expect more of exile writers who were living under very oppressive conditions in the early 1940s as Nazi fascism advanced from one victory to the next. It would have been illusory to dream about the German proletariat's invincible power of resistance or an utopian victory over German fascism. For the time being, it was important to portray left liberals who had made the difficult transition to committed combatants and even show workers involved in the resistance along with middle-class humanists. These novels belong to the best works of German exile literature because they confront the barbarism of Nazi fascism with an art of resistance that does not simply retreat to bourgeois classicism, but, having emerged from contemporary experience, points toward the future.

Theater

Artists who were dependent on an established theater outfitted with stage machinery, a generous advertising budget, and a large German-speaking audience had an even more difficult time than the authors of prose and poetry. And this group was especially large, because in Germany there were traditionally plenty of state-subsidized theaters; during the Weimar Republic, these ensembles had been among the best in the world. Their directors, actors, and actresses were well-known. Because of that, famous Berlin directors such as Leopold Jessner and Max Reinhardt were quite successful after 1933, although they had to confront some anti-Semitic prejudices outside the borders of Germany as well. But where could the many German-Jewish actors and actresses find a new livelihood? The language barrier was usually an insurmountable obstacle, even for the better-known among them. Elisabeth Bergner and Lotte Lenya were able to carve out a career abroad, but in contrast, Albert Bassermann, Fritz Kortner, and Helene Weigel, for example, found hardly any engagements that corresponded to their talents.

Shortly after 1933, countries such as Austria and Switzerland seemed most promising to many theater people because there were no difficulties with linguistic adaptation to overcome. States such as the Soviet Union and Czechoslovakia were also options; they had relatively large German-speaking enclaves that supported a number of theaters in which German plays were produced almost exclusively. In other countries, many exiles were forced to found their own clubs or associations if they wanted to stage plays in German. Of course, then they could have no influence on the local population in the Netherlands, in England, or in Mexico, for example, and were largely dependent on the exile milieu. These efforts also suffered under a chronic shortage of funds and therefore did not necessarily motivate the best actors and actresses to support them. On stages of this kind, it was more important to be well-meaning than professionally skilled.

Some of the leftists among the exiled theater people, such as Ernst Busch, Alexander Granach, Heinrich Greif, Carola Neher, Erwin Piscator, Curt Trepte, and Max Vallentin, went to the Soviet Union in 1933 as expected. In the beginning, they were offered the possibility of appearing in serious German plays both old and new, both in Moscow and in the provincial theater in Dnipropetrovsk. For a short time, they were so enthusiastic about this opportunity that they decided not to stay in the country just temporarily, but for a longer time. Erwin Piscator probably developed the most daring theater plans in the USSR; he wanted to transform the existing theater in Engels, the capital of the German Volga Republic, into a significant German national theater in exile. Because he could not accomplish that with the local ensemble, he asked Wolfgang Heinz, Wolfgang Langhoff, Teo Otto, Leonard Steckel, and Helene Weigel to follow him and collaborate in the development of an antifascist theater where the newest avant-garde techniques could be tested. There were several reasons why Piscator did not succeed in carrying out this project. First, almost no one followed him to Engels. Second, the local population, who preferred to see comedies and Heimat plays, were hard to win over for such challenging theater. Third, Piscator soon noticed that a fundamental transition was taking place in the Soviet Union after 1934–1935 from the avant-garde theater practices of Vsevolod Meyerhold to socialist realism; in the theater, socialist realism employed the older Stanislavsky methods based on psychological empathy that Piscator had rejected. Disappointed by this development, Piscator went to the United States.

For other theater people who wanted to stay in a German-speaking area, Austria, Czechoslovakia, and Switzerland were the only options. The situation was most difficult for them in Austria; the country was German-speaking, it is true, but became ever more reactionary under the autocratic Christian chancellor Engelbert Dollfuß and under the subsequent government of Kurt von Schuschnigg, and thus the invasion by German troops in March 1938 was welcomed by the majority of citizens. Most of the directors, actors, and actresses who had fled there considered Austria as nothing more than a way station. This was true of Max Reinhardt, for example; until 1938, he staged several Shakespeare plays at the Salzburg festivals, which were explicitly boycotted by the Nazi fascists. Otherwise, there was hardly anything performed on Austrian stages between 1933

Gegen die Wühlerei

der Emigranten!

Oeffentliche Protestkundgebung

in der „Stadthalle"

Mittwoch, den 21. November, 20.15 Uhr.

Es sprechen: **Henne, Tobler, Wirz**

Gegen das jüdische Emigrantenkabarett

„Pfeffermühle", in der alles Nationale und Vaterländische in den Schmutz gezogen wird,

Prof. Mannheim, der auf der Bühne des Zürcher Schauspielhauses sein jüdisches Gift verspritzt und die Völker verhetzt,

Dr. Fritz Adler, den Ministermörder und Sekretär der II. Internationale, der die schweizerische Gastfreundschaft mißbraucht und mit frecher Dreistigkeit dem Schweizervolk Lehren erteilen zu müssen glaubt,

Dr. Kurt Löwenstein, der seine minderjährigen Schüler „zu Studienzwecken" in die Bordelle führte und dem Schweizer Arbeiter marxistisch-jüdische Asphalt-„Kultur" beibringen will,

Für die radikale **Säuberung der Schweiz vom ganzen Geschmeiß ausländischer Emigranten,** das sich schon allzulange in unserem Lande breit macht.

Zur Deckung der Unkosten wird eine Eintrittsgebühr von 30 Cts verlangt.

Kartenvorverkauf auf der Gauleitung, Zähringerstr. 25 und an der Abendkasse.

NATIONALE FRONT

Figure 45. "Against the emigrants stirring up the muck." Poster of the Nationale Front in Zurich (1934). From the book by Werner Mittenzwei: *Exil in der Schweiz,* Leipzig 1978.

and 1938 in which leading members of the German exile group participated or that had an antifascist slant.

The head of the Zürcher Schauspielhaus, in contrast, a wine wholesaler
named Ferdinand Riese, did not let anti-Semitic protests by the fascist
members of the Schweizer Front keep him from hiring a number of German actors and actresses for financial reasons; his goal was to transform
what had been a provincial playhouse in Zurich into a first-class theater.
It provided an interesting sphere of activity for actors and actresses such
as Therese Giehse, Ernst Ginsberg, Wolfgang Heinz, Kurt Horwitz, Wolfgang Langhoff, Karl Paryla, and Leonard Steckel; set designers such as Teo
Otto; and the dramaturge Kurt Hirschfeld. The repertoire was not limited
to plays by the classical German writers. Some of the exiles were able to
perform—as early as 1933–1934 and despite some vociferous protests—in
plays such as *Die Rassen* by Ferdinand Bruckner and *Professor Mamlock*
(the title was changed from the earlier *Professor Mannheim*) by Friedrich
Wolf, both of which deal with the Nazi fascists' racist repressive measures.
Oskar Wälterlin, who took over the leadership of the Zürcher Schauspielhaus after 1938, favored Bertolt Brecht and Georg Kaiser among the new
German playwrights. Thus, toward the end of World War II, even plays
like *Mutter Courage und ihre Kinder, Der gute Mensch von Sezuan,* and *Herr
Puntila und sein Knecht Matti* premiered in his theater. Although the plays
were slightly de-politicized so that many people in the audience saw *Mutter Courage* as a Niobe tragedy rather than an antiwar play and did not
catch on at all to the basic anti-capitalist structure of *Der gute Mensch von
Sezuan,* these were productions of exile plays with exile actors and actresses the likes of which were not to be seen anywhere else during these
years. True, Wälterlin had more success with the Zurich audiences when
he staged German classics. But all the same: three Brecht premieres and
Erika Mann's political cabaret "Die Pfeffermühle," which did not mince
words in the difficult years after 1933! That this was even possible in Zurich, where a politics of appeasement toward the Third Reich reigned in
other contexts, was much more than many exiles had expected from the
conservative-minded Swiss citizens.

In comparison, what the exiles achieved before 1938 in the theaters of
Prague seems rather modest. The left-democratic and socialist forces were
substantially stronger in Prague than in Zurich, but there was no large
German-language theater ensemble. The only play performed in Prague
that was really political—meaning that it called for a struggle against the
Nazi fascists—was Bertolt Brecht's one-act play *Die Gewehre der Frau
Carrar,* which was staged with the participation of Erich Freund, Erwin
Geschonneck, and Charlotte Küter. There was even less opportunity to
stage more substantial antifascist plays in England. One ensemble of Ger-

man exiles therefore offered revue-like sequences of scenes in German on their Very Small Stage, whereas another exile group tried to reach the native theater audience with revues in English in their Continental Cabaret. But both failed to achieve any great impact.

Some directors, playwrights, actors, and actresses therefore saw the United States as their last hope for the theater. But even there, fortune did not smile on them. The requirements for theater performances in this country were largely unfamiliar to the German exiles. In the United States, where culture did not enjoy any support from the state, a play could only be staged if the director found a producer who rented a theater and advanced the money necessary for the production; subsequent performances had to gross as much as possible to repay this advance. Here everything was subject to the market-based principle of supply and demand. In a system like this, where almost everything revolved around the amortization of financial investments, political plays, especially ones with a European background, could never become one of the desired blockbusters and thus were not even considered by influential producers. The only great theatrical success by one of the Hitler refugees was Max Reinhardt's sensational open-air production of Shakespeare's *A Midsummer Night's Dream* in 1934 in the spacious Hollywood Bowl; Mickey Rooney played the role of Puck and Olivia de Haviland played Hermia. In the ten evenings on which these performances took place, there were over 150,000 tickets sold, which yielded a spectacular profit.

Leopold Jessner's production of Friedrich Schiller's *Wilhelm Tell* in 1939 in the El Capitan Theater on Hollywood Boulevard had the opposite outcome. Because he used actors whose English was sometimes hard to understand, including Ernst Deutsch as Geßler, Leo Reuss as Wilhelm Tell, and Alexander Granach as Stauffacher, the production was both a financial and an artistic failure. Brecht too had little luck with his plays in the United States. After *The Mother* flopped in New York in 1935, there was no halfway liberal Broadway producer left who would have dared to stage Brecht's *Aufhaltsamer Aufstieg des Arturo Ui* or his *Schweyk im Zweiten Weltkrieg*. Even the production of his *Leben des Galilei (The Life of Galileo)* in Beverly Hills was tolerably successful only because the famous movie actor Charles Laughton played the main role; even so, the play did not recoup the production costs by any means. Productions in Los Angeles by the German Jewish Club and by the Freie Bühne (Free Stage) under Walter Wicclair were somewhat closer to audience expectations. They were sometimes in German, but except for scattered forays into the classical repertoire, they limited themselves to revues and comedies without any pretence of presenting high culture. As a result, these productions should be considered immigrant theater rather than antifascist exile theater.

Film

Is it really worthwhile to include a chapter on exile films in a book about the role of culture in the political-aesthetic conflicts between 1933 and 1945? Film production almost everywhere was part of the commercial leisure industry, whose owners and managers geared everything to the entertainment needs of the masses. So it seemed that films had to be either mysteries, action films, comedies, or melodramas in the native language of the audience and as accessible as possible. There were approximately two thousand people involved in filmmaking who had to leave Germany after 30 January 1933 because of their leftist views or their Jewish ancestry—they were directors, screenwriters, producers, agents, distributors, movie theater owners, cameramen, production assistants, actors, and actresses; where were they supposed to find jobs? It is true that technically gifted cameramen, sound engineers, set designers, editors, and lighting technicians had the best chance of being hired by foreign film companies temporarily or for a longer period because of the good reputation of the German film studios before 1933. But the more famous (and therefore already older) actors and actresses often had great difficulty in surmounting the language barriers with which they were faced. Among them were many Jewish-born Germans who had turned to the new medium during the Weimar Republic; in other countries, they were not necessarily welcomed with open arms. Only if they succeeded in adapting to the new conditions did they sometimes find a decent livelihood, or even a good one.

And another question: where were the directors and the screenwriters working with them supposed to make films in which they could portray their own exile situation—as some of the refugee writers could do in their plays or novels? In other words, was it even possible for them to appear as representatives of the other, better Germany abroad? Instead, it seemed that they were forced to surrender their cultural identity by submerging themselves completely in the alien film milieu of other countries. In terms of their personal fates, they were and remained exiles. But was it possible for them to include their own situations in their film work or even collaborate on antifascist films? To anticipate the answer to these questions: there was almost no opportunity to do so, and that is why it is so difficult to talk about specific exile films at all.

As was the case in considering other German cultural efforts in exile, it is important to distinguish among the various countries with respect to the conditions for working and having an impact they offered the refugees. The directors and actors who went to the Soviet Union shortly after 1933 had the best opportunity to collaborate on films with political themes. A letter from the actor Alexander Granach to his girlfriend in Berlin written shortly after his arrival in Moscow illustrates the high hopes held by many German communists in Russian exile: "I'm simply overwhelmed by happiness—everything is here! A person with strength, with vitality, with faith, with imagination, can live life to the fullest here in artistic terms, in human terms, better than anywhere else!" This enthusiasm was initially shared by all the German exiles who found a position with the Mezhrabpom Film Society. They were offered appealing possibilities for work, and they also made contact with other filmmakers from all over the world in the Moscow House of Cinema, a meeting place in the city center for all the "cinema workers." The Mezhrabpom Film Society had been established in the 1920s as part of the Workers' International Relief and had collaborated with leftist companies such as Weltfilm and Prometheus in Germany before 1933. This film company, with its most important directors Vsevolod Pudovkin and Dziga Vertov, was the real center of the Soviet film avant-garde, and it also invited leftist authors from abroad such as Martin Andersen-Nexö, Haldor Laxness, Upton Sinclair, and Friedrich Wolf to submit scenarios for feature films. Germany had been the principle recipient of the society's films, and when Germany was removed from the scene in 1933, it had to limit its film production somewhat, but still largely retained its international focus.

This film consortium had a staff of approximately twelve hundred people and, along with films that were specifically Russian, also produced films about the Volga Germans, the gypsies, and the people in Birobidzhan, the semiautonomous Jewish Soviet republic that was still under development at the time. Among the German exiles, the leftist director Erwin Piscator and the former film critic for the *Rote Fahne*, Gustav von Wangenheim, as well as the worker-actor Alexander Granach, were active in the consortium. Piscator filmed *Aufstand der Fischer* (Revolt of the Fishermen) based on a story by Anna Seghers in its studios in 1934. And in 1935, Wangenheim made the film *Kämpfer* (Fighters) about the Reichstag fire trial in Leipzig. Other participants in the project were the agitprop group *Kolonne Links* (Left Column), which had fled to the USSR, and Alfred Kurella, who acted as scriptwriter; Heinrich Vogeler, who had lived in the Soviet Union since the late 1920s, designed the sets. The Mezhrabpom Society was too avant-garde in the eyes of the Stalinists committed to the doctrine of socialist realism—in other words too Western,—and was dissolved in summer 1936. Piscator, Wangenheim, Willi Bredel, Alexander Granach, and Julius Hay all had to give up their filmmaking plans. Furthermore, the connections that the film consortium had established in the meantime with exile directors such as William Dieterle, Ernst Lubitsch, and Max Ophüls were severed relatively quickly. After the film *Professor Mamlock* was filmed by Herbert Rappaport in 1937, German exiles were consulted only during the shooting of Soviet films in which the themes were specifically German. Hans Rodenberg was consulted in 1938, for example, for the film *Familie Oppenheim* based on a novel by Lion Feuchtwanger, as was Helmut Damerius, also in 1938, for the film *Die Moorsoldaten* (Moor Soldiers) about one of the Nazi concentration camps. After this, few German exiles were able to work in Soviet film production. Even the former leftist militant Alexander Granach chose exile in the United States over a continued stay in the Soviet Union.

In the two Western democracies of England and France, the filmmakers among the Hitler refugees confronted much less favorable working conditions. In the beginning, many—including directors Ludwig Berger, Kurt Gerron, Fritz Lang, Max Ophüls, Georg Wilhelm Pabst, and Robert Siodmak; producers Paul Kohner and Erich Pommer; and screenwriters Kurt Alexander, Herbert Juttke, Hermann Kosterlitz, Robert Liebmann, and Arnold Lippschütz—had placed great hopes in France, but they remained unwelcome guests. There were many reasons for this. First, the disastrous effects of the world economic crisis were still prevalent even after 1933, so that even many native French film artists and technicians were unemployed. Second, the film scene there was increasingly flooded with Hollywood products. And third, a tangible anti-Semitic mood was spreading through the right-wing press. To avoid open conflicts, the French government issued an edict according to which no more than 10 percent of the artistic personnel of the French film industry could be foreigners. Even famous German directors such as Fritz Lang and Max Ophüls had to struggle—contrary to their expectations—with significant restrictions. They did receive a certain support from exiled producers such as Max Glaß, Hermann Millakowsky, Seymor Nebenzahl, Arnold Pressburger, and Eugen Tuscherer, who had accumulated enough capital in Parisian banks through the export of their films during the Weimar Republic. They employed most of the expelled German filmmakers, and this group succeeded in making fifty films in France between 1933 and 1939. They were mostly films for popular consumption, including comedies, melodramas, crime stories, and other similar genres. All attempts to make an emigrant film or confront the Nazi fascists openly, with the exception of Robert Siodmak's film *Ultimatum* (1938), were destined to fail from the outset because of the appeasement policy dominant in France at the time.

In England, the outlook for the expelled filmmakers was much the same. Some famous stars such as Elisabeth Bergner, Fritz Kortner, Peter Lorre, Conrad Veidt, and Adolf Wohlbrück, as well as the director Berthold Viertel, did succeed in getting a foothold in the marketable genres of the British film industry for a while. But most of them, hoping they would be safer, left Great Britain in 1939–1940 for the United States. The exiled filmmakers in the Netherlands, on the other hand, where there had been no film industry to speak of previously, did make several films that were quite successful. Chief among them were Max Ophül's *Komedie om Geld* (1936; A Comedy About Money) and Ludwig Berger's *Ergens in Nederland* (1940; Somewhere in the Netherlands), which even treated socially critical and antifascist themes. Kurt Gerron, too, who moved to Amsterdam in 1935 after brief stays in Paris and Vienna, achieved a certain success with his film *Het mysterie van de mondscheinsonate*, which is a mystery, not a German musical film as the title might suggest. After the occupation of Holland by Nazi troops, Gerron could only stage musical revues in a Jewish cultural organization; in February 1944, he was deported to Theresienstadt, where he was forced to take over the direction of a film that after 1945 was titled *Der Führer schenkt den Juden eine Stadt* (The Führer Gives a City to the Jews). Shortly before the filming was completed, however, he was transferred to Auschwitz and murdered there in November 1944.

The 120 directors, cameramen, film composers, screenwriters, set designers, movie-house owners, technicians, and distributors who fled to Palestine between 1933 and 1940 were a special case within the emigration of German-language filmmakers. Some of this group, in cooperation with the Jewish Cultural League and the World Zionist Organization, and with the express endorsement of the Nazi authorities, made a dozen Zionist-oriented films between 1933 and 1938 that were intended to promote the emigration of German Jews to Palestine. Under the direction of Erich Brock, Georg Engel, and Hilmar Lerski, films were made in which swamps were drained and agriculturally useful irrigation systems were installed; the heroic aspect of these tasks were usually front and center to give primarily young people an incentive to emigrate to Palestine. Whether these films should be characterized as "exile films" is problematic. But they were made with the assistance of exiles and therefore belong in this context.

From a purely numerical standpoint, the United States was the most important country of exile for this professional group. Approximately eight hundred of the two thousand filmmakers who left Germany after 1933 went there, almost exclusively to Hollywood. Their reactions to the dream factory, or make-believe machine, as Hollywood was often called, varied widely. Many, such as Marlene Dietrich, Fritz Lang, and Billy (Willi) Wilder, quickly carved out successful careers there; others, such as Bertolt Brecht, Curt Goetz, Friedrich Torberg, and Carl Zuckmayer perceived the place as hell, because everything there centered around making money without any higher aspirations. But viewed objectively, the hunger for appropriate film scripts in Hollywood provided a minimal living wage for a number of exile authors, among them Alfred Döblin, Leonhard

Frank, and Heinrich Mann, who thought up stories that were suitable for filming for a hundred dollars a month. These scripts or treatments were very rarely made into films, because they were usually much too artistic or ambitious, as the Americans said. Here—in contrast to France, England, or the Netherlands—being aesthetically challenging counted for much less than being commercially popular. When Fritz Lang, who was a highly respected filmmaker in Europe, arrived in the United States, the *New York Times* wrote, "Those fellows are notorious for being 'arty.' To the future confusion of the natives, he wore a monocle, something to which we cannot become accustomed." Henry Koster, an exile director who wanted to insert a passage of "classical music" in one of his Hollywood films, had to be told, "Nobody in America listens to that kind of music. You mean Wagner and Beethoven? You can't sell that here."

Some of these directors and screenwriters, driven more by necessity than by their own inclinations, were still able to have a substantial influence on the American film industry. In terms of themes for the films, this was possible only within certain limits. Until the end of 1941, before the US entry into World War II, films with a European background and films with antifascist or specifically Jewish themes were not in demand. Avant-garde films, as Oskar Fischinger or László Moholy-Nagy would have liked to make, were equally taboo. What the big companies really wanted were melodramatic society films, comedies, musicals, and science fiction or horror films—everything that Bertolt Brecht and Theodor W. Adorno viewed as base or trivial products of an unculture industry concerned only with making a profit. Nevertheless, some of the exile directors such as William Dieterle, Henry Koster, Fritz Lang, Max Ophüls, Otto Preminger, Robert Siodmak, Edgar Ulmer, Billy Wilder, and Fred Zinnemann did succeed in maintaining certain artistic pretensions even within these genres, although they knew it was not the good, the true, and the beautiful they were expected to produce, it was truly beautiful goods.

Almost none of them made any social-problem films in which they addressed their Jewishness, the loss of their homeland, their culture shock, or their hatred of Nazi fascism. Especially before 1941, while a widespread pro-appeasement mood prevailed in the United States, film was still viewed primarily as an entertainment genre that should be as accessible as possible and where political elements should be avoided. Even the beloved Charlie Chaplin was resented for taking up socially critical subject matter in his 1936 film *Modern Times,* and the *New York Times* suggested that it would be better if he went back to making slapstick comedies. It was even more taboo in the United States to use Jewish themes in developing antifascist propaganda. This was why many American film companies urged their Jewish actors and actresses to change their Jewish-sounding names to something more customary—for business reasons and also because of the anti-Semitism that was prevalent even in the United States. They did not want it to seem like theirs was an industry of Jews, nor did they want to jeopardize the export of their films to Nazi Germany and Italy. Accordingly, Bernard Schwartz suddenly became Tony Curtis; Issur Danielovitch became Kirk Douglas; Jacob Julius Garfinkle, John Garfield; Marion Levy, Paulette Goddard; Judith Tuvim, Judy Holliday; Shirley Schrift, Shelley Winters; Asa Yoelson, Al Jolson; and Nathan Birnbaum became George Burns. As a consequence, when Charlie Chaplin set about making a Hitler satire with his film *The Great Dictator* in 1939, including references to the Reichskristallnacht and the Anschluß of Austria, he met with fierce resistance at every point. The anti-Semites attempted to expose him as a Jew whose real name was Israel Thonstein in their brochure *Jew Star over Hollywood*, while the conservative isolationists attacked him sharply as a warmonger, with the result that the House Committee on Un-American Activities wanted to subpoena him. When the film *Confessions of a Nazi Spy* by Anatole Litvak was released the same year, there were strong protests in several American cities by the German-American Bund, which was sympathetic to the Nazi regime, because of the film's antifascist content.

Films like this became possible only with the entry of the United States into the war in December 1941. At that point, German exile directors, who had mostly made entertainment films and so-called B-movies for the big Hollywood companies, could finally take up antifascist themes. One example is the film that Fritz Lang made in 1942 based on a script by Bertolt Brecht about the murder of Heydrich in Prague; because its original title, *Trust the People*, had a left-critical tone, it was changed to *Hangmen Also Die* to Hollywoodize it, as the process was described in exile circles. One year later, James P. Hogan released his film *The Strange Death of Adolf Hitler*, with a doppelgänger motif that harked back to Chaplin's *Great Dictator*; in it Ludwig Donath and Fritz Kortner played two of the most important roles. German exiles, among them Hermann Millakowsky, Peter

Figure 46. Ludwig Donath (r.) in the film *The Strange Death of Adolf Hitler* (1943) directed by James P. Hogan. © Los Angeles, Margaret Herrick Library Academy Film Archive.

Pohlenz, Hermann Rauschning, Douglas Sirk, and Alfred Zeisler, also worked as directors, screenwriters, and actors in other anti-Nazi films that were made in Hollywood between 1941 and 1943 such as *The Hitler Gang, Enemy of Women, Women in Bondage, To Be or Not to Be, Hitler's Madman,* and *The Man Hunt.* In these films, the Nazi fascists, in contrast to the highly moral Americans, were usually portrayed as trigger-happy gangsters, satanic atheists, or cold-blooded womanizers in the tradition of earlier horror or Wild West films. President Franklin D. Roosevelt and the Office of War Information tried more than once to convince the film industry to produce better and above all more realistic anti-Nazi films, but the big film companies always had their eyes on the profit motive, and therefore they fell back on the proven clichés of melodramatic confrontation between villains and noble individuals with which they hoped to achieve the greatest success with the masses.

That was about the best that could be done in the US film industry even at that time. In short, many exiled filmmakers were in Los Angeles, but the movies they made for the big studios were almost exclusively entertainment films that promised a profit—horror films, costume dramas, science fiction, and comedies. Only a few films were specifically exile films in which they could portray their own situation, their culture, or their antifascist viewpoint—as many works of exile literature during these years were able to do.

Painting, Graphic Art, and Photomontage

Many fewer visual artists went into exile after 1933 than writers, film people, composers, or musicians. At first glance, this seems somewhat surprising. After all, the Nazi leaders had quickly zeroed in on artworks they did not like. As early as spring 1933, a series of well-known German painters such as Otto Dix and Max Beckmann were removed from their teaching positions by the NS authorities, and they were subsequently banned from exhibiting. Even some who held volkish views such as Emil Nolde, who had become an early member of the NSDAP, found no favor in the eyes of the new rulers. Nevertheless, the vast majority of German painters stayed in the Third Reich after 1933; there are many possible reasons why they made the decision not to go abroad. On the one hand, the conditions of their artistic production played a role. These groups were much less dependent than other artists on public institutions—publishing houses, film companies, or orchestras—some of which continued under private ownership in the Third Reich, but were still subject to a relatively strict state control by the censorship authorities. Even painters who were proscribed by the Nazi fascists, if they were already sufficiently well-known, could continue to sell their paintings privately to well-heeled collectors, albeit without exhibits organized by the state or any contact with galleries. This way they could live a relatively undisturbed life even under the swastika. On the other hand, there had been many fewer leftists and Jews among visual artists during the Second German Empire and the Weimar Republic than among creative artists active in the fields of literature and music.

Among the writers, filmmakers, composers, and musicians, it was primarily the leftists and the Jews who were purged from German cultural life beginning in 1933. But only a marginal number of painters had belonged to these groups, so the authorities had to round up some other kinds of scapegoats on which they could vent their overheated Nordic anger. Their targets, it was decided after some internal quarrels at the highest levels of the party, would be the racially degenerate modernists whose work was biased in favor of the low-minded, the formless, the obscene, and even the sluttish. Many Nazi policy statements proclaimed that most of these artists had only been interested in tickling the nerve endings of a metropolitan upper class of connoisseurs eager for artistic little sensations and had thereby failed to use the healthy feelings of the volk as their starting point. The main fury of the Nazi fascist art critics was therefore directed at artistic movements such as expressionism, cub-

Figure 47. Gerd Arntz: *Der Gegensatz Deutschland-Rußland* (The Contrast Germany-Russia, 1935).

ism, and Dadaism. They attacked these movements as manifestations of Weimar Republic internationalism, which had used pseudo-revolutionary means to distort everything deeply and devoutly German in art into something formless—and even to drag it through the mud. Instead, the Nazis favored a kind of painting that emphasized Germanness. By drawing on the noblest traditions of earlier art, this new art was supposed to portray an idealized reality. The first artist they believed had portrayed this idealized reality, and the one they still considered the most exemplary, was Albrecht Dürer, whose etching *Ritter zwischen Tod und Teufel* was seen as a model for every heroically minded German. As the most recent important representatives of this kind of art, they identified Eduard Grützner and Franz von Defregger, regional artists around 1900, and some painters belonging to the right wing of the New Objectivity movement, such as Werner Peiner and Adolf Ziegler.

Figure 48. Hanns Kralik: *Forced Labor in Börgermoor Concentration Camp* (1935). From the book by Wolfgang Langhoff: *Veensoldaten*, Amsterdam 1935.

Most painters who had been living in Germany since the late 1920s favored styles that reflected earlier regional art or the moderate wing of the New Objectivity movement. Therefore they had little to fear from the Nazi authorities, who even supported them energetically as part of their cultural propaganda program and recognized them with commissions. Many of the expressionists had now grown older, and like Erich Heckel, Max Pechstein or Karl Schmidt-Rottluff had moved to a more realistic style of painting even before 1933; they too remained relatively undisturbed. In contrast, artists who had sympathized with the KPD in the context of the Association of Revolutionary Visual Artists of Germany now had almost no possibilities for having an impact. The socially critical verists were equally threatened, as were Jewish artists and everyone who had followed Bauhaus trends and opted for styles of nonrepresentational painting. At first glance, it appears that we are talking about several significant groups, but that would be misleading. In reality, we are just talking about a scattered few, and not all of those few took refuge in exile.

Most of the painters and graphic artists who had belonged to the KPD before 1933 or had agreed with its objectives, such as Otto Griebel, Hans Grundig, Otto Nagel, and Oskar Nerlinger, remained in Germany despite multiple interrogations, arrests, and imprisonments. And even the

Figure 49. John Heartfield: *Werkzeug in Gottes Hand? Spielzeug in Thyssens Hand.* Photomontage for the *Arbeiter-Illustrierte Zeitung aller Länder* (Tool in God's Hand? Plaything in Thyssen's Hand, 1933). © Berlin, Bildagentur für Kunst, Kultur und Geschichte.

graphic artist and sculptor Käthe Kollwitz, who had become well-known even outside the Weimar Republic because of her pacifistic and pro-socialist works, did not go into exile. The antifascist works created by these artists during the Third Reich of course could not be exhibited until after 1945 and therefore remained virtually unknown inside Germany until then.

Outside Germany, only painters and graphic artists with leftist views were politically active, primarily as part of the Oskar-Kokoschka-Circle in Prague or the Union des Artistes Libres in Paris; among them were Gerd Arntz, Hanns Kralik, Max Lingner, Karl Schwesig, and Johannes Wüsten. In other countries, most of them ran into substantial difficulties. In Amsterdam in 1936, they were allowed to participate in the exhibition *De Olympiade Onder Dictatuur,* mounted in opposition to the Olympic games taking place in Berlin. A number of their works contained scenes from Nazi torture chambers and concentration camps that were intended to be provocative, as well as pro-Soviet motifs; due to protests by the German embassy in The Hague, critical statements by Dutch national socialists, and the timid stance of the Dutch authorities, these were purged from the exhibit after just a few days. In contrast, surrealistic or non-representational pictures such as those by Max Ernst, Otto Freundlich, and Heinz Lohmar, which were characterized as true works of art by the administrators responsible for the exhibition, did not offend anyone. The only communist-oriented visual artist in exile who had a significant international impact was the photomontage artist John Heartfield, who has become world-famous in the meantime. In the Hitler satires he completed between 1933 and 1938 for the *Arbeiter-Illustrierte Zeitung aller Länder* in Prague, he tried to expose Nazi fascism initially from a socially critical perspective as a regime of marionettes in the hands of German industrial barons like Fritz Thyssen and then as a brutal regime based on violence that was intervening in world politics. After he fled from Prague to England in 1938, he faced a lack of financial support and also a series of political restrictions, so he was forced to work almost exclusively as a book designer.

Even many of the left-oriented verists among the painters and graphic artists, Otto Dix and Rudolf Schlichter among them, remained in Germany, but after 1933 they migrated to a style of painting that displayed little critical perspective. The exhibition ban issued against them by the Nazi fascists forced them to sell their pictures only to private collectors. The main exceptions within this group were George Grosz and Max Beckmann. Shortly before Hitler's accession to power, Grosz left for the United States. He accepted a teaching position, but because of his deep-seated pessimism, he largely withdrew from politics. Things were made worse by the failure of his antifascist portfolio *Interregnum* (1935); although the well-known antiwar novelist John Dos Passos wrote the preface, only ten copies were sold in the United States. Beckmann lost his professorship at the Frankfurt Städelschule in March 1933 because of his crassly realistic pictures, but continued to live in Germany from the private sale of his pictures until 1937. In 1938, after eight of his paintings were pilloried as un-German at the Munich exhibit *Entartete Kunst*, he finally went into exile, first to Paris, then to Holland, and finally in 1947 to the United States. There, he was not actively antifascist; instead, he stuck to his conviction that all forms of a collective attitude, whether left, right, or just bourgeois, are detrimental to art and that every painter should be concerned primarily with the psychological exploration of the individual.

The few German-Jewish painters adopted a similar position after 1933. Max Liebermann resigned from the Prussian Academy of Arts immediately after the transfer of power to Hitler as a protest against the brown anti-spirit. He died in Berlin in February 1935 after advising some younger Jews to emigrate to Palestine rather than stay in Germany. In the course of the 1920s, Ludwig Meidner, like so many former expressionists, had gradually given up what had been his stirring, revolutionary painting style; he left Berlin in 1935. He taught drawing for a while at a Jewish school in Cologne until deciding in 1939 to emigrate to England. Felix Nußbaum, who was substantially younger, is a special case. In the late 1920s he had belonged to the wing of the New Objectivity movement for which the name magic realism gained currency at the time. He left Germany in 1933 and went first to France and then to Belgium. After he had been interned for a time in Gurs in 1940, he lived in hiding in Brussels. He was arrested again in summer 1944 and transported to Auschwitz a short time later. Before 1938, he had painted primarily portraits and magically de-familiarized genre scenes. Starting in 1939–1940, he decided to paint primarily pictures of loneliness, grief, and horror. After 1943, he also included features in his paintings that were intended to be antifascist, among them the Jewish identification card and the yellow Star of David that identified him as a political outcast. In 1937–1938 Peter Weiss, who was even younger and living in exile in Prague, began to paint pictures that were also indebted to the style of magical realism of the later 1920s, but he refrained from including features that could take on antifascist meanings. He, like Nußbaum, preferred motifs related to solitude, but without underlaying them with any clearly delineated political viewpoint.

The group of painters who had clung to abstract, constructivist, or nonrepresentational styles of painting until 1933 despite the incursion of New Objectivity was somewhat larger. Bauhaus artists who have become famous in the meantime belonged to this group, among them Wassily

Figure 50. Felix Nußbaum: *Selbstbildnis mit Judenstern und Identifikationskarte* (Self-Portrait with Star of David and Identification Card, 1943). © VG-Bild-Kunst, Bonn 2010.

Kandinsky, Paul Klee, and Lionel Feininger. For the art critics with strict modernistic views, these were the most consistent representatives until 1933 of what was referred to as avant-gardism in painting. Kandinsky escaped to France at the beginning of the Third Reich; Klee returned to Switzerland and Feininger to the United States, where they had lived before moving to Germany. In exile or in their earlier home countries, all three continued to paint in the style of international modernism instead of presenting themselves as representatives of an art that was specifically

German. And they held themselves more or less aloof from expressions of antifascism. The same is true of the Hungarian Lázló Moholy-Nagy, who had worked at the Bauhaus before 1933 as a so-called constructivist in the fields of photography, typography, and set design. He emigrated to England in 1935 and then to the United States in 1937, where he was one of the cofounders of the New Bauhaus in Chicago a short time later. The only ones in this group who really created a sensation, however, were Walter Gropius and Ludwig Mies van der Rohe, the two most important Bauhaus architects. As practitioners of the new international architectural style that they had initiated along with others, they went to the United States in 1937, where they found a fertile field for their activities. The question of whether they still viewed themselves as exiles must be left undecided. At this point, the border between German and international culture begins to blur, so that these artists' activities cannot really be viewed as taking place under conditions of exile.

Music

The third largest group of artists who were driven out of the Third Reich, along with writers and filmmakers, was made up of composers, conductors, and practicing musicians. In contrast to many writers and actors, who were often faced with insurmountable barriers abroad because they were German-speaking, it was somewhat easier for them to find new employment opportunities because of the international nature of musical means of expression. However, this was not the case for all of the composers and conductors who had fled Germany and Austria, because they represented very different artistic perceptions that would not be equally appreciated in all countries of exile. The ones who were most successful in identifying a new locus for their activity were advocates of the classical-romantic German musical tradition, which had been especially highly esteemed since the end of the eighteenth century in many European countries and was equally valued in the United States. One example was the Jewish-born conductor Bruno Walter, who liked to boast that he, in contrast to Wilhelm Furtwängler, had never conducted a non-German work. But even a composer classified as semimodern such as Paul Hindemith was able to perform his works in several exile countries and even be appointed to a highly respected position as professor of composition at Yale University in the United States. Composers who began to write music for Hollywood films, such as Erich Wolfgang Korngold, Miklos Rósza, Hans Julius Salter, and Ernst Toch, were even more successful, as was Kurt Weill, who supplied musicals for the Broadway stage. In contrast, there were two much smaller groups who were rejected almost everywhere: hardheaded modernists such as Arnold Schoenberg and Ernst Krenek and leftists such as Hanns Eisler, Paul Dessau, and Stefan Wolpe.

But a discussion of the exiled composers and conductors should not be limited to their artistic and ideological separation into various groups. It is also important to keep in mind the variation from one country to another of the public's readiness to receive the works they composed and played. Classical and romantic music was welcome almost everywhere. This primarily benefited the many German-Jewish conductors who continued to perform works from the German musical tradition that was respected by everyone. In contrast, almost none of the eminent non-Jewish conductors and composers in the classical-romantic tradition went into exile; in fact, they were usually awarded high honors by the Nazi fascists. Among the conductors were Karl Böhm, Karl Elmendorff, Wilhelm Furtwängler, Eugen Jochum, Herbert von Karajan, Hans Knappertsbusch, Clemens Krauß, and Hans Schmidt-Isserstedt; Hans Pfitzner and Richard Strauss were two of the most important composers. Even a former expressionist and objectivist like Paul Hindemith remained in Germany for several years after Hitler came to power, hoping that he would be recognized by the new masters. In 1938, he realized that there were no further opportunities for him in Germany and decided to emigrate to the United States via Switzerland.

There were other composers, conductors, and soloists expelled from Germany who made the decision to seek a position in the United States relatively late. Shortly after 1933, they first tried to look for new positions in countries bordering the Third Reich. In the beginning, Austria seemed to be the best option. It had been renowned as a country of music since time immemorial—as the home of Franz Joseph Haydn, Wolfgang Amadeus Mozart, Ludwig van Beethoven, Franz Schubert, Johann Strauß, Johannes Brahms, Anton Bruckner, Hugo Wolf, and Gustav Mahler. The first to move there were operetta composers who were originally from Austria, such as Paul Abraham and Robert Stolz. They had gone to Berlin in the 1920s and now tried to regain a foothold in Vienna. But by 1938, after the so-called Anschluß, they as Jews were also forced to flee to the United States. Alexander von Zemlinsky, a sympathizer with the Schoenberg Circle, also returned to Vienna from Berlin, but had a relatively difficult time in Austria even before 1938 and left for the United States. Ernst Krenek, who had lived in Vienna since 1928, followed the same path. After completing *Jonny spielt auf* (1927), a *Zeitoper* with jazz elements, he moved closer to Schoenberg's compositional techniques. He composed his opera *Karl V* using a strict twelve-tone technique, and it was therefore viewed by the anti-Semitic Austrian music lovers as Jewish. The opera's premiere in 1934 was blocked at the instigation of the Heimwehr (Home

Guard) and the Vaterländische Front (Patriotic Front), organizations that were closest to the Nazi fascist ideology dominant in Germany. And thus Krenek, too, although he was neither communist nor Jew, decided to emigrate to the United States in 1938.

The situation was not much different in Switzerland, despite the efforts of Hermann Scherchen, an antifascist conductor in exile. The opinion makers interested in music were also cultural conservatives and tried to close themselves off from any kind of left avant-garde music or from modernism à la Schoenberg. Similar conditions held in the Netherlands. As in Switzerland, everything in the German musical tradition that was classical or romantic had always been welcome. Thus, Georg Szell was able to lead the Residentie-Orchester in The Hague from 1937 to 1939, and Erich Kleiber, who had resigned from his position as opera director in Berlin in 1935 because of the banning of a work by Alban Berg, led the Wagner-Vereniging in Amsterdam from 1933 to 1938. In addition, the Busch-Quartett and the pianist Rudolf Serkin, who were also not able to appear in Germany after 1933, gave several concerts of German classical music in the Netherlands after that date. In contrast, works that were modernistic or leftist works that were antifascist had almost no chance of being performed, even in Holland.

The situation in Great Britain was not quite so restrictive. There, too, German classical and romantic music had long enjoyed high esteem. Therefore, the English authorities did not hesitate to invite Wilhelm Furtwängler, who was courted by the Nazis, to rehearse Richard Wagner's *Ring des Nibelungen* at the Covent Garden Opera on the occasion of the coronation festivities for George VI in 1937. Concerts of Bach, Beethoven, and Brahms directed by Furtwängler also received enthusiastic reviews in London. When Richard Strauss gave a guest concert with the Dresden Symphony Orchestra in 1936 in the Queen's Hall in London, the praise from the London *Times* was just as enthusiastic. But there were also many Hitler refugees who were highly esteemed by London music connoisseurs. This is demonstrated by the popularity of the opera festival in Glyndebourne, which was founded in 1934 by German exiles, including Carl Ebert as director, Fritz Busch as conductor, and Rudolf Bing as general manager. There were also a number of German exile composers, musicians, singers, and conductors who found much-envied positions with the British Broadcasting Company. Anyone not employed there could at least appear in the forty concerts organized by the Free German Cultural League beginning in 1939. Even some modernistic-sounding works by Arnold Schoenberg, Alban Berg, and Ernst Krenek were performed in London with the support of Benjamin Britten. However, it was more difficult for the leftists to make their voices heard in England, as in all of the countries where a policy of appeasement toward the Third Reich was in force. This explains the decision of composers and conductors who were sympathetic to communism such as Georg Knepler and Ernst Hermann Meyer, who had previously directed workers' choruses, to withdraw from active musical praxis and become musicologists.

The city of Prague offered the German musicians in exile even better possibilities for living and working. There was already an orchestra connected to the Neues Deutsches Theater (New German Theater), and the exiles were able to found two additional symphony orchestras after 1933, the Prager Philharmonie and the Prager Symphoniker. These orchestras embraced avant-garde and half-modern music as well as classical and romantic music and did not hesitate to invite left-oriented Hermann Scherchen, who had been banned from Germany, as guest conductor. Leo Kestenberg, the once highly influential secretary for music in the Prussian Ministry of Culture, who had given Arnold Schoenberg a position teaching composition in the Prussian Academy of Arts, was even able to continue the reform of music education that he had begun in Berlin until he was forced to flee to Palestine in 1939.

German musicians were less welcome in France, where very few found positions as conductors or orchestra members. Their chances were even slimmer if they wanted to succeed as composers. Even Kurt Weill's "accessible" music met with little response. When Weill staged his *Sieben Todsünden* (Seven Deadly Sins) based on Brecht texts in Paris in 1934, the French composer Florent Schmitt is supposed to have called loudly from the audience, "Vive Hitler!" In the same year, however, a Beethoven concert with Wilhelm Furtwängler and the Berlin Philharmonic was received with enthusiasm by the Parisian audience. Conservative right-wing circles in France very strongly resisted seeing any musical works put in the service of antifascist views, an attitude Hanns Eisler experienced. In 1936, on the occasion of a meeting of the International Society for New Music, he submitted two movements from his *Konzentrationslagersymphonie* (Concentration Camp Symphony) based on texts by Ignazio Silone and Bertolt Brecht to the committee responsible for selecting the works that would be performed. Because of the high quality of the composition, these two movements even won first prize and were supposed to be rehearsed in Paris for performance. But a few weeks before the premiere, the gentlemen of the jury thought worse of it. Fearing a protest from the German embassy, they suggested to Eisler that he replace "the voices which were to sing the offending antifascist song texts with saxophones." Since this was unacceptable to Eisler, he withdrew his score. In consequence, his *Deutsche Symphonie*, as he later called the work, remained unperformed in exile. Yet he had thought that its mixture of Schoenberg twelve-tone technique and antifascist texts, of Bach-like cantata style and echoes of the International, would fit perfectly into the popular front concept that was definitely on the political agenda at the time—especially in the left and left-liberal camps, but in the bourgeois-humanistic camp as well. His *Kantate gegen den Krieg* (Anti-war Cantata), his *Zuchthauskantate* (Penitentiary Cantata), his *Kantate auf den Tod eines Genossen* (Cantata on the Death of a Comrade) and his *Kantate im Exil* (Cantata in Exile) met a similar fate and were performed seldom or not at all in other countries as well. Not even the Soviet Union would take on works like these. Important German exile conductors such as Kurt Adler, Leo Blech, Kurt Sanderling, Fritz Stiedry, and Heinz Unger were welcomed there with open arms because of their familiarity with the German classical tradition. But even in the USSR composers of left avant-garde music, for which the defamatory word "formalistic" was gaining acceptance, encountered increasing opposition. In the end, even Hanns Eisler was forced to emigrate to the United States.

There the exiled musicians' lives were safe, which was the main concern for many of them at that point, but they soon faced many difficulties, both anticipated and unanticipated. Once again, the conductors and soloists had the easiest time in finding a position, as long as they limited themselves to performing classical and romantic works that were the old familiar war horses of symphony orchestras in New York, Boston, Chicago, Cleveland, Pittsburgh, Los Angeles, and other large American cities where exile conductors such as Jascha Horenstein, Otto Klemperer, Erich Leinsdorf, Wilhelm Steinberg, Georg Szell, and Bruno Walter had been able to occupy leading positions relatively quickly. Even half-modern composers were offered lucrative jobs by US universities or colleges.

Composers whose reputation as left or avant-garde preceded them had a substantially more difficult time in the United States. In the United States, anything on the left was taboo in so-called elite music in any case. Hanns Eiser had been the leading exponent of *Rote Kampfmusik* (red music for struggle) in the Weimar Republic and had then accommodated himself in the mid-1930s to the popular front strategy against German fascism. After his arrival in the United States, he had to adapt as a composer once more to compose the kind of functional music the film companies in Hollywood wanted. As a resident alien under the watchful eyes of the FBI, any political activities at all would have been prohibited. And in this country, where the so-called New Music was almost unknown, he could only indulge his earlier penchant for compositions in the style of Schoenberg's twelve-tone technique privately. One example is his septet *Vierzehn Arten den Regen zu beschreiben* (Fourteen Ways to Describe the Rain) that he composed in strict serial technique in honor of the seven-

Figure 51. Arnold Schoenberg in exile (c. 1935).

tieth birthday of Schoenberg, who had been his teacher; it was premiered on 13 September1944 in Schoenberg's house in Los Angeles. But otherwise he was forced to "work the streets," as Bertolt Brecht had put it in his *Hollywood-Elegien*, for the corporate executives of the film industry.

Ernst Krenek and Stefan Wolpe had more or less the same experience in the United States, misunderstood everywhere because of their modernistic compositions. Krenek even had to give up his teaching positions at Vassar College and at Hamline University primarily because he championed Schoenberg's twelve-tone technique too avidly. Stefan Wolpe, once a student of Anton Webern, also ran into difficulties in the United States, where he went after a stopover in Palestine. Since the late 1920s and early 1930s, detours into jazz à la George Gershwin's *An American in Paris* (1928) or into folkloristic elements à la Aaron Copland's *El Salon Mexico* (1934) were increasingly popular, but a left-leaning modernist like Wolpe was viewed as a bizarre misfit.

The best-known victim of this aversion to modernism in music was Arnold Schoenberg, who had come to the United States in 1934, taught for a short time at Malkin Conservatory in Boston, and then in 1936 accepted temporary teaching positions at the University of California in

Los Angeles and at the University of Southern California. Even he, whose music was considered in Europe as the non-plus-ultra of modernistic composition, remained a nobody in the United States. In Berlin in 1931, the great Schoenberg had advanced the self-aggrandizing theory in his essay *Nationale Musik* that his discovery of the twelve-tone technique had secured one-hundred more years of "international reputation" for German music. He had never heard of most film composers in Los Angeles before, but they had much more prestige than he did and usually looked down on him, if they even noticed him. Almost none of his compositions were played anywhere. Schoenberg, full of resentment, blamed the supposed anti-Semitism of the German-Jewish conductors who had migrated to the United States, felt misunderstood, and became reclusive. This attitude led his disciple Theodor W. Adorno, who deemed himself equally misunderstood, to portray Schoenberg in his *Philosophie der Neuen Musik* (Philosophy of New Music), which appeared in 1947, as the most significant composer of the twentieth century, to whom even Béla Bartók and Igor Strawinsky could not hold a candle. Two pieces composed in 1942 were also not helpful for Schoenberg: one was his tonal "*Gebrauchsmusik*" (Functional Music) for concert band and the other was his "Ode to Napoleon Buonaparte" for reciter, string quartet, and piano. The latter, with its cryptic Napoleon-Hitler parallel, was definitely intended to be antifascist, but it required, as did all of his works, an extremely demanding transposition process to be understood as such and therefore went unrecognized. Schoenberg left his opera *Moses und Aron*, which was intended to be Zionist, uncompleted, because there were absolutely no opportunities at all in the United States for the work to be performed. Instead, shortly after the collapse of the Third Reich, he completed his eleven-and-a-half-minute melodrama *A Survivor from Warsaw*, which was one of the most important musical works created in exile. In its pointed form, it evokes more forcefully than a lengthy opera would have done the ghastly fate of a group of Polish Jews who were deported to Auschwitz. After this, Schoenberg fixed his eyes unwaveringly on the state of Israel, cursed any Jewish exile who returned to Germany, and finally died in Los Angeles in 1951, an embittered man.

Few Hitler refugees among the German composers in the United States could bring themselves to assume such an extreme outsider role. If they were offered the possibility of hiring themselves out to one of the many branches of the commercial music industry, they took it, as a means of survival if nothing else. Kurt Weill, for example, who was far removed from everything highbrow and any feeling of being misunderstood, did not hesitate at all to get involved in the business of Broadway. But even he came to realize that some of his works were considered difficult. What the producers expected from him were accessible musicals, in other words, musicals that were designed to produce a profit, whereas he continued to be influenced in part by European opera. At that time, most Americans thought of opera as bombastic and boring, something with which you could definitely not make a fast buck. Reflecting this attitude, a group of potential sponsors rejected Weill's half opera *Down in the Valley* in 1944 with the remark "that they might be accused of submitting an 'opera' to the public." Lotte Lenya explained in reference to a rehearsal of Weill's *Street Scene* in Philadelphia in 1946, "The word 'opera' frightened everybody." This, despite the fact that Weill had done everything he could to conceal his German origins as much as possible and to acculturate to the United States—to conform to the musical conventions of the Broadway scene with musicals such as *Knickerbocker Holiday* (1938), *Lady in the Dark* (1940), *One Touch of Venus* (1943), and *Down in the Valley* (1945).

This attitude provoked the anger of Bertolt Brecht, who saw it as a betrayal of Weill's earlier left-liberal views. It also aroused the displeasure of Theodor W. Adorno, who tended to particularly implacable judgments in the realm of music. In his view, all products of what he described as a totally depraved culture industry were a priori alienated, manipulative, and therefore totalitarian, and he equated them with the mind-numbing products of Nazi fascist propaganda. In his *Philosophie der Neuen Musik* and in *Dialektik der Aufklärung* (Dialectic of Enlightenment), both of which appeared shortly after the end of World War II, he settled accounts with everything that transgressed his German-elitist concept of culture. His hatred of the social engineering tactics employed by the American culture industry, or unculture industry, as it should more appropriately be called, was often so overstated that it only seemed to reflect an outsider's marginal viewpoint, sometimes to the point of absurdity. Once, in his emotional response to the tendency of the mass media to blast us with sound, he stated that we should no longer listen to music, we should read it. The anger underlying such statements can certainly be understood as the expression of an exile-induced psychosis or of a "damaged life," as Adorno called it in *Minima moralia,* his collection of aphorisms. It has lost none of its critical bite in the face of our leisure industry today, which has grown even more trivial. This kind of critique, however, lacks a counter image that would give it a deeper meaning. Even toward the end of the war, Adorno consistently rejected attempts to come up with forward-looking concepts. While others among the exiles were already looking toward a Germany whose culture would need to be reconstructed on the basis of an "aesthetics of anticipation," Adorno still insisted on the principle of negativity. He saw only alienation produced by the capitalist economic and social order, an order in which there was "nothing right within the wrong" and which for the time being was inalterable.

VISIONS OF A LIBERATED CULTURE
IN POSTFASCIST GERMANY

During the time between 1933 and 1939 when Nazi fascism was the sole dominant power in Germany and during the first three war years as it began its victorious advance on all fronts to the east, the west, and the north, the political and cultural manifestations of exile reflected either a depressed waiting room mood or senseless protest. Only after the Battle of Stalingrad in the winter of 1942–1943, which marked a turning point in World War II in the Allies' favor, did scattered exiles or exile groups begin to think about plans for a liberated Germany and a new German culture. They had feared at first that the Western powers and the Third Reich might still reach a compromise peace agreement that would ensure hegemony in large parts of Europe for Hitler, but the insistence on an unconditional surrender by Franklin D. Roosevelt and Winston Churchill in Casablanca on 20 January 1943 suddenly cleared the way for them to think about Germany's future after the collapse of Nazi fascism. Of course these efforts were made in the shadow of the United States and the USSR, which had come out on top as the two political great powers of the era, and they left little room for initiatives on the part of the German exiles.

In the United States, a number of those who had been driven out of Germany because of their liberal views or because they were Jews agreed with the wholesale condemnation of everyone who had remained in the Third Reich expressed by Franklin D. Roosevelt and especially Henry Morgenthau. Only toward the end of the war did they begin to subscribe to the proposition that after the cessation of hostilities a fair differentiation would have to be made between the actual Nazi criminals and the German people, who had been seduced, but had remained deeply honorable. The communists and other leftists among the exiles supported this differentiation most forcefully. They had sided with Roosevelt since the Japanese attack on Pearl Harbor on 7 December 1941 and the United States' subsequent entry into the war, but a total condemnation of the German people had seemed politically unwise to them from the beginning. In the years between 1942 and 1945, they hoped that German soldiers with a proletarian background would revolt or at least desert en masse, but in

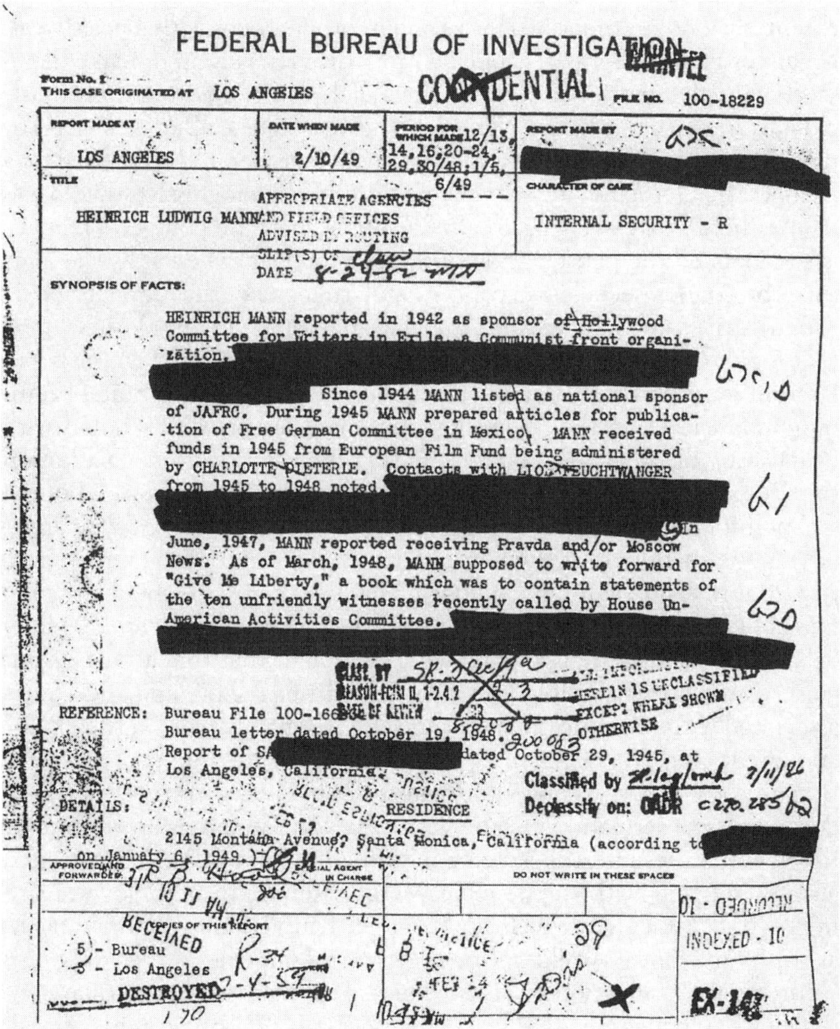

Figure 52. FBI file for Heinrich Mann (1949). © Washington, D.C., National Archives.

contrast to World War I, it never happened. Nevertheless, they clung to the idea that after an Allied victory the majority of Germans could quickly be won over to the ideas of peace, democracy, and even socialism, and that the broad masses of the German population should therefore not be punished or oppressed too severely.

But the German communists could not put their views across within the various exile organizations in the United States for two reasons. First, they were constantly under surveillance by the secret service of the Federal Bureau of Investigation and were therefore intimidated to some extent. Second, in their own ranks and in other groups with a positive attitude toward the German people, nationalist views began to make themselves felt; this patriotism toward the Reich was sometimes disastrously close to the ideology of the Nazis. For this reason, the alliance formed by the various groups of exiles, which had come together in the Council for a Democratic Germany under the leadership of the progressive theologian Paul Tillich, broke apart again after a short time. The bourgeois humanists repudiated the participation of the communists, whereas at the same time the council seemed too pangermanic to many of the German Jews.

Much the same happened to the Nationalkomitee Freies Deutschland (National Committee for a Free Germany), which was based on the popular front ideas of the 1930s and became active in the United States beginning in fall 1943. In the beginning, politicians, artists, and scholars with widely varying ideological backgrounds participated in this organization too. But serious differences of opinion soon arose, just as they had in the Council for a Democratic Germany. A number of committee sympathizers, among them Bertolt Brecht, Lion Feuchtwanger, Bruno Frank, Heinrich Mann, Thomas Mann, Ludwig Marcuse, Hans Reichenbach, and Berthold Viertel, met in Los Angeles on 1 August 1943. After a lengthy debate, they agreed in a programmatic statement that they would distinguish as clearly as possible "between the Hitler regime and the groups associated with it on the one hand and the German people on the other," and at the same time that they would call upon the German people to "force its oppressors to unconditional surrender and to fight for a strong democracy in Germany." But the very next day, Thomas Mann withdrew his signature because the statement seemed to him to be too patriotic, and he felt that with it, the exiles were "stabbing the US government in the back." Like Roosevelt and Morgenthau, Thomas Mann thought at this point that it would not be unreasonable for the "Allies to punish Germany for ten or twenty years." He felt his view was more than confirmed when he learned during a conversation in Washington in October 1943 that the US government did not encourage such premature reconstruction plans and therefore would not recognize a German government in exile—a government that many exiles thought should be headed by Heinrich Mann.

The artists and philosophers in these exile groups—communists, social democrats, members of the group Begin Anew, centrists, bourgeois liberals, and independents—had been concerned not only with the establishment of a democratic German republic after the war; they were also concerned with the role art would play in a culture that was truly close to the people. After the collapse of their interventionist plans, the members of these groups saw themselves thrown back on their own métiers, and so they began to conceive visions of the contribution works of art and philosophy could make in the implementation of a democratically just social order in Germany. Thomas Mann held on firmly to his punishment ideas and ruled out returning to Germany from the outset. Ernst Bloch, on the other hand, was already working on his *Prinzip Hoffnung* (Principle of Hope) at the time, in which he attempted to make his romantic Marxism relatively concrete and therefore productive for a Germany of the future, where there would have to be an indissoluble synthesis of politics, philosophy, and culture. Even Bertolt Brecht, an author previously averse to all utopian thinking, began in 1944 in his *Kaukasischer Kreidekreis* (Caucasian Chalk Circle) to conceptualize an image of the future in which artists would be given a substantial voice in the construction of a socially just society. He did not dare to set the plot of the play in a liberated Germany; instead, he chose Grusinia, in other words Georgia, a country that was already socialist. When solutions to conflicts are needed there, the popular poet Arkadi Tscheidse is given the task of mediating between the party and the people with his politically interventionist works. Up to that point, Brecht had still hoped to see at least some of the plays he had written in exile performed on American stages, but he now realized that if this play were to be performed at all, it would have to be on a stage in liberated Germany, where high culture would once again have an important function in a socialist context.

The German exiles connected to Aurora-Verlag, which had been founded in New York in 1944 by Wieland Herzfelde, nursed similar hopes. Not only had they published Ernst Bloch's *Abriß der Sozialutopien* (Survey of Social Utopias) and Bertolt Brecht's series of scenes *Furcht und Elend des Dritten Reichs* in German; shortly after the end of the war, they also compiled a reader under the title *Morgenröte* (Dawn) with an introduction written by Heinrich Mann. In its 350 pages, Herzfelde included in no particular order texts by leftist exile authors next to texts by older German writers who professed liberal, left-liberal, and socialist views. In the best sense of the popular front concept, the book was intended to offer a guideline to all German readers abroad as well as those in the four allied occupation zones for what should be considered true German literature and culture in the future.

The most important cultural-political stimuli at the time, however, came from those German politicians and writers who had fled to the USSR, not from the exiles in the United States. In mid-1943, the KPD leadership in Moscow had begun to develop plans for how the exiles could participate in the political, economic, and cultural reconstruction of Germany after the war. The National Committee for a Free Germany, which had been established on 13 July 1943 with the cooperation of leading KPD functionaries and exiled writers such as Johannes R. Becher, Friedrich Wolf, and Erich Weinert, played an important role in this effort. They primarily addressed the task of an ideological reeducation of German prisoners of war. With his famous statement on 23 February 1942, "The Hitlers come and go, but the German people, the German state, endures," Stalin absolved the majority of the German population from collective responsibility for Nazi crimes. Following this statement, German exile writers living in the Soviet Union became noticeably more nationalistic. Johannes R. Becher, for example, did not hesitate at the time to speak forcefully about the "guardian spirit of an eternal Germany," which—after Nazi fascism had been wrestled to the ground—would have to be in the forefront during the construction of a new culture. The group's objective was an unambiguously national culture with an antifascist bias that would open a path to a democratic concept of art. In the spirit of popular front policies, they planned for close cooperation between bourgeois humanist and socialist creative artists; they emphasized retaining pan-German attitudes to maintain Germany's cultural unity despite the planned division into four zones of occupation.

These plans were introduced to the postwar German public on 3 July 1945 from the large broadcasting room of Radio Berlin. The initiator of the event was the recently founded Kulturbund zur demokratischen Erneuerung Deutschlands (Cultural Federation for the Democratic Renewal of Germany), which wanted to connect the artists of both inner and outer emigration, in the terminology used at the time. Johannes R. Becher was elected first president of the federation, supported by writer Bernhard Kellermann, painter Karl Hofer, and classical philologist Johannes Stroux as vice presidents. The very old Gerhard Hauptmann was named president emeritus. Other positions of leadership were assumed by theater critic Herbert Jhering, physicist Robert Havemann, SPD politician Gustav Dahrendorf, sculptor Renée Sintenis, actor Paul Wegener, philosopher Ernst Niekisch, CDU politician Ernst Lemmer, professor of French literature Viktor Klemperer, theater director Wolfgang Langhoff, KPD politician Anton Ackermann, educational theorist Eduard Spranger, painters Otto Nagel and Max Pechstein, as well as writers Willi Bredel, Ricarda Huch, Ludwig Renn, Anna Seghers, and Günther Weisenborn. Thanks to this impressive phalanx of important politicians, scholars, and creative artists, forty-five thousand members organized in 394 local groups joined the cultural federation in the first year. The basic program of the federation, agreed to at the founding meeting, followed the earlier popular front strategy on many points: it advocated a "national unity front of all German intellectual workers," whose representatives would above all support "the rediscovery and promotion of the free and humanistic traditions of our people" during the "cultural reconstruction of Germany." First, in cooperation with all democratic ideological, religious, and ecclesiastical movements and groups, it was essential to achieve a "systematic destruction of Nazi ideology in all areas of life, knowledge, and culture."

This kind of program seemed very politically involved, but at the same time rather general. Nevertheless, a two-pronged strategy was surely inevitable in the immediate postwar situation to avoid alienating the majority of those artists who were still under the influence of conservative, volkish, or Nazi fascist ideologies and who had not gone into exile after 1933. A thoroughly revolutionary program would surely have gotten mired in sectarianism at the time. In view of this fact, the federation behaved "without blinders but with determination, objective but not neutral," as it was phrased in *Aufbau*, the federation's own journal. At the same time, it declared repeatedly that in contrast to Nazi fascism it was not attempting to force a particular ideology on anyone; the federation was simply trying to "awaken the true spirit of humanity and to promote it" in all people. But it would not compromise on one point: it insisted that great national, political, and social concerns must be at the core of all future art. For this reason, the federation strictly rejected both the elitist dissociation of art from the broad masses of the population and the production of trivial distraction and entertainment of the kind that had been used culturally to corrupt the lower classes in the Weimar Republic and in the Third Reich.

This internal unity collapsed as early as 1946–1947; after the beginning of the Cold War between the United States and the USSR, there were inevitably fierce political and cultural confrontations between Western bourgeois and Eastern socialist creative artists in the four zones of occupation. This became clearly perceptible at the first Deutscher Schriftstellerkongreß (German Writers' Congress) convened by the Cultural Federation in Berlin in October 1947. Johannes R. Becher invoked the idea of Germany's cultural unity once again and called on all participants to oppose energetically any tendency to schisms. But these statements had an activist sound to them and led a few weeks later to the banning of the Cultural Federation in the three Western sectors of Berlin by the local occupation authorities. In the three Western zones of occupation, where an increasingly conservative spirit was gaining ground, its activities were so hampered that it became meaningless in the end.

It was easy to predict what would happen next. In fall 1949, there was a final division of Germany into two independent states—the Bundesrepublik Deutschland (Federal Republic of Germany) and the Deutsche Demokratische Republik (the German Democratic Republic). The GDR adhered to the leftist orientation of the earlier popular front strategy in matters of culture well into the 1950s; in other words, it excluded all genres of trivial culture and valued almost exclusively Marxist and bourgeois humanist representatives of high culture. In the FRG, on the other hand, an elite culture built on inner emigration or modernist concepts was propagated by the educated middle class, whereas at the level of entertainment culture a commercial unculture was soon permitted to spread—the same unculture that the Cultural Federation for the Democratic Renewal of Germany had wanted to abolish completely only a few years before. Thus, the opportunity for cultural unity in Germany was lost for decades to come. Following this change, of course, a development began in the history of German culture that many on both sides of the Iron Curtain perceived as new, although it was based on events and works portrayed in this volume whose importance cannot be overestimated.

SELECTED BIBLIOGRAPHY

I owe many ideas to my perusal of archival materials and to reading many more books than I included in the following bibliography. Conversations with friends and colleagues such as Helmut G. Asper, Klaus L. Berghahn, Werner Mittenzwei, Klaus Scherpe, and Marc Silberman were also extremely stimulating as I developed the concept for this volume. In addition, I still remember numerous conversations with Walter Grab, Paul Jagenburg, Hans Mayer, George L. Mosse, and Felix Pollak in which we talked again and again about the problems of Nazi fascism and exile; these conversations continue to exert an influence on my thinking.

I am grateful to Adam Woodis for the careful computerization of my manuscript, which was originally in quite a chaotic state; its final format, reduced to the point of a compact textbook, required constant new cuts and transpositions. And last but not least, I have to thank Victoria Hill for the difficult task of translating the German original of this book into a readable English.

The individual contributions within the sections of the following bibliography are ordered chronologically. The intent is to enable readers who are interested in further research in this area to obtain initial information and at the same time permit insights into the development of the secondary literature that has grappled with the cultural ideas of the Nazi fascists, the representatives of inner emigration, and the exiles expelled from the Third Reich.

NS Culture

Adler, Hans G. *Theresienstadt. 1941–1945. Das Antlitz einer Zwangsgemeinschaft*. Tübingen: J.B.C. Mohr, 1955.

Brenner, Hildegard. *Die Kunstpolitik des Nationalsozialismus*. Reinbek: Rowohlt, 1963.

Mosse, George L. *Nazi Culture: Intellectual, Cultural, and Social Life in the Third Reich*. New York: Grosset and Dunlap, 1966.

Vondung, Klaus. *Magie und Manipulation. Ideologischer Kult und politische Religion des Nationalsozialismus*. Göttingen: Vandenhoeck und Ruprecht, 1971.

Damus, Martin. *Kunst und Kultur im deutschen Faschismus*. Stuttgart: J.B. Metzler, 1978.

Schnell, Ralf, ed. *Kunst und Kultur im deutschen Faschismus*. Stuttgart: J.B. Metzler, 1978.

Grimm, Reinhold and Jost Hermand, eds. *Faschismus und Avantgarde*. Königstein: Athenäum, 1980.

Schäfer, Hans Dieter. *Das gespaltene Bewußtsein. Über deutsche Kultur und Lebenswirklichkeit 1933–1945*. Munich: Hanser, 1981.

Herf, Jeffrey. *Reactionary Modernism: Technology, Culture, and Politics in Weimar and the Third Reich*. New York: Cambridge University Press, 1984.

Prinz, Michael, and Rainer Zitelmann, eds. *Nationalsozialismus und Modernisierung*. Darmstadt: Wissenschaftliche Buchgesellschaft, 1991.

Reichel, Peter. *Der schöne Schein des Dritten Reiches. Faszination und Gewalt des Faschismus*. Munich: Hanser, 1991.

Adam, Peter. *Kunst im Dritten Reich*. Hamburg: Rogner und Bernhard, 1992.

Akademie der Künste, ed. *Geschlossene Vorstellung. Der jüdische Kulturbund in Deutschland 1933–1941*. Berlin: Edition Hentrich, 1992.

Geisel, Eike, and Henryk M. Broder. *Premiere und Pogrom. Der jüdische Kulturbund 1933–1945. Texte und Bilder*. Berlin: Siedler, 1992.

Hermand, Jost. *Old Dreams of a New Reich: Volkish Utopias and National Socialism*. Bloomington: Indiana University Press, 1992.

Dahm, Volker. *Das jüdische Buch im Dritten Reich*. Munich: Beck, 1993.

Hewitt, Andrew. *Fascist Modernism: Aesthetics, Politics, and the Avant-Garde*. Stanford: Stanford University Press, 1993.

Steinweis, Alan. *Art, Ideology and Economics in Nazi Germany: The Reich Chambers of Music, Theater, and the Visual Arts*. Chapel Hill: North Carolina University Press, 1993.

Cuomo, Glenn, ed. *National Socialist Cultural Policy*. New York: Macmillan, 1995.

Faustmann, Uwe Julius. *Die Reichskulturkammer. Aufbau, Funktion und rechtliche Grundlagen einer Körperschaft des öffentlichen Rechts im nationalsozialistischen Regime*. Aachen: Shaker, 1995.

Petropoulos, Jonathan. *Art as Politics in the Third Reich*. Chapel Hill: North Carolina University Press, 1996.

Gassert, Phillip. *Amerika im Dritten Reich. Ideologie, Propaganda und Volksmeinung 1933–1945*. Stuttgart: Steiner, 1997.

Reimer, Robert C., ed. *Cultural History through a National Socialist Lens*. Rochester: Camden House, 2000.

Etlin, Richard, ed. *Art, Culture, and Media under the Third Reich*. Chicago: University of Chicago Press, 2002.

Schütz, Erhard, and Gregor Streim, eds. *Reflexe und Reflexionen von Modernität 1933–1945*. Bern: Peter Lang, 2002.

Klee, Ernst. *Das Kulturlexikon zum Dritten Reich. Wer war was vor und nach 1945?* Frankfurt: S. Fischer, 2003.

Koonz, Claudia. *The Nazi Conscience*. Cambridge: Belknap, 2003.

Baranowski, Shelley. *Strength through Joy: Consumerism and Mass Tourism in the Third Reich*. New York: Cambridge, 2004.

Michaud, Eric. *The Cult of Art in Nazi Germany*. Stanford: Stanford University Press, 2004.

Sarkowicz, Hans, ed. *Hitlers Künstler. Die Kultur im Dienst des Nationalsozialismus*. Frankfurt: Insel, 2004.

Seligmann, Matthew. *Daily Life in Hitler's Germany*. New York: Thomas Dunne, 2004.

Berghahn, Klaus L., and Jost Hermand, eds. *Unmasking Hitler: Cultural Representations of Hitler from the Weimar Republic to the Present*. Oxford: Peter Lang, 2005.

Bollmus, Reinhard. *Das Amt Rosenberg und seine Gegner. Studien zum Machtkampf im nationalsozialistischen Herrschaftssystem*. Munich: Oldenbourg, 2005.

Glaser, Hermann. *Wie Hitler den deutschen Geist zerstörte. Kulturpolitik im Dritten Reich*. Hamburg: Ellert und Richter, 2005.

Huener, Jonathan, and Francis Nicosia, eds. *The Arts in Nazi Germany: Continuity, Conformity, Change*. New York: Berghahn, 2006.

Pine, Lisa. *Hitler's "National Community": Society and Culture in Nazi Germany*. London: Bloomsbury, 2007.

Heidenreich, Bernd, and Sönke Neitzel,eds. *Medien im Nationalsozialismus*. Munich: Fink, 2009.

NS Architecture

Teut, Anna. *Architektur im Dritten Reich. 1933–1945*. Berlin: Ullstein, 1967.

Taylor, Robert. *The Word in Stone: The Role of Architecture in the National Socialist Ideology*. Berkeley: University of California Press, 1974.

Petsch, Joachim. *Baukunst und Stadtplanung im Dritten Reich*. Munich: Hanser, 1976.

Rasp, Hans Peter. *Eine Stadt für tausend Jahre. München, Bauten und Projekte für die Hauptstadt der Bewegung*. Munich: Süddeutscher Verlag, 1981.

Stommer, Rainer, ed. *Reichsautobahnen. Pyramiden des Dritten Reiches*. Marburg: Jonas, 1982.

Schmidt, Matthias. *Albert Speer: The End of a Myth*. New York: St. Martin's Press, 1984.

Bartetzko, Dieter. *Zwischen Zucht und Askese. Zur Theatralik von NS-Architektur*. Berlin: Mann, 1985.

Seidler, Franz W. *Fritz Todt. Baumeister des Dritten Reiches*. Frankfurt a. M. und Berlin: Bublies Siegfried, 1988.

Schäche, Wolfgang. *Architektur und Städtebau in Berlin zwischen 1933 und 1945*. Berlin: Mann, 1992.

Schütz, Erhard, and Eckhard Gruber. *Mythos Reichsautobahn. Bau und Inszenierung der "Straßen des Führers" 1933–1941*. Berlin: Link, 1996.

Weihsmann, Helmut. *Bauen unterm Hakenkreuz*. Wien: Promedia, 1998.

Fest, Joachim. *Speer: The Final Verdict*. New York: Harcourt, 2001.

Van Tol, David. *Albert Speer*. Wilston: Farr Books, 2008.

NS Painting and Sculpture

Rave, Paul Ortwin. *Kunstdiktatur im Dritten Reich*. Hamburg: Mann, 1949.

Wulf, Josef, ed. *Die bildenden Künste im Dritten Reich*. Hamburg: Rowohlt, 1966.

Bussmann, Georg, ed. *Kunst im Dritten Reich. Dokumente der Unterwerfung.* Frankfurt: Frankfurter Kunstverein, 1974.

Müller-Mehlis, Reinhard. *Die Kunst im Dritten Reich.* Munich: Heyne, 1976.

Thomane, Otto. *Die Propaganda-Maschinerie. Bildende Kunst und Öffentlichkeitsarbeit im Dritten Reich.* Berlin: Mann, 1978.

Hinz, Berthold. *Art in the Third Reich.* New York: Pantheon, 1979.

Wolbert, Klaus. *Die Nackten und die Toten des "Dritten Reiches." Folgen einer politischen Geschichte des Körpers in der Plastik des deutschen Faschismus.* Gießen: Anabas, 1982.

Merker, Reinhard. *Die bildenden Künste im Nationalsozialismus. Kulturideologie, Kulturpolitik, Kulturproduktion.* Cologne: DuMont, 1983.

Petsch, Joachim. *Kunst im Dritten Reich. Architektur – Plastik – Malerei – Alltagsästhetik.* Cologne: Vista Point, 1983.

Schuster, Peter Klaus, ed. *Nationalsozialismus und "Entartete Kunst." Die Kunststadt München 1937.* Munich: Prestel, 1987.

Backes, Klaus. *Hitler und die bildenden Künste. Kulturverständnis und Kunstpolitik im Dritten Reich.* Cologne: DuMont, 1988.

Wissel, Adolf. *Malerei und Kunstpolitik im Nationalsozialismus.* Berlin: Mann, 1994.

Von zur Mühlen, Ilse. *Die Kunstsammlung Hermann Görings.* Munich: Bayrische Staatsgemäldesammlungen, 2004.

NS Music

Wulf, Josef, ed. *Musik im Dritten Reich.* Gütersloh: Mohn, 1963.

Prieberg, Fred K. *Musik im NS-Staat.* Cologne: Dittrich, 1982.

Heister, Hanns-Werner, and Hans-Günter Klein, eds. *Musik und Musikpolitik im faschistischen Deutschland.* Frankfurt: Fischer, 1984.

Prieberg, Fred K. *Kraftprobe. Wilhelm Furtwängler im Dritten Reich.* Wiesbaden: Brockhaus, 1986.

Splitt, Gerhard. *Richard Strauss 1933–1945. Ästhetik und Musikpolitik zu Beginn der nationalsozialistischen Herrschaft.* Pfaffenweiler: Centaurus, 1987.

Dümling, Albrecht, and Peter Girth, eds. *Entartete Musik. Eine kommentierte Rekonstruktion.* Düsseldorf: Landeshauptstadt, 1988.

Polster, Bernd, ed. *"Swing Heil." Jazz im Nationalsozialismus.* Berlin: Transit, 1989.

Vogelsang, Konrad. *Filmmusik im Dritten Reich. Die Dokumentation.* Hamburg: Facta, 1990.

Kater, Michael H. *Different Drummers: Jazz in the Culture of Nazi Germany.* New York: Oxford UP, 1992.

Levi, Erik. *Music in the Third Reich.* New York: St. Martin's Press, 1994.

Kopffleisch, Richard. *Lieder der Hitlerjugend.* Frankfurt: Peter Lang, 1995.

Schlesinger, Robert. *"Gott sei mit unserem Führer." Der Opernbetrieb im deutschen Faschismus.* Vienna: Löcker, 1997.

Kater, Michael H. *Die mißbrauchte Muse. Musiker im Dritten Reich.* München: Europa Verlag, 1998.

Potter, Pamela M. *Most German of the Arts: Musicology and Society from the Weimar Republic to the End of Hitler's Reich.* New Haven: Yale UP, 1998.

Brinkmann, Reinhold, and Christoph Wolff, eds. *Driven into Paradise: The Musical Migration from Nazi Germany to the United States.* Berkeley: University of California Press, 1999.

Frommann, Eberhard. *Die Lieder der NS-Zeit*. Cologne: PapyRossa, 1999.

Kater, Michael H. *Composers of the Nazi Era: Eight Portraits*. New York: Oxford University Press, 1999.

Sonntag, Brunhilde, et al., eds. *Die dunkle Last. Musik und Nationalsozialismus*. Cologne: Bela, 1999.

Friedländer, Saul, and Jörn Rüsen, eds. *Richard Wagner im Dritten Reich*. Munich: Beck, 2000.

Hamann, Brigitte. *Winifred Wagner: A Life at the Heart of Hitler's Bayreuth*. Munich: Granta, 2002.

Kater, Michael H., and Albrecht Riethmüller, eds. *Music and Nazism*. Laaber: Laaber, 2003.

Koch, Hans-Jörg. *Das Wunschkonzert im NS-Rundfunk*. Cologne: Böhlau, 2003.

Jockwer, Axel. *Unterhaltungsmusik im Dritten Reich*. Konstanz: UP, 2004.

Stiftung Schloß Neuhardenberg, ed. *Das "Dritte Reich" und die Musik*. Berlin: Nicolai, 2006.

Hirsch, Lily E. *A Jewish Orchestra in Nazi Germany: Musical Politics and the Berlin Jewish Culture League*. Ann Arbor: University of Michigan Press, 2010.

NS Literature

Strothmann, Dietrich. *Nationalsozialistische Literaturpolitik. Ein Beitrag zur Publizistik im Dritten Reich*. Bonn: Bouvier, 1960.

Schonauer, Franz. *Deutsche Literatur im Dritten Reich. Versuch einer Darstellung in polemisch-didaktischer Absicht*. Olten: Walter, 1961.

Wulf, Josef, ed. *Literatur und Dichtung im Dritten Reich*. Gütersloh: Mohn, 1963.

Loewy, Ernst. *Literatur unterm Hakenkreuz. Das Dritte Reich und seine Dichtung*. Frankfurt: Europäische Verlagsanstalt, 1966.

Vondung, Klaus. *Völkisch-nationale und nationalsozialistische Literaturtheorie*. Munich: List, 1973.

Denkler, Horst, and Karl Prümm, eds. *Die deutsche Literatur im Dritten Reich. Themen – Traditionen – Wirkungen*. Stuttgart: Reclam, 1976.

Ketelsen, Uwe-Karsten. *Völkisch-nationale und nationalsozialistische Literatur 1890–1945*. Stuttgart: Metzler, 1976.

Hartung, Günter. *Literatur und Ästhetik des deutschen Faschismus*. Berlin: Akademie-Verlag, 1983.

Sauder, Gerhard. *Die Bücherverbrennung. Zum 10. Mai 1933*. Munich: Hanser, 1983.

Ketelsen, Uwe K. *Literatur und Drittes Reich*. Schernfeld: SH-Verlag, 1992.

Scholdt, Günther. *Autoren über Hitler. Deutschsprachige Schriftsteller 1919 bis 1945 und ihr Bild vom "Führer."* Bonn: Bouvier, 1993.

Barbian, Jan-Pieter. *Literaturpolitik im "Dritten Reich." Institutionen, Kompetenzen, Betätigungsfelder*. Munich: Deutscher Taschenbuch Verlag, 1995.

Caemmerer, Christiane, and Walter Delabar, eds. *Dichtung im Dritten Reich? Zur Literatur in Deutschland 1933–1945*. Opladen: Westdeutscher Verlag, 1996.

Schnell, Ralf. *Dichtung in finsteren Zeiten. Deutsche Literatur und Faschismus*. Reinbek: Rowohlt, 1998.

Schoeps, Karl-Heinz. *Literature and Film in the Third Reich*. New York: Camden House, 2003.

Düsterberg, Rolf. *Hanns Johst. Der Barde der SS*. Paderborn: Schöningh, 2004.

Baird, Jay. *Hitler's War Poets: Literature and Politics in the Third Reich*. New York: Cambridge, 2008.

NS Theater

Wulf, Josef, ed. *Theater und Film im Dritten Reich*. Gütersloh: Mohn, 1963.

Rühle, Günther. *Zeit und Theater. Diktatur und Exil 1933–1945*. 2 vols. Berlin: Ullstein, 1974.

Eichberg, Henning, et al. *Massenspiele. NS-Thingspiele, Arbeiterweihespiele und olympisches Zeremoniell*. Stuttgart: Frommann Holzboog, 1977.

Wardetzky, Jutta. *Theaterpolitik im faschistischen Deutschland*. Berlin: Henschelverlag, 1983.

Stommer, Rainer. *Die inszenierte Volksgemeinschaft. Die Thing-Bewegung im Dritten Reich*. Marburg: Jonas, 1985.

Daiber, Hans. *Schaufenster der Diktatur. Theater im Machtbereich Hitlers*. Stuttgart: Neske, 1995.

Rischbieter, Henning, ed. *Theater im "Dritten Reich." Theaterpolitik, Spielplanstruktur, NS-Dramatik*. Velber: Kallmeyer, 2000.

Ketelsen, Uwe-Karsten. *The Swastika and the Stage: German Theater and Society, 1933–1945*. New York: Cambridge University Press, 2007.

NS Radio, Film, and Press

Hagemann, Walter. *Publizistik im Dritten Reich. Ein Beitrag zur Methodik der Massenführung*. Hamburg: Heitmann, 1948.

Wulf, Josef, ed. *Presse und Funk im Dritten Reich*. Gütersloh: Mohn, 1963.

Hale, Oron J. *Presse in der Zwangsjacke 1933–1945*. Düsseldorf: Droste, 1965.

Abel, Karl Dietrich. *Presselenkung im NS-Staat. Eine Studie zur Geschichte der Publizistik in der nationalsozialistischen Zeit*. Berlin: Colloquium, 1968.

Hull, David Stewart. *Film in the Third Reich: A Study of the German Cinema 1933–1945*. Berkeley: University of California Press, 1969.

Hagemann, Jürgen. *Die Presselenkung im Dritten Reich*. Bonn: Bouvier, 1970.

Courtade, Francis, and Pierre Cadars. *Geschichte des Films im Dritten Reich*. Frankfurt: Büchergilde Gutenberg, 1975.

Albrecht, Gerd. *Film im Dritten Reich. Eine Dokumentation*. Karlsruhe: Doku-Verlag, 1979.

Hollstein, Dorothea. *"Jud Süß" und die Deutschen. Antisemitische Vorurteile im nationalsozialistischen Spielfilm*. Frankfurt: Ullstein, 1983.

Rabenalt, Arthur Maria. *Joseph Goebbels und der großdeutsche Film*. Munich: Herbig, 1985.

Drewniak, Boguslaw. *Der deutsche Film 1938–1945. Ein Gesamtüberblick*. Düsseldorf: Droste, 1987.

Loiperdinger, Martin. *Der Parteitagsfilm "Triumph des Willens" von Leni Riefenstahl. Rituale der Mobilmachung*. Opladen: Leske und Budrich, 1987.

Hoffmann, Hilmar, ed. *"Und die Fahne führt uns in die Ewigkeit." Propaganda im NS-Film*. Frankfurt: Fischer, 1988.

Frei, Norbert, and Johannes Schmitz. *Journalismus im Dritten Reich*. Munich: Beck, 1989.

Leiser, Erwin. *"Deutschland erwache!" Propaganda im Film des Dritten Reiches*. Reinbek: Rowohlt, 1989.

Hinton, David B. *The Films of Leni Riefenstahl*. Metuchen: Scarecrow, 1991.

Lowry, Stephen. *Pathos und Politik. Ideologie in Spielfilmen des Nationalsozialismus*. Tübingen: Niemeyer, 1991.

Witte, Karsten. *Lachende Erben, toller Tag. Filmkomödie im Dritten Reich*. Berlin: Vorwerk, 1995.

Rentschler, Eric. *The Ministry of Illusion: Nazi Cinema and its Afterlife*. Cambridge: Harvard University Press, 1996.

Schulte-Sasse, Linda. *Entertaining the Third Reich: Illusions of Wholeness in Nazi Cinema*. Durham: Duke University Press, 1996.

Marßolek, Inge, and Adelheid von Saldern, eds. *Radio im Nationalsozialismus. Zwischen Lenkung und Ablenkung*. Tübingen: Diskord, 1998.

Frei, Norbert. *Journalismus im Dritten Reich*. Munich: Beck, 1999.

Möller, Felix. *Der Filmminister. Goebbels und der Film im Dritten Reich*. Stuttgart: Axel Menges, 2000.

Hake, Sabine. *Popular Cinema of the Third Reich*. Austin: University of Texas Press, 2001.

Welch, David. *Propaganda and the German Cinema 1933–1945*. Oxford: Oxford University Press, 2001.

Kinkel, Lutz. *Die Scheinwerferin. Leni Riefenstahl und das "Dritte Reich."* Hamburg: Europa Verlag, 2002.

Gemünden, Gerd, and Anton Kaes. *Film and Exile*. New York: Telos, 2003.

Segeberg, Harro, ed. *Mediale Mobilmachung I. Das Dritte Reich und der Film*. Munich: Fink, 2004.

Bach, Steven. *Leni: The Life and Work of Leni Riefenstahl*. New York: Knopf, 2007.

Glasenapp, Jörg, ed. *Riefenstahl Revisited*. Munich: Fink, 2009.

Inner Emigration

Paetel, Karl O., ed. *Deutsche Innere Emigration. Antinationalsozialistische Zeugnisse aus Deutschland*. New York: Krause, 1946.

Kantorowicz, Alfred, and Richard Drews. *Verboten und verbrannt. Deutsche Literatur 12 Jahre unterdrückt*. Berlin: Ullstein, 1947.

Frommhold, Erhard, ed. *Kunst im Widerstand. Malerei, Graphik, Plastik 1933–1945*. Dresden: Verlag der Kunst, 1968.

Klieneberger, Hans Rudolf. *The Christian Writers of the Inner Emigration*. Den Haag: Mouton, 1968.

Schnell, Ralf. *Literarische Innere Emigration 1933–1945*. Stuttgart: Metzler, 1976.

Piper, Ernst. *Ernst Barlach und die nationalsozialistische Kunstpolitik. Eine dokumentarische Darstellung zur "entarteten Kunst."* Munich: Piper, 1983.

Ritchie, James M. *German Literature under National Socialism*. London: C. Helm, 1983.

Brekle, Wolfgang. *Schriftsteller im antifaschistischen Widerstand 1933–1945 in Deutschland*. Berlin: Aufbau, 1985.

Bock, Sigrid, and Manfred Hahn, eds. *Erfahrung Nazideutschland. Romane in Deutschland 1933–1945*. Berlin: Aufbau, 1987.

Peukert, Detlev. *Inside Nazi Germany: Conformity, Opposition, and Racism in Everyday Life*. New Haven: Yale University Press, 1987.

Krohn, Claus-Deiter, et al., eds. *Aspekte der künstlerischen Inneren Emigration 1933–1945*. Munich: Text + Kritik, 1994.

Donahue, Neil, and Doris Kirchner, eds. *Flight of Fantasy: New Perspectives on Innere Emigration in German Literature 1933–1945*. New York: Berghahn, 2003.

Denkler, Horst. *Werkruinen, Lebenstrümmer. Literarische Spuren der "verlorene Generation" des 3. Reichs*. Tübingen: de Gruyter, 2006.

Exile

Häsler, Alfred. *Das Boot ist voll. Die Schweiz und ihre Flüchtlinge 1933–1945*. Zürich: Ex Libris, 1967.

Grimm, Reinhold, and Jost Hermand, eds. *Exil und Innere Emigration*. Frankfurt: Athenäum, 1972.

Müssener, Helmut. *Exil in Schweden. Politische und kulturelle Emigration nach 1933*. Munich: Hanser, 1974.

Berendsohn, Walter A. *Die humanistische Front. Vom Kriegsausbruch 1939 bis Ende 1946*. Worms: Heintz, 1976.

Heilbut, Anthony. *Exiled in Paradise: Refugee Artists and Intellectuals in America*. New York: Viking, 1983.

Möller, Horst. *Exodus der Kultur. Schriftsteller, Wissenschaftler und Künstler in der Emigration nach 1933*. Munich: Beck, 1984.

Picard, Jacques. *Die Schweiz und die Juden 1933–1945. Schweizerischer Antisemitismus, jüdische Abwehr und internationale Migrations- und Flüchtlingspolitik*. Zürich: Chronos, 1994.

Krohn, Claus-Deiter, et al., eds. *Handbuch der deutschsprachigen Emigration 1933–1945*. Darmstadt: Primus, 1998.

Langkau-Alex, Ursula. *Deutsche Volksfront 1932–1939. Zwischen Berlin, Paris, Prag und Moskau. Bd. 1, Vorgeschichte und Gründung des Ausschußes zur Vorbereitung einer deutschen Volksfront*. Berlin: Akademie, 2004.

Caestecker, Frank, and Bob Moore, eds. *Refugees from Nazi Germany and the Liberal European States*. New York: Berghahn, 2010.

Exile Literature and Press

Drews, Richard, and Alfred Kantorowicz, eds. *Verboten und verbrannt. Deutsche Literatur – 12 Jahre unterdrückt*. Berlin: Ullstein, 1947.

Pfeiler, William K. *German Literature in Exile. The Concern of Poets*. Lincoln: University of Nebraska Press, 1957.

Sternfeld, Wilhelm, and Eva Tiedemann, eds. *Deutsche Exil-Literatur, 1933–1945. Eine Bio-Bibliographie*. Heidelberg: Schneider, 1962.

Jarmatz, Klaus. *Literatur im Exil*. Berlin: Dietz, 1966.

Wegner, Matthias. *Exil und Literatur. Deutsche Schriftsteller im Ausland 1933–1945*. Frankfurt: Athenäum 1968.

Walter, Hans-Albert. *Deutsche Exilliteratur 1933–1950, "Bedrohung und Verfolgung bis 1933."* Neuwied: Luchterhand, 1972.

Hohendahl, Peter Uwe, and Egon Schwarz, eds. *Exil und Innere Emigration II*. Frankfurt: Athenäum, 1973.

Arnold, Heinz-Ludwig. *Deutsche Literatur im Exil 1933–1945*. Frankfurt: Athenäum, 1974.

Schiller, Dieter. *"...von Grund auf anders." Programmatik der Literatur im antifaschistischen Kampf während der dreißiger Jahre*. Berlin: Akademie, 1974.

Walter, Hans-Albert. *Deutsche Exilliteratur 1933–1950, "Exilpresse I."* Neuwied: Luchterhand, 1974.

Dahlke, Hans. *Geschichtsroman und Literaturkritik im Exil*. Berlin: Aufbau, 1976.

Winkler, Michael. *Deutsche Literatur im Exil 1933–1945. Texte und Dokumente*. Stuttgart: Reclam, 1977.

Herden, Werner. *Wege zur Volksfront. Schriftsteller im antifaschistischen Bündnis*. Berlin: Akademie, 1978.

Kantorowicz, Alfred. *Politik und Literatur im Exil. Deutschsprachige Schriftsteller im Kampf gegen den Nationalsozialismus*. Hamburg: Christians, 1978.

Krispyn, Egbert. *Anti-Nazi Writers in Exile*. Athens: University of Georgia Press, 1978.

Stephan, Alexander. *Die deutsche Exilliteratur 1933–1945*. Munich: Beck, 1979.

Hoffmann, Ludwig. *Exil in der Tschechoslowakei, Großbritannien, Skandanavien und Palästina*. Leipzig: Reclam, 1980.

Middel, Eike. *Exil in den USA, mit einem Bericht "Schanghai – Eine Emigration am Rande."* Leipzig: Reclam, 1980.

Fritsch, Christian, and Lutz Winckler. *Faschismuskritik und Deutschlandbild im Exilroman*. Berlin: Argument, 1981.

Hermsdorf, Klaus, et al. *Exil in den Niederlanden und Spanien*. Leipzig: Reclam,1981.

Kiessling, Wolfgang. *Exil in Lateinamerika*. Leipzig: Reclam,1981.

Mittenzwei, Werner. *Exil in der Schweiz*. Leipzig: Reclam, 1981.

Schiller, Dieter. *Kunst und Literatur im antifaschistischen Exil. Exil in Frankreich*. Leipzig: Reclam, 1981.

Pike, David. *German Writers in Soviet Exile, 1933–1945*. Chapel Hill: University of North Carolina Press, 1982.

Walter, Hans-Albert. *Deutsche Exilliteratur. Europäisches Appeasement und überseeische Asylpraxis*. Stuttgart: Metzler, 1984.

Jarmatz, Klaus, and Simone Barck. *Kunst und Literatur im antifaschistischen Exil. Exil in der UdSSR*. Leipzig: Reclam, 1989.

Stephan, Alexander. *"Communazis": FBI Surveillance of German Emigré Writers*. New Haven: Yale University Press, 2000.

Exile Theater

Wächter, Hans-Christoph. *Theater im Exil. Sozialgeschichte des deutschen Exiltheaters 1933–1945*. Munich: Hanser, 1973.

Haarmann, Hermann, et al. *Das "Engels"-Projekt. Ein antifaschistisches Theater deutscher Emigranten in der UdSSR (1936–1941)*. Worms: Heintz, 1975.

Mittenzwei, Werner. *Das Zürcher Schauspielhaus 1933–1945*. Berlin: Henschel, 1979.

Schneider, Hansjörg. *Exiltheater in der Tschechoslowakei 1933–1938*. Berlin: Henschel, 1979.

Lyon, James K. *Bertolt Brecht in America*. Princeton: Princeton University Press, 1980.

Trabb, Frithjof, et al., eds. *Handbuch des deutschsprachigen Exiltheaters 1933–1945*. Berlin: De Gruyter, 1999.

Exile Film

Hilchenbach, Maria. *Kino im Exil. Die Emigration deutscher Filmkünstler 1933–1945*. Munich: Saur, 1982.
Elsaesser, Thomas, and Ginette Vincendau, eds. *Les cinéastes allemands en France. Les années trente*. Amsterdam: Goethe Institute, 1983.
Horak, Jan-Christopher. *Anti-Nazi-Filme der deutschsprachigen Emigranten von Hollywood 1939–1945*. Münster: Maks, 1984.
———. *Fluchtpunkt Hollywood. Eine Dokumentation zur Filmemigration nach 1933*. Münster: Maks, 1986.
Asper, Helmut G. *"Etwas Besseres als den Tod...." Filmexil in Hollywood. Porträts, Filme, Dokumente*. Marburg: Schüren, 2002.
———. *Filmexilanten im Universal Studios 1933–1960*. Berlin: Betz + Fischer, 2005.

Exile Painting

Hahn, Manfred, ed. *Künstler und Künste im antifaschistischen Kampf*. Berlin: Kulturbund, 1983.
Bartmann, Dominik, ed. *Die Olympiade unter der Diktatur. Rekonstruktion der Amsterdamer Kunstolympiade 1936*. Berlin: Stadtmuseum, 1996.

Exile Music

Schebera, Jürgen. *Hanns Eisler im USA-Exil*. Berlin: Akademie, 1978.
Maurer Zenck, Claudia. *Ernst Krenek – ein Komponist im Exil*. Vienna: Lafite, 1980.
Traber, Habakuk, and Elmar Weingarten, eds. *Verdrängte Musik. Berliner Komponisten im Exil*. Berlin: Argon, 1987.
Heister, Hanns-Werner, ed. *Musik im Exil. Folgen des Nazismus für die internationale Musikkultur*. Frankfurt: Fischer,1993.
Geiger, Friedrich, and Thomas Schäfer, eds. *Exilmusik. Komposition während der NS-Zeit*. Hamburg: Von Bockel, 1999.
Petersen, Peter, and Claudia Maurer Zenck, eds. *Musiktheater im Exil der NS-Zeit*. Hamburg: Von Bockel, 2006.

INDEX

A

Abraham, Paul, 73, 239
Abusch, Alexander, 190, 196
Ackermann, Anton, 250
Ackermann, Max, 157
activists in exile, 178–80, 204–10, 235
    trust in German working class, 179–80
Adorno, Theodor W., 129, 200, 229, 245
advertising, 135–37, *136*, 138, 200
agitprop, 8, 73, 105, 179, 181, 190
agrarian culture, 21–23, *22. See also* peasant,
    cult of
air planes, 134
Albendroth, Walter, 72
Albers, Hans, 85
Albiker, Karl, 52, 70
Allert de Lange publishing house, 215
All Union Congress, 185
Amann, Max, 40
American Guild for German Cultural Free-
    dom, 197, 206
Amsterdam, Holland, 235, 240
Ančerl, Karel, 83
Andres, Stefan, 149
Anschluß of Austria, 180, 182, 195, 230,
    239
antifascism, 202–10
    associations, 204–6
    bourgeois liberals, 203. *See also* liberal-
      ism
    exile literature, 211–20
    films, 229–30
    leftist, 204–10 *passim*
    publications, 203, 208–9
anti-Semitism
    anti-Jewish boycotts, 10, 36, 124
    dollar imperialism, 12
    linking communism and Jews, 12
    music and, 73
    sexual intercourse laws, 10
    slogans, 12

    writings, 9–10
    See also enemy stereotypes; Jews
apolitical as political, 128, 137, 177, 215
appeasement, 180, 181, 199, 208, 211,
    241
architecture, 46–55, 238
    classicism, 48, 53, 54
    modernism, 48. *See also* modernism
    monumentality, 48, 50, 54
    realpolitik, 53
    See also specific architects, cities, and
      styles
Arendt, Erich, 213
Armstrong, Louis, 129
Arntz, Gerd, *232*, 235
Arp, Hans, 69
art, visual, 40, 55–72, 156–62
    activist, 145, 235
    art critics, 232
    art history, 19, 38
    censorship, 37, 56, 60, 161, 231. *See*
      also censorship
    class issues, 63–68
    collections, 68
    exile art, 56, 231–38
    influence of Nazi fascists on, 55–72
    inner emigration group and, 143–46
    "of the people," 60–61
    resistance art, 145
    shame exhibits, 58–59
    social criticism, 234
    theories of, 4
    See also architecture; censorship;
      graphic art; painting;
      photomontage; sculpture
Artaman League, 21
Art from Blood and Soil (Schultze-
    Naumburg), 19
Aryans, 28, 37, 125
    Aryan certificate, 103, 109
    See also Nordic superiority

asphalt literati, 171
ASSO (Association of Revolutionary Visual
    Artists of Germany), 36, 58
Association for the Protection of German
    Writers, 188, 204, *205*
Association of Revolutionary Visual Artists
    of Germany, 234
Attack, The, 6
Attacker, The, 6
Aufbau, 209
Augsburg, Germany, 52
Aurora Verlag, 208, 249
Auschwitz, 12, 183, 236
Ausländer, Rose, 213
Austria, 184–85, 222–23, 239
    Anschluß of Austria, 180, 182, 195,
        230, 239
    German invasion, 222
authority, 139
Autounion, 134
avant-garde, 226, 229, 237, 242
    expressionist debate, 182
Avenarius, Ferdinand, 63

B

Bade, Wilfried, 97
Bangert, Otto, 21, 32, 90
Barbusse, Henri, 88
Barlach, Ernst, 38, 56, 57, 69, 160, 161, *161*,
    162
Bartels, Adolf, 9, 42
Bartók, Béla, 74, 167, 244
Bassermann, Albert, 221
Bauhaus, 13, 55, 157, 234, 236
    New Bauhaus, 238
Baum, Carl, 67
Baum, Vicki, 214
Baumann, Hans, 93
Baumeister, Willi, 157
Baumgartner, Thomas, 67
Baum Group, 9
Baümler, Alfred, 88
Bavaria, 6, 48
Beauty of Labor organization, 130–31, 132
    office, *133*
Beaux Arts style, 67
Becher, Johannes, 165, 174, 185, 189, *191*,
    250, 251
Becher, Ulrich, 175
Beckmann, Max, 69, 156, 231, 235, 236
Beer-Hofmann, Richard, 175
Begin Anew group, 209, 249
Behrens, Peter, 54
Belgium, 236
    invasion, 195

as refuge for German exiles, 191–92
Belief and Beauty organization, 135
Belling, Rudolf, 69
Beneš, Eduard, 187
Benjamin, Walter, 189, 212
Benn, Gottfried, 89, 104, 151, 163
Berendsohn, Walter, 177
Berg, Alban, 75, 240
Bergengruen, Werner, 153, 154
Berger, Ludwig, 228
Bergner, Elisabeth, 221, 227
Berlau, Ruth, *198*
Berlin, Germany, 52, 104, 160, 164,
    251–52
    amphitheater, 93
    athletic grounds, 52
    Berlin Philharmonic, 127
    Berlin State Opera, 164
    book burning, 88
    Great Hall, *51*
    public buildings, 48, 52
    trains, 134
Bermann Fischer publishing house, 215
Bertolt Brecht Club, 187
Beumelburg, Werner, 99
Biedermeier style, 67
Binding, Rudolf G., 101, 148
Bing, Rudolf, 240
Birgel, Willy, *117*
Bismarck, Otto von, 171
Blacher, Boris, 77
Black Brigade, The (newspaper), 89
Blaupunkt firm, 129
Bleeker, Bernhard, 69
Bloch, Ernst, 179, 189, 196, 199, 249
blood and soil slogan, 13, 19, 22, 56
Blum, Klara, 185
Blume, Friedrich, 72, 80
Blumenthal, Hermann, 160, 161
Blunck, Hans Friedrich, 40, 88–89, 95, *95*, 96,
    99
Bochmann, Werner, 83, 85
Boehle, Fritz, 67
Böhm, Karl, 79
bolshevism, 12
    cultural, 48, 87, 157
    See also communists
Bolvary, Géza von, *119*
Borgmann, Hans Otto, 79
Börne, Ludwig, 187
bourgeoisie. *See* class issues; liberalism
BPRS. *See* League of Proletarian and
    Revolutionary Writers
Braun, Alfred, *110*
Braunfels, Walter, 73

Brecht, Bertolt, 8, 36, 88, 163, 165, 178, 182, 187, 189, 190, *191*, 205, 217, 228, 229, 241
    exile performances of plays, 191, 214, 223, 224
    humor of, 214
    poetry of, 174, 211, 213
    tui behavior of intellectuals, 175, 189, 199
    in United States, 197, 198, *198*, 199, 200, 214, 243, 245, 248, 249
Brecker, Arno, 161
Bredel, Willi, 8, 185, 213, 216, 251
breeding, 152
Brehm, Bruno, 64, 99
Breker, Arno, 51, 52, 69, 69–70
Brentano, Bernard, 174
British Broadcasting Company, 240
Britten, Benjamin, 240
Broch, Hermann, 197
Brod, Max, 177, 194
Bronnen, Arnolt, 89
Bruch, Max, 73
Bruckner, Ferdinand, 178, 190, 196, 214, 223
Brüning, Elfriede, 147
Buber, Martin, 42
Buchenwald concentration camp, 153
Budzislawski, Hermann, 186
Burns, George, 230
Burte, Hermann, 90
Busch, Ernst, 185, 221
Busch, Fritz, 240

C
capitalism, 26, 123, 137, 179
Carossa, Hans, 210
Cassirer, Ernst, 177
Catholic church, 175, 212
    pope's signing of concordat, 180
censorship, 36–37, 56, 231
    art, visual, 37, 56, 60, 161, 231
    burning books, 37, 87, 88, 204
    literature, 94–95
    music, 37
Chamberlain, Houston Stewart, xiii, 9, 58
Chaplin, Charlie, 229, 230
Chelmno, 12
Chicago, Illinois, 238
chosen people of Grail, 28. See also knights, German
Christianity, 154–55
    heroic Christianity, 19
Churchill, Winston, 193, 246
Cissarz, Vinzenz, 67

city planning, 49–55
classicism, 48, 53, 54, 126, 143–44
class issues, xv, 4, 30–35
    by class
        middle class, 8, 34, 123, 126, 137, 139, 252
        petty bourgeoisie, 123, 180. See also liberalism
        proletariat, 123, 130, 139
        underclass, 7, 34
        upper class, 8, 123, 126, 139
        white-collar workers, 34, 35, 123, 137
        workers of head *versus* workers of fist, 126
        working class, 179–80
    by genre
        art, 63–68
        entertainment, 31, 34, 100–101, 111, 116, 127–28, 135, 225
        literature, 100–101
        mass media, 113
        music, 77–86
    splits in culture, 44, 125
    success of Nazi cultural policies, 122–40
Claudius, Hermann, 90
Claudius, Matthias, 218
Coca-Cola, 129
Cold War, 251
collective consciousness, xi
    false consciousness in masses, xv
collective guilt, 183
collective responsibility, 250
collectivism, 213
Cologne, Germany, 236
    trains, 134
Communist Party. See KPD (German Communist Party)
communists, 19, 143, 247, 248
    antifascist movements, 204–10 *passim*
    arrests of, 8–9
    as enemy stereotype, 6, 7–9, 172
    linking communism and Jews, 12
    party organs, 8
    as refugees, 173–83 *passim*
concentration camps, 12, 42, 139, 183
Concentration Camp Symphony, 241
constructivist art, 236
consumerism, xi–xii, 128–29, 132, 135–37, 200. See also advertising
Copland, Aaron, 243
cosmopolitan intellectual, 13–14, 177
Council for a Democratic Germany, 248
cubism, 56, 143, 232–33

cult of Führer. *See* personality cult
Cultural Federation for the Democratic
  Renewal of Germany, 250–51, 252
Cultural Federation of German Jews, 41–42
culture, xi
  advertising and, 135–37, *136*, 138,
    200. *See also* advertising
  avant-garde, 182, 226, 229, 237, 242
  class issues, 30–33, 44, 122–40. *See
    also* class issues
  consumer perspective, xi–xii, 128–29,
    132, 135–37, 200
  cultural theory, 15, 30–31, 55, 56
  entertainment, 31, 34, 100–101, 111,
    116, 125, 127–28, 130–32, 144, 225
    vacations, 130
  high culture, xi, 5, 8, 10, 31, 37, 44,
    87, 125, 132, 145, 180, 182
  implementation of, 34–45
  inner emigration group and, 143–46
  low culture, 5, 44, 125, 127–28, 132,
    144
  meaning of, xi
    false community and, 139
    ideology, 137
    as term in Nazi propaganda, 3
  militant *versus* resigned, 174
  periodicals, 31. *See also* press
  political culture, 128, 137, 145, 177,
    215
  See also German culture
Curtis, Tony, 230
Czechoslovakia
  German refugees in, 186–87, 222,
    223, 241
  occupation, 180, 182, 186
  publications, 186

D
Dachau Concentration Camp, 166
Dadaists, 35, 56, 143, 233
Dahn, Felix, 96
Dahrendorf, Gustav, 250
Damaschke, Otto, 21
Danzig, 180
DAP (German Workers' Party), 6
da Ponte, Lorenzo, 73
Darré, Walter, 21, 23
Das Wort, 185
Day of Potsdam, 104
Defense of Culture conference (Paris). *See*
  In Defense of Culture conference
Defregger, Franz von, 65, 233
Degenerate Art exhibit, 37, *57*, 59, 157
Degenerate Music exhibit, 37, *75*

degeneration, civilizational, 3, 16, 141
  degenerate artists, 156
de Lagarde, Paul, 9, 63
Der Angriff newspaper, 120
Der Stürmer newspaper, 121
Desseu, Paul, 239
destiny, 64
Deutscher Werkbund, 54
Dichtung, 86
Diderot Society, 205
Dietrich, Marlene, 228
Dietrich Eckart-Bühne, 7, 93, 104
Dinter, Artur, 9
Disney, Walt, 129
Distler, Hugo, 163
Dix, Otto, 156, 158–60, *159*, 231, 235
Döblin, Alfred, 174, 176, 189, 194, 197,
  228
Doktor Faustus (Mann), 218–19
Dollfuß, Engelbert, 222
Domin, Hilde, 213
Dominik, Hans, 101
Donath, Ludwig, 230, *230*
Dörries, Bernhard, 65
Dos Passos, John, 236
Douglas, Kirk, 230
Dresler, Adolf, 59, 63
Dreßler-Andreß, Horst, 40, 110
Dürer, Albrecht, 23, 181, 233
Düsseldorf, Germany, 37, 75, 106.165
dystopia, 26–27

E
eagle as emblem, 54, *133*
Eberlein, Kurt Karl, 58
Ebert, Carl, 240
Ebert, Friedrich, Jr., *110*
ecstatics. *See* expressionists
Eggebrecht, Axel, 116
Egger-Lienz, Albin, 67
Egk, Werner, 82
Ehrenburg, Ilja, *191*
Eichenauer, Richard, 72, 80
Eifel region, Germany
  castles, 48
Einstein, Albert, *176*
Einstein, Carl, 212
Eisenstein, Sergei, 8
Eisler, Hanns, 8, 36, 73, 165, 174, 185, 186,
  190, 197, 199, 239, 241, 242
Elmendorff, Karl, 79
emigration, 97. *See also* exile community;
  inner emigration group
enemy stereotypes, 4, 6–14
  communists, 6–9

cosmopolitan intellectual, 13–14
Jews, 6, 9–14
England
as refuge for Germans in exile, 193,
212, 223–24, 227, 235, 236, 240
Entartete Musik exhibition, 165
Epp, Franz von, 6
Erler, Fritz, *17*
Ernst, Max, 235
escapism, 175–76
Essler, Johann, 148
Eternal Jew exhibition, The, 10
Euringer, Richard, 7
euthanasia, 16, 117, 139, 152, 153
Ewers, Hanns Heinz, 210
Exile (Feuchtwanger), 219
exile community
activists, 178–80, 202–10
alienation, 172, 225
antifascism efforts, 202–10
appropriation of German culture, xii,
xiv, 176–78, 203
displacement from Europe, 183
escapism, 175–76
exile film, 225–31
exile literature, 211–20
exile music, 238–45
exile theater, 220–24
exile visual art, 231–38
fragmentation of, xiv–xv, 171–83, 212
humanists, 176–78
Marxists, 174, 185, 202
militant *versus* resigned art, 174
poster, *222*
refugee countries, 184–201
suicide among, 212
testimonials, 174
expressionists, 35, 38, 39, 42, 55, 56, 65, 89,
126, 143, 176
debate, 182
extermination camps. *See* concentration
camps

F
Fahrenkrog, Ludwig, 65
Falke, Konrad, 190
Fall, Leo, 73
Fallada, Hans, 116, 151
fascistoid, 129
FBI. *See* Federal Bureau of Investigation
(United States)
Fechter, Paul, 56
Feder, Gottfried, 7, 9
Federal Bureau of Investigation (United
States), 200, 242, *247*, 248

Federal Republic of Germany (FRG), 252
Feininger, Lyonel, 157, 237
Feistel-Rohmeder, Bettina, 59
Feuchtwanger, Lion, 10, 174, 185, *188*, 189,
196, 197, *198*, 204, 214, 215, 219, 248
film, 40, 114–19, *117*, *119*
actors, 117–18, 227, 231
antifascist, 229–31
comedies, 128, 134
directors, 227, 230, 231
entertainment, 116, 225
exile community in film, 175, 199,
225–31
historical, 118
Hollywood films, 129, 228–31
Jewish themes, 229–30
propaganda, 115, 117–18
scriptwriters, 116
social realism, 226, 231
state controls, 116
statistics, 119
Fischer, Ernst, 185
Fischer, Samuel, 150
Fischinger, Oskar, 229
Flesch, Hans, *110*
Flying Dutchman, 134
Forster, Georg, 187–88
France, 195, 236
invasion, 195
popular front movement, 180
as refuge for Germans in exile, 187–90,
212, 227, 241
Franck, Wolf, 172
Frank, Bruno, 197, 248
Frank, Leonhard, 197, 228–29
Frankfurt, Germany, 47, 87, 127
Free German Cultural League, 193, 206, 240
Free Germany (Mexico), 196
Free Stage, 224
Frei, Bruno, 196
Freud, Sigmund, 218
Freundlich, Otto, 69, 235
New Man, The, 57
Frick, Wilhelm, 56
Friedrich Wilhelm I, 154
functionalism, 13, 16
Fürchtegott Reemtsma, Hermann, 162
Fürnberg, Louis, 194
Furtwängler, Wilhelm, 74, 79–80, 82, 127,
164, 238, 240, 241
futurism, 56, 143

G
Gabelentz, Hans von, 148
Gall, Leonhard, 48

Garfield, James, 230
George, Heinrich, 116
George, Stefan, 90
George Circle, 207
Gerhard, Heinz, 97
German Academy of Art, 197
German American Bund, 230
German-American Cultural Association, 206
German-American Emergency Conference, 206
German-American Writers' Association, 206
German culture
    American influences on Germany, 129
    ancient Germanic tribes, 19–21, 20, 23
    cultural unity after war, 252
    eternal German culture, 28–33
    Germanic intuition of essence, 19
    German verus un-German rubric, 4
    intra Nazi party conflicts about, 124
    splits in unified culture, 44, 125
    success of Nazi policies, 122–40
    superiority of, xii–xiii, 3
    See also culture; volk, concept of
German Democratic Republic (GDR), 252
German for Germans anthology, 178–79
German Jewish Club, 224
German Labor Front, 39, 54, 105, 130
Germanness, concept of, 15
German-Soviet Nonaggression Pact, 182, 185, 209, 212
German verus un-German rubric, 4
German Volga Republic, 185
German Writers' Academy, 90
German Writers' Congress, 251
Germany
    under fascists, 46–114. See also specific people and topics
        education level of country, 122–23
        population statistics, 122–23
    postfascist, 246–52
        condemnation of everyone after war, 246–52 passim
        distinction between people and government after war, 246–52 passim
        division into two states, 252
    Weimar Republic, 3, 9, 34–35, 48, 58, 63, 203. See also Weimar Republic
    See also specific topics
Gershwin, George, 243
Gerster, Ottmar, 82

Gide, André, 189
Giehse, Therese, 191
Giesecke, Hermann, 110
Giesler, Hermann, 48, 52
    Hohe Schule, 49
Glaeser, Ernst, 174
Godard, Paulette, 230
Goebbels, Joseph, xiii, 39, 83, 88, 144, 202
    avoidance of revolutionary approach, 44, 104–5
    pluralism and, 44–45, 125
    pragmatism of, 11, 37–38, 40–41, 43, 65, 128
    as propaganda minister, 38, 39, 79, 105, 109, 120, 121, 125
    role in architecture, 53
    role in art, 57, 65
    role in literature, 89, 90, 101, 150
    role in mass media, 109, 111, 114–15, 119, 120
    role in music, 76, 77, 85–86, 164
    role in theater, 104–5
    "romanticism made of steel," 18–19, 82
Goes, Albrecht, 153
Goethe, Johann Wolfgang von, 28, 29, 107, 177–78, 181, 182, 194, 220
Goetz, Curt, 116, 228
Göring, Hermann, 38, 60, 76, 120
Gorki, Maxim, 88, 185
Graf, Oskar Maria, 177, 185, 186, 196, 197, 217
Granach, Alexander, 185, 221, 225, 226
graphic art, 231–38
Great Britain. See England
Great Dictator (Chaplin), 230
Great German Art Exhibit (Munich, 1937), 66, 67, 93
Greif, Heinrich, 221
Griebel, Otto, 234
Gries, Karl, Summer tapestry, 62
Grimm, Hans, 148, 210
Grimmelshausen, Hans Jakob Christoffel von, 166
Gropius, Walter, 48, 238
Grosz, George, 8, 56, 175, 235–36
Grothe, Franz, 84, 85
Grundig, Hans, 157, 234
Grützner, Eduard, 65, 233
Guthmann, Heinrich, 38–39

H
Haavara Agreement, 180
Habsburg empire, 187
Hadamovsky, Eugen, 110, 111

Haider, Karl, 67
Halle an der Saale, 48
Hangman Also Die (Brecht), 230
Hans Otto Club, 187
Hartmann, Karl Amadeus, 163, 165–68, 186
Hasenclever, Walter, 10, 175, 212
Hauerstein, Georg, 21
Hauptmann, Gerhard, 150–51, 250
Haushofer, Albrecht, 148
Havemann, Robert, 250
Hay, Julius, 185
Heartfield, John, 8, 179, 187, 234, 235
Heckel, Erich, 234
Heesters, Johannes, 85
Heidegger, Martin, 61
Heilmann, Ernst, *110*
Heine, Heinrich, 184, 187
Heinkel, 134
Heinrich Heine Club, 206
Heinz, Wolfgang, 221
Hentschel, Willibald, 21
Hermann, Georg, 42
Hermann-Neiße, Max, 174, 175, 213
heroism, 16–19, *17*, 28, 64
Herzfelde, Wieland, 186, 187, 205, 208, 249
Herzmanowsky, Bernhard, 83
Hess, Rudolf, xiii
Heyck, Hans, 97
Heydrich, Reinhard, 12
high culture, xi, 5, 8, 10, 31, 37, 44, 87, 125, 132, 145, 180. *See also* culture; German culture
Hildebrand, Adolf von, 69
Hiller, Kurt, 178, 193, 215
Hilz, Sepp, 67
Himmler, Heinrich, 11–12, 21, 23, 151
Hindemith, Paul, 74–75, 163, 164–65, 167–68, 197, 200, 238, 239
Hinkel, Hans, 41
Hippler, Fritz, 56, 88
Hirschfeld, Kurt, 223
Hitler, Adolf, *80*, *128*
    as actor, 109
    anti-communism, 7
    architecture views, 48–50
    art views, 56–57, 65–66, 69–70
    imperialist objectives, 24
    maxims, *xiii*, 126–27
    as painter, xii–xiii, 156
    personality cult, 16–18, *17*, 64, 90–91, 202
    on radio, 111
    speech at Nuremberg party conference (1934), 65

See also Nazi fascists; NSDAP (National Socialist German Workers' Party)
Hitler Youth, 79, 85–86, 88, 92, 93, 105, 115
    trumpet parade, 78, *78*
Hofer, Karl, 56, 156, 158, 250
Hoffman, Heinrich, 130, *131*
Hofmannsthal, Hugo von, 76
Hogan, James P., 230, *230*
Holland
    invasion, 195
    as refuge for Germans in exile, 192–93, 228, 240
Holliday, Judy, 230
Holt, Hans, *119*
Homeland-Art Movement, 22
Honegger, Arthur, 74
Hönig, Eugen, 40, 57
"Horst-Wessel-Lied," 77–78
Hubbuch, Karl, 160
Huch, Ricarda, 155, 251
Huchel, Peter, 116
Huebsch, Benjamin, 198
humanists, 176–78, 213
    as emotional, 177
    See also liberalism
Hungary, 185

I
Ilberg, Werner, 147
In Defense of Culture conference, xv, 189, *191*, 205
inner emigration group, 218
    accommodation and, 146, 165
    appropriation of German culture, xii, xiv
    art, 143–46, 156–62
        inner emigration *versus* resistance art, 145
    defining, 143–46
    eternal values, xiv
    literature, 146, 147–56
        publishing houses, 150
        social criticism, 150–56
    as marginal, 146
    music, 146, 162–68
    painting, 156–62
    sculpture, 160–62
Internationale Literatur, 185
internationalism, 13, 38, 48, 233, 237, 238
International PEN club, 204
International Socialist Combat League, 209
International Style of architecture, 55. *See also* Bauhaus
International Writers' Congress, *191*

J

Jahn, Turnvater, 135
Jank, Angelo, 67
Jary, Michael, 85
jazz, 73–74, 126
Jelusich, Mirko, 99
Jessner, Leopold, 10, 220, 224
Jewish Cultural Federation, 41–42, 83, 103
Jewish Cultural League, 228
Jews, 19
    censorship of publications, 126
    as enemy stereotype, 6–15, 171
    as honorary Aryans, 120
    Jewish boycotts, 124
    linking communism and Jews, 12
    name changes in film industry, 230
    orthodox Judaism, 212
    painting collections, 68
    as refugees, 173–83 *passim*
    spheres for cultural activity, 41–42
    See also exile community
Jhering, Herbert, 250
Jöde, Fritz, 163
Johst, Hanns, 89, 90, 94
Jolson, Al, 230
July 20 plot, 217, 218
Jünger, Ernst, 90, 151, *152*

K

Kadinsky, Wassily, 56
Kaiser, Georg, 151, 190, 214, 223
Kálmán, Emmerich, 73
Kampf, Arthur
    Hildebrand Overpowers Odoaker's Son,
    95
Kampfbund für deutsche Kultur. *See*
    Militant League for German Culture
Kandinsky, Wassily, 157, 236–37
Kantorowicz, Alfred, 213
Karajan, Herbert von, 80
Karsch, Joachim, 160–61
Kaspar, Hermann, 52
Kästner, Erich, 100
Katz, Leo, 196
Kaufmann, Louis, 147
KdF. *See* Strength Through Joy organization
Kellermann, Bernhard, 250
Kerr, Alfred, 10, 193
Kesten, Hermann, 178, 214
Kestenberg, Leo, 10, 75
Keun, Irmgard, 217
Khachaturian, Aram, 82
Kirchner, Ernst Ludwig, 56, 69
Kirsch, Joachim, 69
Kisch, Egon Erwin, 196, 213

kitsch, 84, 94
KJVD (Communist German Youth League),
    9
Klee, Paul, 157, 174, 237
Kleine, Werner, 85
Klemperer, Viktor, 250
Klepper, Jochen, 153, 154
Klimsch, Fritz, 69
Klopstock, Friedrich Gottlieb, 218
Klotz, Clemens, 48
Knappersbusch, Hans, 80
Knepler, Georg, 241
knights, German, 23–25, *25*, 28
Knights of the Rose festivals, 148
Knopf publishing, 215
Koeppen, Wolfgang, 116
Koestler, Arthur, 209
Kokoschka, Oskar, 193
Kolbe, Georg, 69
Kolbenheyer, Edwin Guido, 99
Kollwitz, Käthe, 58, 157, 161, 162, 235
Korngold, Erich Wolfgang, 73
Kortner, Fritz, 221, 227, 230
KPD (German Communist Party), 7, 35,
    124, 147, 157, 180, 185, 234, 250
Kralik, Hanns, 235
Krauss, Clemens, 80
Krauss, Werner, 105, 156
Kreisau Circle, 154, 217
Krenek, Ernst, 74, 197, 199, 239–40, 243
Kreuder, Peter, 85
Kristallnacht. See Night of Broken Glass
    (*Reichskristallnacht*)
Kroll, Bruno, 63
Kuckhoff, Adam, 155
Künneke, Eduard, 77, 85
Kurella, Alfred, 182, 185
Kursell, Otto von, 6

L

Labor Front, 110
Lachmann Mosse, Hans, 120
Landauer, Walter, 192
Landshoff, Fritz, 192
Lang, Fritz, 114, 227, 228, 229, 230
Langenbucher, Hellmuth, 86, 151
Langgässer, Elisabeth, 153, 155
Langgbehn, Julius, 21–22, 63
Langhoff, Wolfgang, 148, 191, 221, 250
Lasker-Schüler, Else, 174, 175, 194, 213
Laubinger, Otto, 40, 105
Laughton, Charles, 224
Law for the Protection of German Blood
    and Honor, 10
League of American Writers, 206

League of Conspirators, 39
League of German Girls, 92
League of Proletarian and Revolutionary
	Writers, 36, 147, 187, 203
Leander, Zarah, *117*
Lebensraum, 18, 23
Le Corbusier, 48
Leer, Johannes von, 9
Le Fort, Gertrud von, 153
Lehar, Franz, 42, 77, *83*, 116
Leipzig, Germany, 127
Lemmer, Ernst, 250
Lenin, Vladimir, *186*
Lenk, Franz, 160
Leonhard, Rudolf, 179, 189
Lepac Cultural Federation, 206
Lessing, Ephraim, 218
Ley, Robert, 39, 53, 130
liberalism, 13, 19, 35, 36, 60, 87, 102, 105,
	106, 110, 123, 180, 203, 206, 249. *See
	also* humanists
libraries, 88
Libro Libre publishing house, El, 196
Liebenfels, Jörg Lanz von, 9
Liebermann, Ernst, 67
Liebermann, Max, 10, 42, 150, 236
Liepmann, Heinz, 216
Liga V, 206
Lingner, Max, 235
Linz, Germany, 52, 53
Lippoldsberg writers' congress, 148
literature, 40
	audience, 86
	censorship, 36–37, 87–88, 94–95, 147,
		154, 204
		blacklists, 36, 87
		book burnings, 37, 87, 88
		encoded literature, 147
	by genre
		activist literature, 92, 151–56,
			174, 185, 189, 202, 216–18
		biographies, 215
		novels, 94–103, 214–20
		playwrighting, 213–14
		poetry, 149, 213
		religious writing, 153, 154–55
		resistance, 147
		song writing, 92–93
	by group
		exile literature, 173–83 *passim*,
			186–87, 211–20
		inner immigration group, 146,
			147–56
		Nazi fascist influence on
			literature, 86–103

literary theory, 10, 94, 211–20 *passim*
publishing houses, 10, 150, 190, 192,
	192, 196, 198, 215
	translations, 215
Litvak, Anatole, 230
Lohkamp, Emil
	Hans Westmar, 116
Lohmar, Heinz, 235
London, England, 193, 211
London, Jack, 88
Loos, Adolf, 48
Lorre, Peter, 227
Los Angeles, California, 199, 243, 248
Louis, Joe, 135
low culture, 5, 44, 125, 127–28, 132, 144.
	See also class issues; culture; German
	culture
Ludwig, Emil, 183, 198, 215
Lukács, Georg, 182, 215

M
Mackeben, Theo, 85
Mackensen, Fritz, 67
Magnus, Kurt, *110*
Mahler, Gustav, 73
Majdanek camp, 12
Mann, Erika, 190
Mann, Heinrich, 177, 178, 179, 187, 189,
	197, 199, 204, 215, 229, *247*, 248, 249
Mann, Klaus, 88, 177, 204, 210, 216
Mann, Thomas, 174, 176, *176*, 177–78,
	181, 182, 187, 190, 197, 198, 213, 215,
	218, 248, 249
March, Werner, 7, 48, 52
marches, 77–79, *78*
March to the Feldherrnhalle, 48
Marcks, Gerhard, 161
Marcuse, Ludwig, 177, 248
Maron, Karl, 147
Marx, Karl, 165, 187
Marxist analysis, 203–10 *passim*
	superstructure, 203
Masaryk, Tomáš, 187
mass media, xii, 109–21, 128–29, 139
	class issues, 113
master race, 24. *See also* race issues
May, Ernst, 55, 185
May, Karl, 100
Mayen, Germany, 63
Mehring, Franz, 182
Meidner, Ludwig, 236
Mein Kampf (Hitler), 7, 9, 21, 42, 48–50,
	56–57, 216
Meisel, Willy, 85
Meistermann, Georg, 157

Meller, Willy, 70
memorials, 53
Mencken, H. L., 129
Mendelssohn, Erich, 55
Mendelssohn-Bartholdy, Felix, 73
Mephisto (Mann), 216–17
Mercedes-Benz, 134, 138
Messerschmitt, 134
Mexico, 206
    as refuge for German's in exile, 196
Mexico City, Mexico, 211
Meyer, Ernst Hermann, 241
Meyerbeer, Giacomo, 73
Meyerhold, Vsevolod, 221
Mezhrabpom Society, 226
Midsummer Night's Dream (Reinhardt,
    Shakespeare), 224
Mies van der Rohe, Ludwig, 48, 238
Militant League for German Culture, 8, 23,
    35, 38, 55, 105
Millakowsky, Hermann, 230
Ministry for Propaganda, 79, 105, 121
modernism, 13, 19, 35, 48, 126, 137, 143,
    232, 237, 239, 240
    critical reflection, 13
    crusades against, 55, 56
    secessionist modernity, 13
Modern Times (Chaplin), 229
Modersohn, Otto, 67
Moholy-Nagy, László, 229, 238
Möller, Karl von, 97
Morgenthau, Henry, 210, 246
Moscow, Soviet Union, 211
Moscow Group, 182, 185
Moser, Hans Joachim, 42, 72
Mosse publishing, 10
Movement for a Free Territory, 194
Mühsam, Erich, 204
Müller, Bernhard, 67
Münchhausen, Börries von, 148
Munich, Germany, 10, 29, 37, 48, 57, 160
    art exhibits, 66, 70, 157, 236
    public buildings, 52–53, 127
Munich Agreement, 180, 181, 182, 193
Münzenberg, Willi, 186, 188, 209, 212
music, 37, 40, 41, 72–86, 162–68
    atonal, 73
    baroque, 163
    censorship, 164
    classical, 163, 238, 239, 240
    class issues, 77–86
    composers as refugees, 173–83 passim,
        238–45
    conductors, 239
    dance, 74

exile music, 238–45
    for films, 238
    history of German music, 72–73, 238
    inner emigration group and, 146
    Jewish folk melodies, 165
    marches, 77–79, 78, 163
    modernism, 239, 240
    New Music, 242
    opera, 73–74, 77, 82, 163–64, 166–68,
        239–40
    pop songs, 77, 84
    Protestant church music, 163
    racist thinking about, 73
    romantic, 163, 238, 239, 240
    theory of music, 72
    twelve-tone scale, 241–42, 244
Musil, Robert, 174, 175, 189, 213
Mythus des 20. Jahrhunderts (Rosenberg),
    12, 38, 58

N
Nagel, Otto, 157, 234, 251
National Committee for a Free Germany,
    206, 248, 250
National Socialist Culture Community, 23,
    38, 39, 54, 57, 106
National Socialist German Students'
    League, 38, 57
National Socialist Public Welfare
    Organization, 129
National Socialist Society for German
    Culture, 55
National Socialist Student Society, 37
Nazi fascists
    anti-communism, 7, 9
    appropriation of German culture,
        xii–xiii
    awakening versus revolution, 91
    class issues, xv, 4–5, 7–8, 30–33. See
        also class issues
    coexistence of high and low cultures, 5
    consequences for architecture, 46–55
    consequences for film, 114–19
    consequences for literature, 86–103
    consequences for music, 72–86
    consequences for painting, 55–68
    consequences for radio, 109–14
    consequences for sculpture, 68–72
    consequences for theater, 103–9
    debasement of culture, xv, 4
    democratic election of, 123
    enemy stereotypes, 4, 7–14
    ideology, 123
    interpretation of German history,
        28–29

intra party conflicts, 124
law and order, 9
leaders as artists, xii–xiii
Nazi theorists, 15–27
pragmatists *versus* radical, 4–5, 37–38, 124
See also Hitler, Adolf; NSDAP (National Socialist German Workers' Party)
Nazi publications, 6. *See also* press
Negroid label, 19, 56, 73–74, 157
Negro spirituals, 129
Neher, Carola, 221
Neithardt, Mathis, 164
neoliberal criticism, xi
Nerlinger, Oskar, 157, 234
Netherlands. *See* Holland
Neukrantz, Klaus, 8
New Horizons, 117
new media, 10
New Objectivity, 35, 48, 65, 73, 126, 132, 137, 157, 160, 163, 164, 233, 236
New York City, New York, 199, 214, 224, 238, 244, 245, 249
New York Times, 229
Niekisch, Ernst, 250
Niemöller, Martin, 153–54
Nierendorf Gallery (Berlin), 160
Nietzsche, Friedrich, 64, 91, 218
Night of Broken Glass *(Reichskristallnacht)*, 12, 42, 182, 195, 230
Nolde, Emil, 38, 56, 57, 156, 231
Norden, Hans von
    postcard, *91*
Nordic superiority, 48, 63, 72, 77, 81, 104.
    See also German culture
Norm and Value (Switzerland), 190
novels, 94–103
    agrarian, 95, 96–97
    detective novels, 100
    entertainment, 100–101
    historical, 99–100
    Teutonic, 96
    war, 95, 98–99
November art exhibit, 37
November republic, 125, 139–40
NSDAP (National Socialist German Workers' Party), xiv, 6, 12, 85, 108
    architecture and, 48–55
    attitudes toward labor, 6–7
    class issues, 30–33. *See also* class issues
    cult of peasant, 21–22, *22*
    cultural conference of 1933, 18
    elections, 99, 203
    Germanic intuition of essence, 19

Hohe Schule, 49
    left wing of, 26
    statistics, 26–27
    See also Hitler, Adolf; Nazi fascists
Nuremberg, Germany, 48, 70
Nußbaum, Felix, 174, 236, *237*

O
Office for the Beauty of Work, 54–55
Olympics (1936), 52, 104, 134, 135, 180, 235
    exhibition in protest against, 235
opera, 77, 82, 163–64, 166–68, 239–40
    libretto, 164
operas, 73–74
Ophüls, Max, 227, 228
Oppermanns, The (Feuchtwanger), 215–16
Oprecht publishing house, 190, 215
Oranienburg concentration camp, *110*
order-state, 28. *See also* knights, German
Orff, Carl, 73, 77, 82
Orient, 194, *195*
Ossietzky, Carl von, 204
Oswald, Richard, 10
Otto, Teo, 221
Oympia (Riefenstahl), 52

P
Pachter, Henry, 177
painting, 156–62
    abstract, 236. *See also* modernism
    exile painting, 231–38
    female nudes, 67
    field, forest, and meadow painters, 65
    inner immigration group and, 146
    landscape, 67, *159*
    magic realism, 236
    painters as refugees, 173–83 *passim*, 231–38
    realistic genre painting, 65
    revolutionary art, 65
    traditional art, 65
    See also art, visual
Palestine
    as refuge for Germans in exile, 193–94, 228
Pan-German league, 21, 97
parade grounds, 47–48
Paris, France, xv, 187–90, *189*, 205, 211
    Library of Burned Books, *188*, *189*
parliamentarianism, 13
peasant, cult of, 21–22, *22*, 23, 28
    tribal consciousness, 23
Pechstein, Max, 156, 234, 251
Peiner, Werner, 52, 65, 233
    German Soil, 98

Peppermill, The, 190
Pepping, Ernst, 163
personality cult, 16–18, *17*, 28, 64
Pétain, Marshall Philippe, 195
Petersen, Jan, 147–48, 189
Pfizner, Hans, 76, 239
Phitzner, Hans, 163
photomontage, 231–38, *234*
Piscator, Erwin, 105, 185, 221, 226
Plivier, Theodor, 185, 196
pluralism, 13, 44–45, 77, 121, 125
Pohlenz, Peter, 230–31
Poland, 185
    invasion of, 182–83
Polgar, Alfred, 173
Pomerania, Germany, 48
Ponten, Josef, 97
popular front movement, 180, 205, 249. *See
    also* antifascism
Portrait of the Führer (Erler), *17*
Prague, Czechoslovakia, 186, 187, 211, 235,
    241
press, 40, 120–21
Prokofiev, Sergei, 82
propaganda, 3, 79, 105, 115, 121, 234
    apolitical as political, 128
    false community and, 139
Prussian Academy of Arts, 155, 162, 241
public buildings, 47–55, 127

Q
Quatre, Henry, 215
Querido-Verlag publishing (Holland), 192,
    192, 215

R
Raabe, Peter, 76–77
race cars, 134
race issues, 30, 161
    arguments in art, 55–56
    Germanness, 15
    international mixing of races, 16
    music, 73
    mythos of blood, 27
    as term in Nazi propaganda, 3
    theater, 103–4
radio, 40, 109–14
    entertainment, 111
    German Freedom Station 29.8, 179
    listener statistics, 112
    music, 113
    programming, 113
    volk receivers, 110, *112*, 129
Radio Berlin, 250
Radziwill, Franz, 160

Rappaport, Herbert, 226
Rauschning, Hermann, 24, 82, 180, 231
Ravel, Maurice, 74
realism, 157, 160
    socialist realism, 185, 186
real-politik, 139
Red Orchestra, 155, 156, 217
refugees. *See* exile community
Regler, Gustav, 185, *191*, 209
Reich, concept of, 25–26
Reich Armed Forces, 43
Reich Chamber for Visual Arts, 40, 57
Reich Chambers of Culture, 10, 18, 39, 41,
    125, 160
Reichenbach, Hans, 248
Reich Film Chamber, 39, 40, 109, 114–15
Reich Labor Service, 92
Reich Literature Chamber, 40, 86, 88, 89,
    90, 148, 154
Reich Music Chamber, 41, 76, 164
Reich Press Chamber, 40, 109
Reich Radio Chamber, 40, 77, 109, 111
Reichsautobahn, 46–47
Reichs Protectorate of Bohemia and
    Moravia, 106
Reichstag, 123
    fire, 172
Reichswehr, Ulm, 123
Reich Theater Chamber, 40, 105
Reinhardt, Max, 10, 220, 224
Remarque, Erich Maria, 99, 197
Renn, Ludwig, 88, 213, 251
Rentschler, Eric, *116*
resistance, 145, 147, 211
Reutter, Hermann, 82
Revolution in the Visual Arts (Rosenberg),
    19
Revolution of 1848, 171
Rhine-Ruhr industrialists, 202
Riefenstahl, Leni, 50, 79, *108*, 116–17
    Oympia, 52, 134
Rinser, Luise, 153
Rittich, Werner, 48
road construction, 46–47, 137
Röhm, Ernst, 39, 57
romanticism, 126, 163, 238, 239, 240
    "romanticism made of steel," 18–19,
    82
"romanticism made of steel," 18–19, 82
Rooney, Mickey, 224
Roosevelt, Franklin D., 246
Rosemeyer, Bernd, 134
Rosenberg, Alfred, xiii, 35, 48, 104, 164,
    202, 210
    anti-communism, 7, 8

anti-Semitism, 9, 10–11
Der Mythus des 20. Jahrhunderts, 12, 38, 58
as painter, 156
radical approach, 37–38, 58, 60, 106, 124–25
Revolution in the Visual Arts, 19
role in art, 55, 57–58, 65, 161–62
role in literature, 89, 150, 151
role in music, 77, 81
Teutonic knights and, 23–24
Roses in Tyrol (comedy), *119*
Rühmann, Heinz, 85, *128*, 134
Russia, 7. *See also* Soviet Union

S

Saar region, Germany, 180
Sachs, Hans, 81
Sachs, Nelly, 213
Salomon Ernst von, 116
Samberger, Leo, 67
Scala, 128
Schad, Christian, 160
Schaeffer, Albrecht, 175
Schaub, Julius, *128*
Schauwecker, Franz, 99
Scheibe, Richard, 69
Schenzinger, Karl Aloys, 102
Scherchen, Hermann, 75, 166
Scheuermann, Fritz, 39
Schiffer, Marcellus, 85
Schilling. Heinar, 21
Schirach, Baldur von, xiii, 78
Schlamm, Willi, 186
Schlemmer, Otto, 56
Schlichter, Rudolf, *152*, 235
Schmeling, Max, 134
Schmidt-Rotluff, Karl, 57, 156, 234
Schmitt, Carl, 13
Schmitt, Florent, 241
Schneider, Reinhold, 153, 154
Schnitzler, Arthur, 88
Schoenberg, Arnold, 10, 73, 75, 126, 174, 176, 194, 197, 198, 199, 239, 240, 241, *243*, 243–44
Scholl, Hans, 217
Scholl, Sophie, 217
Schönerer, Georg von, 9, 21, 97
Schönstedt, Walter, 216
Schorer, Georg, 63
Schrade, Hubert, 19
Schramm-Zittau, Rudolf, 67
Schreiber, Otto Andreas, 56
Schreker, Franz, 10, 73, 75
Schrifttum, 86

Schultz, Norbert, 84, 85
Schultz, Wolfgang, *20*
Schultze-Naumburg, Paul, 13, 19, 32, 48, 55, 56, 58
Schuschnigg, Kurt von, 222
Schwarzkopf, Richard
  German Passion, 93
Schweitzer, Hans, 6
Schwesig, Karl, 235
sculpture, 68–72, 160–62
  Hildebrand school, 69, 70
  monumentalism, 69
Seghers, Anna, 88, 174, 178, 185, 186, *188*, 196, 217, 219–20, 251
Seidel, Ina, 90, 101
Senger, Alexander von, 48
Shanghai, 195
Shostakovich, Dmitri, 82
Siebert, Georg, 65
Siemens Corporation, 127
Sierck, Detlef, *117*
Silone, Ignazio, 241
Silver Arrows, 134
Sinclair, Upton, 88
Sintenis, Renée, 250
Sirk, Douglas, 231
Slash and Thrust newspaper, 147
Slavs, 23, 130
Slezak, Leo, 42
slogans, 12, 123, 126, 195–96
Sluytermann von Langeweyde, Georg, 19, *25*, 63
social Darwinism, 26
Social Democratic Party, 209
social democrats, 212
Socialist Workers' Party, 209
Sohibor camp, 12
song writing, 92–93. *See also* music
Soviet Paradise exhibit, 9
Soviet Union, 130
  German refugees in, 173, 185–86, 221, 225–27, 242, 250
  repression, 211–12, 250
  Soviet Judea, 12
Spain, 196
Spanish Civil War, 180, 213
Speer, Albert, 50, 132
  German Stadium, 50
  Great Hall, 51, *51*
  New Congress Hall, 50
  New Reichs Chancellory, 52
  Paris International Exposition, 50–51
  sculpture commissions, 70
Spengler, Oswald, 203, 210
Sperber, Manès, 209

Spoerl, Heinrich, 100
Spoliansky, Mischa, 85
sports, 132, 134–35
    relation to military, 135
Spranger, Eduard, 250
Stalin, Joseph, 212, 250
Stapel, Wilhelm, 9
Stassen, Franz, 65
Steckel, Leonard, 191, 221
Stege, Fritz, 72, 80
Stenzel, Hermann, 63–64
sterilization, 16, 139
Stolz, Robert, 239
Stramm, Gustav, 163
Strange Death of Adolf Hitler, The (Hogan),
    230, 230
Strasser, Otto, 26, 57
Strauss, Oscar, 73, 163
Strauss, Richard, 40, 41, 76, 82, 239, 240
Stravinsky, Igor, 74, 75
Streicher, Julius, 12, 121
Strength Through Joy organization, 39, 63,
    105, 110, 130–31, 135
Stroux, Johannes, 250
Strzygowski, Josef, 21
surrealism, 56
swastika as emblem, 54
Switzerland
    as refuge for German exiles, 190–91,
        214, 222, 223, 240
synchronization, 65, 122, 125

T
Taut, Bruno, 55, 185
technology, cult of, 132–34
Teetjen, Albert, 217
Temple of Honor, 48
Tessenow, Heinrich, 54
Teutons, 21, 28, 48, 124
    Teutonic knights, 23–24, 25
Thälmann Brigade, 213
theater, 40, 103–9
    actors, 103, 223, 224
    antifascist theater, 221
    directors, 103, 107, 223, 224
    exile group, 220–24
    laws, 105–6
    managers, 103, 221, 224
    race issues, 103–4
    social realism, 221
    subsidies, 106
    theory, 105
    variety shows, 128
Theresienstadt camp, 42, 83
Thing sites, 48, 104

Thingspiel, 93, 94, 104, 105
    amphitheaters, 104
Thoma, Hans, 67
Thorak, Josef, 69–70
    studio, 71
Thüringen, Germany, 55–56
Thyssen, Fritz, 202, 235
Tillich, Paul, 248
Toch, Ernst, 73
Todt, Fritz, 46–47, 132
Toller, Ernst, 10, 178, 185, 204, 212, 214
Torberg, Friedrich, 228
trains, 134
Transit (Seghers), 219–20
Treblinka camp, 12
Trepte, Curt, 221
Triumph of the Will (Riefenstahl), 50, 79,
    108, 116–17
Troost, Paul Ludwig, 48, 50
Trotsky, Leon, 196
Trotskyites, 185
Tucholsky, Kurt, 10, 85, 175, 181, 212
tui behavior of intellectuals, 175
Two Thousand Years of German Culture
    (Munich, 1939), 29

U
Uhse, Bodo, 188, 196, 213
Ullmann, Viktor, 83
Ullstein publishing, 10
Union of the Twelve, 205
United States
    anti-communism in, 183
    anti-Semitism, 230
    appeasement, 199, 229
    entrance into World War II, 230
    Hollywood films, 129, 228–31
    mass media, 128–29
    as refuge for Germans in exile,
        196–201, 206, 210, 212, 224, 227,
        228–31, 239–40, 242–45
    xenophobia, 196
urbanization, 22
USSR
    Soviet Judea, 12
U.S.S.R. See Soviet Union
utopia, 24–25, 38

V
vacations, 130, 131
Vallentin, Max, 221
Vansittart, Robert, 210
Veidt, Conrad, 227
Versailles, shame of, 36
Vesper, Will, 90, 151

Viertel, Berthold, 193, 227, 248
Viking Press, 198, 215
volk, concept of, 36, 88, 104, 106, 124
    art, 60–61, 62
    authoritarian ideas and, 61
    class issues, 30–35, 44
    community, 5, 7, 42–43, 64, 89, 122,
        125, 132, 137, 139
    literature, 90, 98
    versus modernism, 56
    origins, 13
    as term in Nazi propaganda, 3
    threatened by urbanization, 22
Voll, Christopher, 160–61

W
Wackerle, Josef, 52, 70
Wagner, Richard, 9, 29, 64, 81–82, 240
    Parisfal, 24
Wagner, Wolfgang, 80
Wagner-Régeny, Rudolf, 82
Waldmann, Guido, 72
Walter, Bruno, 238
Wamper, Adolf, 70
Wangenheim, Gustav von, 185, 226
Wansee Conference, 12
Wasserman, Jakob, 42, 88
Webern, Abtib, 166
Webern, Anton, 243
Wegener, Paul, 250
Wehner, Josef Magnus, 99
Wehrmacht, 44
Weigel, Helene, 221
Weill, Kurt, 10, 73, 74, 238, 244–45
Weimar, Germany, 52, 56, 84, 132
Weimar Republic, 3, 203
    anti-communism during, 9
    class issues in, 34–35
    communism and, 7
    consumption in, 137
    culture
        architecture, 48
        art, 58, 63
        coexistence of high and low
            cultures in, 5
        entertainment, 127, 144
        films, 227
        German culture, 29
        literature, 86–87, 88, 102, 149,
            213
        mass media, xii, 128, 172
        music, 37, 73–74, 75, 242
        painting, 158, 232, 233, 235
        sculpture, 69
    education policy of, 123

ideological conflict in, 207
internationalism in, 13, 233
press in, 121
technology in, 132
Weinert, Erich, 213, 250
Weinheber, Joseph, 151
Weisenborn, Günther, 155–56, 251
Weiss, Ernst, 212
Weiss, Peter, 236
Wells, HG, 204
Wendland, Winfried, 58
Werfel, Franz, 174, 176, 178, 183, 197, 215
Werner, Theodor, 157
Wessel, Horst, 77
Westecker, Wilhelm, 64, 64
Western democracies
    anti-communism in, 173, 183
    appeasement, 180, 181, 211, 241
Westheim, Paul, 196
White Rose Group, 217
Wicclair, Walter, 224
Wiechert, Ernst, 153
Wilder, Billy, 228
Willrich, Wolfgang, 59, 63, 126
    U-Boat Comander Joachim Schepke, 64
Winter, Fritz, 157
Winter Aid Organization, 128, 129
Wintergarten, 128
Winters, Shelley, 230
Wirth, Hermann, 21
Wittstock, Erwin, 97
Wohlbrück, Adolf, 227
Wolf, Friedrich, 8, 10, 185, 189, 190, 213,
    214, 223, 250
Wolf, Theodor, 120
Wolfskehl, Karl, 175, 213
Wolpe, Stefan, 73, 199, 239, 243
World's Zionist Organization, 180, 228
World War II, 130, 132, 139, 182
    Battle of Stalingrad, 246
    See also specific countries
Worringer, Wilhelm, 38
Wüsten, Johannes, 186, 235

X
xenophobia, 196

Y
Young German Order, 21

Z
Zeisler, Alfred, 231
Zeitoper, 126, 163
Zeller, Carl, 77
Zemlinsky, Alexander von, 239

Ziegler, Adolf, 37, 52, 59, 67, 233
    Goddess of Art, 66
Ziegler, Hans Severus, 37
Zille, Heinrich, 157
Zionism, 175, 194, 244
    World's Zionist Organization, 180

Zuckmayer, Carl, 178, 197, 214, 228
Zurich, Switzerland, 190, 223
    poster, *222*
Zweig, Arnold, 181, 194, 198, 205, *205*,
    215, 217
Zweig, Stefan, 10, 76, 99, 178, 193, 212, 215